THE WORLD *of*

ANDREW CARNEGIE:

1865–1901

By

Louis M. Hacker

The World of Andrew Carnegie: 1865–1901

Major Documents in American Economic History, 2 vols.

The Larger View of the University

American Capitalism

Alexander Hamilton in the American Tradition

The United States in the Twentieth Century (with H. S. Zahler)

Capitalism and the Historians (with others)

Government Assistance to Universities in Great Britain
(with H. W. Dodds and Lindsay Rogers)

England & America: The Ties That Bind (an Oxford Inaugural Lecture)

The New Industrial Relations (with others)

The Shaping of the American Tradition, 2 vols.

The United States and Its Place in World Affairs, 1918–1943
(with others)

The Triumph of American Capitalism

American Problems of Today

The United States: A Graphic History
(with Rudolf Modley and G. R. Taylor)

A Short History of the New Deal

The Farmer Is Doomed

The United States Since 1865 (with B. B. Kendrick)

THE WORLD of ANDREW CARNEGIE: 1865-1901

LOUIS M. HACKER

J. B. LIPPINCOTT COMPANY
Philadelphia & New York

Thanks are given to Princeton University Press for permission to reprint passages from the following two books:

Socialism and American Life, Vol. 1, edited by D. D. Egbert and Stow Persons, copyright 1952, by Princeton University Press. (From the article "The Background and Development of Marxian Socialism in the United States," by Daniel Bell)

Merger Movements in American Industry, 1895–1956, by R. L. Nelson; National Bureau of Economic Research, #66 General Series, copyright 1959, by Princeton University Press

To Beatrice

FOREWORD

Although this book is about the United States in the greatest period of its growth, that is, from 1865 to 1901, what I have written is not history in the formal sense. I have had a specific intention, and that is to explain why this country, a young, developing nation at the outbreak of the Civil War, became the mightiest industrial power in the world in less than forty years. The book, really, is a continuation and amplification of the earlier essay I wrote in 1940 which I called *The Triumph of American Capitalism*. They are much of a piece, for both are selective and not systematic in their analyses, are based on a set of theoretical assumptions, and try to prove an argument. Honest controversy breaks no bones; sometimes indeed it compels the re-examination of long-received belief and the formulation of new attitudes. I think *The Triumph of American Capitalism* has had that effect. At any rate, its publisher, the Columbia University Press, has kept it in print for these twenty-five years; it has continued to be read and has even been translated into Spanish and Japanese.

Since the 1950s, economists (lately, sociologists, anthropologists, political scientists, and historians have been joining their company) have been seeking to establish the principles or laws that convert traditional societies into developing and then mature and progressing ones. This preoccupation is more than an academic exercise. Earlier economists— Adam Smith, John Stuart Mill, Karl Marx, occasionally and peripherally Alfred Marshall—were also involved in such a hunt, for they understood that human welfare or improving standards of living or social justice could be accomplished only when economic progress occurred. The classical and neoclassical economists, by and large, however, with an increasing refinement of analysis, could see only a stationary economic world with the occasional intrusion of factors and forces that from time to time disturbed its equilibrium. The plight of traditional societies that had been stagnating for millenniums—where there was no efficient allocation of the resources of land, labor, and capital, where the dread Malthusian population laws inexorably worked—was outside their ken. Curiously enough, that most exciting economist of modern times, John Maynard Keynes, too, in his search for stability in a capitalist society bedeviled by disemployment and unused plant capacity, never looked at the other and dark side of the moon where more than two-thirds of the world's people lived in abject poverty.

Today, because of population explosions, national upheavals, and, even more important, the revolution of rising expectations everywhere, it is imperative that the ways and means by which traditional societies can be propelled out of their sloth and grinding poverty be analyzed and applied. To the great credit of economists all over the world, it is they who have assumed this task. Too many of their efforts, however, have centered in the construction of purely theoretical economic models in the belief that these could have a universal applicability. If the rate of investment, and therefore capital creation, could be encouraged to rise to such and such a proportion of the national income—whether by deficit financing and the monetization of public debt, or by foreign borrowings, or by taxation or confiscation; by the encouragement of key heavy industries or by balanced growth—then a people would be on the move. But what if investments were in public monuments or in large steel plants and electrification works, or in war-making industries, or even in health and education—when the economic and social returns would be long deferred, to put the kindest face on the matter? Honesty demands the admission that many such outlays really have been wasted. A rule of thumb as easy and all-encompassing as this (with its application having many choices) has turned out to be too simple and alas! not too successful, as experiences over the last decade or so have demonstrated.

It has been at this point that the anthropologists, sociologists, and political scientists have entered the debate. A proper rate of investment (assuming efficient employment of resources) might be possible—given, however, the existence or creation of institutions through which not only savings and investment but also a modicum at least of free consumer choices could grow. There are, in other words, many kinds of theoretical models that need studying—many more in fact than those the economists alone can supply.

This understanding is the basis of this book. In an effort to explain how one developing nation, the United States, which had begun on the road to industrialization as far back as the 1820s, cleared away the obstructions in its path after the Civil War, I have sought to create a model that is made up more heavily of institutional than of purely economic factors. I have made it my purpose to isolate and examine those attitudes, ways of life, commitments—what William Graham Sumner in his extraordinary book *Folkways* called the mores—of the American people in the years following the Civil War which made possible both investment and the efficient allocation of resources.

Such a study, in consequence, has had to do with the role of government and the public policies it developed, with the kinds of people who created a climate of assent in which capitalism—entrepreneurship, private investment, the determination of costs and prices by a free market—could flourish, and with the ways by which such attitudes, or mores, made possible the development of efficient agricultural, transportation, and banking organization. As Marx did to Hegel's dialectic, I have stood theory on its head, arguing that the creation of the American economic structure, in all its manifold aspects, had to be preceded by the appearance and acceptance of those mores in which the processes of capitalism could flourish and expand. Finally, I have examined the attitudes and accomplishments of the greatest entrepreneur of the period, Andrew Carnegie, as an example of the wonders that innovation—working in a climate which approved of private accumulation and decision-making—could achieve.

The broad result of mores and innovation was the emergence and triumph of American industrial capitalism. A developing nation had become mature and, as a consequence, it now possessed the means by which economic progress, human welfare, even social justice could hopefully follow.

I have written this book as an essay, and so I have not loaded down its pages with footnotes referring to authorities and public documents. Works I have leaned on I cite in the text itself; the bibliography in the back lists all the other books I have used and which students wanting more precise information may consult.

I am obliged to the Guggenheim Foundation and to the Relm Foundation for giving me the leisure and the financial assistance to permit me to write this book in the summers and the few holidays I have been able to take from my classroom teaching. I wish to thank at the Lippincott Company my general editor Miss Tay Hohoff and my copy editor Mrs. Peggy Dowst Cronlund for the care, skill, and delicacy for my feelings with which they have prepared my manuscript for the printer; they have saved me from many gaucheries, habits one falls into over a long lifetime of writing. And I thank my son Andrew Hacker, professor of government at Cornell University, and my old friend Frederic G. Donner, chairman of the board of the General Motors Corporation, for having read the proofs; their comments invariably have been wise, and if I have not always followed them, the fault is mine and not theirs.

I am indebted to my hundreds of students, graduate and undergraduate —and this is a proper *quid pro quo,* for I have given my teaching year wholly to them—for the essays and papers they have written for me on many of the themes discussed here. One of the advantages in being a university lecturer is the opportunity to air fancies and conjectures in the classroom and have the students help in converting those that have merit into hard fact. Under my direction, students have written and written and I have read and read; some of their notions I have caught and imprisoned here.

My thanks in particular go to the following of my students whose researches have been of help to me. *Engineering Education:* Paul De Rosa, R. P. Goldwasser; *The Protestant Churches:* R. E. Johnson, Irving Spitzberg; *Railroads and the West:* J. W. Larson, Cindy Marriott, M. W. Schultz; *The South and Capitalism:* F. A. Santos; *State Banking:* Gary Burkhead, R. K. Kraft, B. D. Sargent, M. B. Sargent; *Urban Growth and Development:* Joseph Beckman, Barbara Insel, R. B. Jaeger, B. B. Sneed, R. D. Whitman.

I express my thanks to the following authors and to the publishers of these books for permission to quote passages from them:

Main Currents in American Thought, Vol. 3, by V. L. Parrington. Harcourt, Brace & World, Inc., 1930.
American Conservatism in the Age of Enterprise, by R. G. McCloskey. Harvard University Press, 1951.

FOREWORD

Folkways, by W. G. Sumner. Waltham, Massachusetts: Blaisdell Publishing Company, A Division of Ginn and Company, 1907.

The Theory of Economic Development, by J. A. Schumpeter. Harvard University Press, 1934.

Origins of the New South, 1877–1913, by C. Vann Woodward. Louisiana State University Press, 1951.

Business Cycles, by J. A. Schumpeter. McGraw-Hill Book Company, 1939.

Transcontinental Railway Strategy, 1869–1893: A Study of Businessmen, by Julius Grodinsky. University of Pennsylvania Press, 1962.

Jay Gould: His Business Career, by Julius Grodinsky. University of Pennsylvania Press, 1957.

The Emergence of the American University, by L. R. Veysey. University of Chicago Press, 1965.

Iron and Steel in Nineteenth-Century America: An Economic Inquiry, by Peter Temin. The M.I.T. Press, Cambridge, Massachusetts, 1964.

The Life of Andrew Carnegie, Vol. 1, by Burton J. Hendrick. Doubleday & Company, Inc., 1932. Reprinted by permission of Dr. Ives Hendrick.

The Autobiography of Andrew Carnegie. Houghton Mifflin Company, 1920.

LOUIS M. HACKER

Columbia University
June 30, 1967

CONTENTS

CONTENTS

CONTENTS

INTRODUCTION

THE BROAD FRAME OF REFERENCE

The Legend of the "Robber Barons"   The term "Robber Baron" not only has become a dirty word used to characterize America's industrial, railroad, and banking leaders from the outbreak of the Civil War until the end of the nineteenth century, but has been absorbed into our popular writing and into too much of our historical literature. It has also become synonymous with American capitalism itself. The assumption has been that the forays of the "Robber Barons" violated all standards of common decency, and that the general outcry which arose properly led to growing intervention in economic affairs by public authority, first by the States and then by the federal government.

This post-Civil War era—so the tale runs—were the bedraggled years when the new lords of the mines, furnaces, mills, factories and counting houses dominated the United States. They destroyed the social balance of the country. Usurping leadership everywhere, they shouldered aside the spokesmen of an earlier and simpler time which had been based on self-help, rectitude in politics, and devotion to a way of life firmly founded on moral values and devotion to an awful yet just deity. Not only was the rural America of independent yeomen and the small towns of merchants and local shops finished. These captains of industry, transportation, and finance were industrializing, urbanizing, and mongrelizing the nation; they encouraged the heavy waves of non-Anglo-Saxon and non-Protestant immigrants who flooded the country.

In the process of making money (for the creation of goods and services

[xvii]

was only incidental to the hunt for profits), they debauched our tastes, corrupted our political life, despoiled our natural resources, and exploited our farmers and workers. Instead of the voice of the turtle, the clink of the almighty dollar now was heard in the land. More specifically, the bill of particulars has run as follows:

They were pre-emptive. Because of badly written laws and a lax officialdom, for which they were responsible, they were able to enter America's public lands and by wholesale waste despoil the natural heritage of the American people.

They were predatory. Presumably energetically competitive among themselves, actually acting collusively and always aided by subservient legislatures and courts, they drove independent producers out of business, farmers into bankruptcy, and workers to the brink of penury and want. The slums of America's cities—breeding poverty, violence, and crime—represented one of the many prices the United States had to pay for their greed.

They were presumptuous. Both major parties were in their thrall. When necessary to effect their purposes, legislators and judges were openly bought. The consumer was flouted. (Had not William H. Vanderbilt, the head of the New York Central system, said, when complaints were made about the services of his railroad: "The public be damned"?) Vulgarly, they spent great sums on personal entertainment, erected ugly monuments to themselves, and were served by a compliant and complacent clergy and world of learning.

"Robber Barons," as a general title, first appeared in Matthew Josephson's book of that name in 1934, but the attack on American capitalism and its outstanding exemplars and beneficiaries had an earlier origin. If one has to seek an initial date for the personal (as opposed to the ideological) rejection of American businessmen, or entrepreneurs, the year 1892 probably furnishes a kind of watershed.

It was then that Ignatius Donnelly, an unsuccessful Minnesota politician, businessman and farmer, prevailed upon the newly formed People's Party to accept the preamble which he had written to the party's first national platform. He had flirted with both the Republican and Democratic Parties, had participated in many of the third-party movements of the 1870s and 1880s, and at various times had been on one side or the other of the tariff (high or low) and money (hard or soft) controversies of the period. Neither Donnelly nor the leaders of the People's Party were socialists; nor, except for a scattered few, were the other writers who took up the same burden.

Thus, Donnelly, writing in the best tradition of political rodomontade, filled with sound and fury, declared:

The conditions which surround us best justify our cooperation. We meet in the midst of a nation brought to the verge of moral, political, and material ruin. . . . The fruits of the toil of millions are boldly stolen to build up colossal fortunes for a few, unprecedented in the history of mankind; and the possessors of these in turn despise the republic and endanger liberty. From the same prolific womb of governmental injustice we breed the two great classes—tramps and millionaires.

Two years later, Henry Demarest Lloyd in his *Wealth Against Commonwealth* struck the same outraged note. Lloyd was no socialist either. A journalist, he had married into great wealth and was able to follow the will-o'-the-wisp of reform—generally, it took the form of producers' cooperatives—into many parts of the world. *Wealth Against Commonwealth* started from an earlier article on the Standard Oil Trust which blossomed into a broad condemnation of American business.

Said Lloyd in a typical high-flown passage:

If our civilization is destroyed as Macaulay predicted, it will not be by his barbarians from below. Our barbarians come from above. Our great moneymakers have sprung in one generation into seats of power kings do not know. The forces and the wealth are new, and have been the opportunity of new men. Without restraints of culture, experience, the pride or even the inherited caution of class or rank, these men, intoxicated, think they are the wave instead of the float, and that they have created the business which has created them. To them science is but a never-ending repertoire of investments stored up by nature for the syndicates, government but a fountain of franchises, the nations but customers in squads. . . . They claim a power without control, exercised through forms which make it secret, anonymous, and perpetual.

Lloyd, despite all his pretenses to intellectuality, made no careful or systematic analysis of the economic processes he was attacking; one may doubt his ability to have done so. He was in fact the first of the large company of muckrakers, those journalists who exposed evidences, they assumed, of fraud, cupidity, venality in business without suggesting or indeed knowing what was to be done about them. The inexpensive popular magazines—*Munsey's, McClure's, Collier's,* the large Hearst string—from about 1904 to about 1912 carried scores if not hundreds of articles containing all sorts of sensational tales of business corruption and worse. Some of them were thoughtful and revealed inequities that cried out for correction. A very few were written by socialists, although even in their case—so rare was a knowledge of theoretical Marxism in the United States of the time—the tales were pitched in the same tones of moral indignation over human excesses, rather than in the Marxian terms of industrial capitalism's decline into monopoly with the ensuing polarization of society, the enfeeblement and immiserization of the working classes, and deepening crisis. The best of the socialist analysts was Gustavus Myers, who did not write for the popular press but whose *A History of the Great American Fortunes,* published in 1907, turned out to be cut from the same cloth. His book was based upon painstaking research in public documents and court records; it commanded, however, a small audience. It was from this work, ironically, that Josephson's book was largely derived; and it was Josephson's that became sensationally successful because it caught the temper of a time when once again Franklin D. Roosevelt's economic royalists were regarded as the devils of the piece.

The intellectuals of the 1930s—again, those who were not radicals in the ideological sense—found Vernon Louis Parrington their chief stay and support. Parrington, a socialist of sorts in his youth, had become a professor of literature at Washington University and sat down to write what he called *Main Currents in American Thought.* The first volume appeared in 1927; the third and last, a fragment, was published posthumously in 1930. The book was presumed to be—it was so planned and was so initially hailed—a serious intellectual history of the United States from the dawn of settlement. A closer and more objective reading showed it to be informed with curious, biased, and narrow emotional overtones. Jefferson was its hero; the Jeffersonian way of life—ruralist, hostile to cities and their heterogeneous masses, anti-industrial and antifinancial, suspicious of government—largely was the pole star by which Parrington steered. He had no economics or any awareness of the necessary intricate lines between public policy and economic affairs.

[xx]

INTRODUCTION

Parrington's bravura passages about capitalism and the "Robber Barons" suited a period that, despite all the brave words and reforming zeal of Franklin D. Roosevelt, saw no way out of the deep pit of depression. Here are some characteristic passages from Parrington's third volume:

This bustling America of 1870 accounted itself a democratic world. . . . Its social philosophy, which it found adequate to its needs, was summed up in three words—preemption, exploitation, progress. Its immediate and pressing business was to dispossess the government of its rich holdings. . . . Preemption meant exploitation and exploitation meant progress. It was a simple philosophy and it suited the simple individualism of the times. The Gilded Age knew nothing of the Enlightenment, it recognized only the acquisitive instinct.

Analyze the most talked-of men of the age and one is likely to find a splendid audacity coupled with an immense wastefulness. A note of tough-mindedness marks them. They had stout nippers. They fought their way encased in rhinoceros hides. There was the Wall Street crowd . . . blackguards for the most part, railway wreckers, cheaters and swindlers, but picturesque in their rascality.

Freedom had become individualism, and individualism had become the inalienable right to preempt, to exploit, to squander. Gone were the old ideals with the old restraints. The idealism of the forties, the romanticism of the fifties—all the heritage of Jeffersonianism and the French Enlightenment—were put thoughtlessly away, and with no social conscience, no concern for civilization, no heed for the future of democracy . . . the Gilded Age threw itself into the business of money-getting. From the sober restraints of aristocracy, the old inhibitions of Puritanism, the niggardliness of an exacting domestic economy, it swung far back into reaction. . . . It was an anarchistic world of strong, capable men, selfish, unenlightened, amoral. . . . In the Gilded Age freedom was the freedom of buccaneers preying on the argosies of Spain.

Congress had rich gifts to bestow—in lands, tariffs, subsidies, favors of all sorts; and when influential citizens made their wishes known to the reigning statesmen, the sympathetic politicians were quick to turn the government into the fairy godmother the voters wanted it to be. A huge barbecue was spread to which all presumably were invited.

Strangely enough, Parrington represented no passing mood. The 1950s, despite a returning prosperity that had all the aspects of permanence, indicated that Parrington had left an ineradicable mark upon the minds of many American intellectuals. Even the clamor and clangor of his style remained unchanged.

Thus Daniel Bell, in an essay published in 1952:

On the national scene a new industrial plutocracy was flexing its muscles in a crude and powerful way. Economically, it was exerting powerful leverage against the farmer while heavily squeezing the worker; politically it was buying up State legislatures and exercising a dominant influence in the Republican Party; culturally, it was spawning the gilded architectural monstrosities and displaying a grossness of taste that was to turn against it both the scions of the older upper-middle classes, such as Brooks and Henry Adams, and the rising intellectual class. . . .

These were the jungle years. The Supreme Court had written Herbert Spencer's Social Statics into the law of the land, and the iron-jawed capitalists prepared to demonstrate that the philosophy of natural rights meant their God-given authority to rule untrammelled. Social Darwinism was a congenial doctrine for the new plutocracy.

And very much in the same vein was Robert Green McCloskey's *American Conservatism in the Age of Enterprise,* published in 1951. He was writing about William Graham Sumner, one of the few men in the 1880s and 1890s who saw a sound, indeed an imperative, economic justification for the processes of wealth accumulation:

Now an argument that takes these directions must inevitably issue in a glorification of the successful businessman as such. He and his fellows constitute the anointed elite of the social order Sumner is describing, and no amount of incidental qualification of this main judgment can change its central character. . . .

For by the terms of that argument the Protestant virtues do not justify themselves; they are justified because they promote the material welfare of society, and they are therefore dependent on that standard. Material value is the controlling norm, and since, by definition, the best measure of such value is success, the successful businessman is meritorious whether he practices Sumner's Protestant virtues or not. The more he aggregates wealth, the more the industrialist serves the community; and the methods he employs are morally unimpeachable because no moral standard for impeaching them exists. . . . The logic of his [Sumner's] materialist ethic was to exalt "the man who can do things" to the level of social heroism.

[xxii]

INTRODUCTION

Individual Enterprise Versus State Planning   What had Sumner said that brought forth such ridicule and contempt, and that, incidentally, vulgarized the thoughtful things Sumner was seeking to do? Sumner had written in two of his essays, published around the turn of the century, as follows:

It is idle folly to meet these phenomena with wailings about the danger of the accumulation of great wealth in few hands. The phenomena themselves prove that we have tasks to perform which require large aggregations of capital. Moreover, the capital, to be effective, must be in few hands, for the simple reason that there are very few men who are able to handle great aggregations of capital. . . . The men who are competent to organize great enterprises and to handle great amounts of capital must be found by natural selection, not by political election. . . . The aggregation of large amounts of capital in few hands is the first condition of the fulfilment of the most important tasks of civilization which now confront us.

If we should set a limitation to the accumulation of wealth, we should say to our most valuable producers, "We do not want you to do us the services which you best understand how to perform, beyond a certain point." It would be like killing off our generals in war.

Today, to economists (if not to historians), all these are truisms. Sumner, more so than anyone of his age, whether in America, England, or on the European continent, caught a fundamental point. And this is interesting, for he was no technically trained economist. Underdeveloped or developing nations, beginning or in the early processes of industrialization—as the United States then was—must bend every energy and make every sacrifice to further capital accumulation for investment. Higher standards of living, a better distribution of income, even wealth, cannot be accomplished until an economy and a polity understand that capital creation—in modernized plants, machinery, transportation, and agriculture—must be first on the order of the day: this is what Sumner meant when he said, "we have tasks to perform." Individuals, free and unrestrained, rather than government, are the agents for such a mighty and imaginative enterprise; and Sumner, for the time being, was willing to run the risks of the emergence of millionaires and even monopolists to start the economic engine going.

I have said that now, in the 1960s, all economists know this; although to many (except in the United States, where the commitment to capitalism still continues), capital accumulation and investment in developing countries must take place only as the result of over-all governmental planning. Thus Gunnar Myrdal, the Swedish economist and Socialist, writing in 1957:

A main element of every national development plan is a decision to increase the total amount of investment, aimed at raising the productive powers of the country, and to procure the capital formation necessary for this purpose. The plan must determine this over-all amount and must, in addition, determine the proportions of the capital which should be allocated in different directions: to increase the over-all facilities in transport and power production; to construct new plants and acquire the machinery for heavy industries and for light industries of various types; to raise the productivity level in agriculture. . . .

In the United States, the "Robber Barons" did all this and more besides, for they were able to carry on by the rules of private business calculation—of costs and profits. Of course, a price was paid in the short run: a governmental fiscal policy that held taxation and public expenditures tightly in leash could not lead to the cleaning out of dirty and unhealthy urban slums or the spending of large sums on public education. It is doubtful if Western and Southern farmers and urban workers, notably the newly arrived immigrants, received immediate cash incomes commensurate with the advancing productivity of industry, transportation, and agriculture. Consumer goods certainly were cheap, but cheap in quality as well as price. And if the freedom for enterprise Sumner so fiercely defended prevented large-scale government intervention to misdirect and stultify the economic processes, it also led to the badgering and often the destruction of working-class organizations. In the long run, both farmers and immigrant workers (or their sons and daughters, at any rate) reaped deferred rewards from the capital growth of the country.

Myrdal, in effect, is saying, or praying for, the same ultimate consequences when, in talking of his over-all national planning mechanism, he declares: "The national plans cannot be made in terms of costs and profits for the individual enterprises; they can, in fact, not be made in terms of the prices in the markets. . . ." Who, then, pays the piper? The same farmers and workers, the great bulk of the producers and consumers, who are taxed heavily, paid little, furnished shoddy goods; by and by, possibly, they will live better. Myrdal will not say this, for he is a Western Socialist to whom freedom is dear: the planning he is talking of can be inaugurated only through totalitarian governments, whether they are Russian or Chinese Communist or Egyptian or Ghanaian Socialist. The new national states of the contemporary world which Myrdal hails are the result of more than political revolutions: they come, also, from a general demand for better standards of living. This is the age of rising expectations. But Myrdal knows, as do all honest economists, that rising expectations must be postponed—possibly for a long, long time, given the inevitable and costly mistakes state planners must make—if "the total amount of investment, aimed at raising the productive powers of the country" are to be sensationally and suddenly increased.

A Theory of Growth for Developing Nations   The burden of my argument in this book begins to emerge. The "Robber Barons" were not the despoilers we have been led to believe. The United States of the post-Civil War period, a developing country, was transformed in not more than a single generation into the greatest industrial nation of the world. At the same time, balanced growth took place—thanks to a free market, private accumulation and investment, and the unhampered activities and leadership of a sizable company of entrepreneurs, or innovators. A complete transportation net, the beginnings of the generation of electrical power and its transmission, the creation of new industries, the modernizing of farm plant: all these were accomplished in this brief time. In consequence all sectors of the economy benefited; indeed, they were intermeshed, so that the country was not at the mercy of or a prey to the overtowering strength or the weaknesses of one or the other.

The desire to accumulate and invest, the presence of individuals ready to start and others to back risky ventures, the appearance of financial institutions to create the money and credit necessary for such enterprises: all of these would have been futile had there not existed a climate of approval which, quite universally, gave its assent to the capitalist processes. An examination of these attitudes and institutions, in an effort to explain why the "Robber Barons" could arise and flourish, is also part of the argument I am seeking to develop.

The problem, then, is, What were those circumstances in the America of the post-Civil War years that were so favorable to the astounding growth and development of the United States? Climate, physiography, and natural resources aside, the chief answers must be two: First, government and the American people rarely placed obstacles in the way of a freely operating private enterprise system or imposed any important restraints or penalties on its practitioners. Second, the structural character of the American economy and polity—the growing size and nature of the working population, the banking system, the law courts and their attitudes toward property and liberty of contract, the absence of challenges politically and industrially from working class organizations—inevitably was a response to the existing favorable attitudes. To use William Graham Sumner's imaginative and useful formulation: these attitudes and institutions constituted the mores of the time.

My intention, it must be apparent, is not to gild the lily. I do not intend to engage in an exercise in hagiology to replace the regnant demonology, to make heroes out of today's antiheroes, to seek to understand what Jay Gould and Andrew Carnegie were trying to do while I am really involved in the disingenuous exercise of justifying all their methods, to substitute for the rough laws of the market place—which I recognize were harsh—an ethics that argues that distributive justice actually existed. Nor am I saying that what took place in the United States a hundred years ago and led to such grand results is the general prescription that must be followed by developing nations today if they seek comparable accomplishments. I am aware, as Gunnar Myrdal is, that the political revolutions and the rising expectations of the world in which we live make growth and development more complex: that social reforms and education, health and welfare must be pushed along with capital creation and balanced growth. On the other hand, I am not the victim of his naïvety.

Economists, perhaps more so the econometricians among them, like to assume that, given a general theory, or a congeries of special theories, of growth and development, and their testing mathematically, it is possible to create models which can be everywhere applied and, in fact, have the force of invariant law. Two observations here are in order. No general theory of growth and development has emerged that really satisfies the thoughtful. And where models that are the outcome of special theories have been drawn and efforts to apply them have been made, none of them to date has met with conspicuous successes. The stubborn realities of national aspirations, politics, personal hostilities and rivalries, religion, social classes and castes—attitudes and institutions again—just do not fit into neatly drawn models or, to change the figure, even into Procrustean beds with the violence they entail. I am not denigrating such analytical exercises, of course; I am simply saying that the tasks are great and many and the travail, errors, and failures equally burdensome.

The following observations, however, from an examination of the American experience, I would like to believe have universal applicability for the developing nations today, as for the United States when it was so swiftly on the march. Peoples will have a better chance to improve their lot, creating welfare as they prosper economically, in a climate that respects liberty and the integrity of the private individual. This means more rather than fewer free markets, more free consumer choices, and more private decision-making by entrepreneurs, or innovators, whose financial backers are willing and are permitted to take risks. This also means free political institutions; most particularly, a system of courts where judges are incorruptible and in which the rule of law reigns. That rule of law protects property but, even more important, the procedural rights of individuals when they choose to dissent. This means, finally, full societal mobility where opportunities to rise (and fall) are generally available to talent and where discrimination because of race, religion, color, national origins, sex—just because discrimination squanders talent— is sternly suppressed. I am not repeating William Graham Sumner. (I am realistic enough to understand the parts modern government can play, through fiscal and monetary policy economically, and in creating— notably through education—those opportunities socially, which, in time, will make any evidences of discrimination obscene.) Such were part of the mores of the post-Civil War America, which, given their own heritages and cultural commitments, developing nations might well emulate. To this extent, I am offering a theory of growth in institutional terms.

The Real "Take-off" in the Post-Civil War Period   I have said that the real leap forward in the United States began with the end of the Civil War. Not only do the statistical evidences demonstrate this; the structural changes, political and economic, to make unimpeded progress possible, occurred only in that era.

INTRODUCTION

I am not unaware of the recent exercises of economists, more particularly of the econometricians, which seek to demonstrate that as early as 1820 significant changes in America had begun and a so-called industrial revolution was on its way. I say econometricians, because the statistical data to prove this are less than fragmentary and only mathematical reconstructions, in part imaginative, in part fanciful, can be offered to make the case. From these, the conclusion is being drawn that Gross National Product per capita in real dollars was beginning to move upward, starting with 1820. Other economists, aware of the essentially mercantile character of the American economy in these earlier years—aware that capitalists were merchants rather than industrialists; that wealth, when produced from trade, was less likely to be invested in the industrial productive processes (of course, there were exceptions) and more likely to be put in banking and rural and urban lands—look to the 1850s as the real "take-off" period into industrialization. Again, statistics are being marshaled: of investment as a significant rate of the total national income; of the increase in railroad mileage; of the rapid development of industry (light industry, it should be pointed out, rather than heavy); of the sudden great increase in the labor force.

These efforts will not do, apart from the dubious nature of the statistical evidence, because they disregard the existent mores of the time. The country was divided hopelessly and tragically into the slave South and the free North. For the slave South to survive, not only must it adhere to a noncapitalist ideology (that industrial capitalism was exploitative, that it was bound to produce a sharply polarized class society—Jefferson had his heirs in John C. Calhoun, George Fitzhugh, Edmund Ruffin), not only must it resist the expansion of the free capitalist institutions into the Territories of the farther West, while it itself encouraged territorial adventure in Central America and the Caribbean, where slavery could be maintained, but it had to oppose those national policies which inevitably would have permitted the triumph of American industrial capitalism everywhere in the nation.

So-called statistical demonstrations of steady growth notwithstanding, a real "take-off" could never have occurred until, as national policy evolved, Congress opened the vast Western public domain to free or easy settlement and permitted the quick exploitation of its natural resources of timber, stone, coal and other minerals; laid out a plan and supported

the building of trunk railroads to the Pacific across lands still un-
inhabited; set up high tariff walls behind which infant industries could
thrive; threw open America's doors to the immigrants of Europe to take
up farms in the public domain and to furnish that large, young and eager
working force so necessary for the development of heavy industry;
established national control over banking to expand and regularize the
money supply. All of these the slave South opposed; and by controlling
the Presidency, the Congress, and the Supreme Court for the greater part
of the ante-bellum period, it was able to prevent the adoption of a program that the Whigs had urged as early as the 1830s and that the Republicans were taking over in the 1850s.

The outbreak of the Civil War permitted a Republican Congress
swiftly to lay out the main lines of the grand design with which and
through which mercantile capitalism could be converted into industrial
capitalism. With the war over the anticapitalist ideology in the South as
well as in the North had been overthrown, the political power of the
Southern slave lords destroyed, and the political institutions and public
policies were already there to make the changeover possible. I am not
saying that during the Civil War itself large-scale industrial growth began;
I am saying that the Union's defeat of the slave South cleared the way for
industrialization. The mores of the nation, for good or ill, had radically
changed.

The statistics from 1869 on are good and reliable, and these we must
now examine. Here all economists the world over are deeply in the debt
of Simon S. Kuznets and Raymond W. Goldsmith, both professors of
economics and both working through the National Bureau of Economic
Research. Kuznets not only devised the operating methods by which a
nation's Gross National Product—the goods and services it turned out—
could be measured in monetary terms; he was also responsible for the
pioneering studies of this Gross National Product in the United States
by decades starting with 1869, and for studies comparing the American
experiences with those of other nations. Goldsmith was able to refine
Kuznets' figures even further so that rates of growth could be examined
on an annual basis instead of a decadal one.

Table 1 is based on Kuznets' constructions. It shows percentage changes
per decade from 1869 to 1913 for the Gross National Product, for the
GNP per capita, in constant dollars, and for population.

INTRODUCTION

TABLE 1

Country	Period	GNP, %	GNP per capita, %	Popula-tion, %
United States	1869–78 to 1904–13	56.0	27.5	22.3
United Kingdom ..	1860–69 to 1905–14	25.0	12.5	11.1
France	1841–50 to 1901–10	18.6	16.3	1.9
Germany	1860–69 to 1905–14	35.6	21.6	11.5
Canada	1870–79 to 1905–14	47.1	24.7	17.8
Japan	1878–87 to 1903–12	49.2	33.7	11.6

SOURCE: S. S. Kuznets, in *Economic Development and Cultural Change*, v. 5, October, 1956, p. 13.

The contrast between the United States, Canada and Japan on the one hand—all countries where mores had sharply changed at the beginning of the periods of their growth—and on the other hand the United Kingdom, France and Germany—all settled and mature countries—is apparent. Undoubtedly the great growth in America's population, and the consequent increase in the labor force, because of immigration, were important factors in the leap forward.

Goldsmith's figures, shown in Table 2, give annual rates of growth, again in constant dollars, for the United States.

TABLE 2

Period	Population, %	GNP, %	GNP per capita, %	Consump-tion, %	Consumption per full consumer, %
1869–98	2.17	4.32	2.11	4.75	2.33
1869–1913	2.03	4.24	2.16	4.49	2.26

SOURCE: U.S. Congress, *Hearings Before the Joint Economic Committee, 86th Cong. 1st Sess.*, Part 2—Historical and Comparative Rates of Production, Productivity, and Prices, pp. 232, 234, 236, and 3456, Washington, 1959.

One interesting observation is in order. A comparison of 1869-98 with 1869-1913 shows that sustained growth, at the same high rates, continued from 1898 to 1913: that period of giant industrial combinations which—so the Progressives of the time were arguing—was leading to trustification, the withholding of efficiency, and the grinding down of labor. One must always remember that figures like these are aggregates and part are based on mathematical calculations; to this extent, weak and soft spots in the economy cannot be revealed.

INTRODUCTION

Some figures of increases in the production of basic raw materials, on which growth was so heavily dependent, tell much the same story. The comparison in Table 3 is between 1860 and 1900; during those forty years the country's population increased 140 per cent.

TABLE 3

Commodity	1860, millions	1900, millions	Increase, %
Anthracite coal (short tons)	11.0	57.4	422
Bituminous coal (short tons)	9.0	212.3	2,260
Crude petroleum (barrels)	.5	45.8	9,060
Pig iron (short tons)	.9	15.4	1,600
Crude steel (long tons)	.01	10.2	10,190
Wheat (bushels)	173.1	559.3	223
Wheat exported (bushels)	4.0	102.0	2,700
Corn (bushels)	838.8	2,662.0	217
Cotton (bales)	3.8	10.1	170

SOURCE: U.S. Department of Commerce. *Historical Statistics of the United States,* 1960, *passim.*

The Mores and Entrepreneurship of the Time In these preliminary observations in which I set the stage for the full discussion of the accomplishments of the "Robber Barons" era, I have used two constructs—that of mores and that of entrepreneurship, or innovation. The first was systematically developed by William Graham Sumner, who, by the 1890s, was beginning to move away from his concerns with economics and public affairs to a study of cultural and comparative anthropology; in 1907 he published his seminal work, *Folkways,* in which the theory of the mores is fully explored with a dazzling learning. The second was the work of that brilliant young Viennese economist Joseph A. Schumpeter. When only twenty-eight years old, in 1911, he published in German his *The Theory of Economic Development,* which did not appear in an English translation until 1934. Schumpeter saw the circular flow of economic activity interrupted by the business cycle; this was so because entrepreneurs, as innovators, appeared in swarms to start new kinds of business ventures or to use new methods in old ones. A static economic world had become dynamic, and change meant improvement so long as the innovators had free rein.

Sumner started, in his analysis of a society, no matter how primitive nor how advanced, with its "folkways." These were the customary or habitual ways a people had devised for living together; they were traditional largely because they had been tested and adapted by experience. As he says in paragraph 31 of *Folkways:*

The folkways are the "right" ways to satisfy all interests, because they are traditional, and exist in fact. They extend over the whole life. . . . The "right" way is the way which the ancestors used and which has been handed down. The tradition is its own warrant. . . . The notion of right is in the folkways. It is not outside of them, of independent origin, and brought to them to test them. In the folkways, whatever is, is right.

As a society evolves to reach the stage of conscious reflection, as it works out a theory of "societal welfare" with an ethics and a law, the "folkways" become "mores." The mores are the rules of conduct which determine right and wrong; they are not absolute and eternal, and change takes place, but slowly and only in terms of those standards a society has already tested. Thus Sumner in paragraph 34:

When the elements of truth and light are developed into doctrines of welfare, the folkways are raised to another plane. Then they become capable of producing inferences, developing into new forms, and extending their constructive influence over men and society. Then we call them the mores. The mores are the folkways, including the philosophical and ethical generalizations as to societal welfare which are suggested by them, and inherent in them, as they grow.

And more fully, in paragraph 66:

They [the mores] are the ways of doing things which are current in a society to satisfy human needs and desires, together with the faiths, notions, codes and standards of well being which inhere in those ways, having a genetic connection with them. By virtue of the latter element the mores are traits in the specific character (ethos) of a society or period. They pervade and control the ways of thinking in all the exigencies of life, returning from the world of abstractions to the world of action, to give guidance and to win revivification.

The mores justify themselves; for their "goodness" or "badness" is based on their adjustment to the life conditions and the interests of the time or place. Thus in paragraph 65:

It is most important to notice that, for the people of a time or place, their own mores are always good, or rather that for them there can be no question of the goodness or badness of their mores. The reason is because the standards of good and right are in the mores. . . . Everything in the mores of a time and place must be regarded as justified with regard to that time and place. . . . We do not study them in order to approve some of them and condemn others. They are all equally worthy of attention from the fact that they existed and were used.

Part and parcel of this scheme of "truth and right" are rights themselves—customary in the folkways, written into laws and institutional arrangements in the mores. In a short essay, written about 1900, called "Rights," Sumner expounded the idea:

It is certainly far wiser to think of rights as rules of the game of social competition which are current here and now. They are not absolute. They are not antecedent to civilization. They are a product of civilization, or of the art of living as men have practiced it and experimented on it, through the whole course of history. They must be enjoyed under existing circumstances, that is, subject to limitations of tradition, custom, and fact. To be real they must be recognized in laws and provided for by institutions, but a great many of them, being inchoate, unsettled, partial, and limited, are still in the mores, and therefore vague and in need of further study and completion by courts and legislatures. This further work will be largely guided by the mores as to cognate matters, and by the conceptions of right and social welfare which the mores produce.

It is idle to argue that by "welfare" Sumner meant only material well-being; that by his insistence that institutions could change only slowly and then in conformance with the mores, he was underwriting inequality and exploitation; that his idea of rights or law meant only the law of private property and liberty of contract, and not the right of the weak to be protected from the strong.

The point is, these were the conceptions of societal welfare, of the mores, of the times. The mores of the post-Civil War period—in the articulations of its spokesmen, economists, spiritual leaders, academics; in the work of its legislatures and the rulings of its courts—gave approval to acquisition, unequal wealth, the competitiveness and ruthlessness of the period's entrepreneurs, or innovators. If there were victims and if many fell by the wayside, the dynamic change that resulted meant progress by all the economic indicators. Sumner had said: In the folkways, and also in the mores, "whatever is, is right." Most Americans agreed.

INTRODUCTION

To Schumpeter the key figures in the processes of economic development were the innovators. They were usually new men, often born obscurely and humbly—in an older vocabulary, they were interlopers and adventurers—who were able to seize the main chance and effect what Schumpeter called "the new combinations" that gave economic life its dynamic character. Schumpeter's argument ran as follows.

First, such new combinations could appear in one or all of a variety of ways. Schumpeter enumerated five. 1) The introduction of a new commodity, one with which consumers were not yet familiar, or of a new quality of a commodity. 2) The introduction of a new method of production or a new way of handling a commodity commercially. 3) The opening up of a new market. 4) The conquest of a new source of supply of raw materials. 5) A new form of organization of an industry, this might be the creation of a monopoly or the breaking up of an old one. It can be seen that innovations were not necessarily inventions and that inventors did not inevitably become innovators. Nor was innovation wholly technological. Innovators were businessmen (Schumpeter in fact called them captains of industry) who were able to start a whole new economic round which had linkage effects with other parts of the economy.

New combinations, as a rule, come through new firms, and, says Schumpeter:

[They] generally do not rise out of the old firms but start producing beside them; to keep to the example already chosen, in general it is not the owner of stagecoaches who builds railroads. This fact not only puts the discontinuity which characterizes the process we want to describe in a special light . . . but it also explains important features of the new course of events. Especially in a competent economy, in which new combinations mean the competitive elimination of the old, it explains on the one hand the process by which individuals and families rise and fall economically and socially and which is peculiar to this form of organization, as well as a whole series of other phenomena of the business cycle, of the mechanism of the formation of private fortunes, and so on.

Secondly, entrepreneurs appear in swarms: first in the particular industry in which the initial innovational step takes place; then in other sectors—and thus in widening circles through much of the economy. Competition also appears among these innovators, within the pioneering industry and between industries. "Hence," says Schumpeter of the consequences,

the first leaders are effective beyond their immediate sphere of action and so the group of entrepreneurs increases still further and the economic system is drawn more rapidly and more completely than would otherwise be the case in the process of technological and commercial reorganization which constitutes the mean of periods of boom.

Thirdly, new combinations require financing: the capitalist, then, is an agent apart who either puts together accumulated savings or—the more effective way—obtains the creation of credit through banks. It is the capitalist, in consequence, who is the risk-taker. Another source of financing, particularly in the very early stages of the innovational process, when the pioneer virtually commands the field, is "entrepreneurial profit": such profits can be and frequently are plowed back into the enterprise in order to maintain the initial competitive advantage.

Finally, the entrepreneur is a special type, and Schumpeter, in a fascinating analysis, sought to indicate his distinctive psychological and social qualities. He must be ready to back his hunches, to have the courage and will to single out the essential and disregard the unessential "even though one can give no account of the principles by which this is done."

He must be able to overcome the inertia of habit and have the energy and will to pursue his idea, to bring himself to look upon it "as a real possibility and not merely as a day-dream."

He must be strong enough to disregard the resistance of his fellows; committed as they are to habitual ways of acting and thinking, their hostility may take violent forms—ostracism, physical obstruction, even personal attack.

What are his motives? They are not hedonistic, in the sense that the entrepreneur is concerned only or largely with the satisfaction of his personal wants. In fact, his conduct is really nonhedonist because prominent among his characteristics is a willingness to avoid conspicuous consumption and more particularly leisure.

Rather, the entrepreneur, because his origins are frequently humble, seeks social recognition and social distinction. There is the will to conquer: "the impulse to fight, to prove oneself superior to others, to

succeed for the sake, not of the fruits of success, but of success itself."
Then there follows this striking passage:

The financial result is a secondary consideration, or, at all events,
mainly valued as an index of success and as a symptom of victory, the
displaying of which very often is more important as a motive of large
expenditure than the wish for the consumers' goods themselves.

And, perhaps most important of all, the entrepreneur is a creator,
working hard and imaginatively because of the pleasure to be derived
from getting things done. Says Schumpeter: "Our type seeks out difficulties, changes in order to change, delights in ventures. This group of
motives is the most distinctly anti-hedonist of the three."

This keen and perceptive analysis of the part played by innovation in
the economic life and of the social and psychological characteristics of
the innovator—when the prevailing mores were prepared to look upon
entrepreneurship and the entrepreneur as just and right—helps to explain
the emergence, acceptance, and triumph of that extraordinary company
of captains of industry of the "Robber Baron" period. To name but a
few: Jay Gould and J. J. Hill in railroading; Andrew Carnegie and
Henry C. Frick in iron and steel; John D. Rockefeller in oil refining;
Cyrus H. McCormick in agricultural implements; George Westinghouse,
Thomas Edison and Frank J. Sprague in electrical equipment; J. P.
Morgan and Jacob H. Schiff in investment banking; Philip Armour and
Gustavus F. Swift in meat packing; William Clark of the Singer Sewing
Machine Company in marketing.

In 1896, in the first volume of the *American Journal of Sociology,* C. R.
Henderson of the University of Chicago wrote, in a sense almost anticipating Sumner and Schumpeter:

It would be strange if the "captain of industry" did not sometimes
manifest a militant spirit, for he has risen from the ranks largely because
he was a better fighter than most of us. Competitive commercial life is . . .
a battlefield where the "struggle for existence" is defining the industrially
"fittest to survive." In this country the great prizes are not found in
Congress, in literature, in law, in medicine, but in industry. . . . The
social rewards of business prosperity, in power, praise and luxury, are
so great as to entice men of the greatest intellectual faculties. . . . The

very perils of the situation have a fascination for adventurous and inventive spirits. In this fierce though voiceless contest, a peculiar type of manhood is developed, characterized by vitality, energy, concentration, skill in combining numerous forces for an end and great foresight into the consequences of social events.

A final thought about the writing of history. In 1931, Herbert Butterfield, the distinguished Cambridge historian, entered the lists against the historical writers of his day with the publication of his *The Whig Interpretation of History*. He was disturbed over the prevailing tendency of looking at the past in terms of the values and the needs of the present—accepting what had gone on before, if it was in the contemporary scheme of things (democracy, equality, religious liberty, internationalism), or rejecting the past if its thinking and conduct ran counter to such emotional commitments. Said Butterfield, "The Whig historian stands on the summit of the twentieth century, and organizes his scheme of history from the point of view of his own day. . . ."

And Butterfield, more fully, went on to voice his protest as follows—and it is this attitude that informs the book I have written:

Real historical understanding is not achieved by the subordination of the past to the present, but rather by our making the past our present and attempting to see life with the eyes of another century than our own. It is not reached by assuming that our own life is the absolute to which Luther and Calvin and their own generation are only relative; it is only reached by fully accepting the fact that their generation was as valid as our generation, their issues as momentous as our issues and their day as full and as vital to them as our day is to us.

1

GOVERNMENT AND POLICY

CHAPTER ONE

GOVERNMENT, POLITICS, AND THE ECONOMY

Why the Civil War Was Fought   The thirty years before the outbreak
of the Civil War had involved all of the best men of the nation—in the
North as well as in the South—in the struggle over slavery. It was small
wonder that the country's elite had entered politics or gone into the
churches or had become publicists and pamphleteers, for here they had
platforms, and the press, the North had Emerson, Thoreau, Parker,
Webster and Clay and later Seward and Lincoln spoke for the North; and
Calhoun, Davis, Benjamin, and Stephens for the South. In pulpits, lecture
platforms, and the press, the North had Emerson, Thoreau, Whittier,
Wendell Phillips, and Horace Greeley; and the South, D. B. De Bow,
Edmund Ruffin, and George Fitzhugh. These, all first-class men, were
naturally and inevitably attracted to the tragic issue. That they were not
able to work out an accommodation—that they were less successful than
Washington, Hamilton, Madison, in an earlier critical period—does not
belie their talents or the total involvement of their hearts and minds.

Once need only contrast the state of political discussion, the position of
the churches, the moral commitment to question-raising and answering of
the following two generations. Except for a Blaine in politics and a
Beecher in the pulpit (and he followed rather than led) one is in the
presence of second-class men in public life. There were giants in those
days, of course (Henry Adams and Charles S. Peirce at once come to mind)
but their impact upon the roistering, unruly, exciting world in which
they lived, either in terms of rejection or acceptance, was nil. The best
thinking, the work of the imaginative, creative, innovational men, was
to be found in the areas of greatest activity, in industry and finance and in

[3]

those ancillary pursuits of engineering, journalism, and education which supported the complex processes of making goods and making money.

The Civil War had settled not only the slavery question, but all those matters of public policy which had been linked with it. North and South once more were reunited as a result of their acceptance of the verdicts of the battlefield. And they were united because of their agreement that public fostering of railroad construction, opening up of the vast public domain to agriculture, unhampered entry of European immigrants, national regulation of money and banking, creation of high tariff walls—in fact, all those devices that would speed up the industrialization of the nation—were desirable and salutary. Nor was this all. From every quarter assent was given; from the law courts, the churches, the writers of economic texts, the spokesmen for the workers (I am referring to the leaders of the national trade unions and of the American Federation of Labor). Society, generally, accepted the verdict which politics had endorsed. There was agreement that the new masters of industry and finance, who of course built up overtowering fortunes, were working for the common good: in opening up new avenues of employment; in producing goods on a mass basis and thus lowering their costs and making their availability general; in creating endless opportunities for talent.

Government approved and encouraged. Its greatest gifts were those public policies which have already been mentioned. At the same time, government did not encumber the newly created fortunes with heavy taxation (as Britain already was doing) or intervene to curb the cutthroat competition of the market place (as Germany and Japan were doing) or impose limitations on the quantity of money, in its broadest sense, so that the States were free to create new credit agencies. The absence of taxation upon personal incomes and inheritance and upon the property and earnings of companies, the absence of order and restraint in the business world, the absence of central banking—although all these led to wild swings in the business cycles—were precisely the key factors responsible for the growth and development of the United States. (A single curious phenomenon helps give an important clue to this extraordinary era: the United States was the only country in the world where even railroading, with its heavy capital investments, continued to be on a competitive footing). Coupled with these was the fact that American business (except for banks, railroads, insurance companies) was largely noncorporate: com-

[4]

panies were owned by individuals or partnerships, and because they were nonpublic in nature, profits did not have to be distributed among shareholders and could be plowed back into new plant and improvements.

It is true of course that a significant start toward industrialization had taken place during the decade before the outbreak of the Civil War; it is doubtful if these processes would have been accelerated had it not been for the war itself. The war freed men of the obsessive involvement in politics; the war, in fact, cleared the air everywhere.

It would be difficult to demonstrate that war in itself adds anything directly to research and industrial development. The enormous consumption and destruction of war materials require great additions to the processes of production—the utilization to full capacity of existing plants, the opening up of plants that previously would have been only marginal, the employment of marginal workers (for cost, obviously, is no factor)— but as a rule no real contributions during a period of war are made to techniques of business organization and management.

During the Civil War, iron and not steel continued the mainstay for the war industries and in railroading, although the Bessemer process was already known. There was no significant change in railroad operations themselves: the introduction of a standard gauge, the speeding up of through freight movements, the development of the air brake, the manufacture of heavier locomotives; all these came later. Electrification to any real extent—although the basic scientific ideas were common knowledge did not occur. Nor were there radical changes in the manufacture of cloth and clothing or in the preparation and movement of foodstuffs. All of these revolutionary innovations awaited the coming of peace.

There was one exception, and that was in agriculture. Heavier plows and the mechanical reaper had appeared before the Civil War: in order to overcome the shortage of labor on the land (the excitements of war naturally attract farming youth—their lives are ordinarily so humdrum), both acreage in wheat and corn and productivity due to mechanization sharply increased. The North, unlike the South, continued to be well fed; also, surpluses were available for export, usually to Britain, to help meet the unfavorable balance of payments and to shift British opinion over from hostility to at least neutrality. It can be argued (as it has been) that it was wheat that won the war for the North; the South's hope that cotton would win it for the South was quickly ended by the effectiveness of the

Northern naval blockade. Lancashire's mills were idle; but at least its working populations had cheap bread.

True, despite income taxes and high excises and the purchase of war bonds, profits during hostilities are made and can be utilized as part of the capital fund for expansion after the war—assuming that victory has occurred and government therefore is in a position to put an end to the wartime inflationary forces. So, in fact, it turned out during the Civil War and in the immediate postwar period.

The peace, when it comes, is faced by entirely new problems if significant advances are to take place. Will the vanquished accept the outcome of the war, harsh as the terms of the settlement may be? Will those policies have general acceptance that were adopted during the war, in part to assure victory, in part to accomplish those national purposes that previously had been thwarted because of inertia or domestic opposition? Will the radicalism that a time of war invariably unleashes be diverted or stilled so that the voices of moderation will prevail? Usually, no matter how complete the victory, an accommodation will have to be worked out with the defeated foe to gain its support for the general program, the only basis on which domestic tranquility can assure those fundamental changes society needs for its progress. All these considerations are particularly important if the war is a civil war, as it was in the United States during 1861-1865.

The Civil War and the Triumph of the Republican Party   The Civil War had been fought to preserve the Union; this was the official view and Lincoln had pressed it until he wrote the Emancipation Proclamation. But there were two other reasons why the war had taken place: to free the Negro slaves and to establish once and for all a governmental policy which would hasten industrialization in the United States. On the last, all Republicans joined together. The freedom of the Negroes and the grant to them of full legal and civil rights (plus equality of economic opportunity) was the particular concern of the Radical Republicans, with whom Lincoln was out of sympathy, at any rate until 1864. He was moving closer and closer to their position, however, and, had he survived, the Radical policy of Reconstruction—to maintain the South as a conquered province until Negro rights had been fully secured—might have been his, too; for Lincoln, unlike Andrew Johnson, was a skilled and realistic politician, and saw that the Radicals dominated Congress and meant to ride roughshod over all opposition.

But there were forces dividing the Radicals, and as soon as the war was over the common purpose that had held them together began to weaken. The Radicals were egalitarians to this extent: many of them prewar abolitionists, they regarded slavery as morally evil and at the same time they pressed for the creation of a society and a polity in which the less privileged—Southern whites as well as blacks—would have a decent chance to rise. They saw the instrumentalities of this new freedom in the economic program of the Republican Party if it was, in the postwar period, supplemented by a thoroughgoing scheme of internal reform or reconstruction in the South itself. It is one of the ironies of history that only part of this grand design could be realized; and, indeed, the egalitarianism to which the Radicals were so committed had to be surrendered to assure that internal peace which was so necessary for the industrial growth of the nation.

The economic program that had to be pressed once the Civil War had started—a program the Southerners had fought against so successfully in Congress for fully three decades before the outbreak of hostilities—included the following: the establishment of a firm and high protective tariff system; the passage of an agricultural homestead act with, at the same time, easy entry into mineral and timber lands; provision, by land grants and financial assistance, for the construction of a series of trunk railroad systems that would reach to the Pacific; generous public support for river and harbor improvement and flood control; a uniform currency; and the opening of American doors to the unrestricted flow of free labor from Europe and Asia, aided by a contract-labor law.

On the questions of money and banking—whether the necessary wartime policy of currency expansion should be continued; whether the newly created national banks should be left alone in the field as the issuer of notes—there was wide division in the ranks of the Republican Party. Roughly, it may be said that those who spoke for the newer men and for fresh opportunities in enterprise were for both high tariffs and soft money: behind high tariff walls, domestic manufacturers could grow and expand, and a larger money supply would furnish that broadened credit base needed to finance risky ventures. The position taken by their opponents—and it was to be the dominant one—had been essentially laid down by Alexander Hamilton eighty years previously: given a sound banking system based on specie payments and the return to the gold standard, national solvency would restore American credit in the eyes of the world, permit the flow once more of foreign investments into the United States, and make it possible, through the expansion of exports, for America to achieve a favorable balance of trade.

Once the South had been brought back into the national system (at the price of the abandonment of Radical egalitarianism), the Republican economic program was to prevail. Only on the question of money and banking did disagreements continue, but even here, by the formal end of the Reconstruction period in 1877, dissident voices were muted. They were to remain unimportant for two decades. It was not until the opening of the 1890s that Southern farmers and the Populists—largely from the wheat-growing trans-Mississippi West—raised once more the money and banking questions. The Democratic Party was taken over by these forces in 1896, but their victory was brief.

Thus, by the middle 1870s, the United States was committed to the return to the gold standard. Efforts to expand the fiat money of the Civil War, the greenbacks, were curbed. The Civil War short-term Treasury notes, really part of the inflated circulating medium, were consolidated into long-term bonds and the process was begun of reducing their volume. The straitjacket in which the National Banking system found itself—on note issue particularly in newer regions where there was a dearth of bank-note currency—was eased; more important, the State banks, which had been threatened with extinction by the imposition of a 10 per cent excise tax on their notes in 1865, were revived by new functions granted them by generous State legislation.

Pursuing a program of rigorous economy—which, of course, made possible the quick dismantling of the Civil War tax structure—and steadfastly rejecting the expansion of the federal authority, the central government did everything it could to encourage business confidence: of manufacturers, bankers, merchants engaged in the export trade.

By 1877—in fact, even earlier in the 1870s, when dedicated and intransigent Radicals like Charles Sumner, Thaddeus Stevens, George Julian, and Benjamin Wade had finally disappeared from the political scene— Radical Republicanism, with its broad commitment of Negro equality and economic opportunity for small business enterprises through protectionism and soft money, was finished. The crusading fervor, the idealism, the political and economic Jacobinism of the original Republican Party was dead and unmourned. With the election of Rutherford B. Hayes, the Republicans had become the party of business—big rather than small, the party that was to be the spokesman for manufacturing, the great trunk railroads, the national banks, the investment bankers, the merchants constantly expanding the American export trade.

The post-Civil War Democratic Party did not oppose. In the North and in the South, it accepted the Republican economic program. Similarly, in the States, there was agreement, and this included the liberalization of corporation and banking laws, the generous treatment of railroads, notably as far as easy tax assessments were concerned, and the grant of charters, frequently with rights in perpetuity, to promoters seeking to develop municipal traction facilities, gas and electricity for power and light, water companies. Of equal importance was the fact that the State courts were the first to move firmly to defend property rights against the encroachments of State legislatures trying, under the guise of the police power, to expand their rights to regulate industry and write social legislation.

There were some exceptions to this broad application of the general compromise in politics under which business growth was made possible without serious interference on the part of governments. In the Congress, Democrats regularly presented tariff bills that called for revision of the high protectionism that had become accepted policy by 1864, but these were demands for modifications only in detail. In 1894, when the Democrats—for the only time until 1913—were in control of both houses of the Congress and Grover Cleveland was President, a so-called reform tariff was passed. But it changed schedules only slightly, and this was because Democratic Senators voted with Republicans against essential tinkering with a system to which they had become committed and of which their constituents too were the beneficiaries. True, the tariff act of 1894 incorporated an income tax provision; in a year, the Supreme Court had declared it unconstitutional. So incensed was President Cleveland with the tariff tinkering of his fellow Democrats that he permitted the bill to become law without his signature, declaring caustically, "the livery of Democratic tariff reform has been stolen and worn in the service of Republican protection."

[9]

Similarly, in the case of the public lands, in the two Democratic administrations of Grover Cleveland, efforts were made to halt the rush into the public lands of the pre-emptors of mineral, timber and water rights, but these were slight and unavailing. On the other hand, Grover Cleveland was a hard-money man who, as soon as he had legislative backing in the Congress, had the Sherman Silver Purchase Act of 1890 repealed in 1893; and he was open and violent in his condemnation of Bryan's soft-money heresies.

True, two pieces of federal legislation were passed, the Interstate Commerce Act in 1887 and the Sherman Antitrust Act in 1890, to impose restraints on business combinations and concentrations. The first, President Cleveland was indifferent to, and the law really did not have any significant effect until the enactment of the Hepburn Act of 1906; while the second was quickly narrowed in its application by the Supreme Court.

It is important to have in mind that such efforts at restriction and restraint as emerged in the States—the Granger legislation regulating railroads and warehouses in the late 1870s and early 1880s—were ineffectual. Even before the Supreme Court's reversal—originally it had declared the laws constitutional and then in 1886 unconstitutional—these statutes had fallen into desuetude. The initial moves in the States to shift the base of taxation from real property to corporate improvements and capitalization did not come until the 1890s. It was not until the courts had finally cleared away all the technical objections that a radical recasting of the tax system began to take place—and this clearing away took more than a decade, in New York State for example.

One should observe, further, that reform governors, like Robert La Follette in Wisconsin and Albert Cummins in Iowa (both Republican, incidentally), did not appear until the turn of the century. Except for the threat of Populism—and in the South this went hand in hand with the appearance of new leaders of the white masses like Benjamin Tillman in South Carolina and Jeff Davis in Arkansas who were more interested in taking over the Democratic Party than in social and monetary reform—there was no cloud, not even one as big as a man's hand, to threaten the fair skies. Public nonintervention prevailed; business development and growth, by whatever means, had the blessing of government.

A word, in passing, about agricultural discontent, a subject to which a return will be made later in greater detail. Farmers' organizations did not participate in the great money debates of the late 1860s and the 1870s, that had to do with the expansion of the currency, the return to the gold standard, and the limited powers of the national banks in the creation of currency. When farmers took alarm and mobilized for legislative action, it was to pass the Granger Laws.

The initial demand for silver coinage that ended in the Bland-Allison Act of 1878 really stemmed from the silver-mining interests, and they obtained only a limited relief. There is no doubt that agricultural credit was restricted. More important, perhaps, was the fact that interest rates were high and in the case of farm mortgages they were certainly too high, particularly where farmers were overexpanding speculatively, as they were in the trans-Mississippi West. There were a number of reasons for hostility to the national banking system: the banks under it could not lend on mortgages; the amount of note issue was fixed by law; the capitalization demanded for the establishment of such banks was too high to encourage their appearance in the rural districts of the South and the trans-Mississippi West; and the right to issue notes and the proportions allotted favored the well-established mercantile and industrial centers of the East and the Middle West. The South and the West also had had an early and unhappy experience during the 1840s and 1850s with rapidly depreciating and even worthless bank notes.

This is why the farmers distrusted the national banks (the only ones which could issue notes; the State banks could not) and demanded public money instead. The Southern Farmers' Alliance in the last years of the 1880s was the first to raise this cry; the idea was written into the Sherman Silver Purchase Act which called for the issue of Treasury notes; and it of course became a fundamental demand of the Democratic Party in 1896. The notion of public money and hostility to bank money lingered on: Bryan, in 1913, for example, before he would accede to the Federal Reserve bill, insisted that the notes of the federal reserve banks be made an obligation of the federal government; and as late as 1933, in the writing of the first Agricultural Adjustment Act, a section was included that authorized the federal government to issue up to three billions of dollars in paper notes.

Relief, as far as short-term credit was concerned, and to a greater extent than is commonly realized for long-term credit as well, came from another quarter: the revived State banks. States passed laws allowing more liberal charters; banks were permitted to lend on longer-term paper and on mortgages. The fact is, bank loans, or deposits, before the nineteenth century was over far exceeded the amount of bank notes in circulation—and the new State banks played an important role here. Farmers in the South and trans-Mississippi West undoubtedly benefited from this expansion of money, as they did from the mortgage loans they could obtain from the State banks and trust companies, which also were State-chartered. Funds for mortgages also appeared from the growing insurance companies and from foreign corporations set up for this purpose.

It was not so much a dearth of credit (except, probably, in the South) as the fact that interest rates (plus commissions) were too high that caused the Populist to raise the cry of the "money power" and charge the banks with usurious practices. The farmers also wanted another kind of credit—the sort the banks could not extend them. They wanted ways and means to permit them to hold nonperishable crops off the market until prices were in their favor, instead of being compelled to dump their products, as soon as the harvests were over, into what quickly became a glutted market. This demand was at the heart of the Southern Alliance's Sub-Treasury Plan (incorporated into the Populist platform of 1892). It was a particular kind of credit, in short, that the farmers sought rather than a broad and general expansion of the money supply. Certainly the growers of agricultural export staples—cotton, wheat, meat products—knew that an inflated currency and therefore higher prices would jeopardize the commanding position they were holding in world markets. As it was, by the 1890s, foreign competition was beginning to appear in serious form from the new grass and arable lands being opened up by railroads in Canada, Australia and New Zealand, South Africa, Argentina, even Russia. This factor, as much as any other, gave urgency to the demands for relief coming from the militant agricultural leaders; if foreign markets were going to taper off (except for cotton), at least the domestic market would be favorable if prices were higher as a result of the augmentation of the money supply.

There was one point, notably, where farmers suffered—in addition to being the victims of railroad practices—and that was as regards taxes. One wonders why this subject has not been explored completely, as have other phases of agricultural discontent. Everywhere in the United States, real property (and this meant agricultural lands) bore a disproportionate share of the tax burden, for there were neither income taxes nor taxes of any consequence on companies and public-utility corporations. The railroads, particularly, were the beneficiaries of those generous programs which not only the federal government but States and cities as well had given their blessings to in order to hasten construction. Cities gave them rights of way and sites for terminals and yards; the federal government made enormous land grants from the public domain, as did the States, too; Texas and Missouri were notably generous. Lieu lands—to replace the sections granted which already were pre-empted—were a particular source of irritation, for railroads were slow to take up their claims in them. They remained therefore undeveloped; many of the railroad grants turned out to be rich in minerals and lumber. All of this escaped taxation either entirely or at any real worth. And as far as road-building was concerned, there was no federal program, carrying appropriations with it, until 1916. Roads had to be paid for locally and with such slight contributions as could be extracted from the States, and therefore, in addition to schools and poorhouse relief, were local responsibilities. All this was added to the load of taxation that real property (which meant farms) had to carry.

These factors were at the heart of farmer discontent and agitation rather than the decline in prices, which continued from 1873 to 1897, for farm productivity was steadily improving and industrial prices were dropping even more sharply than the prices of agricultural goods. Bryan persuaded farmers—who had their misgivings; Populist leaders and middle-class sympathizers like Henry Demarest Lloyd in 1896 felt they had been the victims of smart political maneuvering. They were dubious that cheap money, through the free and unlimited coinage of silver rather than the Sub-Treasury plan, was going to end all their troubles.

The South and the Radical Republicans   It has been pointed out that the South not only had to be brought back into the Union, in its "normal relations"; the South had as well to accept the economic program of the Republican Party and understand that its future lay in industrial expansion—railroad construction, mineral exploitation, the development of manufactures, the creation of sound banking systems—rather than its continuance exclusively as a producer of raw materials, largely agricultural. The processes of Southern "redemption," the taking over of

[13]

governments out of the hands of Scalawags and Carpetbaggers (many of whom were honest and sincere Radicals) and their Negro allies, began as soon as the Presidency of Andrew Johnson was over.

The slacking of interest from the center in Washington—due in large measure to the increasing disappearance of the Old Radicals from Congress and the administrative offices—played a major part. The Freedmen's Bureau and the Union League Clubs, which had been powerful agencies for assuring the political participation of the Negroes, the creation of welfare programs, and the safeguarding of their civil and economic rights, began to dwindle in influence. The Freedmen's Bureau was abolished in 1872. The Union League Clubs ended by becoming rich men's clubs. Thus the burning passions and social commitments of men cool off and ossify. The great program of Stevens and Sumner to assure economic egalitarianism in the South—the confiscation of the lands of those who had been in active rebellion and their redistribution among the landless, whites as well as blacks ("Forty Acres and a Mule" became the cry of these Jacobin Radicals)—was permitted to languish in committee. The thought of confiscation of real property frightened Northerners as much as it did Southerners.

Terror in the South was invoked. Intimidation by armed men and night riders and finally the organized floggings, mutilations and murders by the Ku Klux Klan and similar organizations began to have their effect. More and more Negroes stayed away from the polls; more and more Southern States fell into the hands of the "Redeemers"; indeed, by 1870 the process was already under way and this despite the enactment of federal Force Acts in 1870 and 1871, which authorized federal authorities—courts, marshals, troops—to take over where civil disturbances broke down law enforcement and led to the revocation of civil rights. The second Force Act of 1871 aimed at "armed combinations" and permitting the suspension of habeas corpus, broke the back of Klan resistance; but white terror in the South had already achieved its purpose.

What is being called here Old Radicalism was gone and its influence already stripped by the early 1870s. It was one of those only too rare interludes in human history—a moment of truth. It embodied an unyielding, dedicated commitment to decency and national honor, which insisted that slavery had to be destroyed root and branch and which pushed Lincoln during the war into extreme measures, the ultimate one of which was the induction of Negroes into the Unionist armed forces. It was revolutionary in the Jacobin sense in its insistence upon full and equal political, civil and economic rights for the white masses and the freed Negroes of the South. It wrote the excellent Reconstruction State constitutions embodying all these ideas, including the one of nonsegregated schools and colleges.

This Old Radicalism was replaced by the New Radicalism, made up of younger men in Congress and in public life who during the war had followed the lead of Stevens, Sumner, Wade and the rest in pushing the energetic prosecution of the war. They also had supported the Republican economic program; had, in the beginning, insisted upon Congressional Reconstruction with its stern policies of the Fourteenth Amendment. The split that occurred in the ranks of the Radicals followed two lines: first, on the money question, as has been pointed out; and, secondly, on the protection of the rights guaranteed in the Fourteenth Amendment and in the Southern Reconstruction constitutions.

The New Radicals—Roscoe Conkling of New York, James A. Garfield and John Sherman of Ohio, James G. Blaine of Maine—were the spokesmen for capitalism, too, but not of small business and equality of opportunity; it was a capitalism of combinations and concentrations, railroad and other public service corporations, sound banking, and sound money. The emotional tensions and drives of the Old Radicals, which devotion to abolition had produced, were alien and remote to these newer men. An agreement had to be made with the South—and it was not to be through the Force Acts—to make possible the orderly penetration of Northern capital and enterprise into it and to bring it back into a national market. Only on such a basis could they expect the new and rapidly growing industrial enterprise, now released from its earlier restraints as a result of the war's victory, to thrive.

The "Redeemers" of the South—those who controlled Southern governments and the Democratic Party until the 1890s—completely fell in with such plans. The "Redeemers" were not the old plantation class; rather they represented a combination of landlords and business enterprisers allied with Northern financial, railway, and mineral interests. Many of them, and in this sense they resembled the Scalawags and Carpetbaggers, were men on the make; but unlike the spokesmen for the Old Radicals in the South, they were nonegalitarians, as much concerned lest

[15]

the poorer Southern whites seek political power as they were hostile to Negro equality. To divide poorer whites and Negroes—and themselves obtain control of State governments and the Democratic Party—was a key to their conduct. It was not uncommon for these leaders of the New South to vote Negroes against white candidates hostile to them. It is important to have in mind that the legal disfranchisement of the Negroes in the South did not begin occurring until the 1890s; and this, ironically enough, was accomplished by the spokesmen for the white masses, exactly those whom the Radicals had sought to raise in status and economic position along with the blacks.

In any event, the "Redeemers" succeeded in driving a wedge between whites and blacks; the whites were won over and began to desert the Reconstruction governments; and this, plus the fact of growing indifference in Washington, made the processes of "redemption" easy. The first States to be recaptured were Tennessee, Virginia, and North Carolina, during 1869-71; later, during 1874-76, followed Mississippi, Alabama, Texas, and Arkansas. As has been said, the Freedmen's Bureau in 1872 was permitted to die; in the same year, Washington stopped sending federal troops into the South to assure the observance of federal election laws; and in the same year, too, all but a very small remnant of the former Confederate leaders were restored all their civil rights. The South again had a leadership; but rather than reviving old hatreds, it was prepared to come to terms with the victorious North. Finally, in 1877, as a result of a bargain made following the contested election of 1876, federal troops were withdrawn from South Carolina, Florida, and Louisiana, and Reconstruction, with its high hopes of the creation of an egalitarian society, was abandoned. This is the struggle that today has been renewed with fairer chances of success. It is apparent that the ghosts of the unfinished business of history will continue to trouble men until these uneasy spirits are finally satisfied and laid to rest.

Industrial Capitalism and the South   This analysis of the willingness of the Southern "Redeemers" to work hand in glove with the New Radicals, in economic terms, at any rate, is confirmed by the acute comments of C. Vann Woodward in his *Origins of the New South, 1877-1913.* He points out that many of the "Redeemers" looked to that great Whig spokesman, Henry Clay, for their inspiration (his "American System" had been based on high tariffs, internal improvements, and sound money and banking), and he cites the example of General John C. Brown, the governor of the first Confederate State, Tennessee, to have been redeemed. Brown had been an ante-bellum Whig; after the War he became vice-president of the Texas and Pacific Company (that ambitious scheme fathered by Thomas A. Scott, who too was president of the Pennsylvania Railroad, to construct a Southern transcontinental rail system) and also was made president of the Tennessee Coal, Iron and Railroad Company. There were many others of these new men, like Brown, throughout the South, who eagerly allied themselves with Northern capital to exploit the section's great opportunities for fresh fortunes in transportation, mining, banking and manufactures and who hoped for federal subsidies for Southern shipping companies and for river and harbor improvement and flood control.

In bringing about the reconciliation between North and South, the decision to name Rutherford B. Hayes of Ohio, the Republican candidate, President of the United States, was the keystone to the arch. The Hayes-Tilden election of 1876 had ended with not only a popular majority for the Democratic Tilden but his capture of 184 uncontested electoral-college votes; Hayes had only 166, but he claimed the 19 votes of South Carolina, Florida, and Louisiana (the only remaining Southern States where there were Reconstruction governments bolstered up by federal troops). Today, there is general agreement among historians that Tilden had carried Florida with its four votes and possibly Louisiana as well, and had therefore been honestly elected. But because separate certificates were filed by the Republican and Democratic returning boards of the three contested Southern States, the election was thrown into the Congress, which in turn set up an Electoral Commission. (It was headed by James A. Garfield of Ohio; he was to receive his reward four years later when he was given the Republican nomination for the Presidency.) Tilden needed but one of the disputed votes to be declared President, while Hayes needed all of them.

The complex and frequently quite cynical negotiations that went on behind the scenes between Republican politicians and concession-and-subsidy-hungry Southern Democrats need not concern us here. As Woodward demonstrates, many of the Southerners were Whig rather than (Jacksonian) Democrat in their orientation; they were distrustful of their Northern Democratic brethren; and they felt realistically that their chances of getting financial help were better in Republican than in Democratic hands. In any event, Hayes let it be known that, if chosen, he would withdraw federal troops from the South, appoint a Tennessean postmaster general (as the chief dispenser of the federal patronage) and support financial aid to the South. Hayes, in consequence, was named President by the Electoral Commission, and the desperate efforts of Northern Democrats in Congress, through filibuster, to reject its decision failed, because Southern Democrats refused to stand shoulder to shoulder with their Northern colleagues. When Hayes withdrew the federal troops from the capitals of Louisiana and South Carolina, Southern Reconstruction—which had started out so loftily, with so much participation on the part of so many devoted men and women—ended shabbily. It went out with a whimper. So the curtain was rung down on the bitter drama; it turned out, however, to be only the second act; the third and final one is still being played out today.

The fact that Hayes could not carry out the other part of the bargain that had brought him the Presidency—the building of the Texas and Southern Railway with large public subsidies and the enactment of Southern river and harbor legislation—was a temporary setback. There were too many other opportunities for business promotions and money-making in what came to be called the "New South" to hold fast the loyalties of Southern businessmen and politicians to the agreements that had been beaten out in 1877. Certainly, renewing the old alliance with the agricultural West rather than with the industrial and financial East would be suicidal. Woodward quotes the Charleston *News and Courier* of December 13, 1878:

With one section or the other the South must go, and our fixed opinion is that the *permanent interests of the South lie with the East rather than with the West.* The aim of this being to . . . avoid whatever is revolutionary in politics, sociology, or finance, the South must go with the East, despite its aggregating self-assertion, rather than join hands with the West, which is learning the A.B.C. of statesmanship. [Italics in original.]

And Woodward comments: "The reconstructed South came to be regarded in the eighties as a bulwark of, instead of a menace to, the new economic order."

Northern (and Southern) capital moved on many fronts to open up the rich economic opportunities of the South, among them its timbering and coal and iron resources, railroad construction and consolidation, and factory development and expansion. There were still unpre-empted public lands in the South (in Alabama, Arkansas, Florida, Louisiana, and Mississippi); during Reconstruction, entry into them had been virtually stopped pending the passage of a Southern Homestead Act which, as we have seen, never got Congressional approval. In 1876, all the restrictions, particularly that of cash sale, were lifted; and, in consequence, large tracts of timber and mineral lands went quickly to Northern and Southern land jobbers (and to British companies) and to timber and mining concerns. Between 1877 and 1888, more than 5½ million acres of federal lands were sold in the Southern States. The Southern States themselves, virtually for a song, disposed of large portions of what was left of State-held lands; at the same time, following the federal pattern, they granted free great tracts of land to railroad companies. Texas, for example (Missouri almost matched this prodigality), turned over to twelve railroad companies more than 32 million acres, an area larger than the whole state of Indiana. The increase in lumbering in the South tells in little the characteristics of the general tale: between 1880 and 1900, in the five Gulf States alone, the value of lumber production increased from $13 million to $73 million.

The 1880s saw the launching of a great railroad boom in the South; here, Northern and European capital played the leading roles, although the South assisted manfully by land grants and subsidies, favorable tax treatment, the refusal to pass regulatory and restrictive legislation. East of the Mississippi, in the single decade, the South laid down more than 14,000 miles of track; in the South as a whole, mileage increased from 16,600 miles in 1880 to 39,000 miles in 1890—a rate of growth that was almost twice that of the whole country's.

Many of the small railroad companies thus begun were inefficient and unnecessarily competitive; it was inevitable that consolidations should take place. By 1890, possibly half of the railroads' mileage in the South was under the control of a dozen or so such integrations. The most important of these was the Richmond Terminal Company, which, starting with the Richmond and Danville Railroad, before the 1880s were over, through the absorption of the East Tennessee and the Virginia and Georgia Railroad, controlled 6,000 miles of rail lines.

The depression of the 1890s laid low the Richmond Terminal system as it did so many of the other railroad consolidations of the country; it was the House of Morgan, starting in 1893, that reorganized it and, as the Southern Railway, made it one of the outstanding railroading properties of the country. Stockholders of the bankrupt or financially embarrassed lines in the consolidation were heavily assessed to obtain new capital (but they were given in exchange preferred stock); new bonds and stock were issued. The floating debt and its carrying charges were scaled down and fresh funds were immediately allotted for new construction and modernization. In September, 1894, when the reorganization was completed, the new Southern Railway was running 4,500 miles of road; by the end of 1895 another 3,000 was added, this including the Central of Georgia. Placed in charge of the rehabilitated system was Samuel Spencer, a native Georgian and a trained railroad man, who had become Morgan's railroad expert and a partner in the firm. It was generally agreed that not only had the reorganization been one of Morgan's greater accomplishments but it gave the South a model transportation system.

The expansion of the railroad net, connecting more and more back country with Atlantic and Gulf cities, brought on an impressive increase in exports from Southern ports. Between 1880 and 1901 exports from the section grew almost 100 per cent in volume, as compared with 65 per cent for the rest of the country. New Orleans and Galveston notably benefited from the movement of interior products to the sea, the most important being cotton, flour, and lumber, and increasingly coal, iron, and petroleum. The federal government now stood by generously; between 1891 and 1906, river and harbor appropriations allotted $8 million for the Mississippi River below New Orleans, $7.5 million for Galveston, and $3 million for Mobile.

A new iron and coal industry also emerged, beginning with 1879 and thanks to the appearance of British and Northern capital. The Louisville and Nashville Railroad, largely foreign-owned, was a leader in the opening up of the rich mineral resources of Alabama, in twenty years expending more than $30 million in railroad extensions and improvement and in iron mines and furnaces. To quote Woodward:

By the late eighties the South was producing far more pig iron than the nation produced before the war, investment in blast furnaces was mounting faster than in any Northern State; and between 1876 and 1901 pig-iron production increased seventeen times in the South and only eight times in the country at large.

Tobacco manufacture took on a new lease of life, thanks to the spread of a lighter leaf (the so-called bright tobacco), the growing popularity of cigarettes, and the mechanization of the whole industry. Leadership here was almost entirely in Southern hands. A Southerner invented the cigarette machine; other innovations, in processing, packing, bagging, and labeling, were the work of Southerners; and the modernization and great expansion of the industry was the product of the ingenuity, daring, and ruthlessness of Southerners like James R. Day, Julian S. Carr, R. J. Reynolds, and Washington and James Duke.

The same was true of cotton textiles. The year 1880 was not a turning point, for cotton manufactures had continued in the Southern States during Reconstruction; but there can be no doubt that the two decades of the 1880s and 1890s saw a vast expansion of the industry. The number of mills increased impressively; more important was the growth in number of spindles; but—and this was the heart of the matter—with fresh capital, new plants and therefore improved machinery could be erected and installed. From 1880 to 1900, in the four outstanding textile States of North Carolina, South Carolina, Georgia, and Alabama, the number of spindles increased from 423,000 to 3,792,000. In all the Southern States, in the same twenty years, the number of operatives grew from 16,741, to 97,559 and the capital invested from $17,376,000 to $124,597,000. A good deal of this capital came from small investors in the South who, spurred on by promotional campaigns that frequently took on an evangelical fervor (and encouraged by high profits, for modern Southern mills were competing with obsolescent Northern ones), poured their savings into the new enterprise. But Northern capital contributed heavily, notably in furnishing the textile machinery and in financing the factoring houses which finished the gray textiles and sold the cloth.

Side by side with these new industrial activities, new towns emerged from what had been country crossroads or sleepy river communities: Birmingham, Anniston, Bessemer, and Sheffield in Alabama; Chattanooga and Memphis in Tennessee; Roanoke in Virginia; Winston-Salem,

Greensboro, Gastonia, and Durham in North Carolina; Natchez in Mississippi. And as they expanded, real-estate booms appeared to tempt, to their sorrow, the unwary and covetous with dreams of fabulous profits. But, at least, in many of the towns there began the processes of urban improvement—paved and lighted streets, water-supply systems, and municipal traction.

Was the South a "Colonial" Dependency of the North? These were dramatic changes, and while they did not revolutionize the South's economy in a generation—for the South continued largely agrricultural in its activities and interests—they kept pace with the general industrial growth of the nation. When measured by per capita wealth and income, however, the South continued to be the poorest section of the country; but it is fanciful to assume that this was so because the South was now in a "colonial" relationship to the East. So runs the theory of colonial exploitation (first advanced by the English economist John Hobson and later put in its most sensational form by Lenin): not only had so many of the improvements been financed by Northern (and British) capital, but the profits of the new enterprises were constantly being drained off by absentee management and ownership. To put the charge in its most spectacular terms, the Houses of Morgan and Rockefeller were holding the South in thrall, for increasingly they were speaking for the great railroad, steamship, iron and steel, coal (and later petroleum) integrations.

Enough has been said here to make this assumption a highly dubious one. The new industrialization was not imposed from the outside without consent; quite the reverse, for the leaders of the new South did everything in their power—by direct representation, by cajolery, by entreaty—to encourage extrasectional capital investment. They themselves participated in the movement, investing when they had the funds. Indeed, they assumed leadership themselves in initial postwar railroad construction, the cotton-textile industry, tobacco manufacture, and they benefited directly and indirectly. They became the functionaries (the management, the technicians) of the new industries; they developed the needed ancillary service enterprises; they took part in and many waxed rich from urban booms and growth.

Again, the new factories, mills, and mines of the South did not thrive because of labor exploitation. We should remember that trade unionism was weak everywhere throughout the country at this time. That new Southern enterprises were successful, therefore, was not because they were "runaway" (non-union) shops or because the wage differentials were marked. Allowing for differences in cost of living, the wages of skilled and semiskilled workers in Southern railroads, coal and iron, steel, cotton textiles and tobacco manufacture did not deviate markedly from national standards. Initially, one may assume, wages would be low, for country, and frequently hill, people had to be trained to master sometimes complex mechanical processes; but once skills were acquired, wage rates were reaching prevailing levels.

We should note too that, rather than skimming off the cream, the capitalist outsiders reinvested earnings—and fresh capital—in the section's companies and developments. The great improvements that took place in the Southern Railway Company and the steady advance of the Tennessee, Coal, Iron, and Railroad Company (which did not content itself with mining coal and iron but which sat down to create a great industrial complex in Alabama and Tennessee that was beginning to make Northern steelmen more and more uneasy) are only two cases in point. In fact, the continued decline of Northern textiles was as much due to greedy profit-taking by the scions of the New England founders (many of whom had become absentee *rentiers*), and the consequent neglect of modernization, as to the commonly advanced reasons of unfair Southern wage, tax, and rent differentials; while the steady advances of Southern textiles and the first great change-over to synthetic fibers which took place in their mills—undoubtedly went hand in hand with the plowing back of earnings.

An aside devoted to the Tennessee, Coal, Iron, and Railroad Company will prove illuminating. By 1887, it was recognized as the largest single owner of iron ore lands and furnaces in the United States. (This was before Carnegie's great forward push in the 1890s.) In 1892 the company expanded enormously by consolidation, among its new properties being the big De Bardeleben interests which were Southern in origin. Not only did it possess 400,000 acres of coal and iron lands in Alabama and Tennessee; it had seventeen iron furnaces. As a result, it was exporting pig iron to England, Europe and Japan, and Birmingham had become the largest pig-iron shipping point in the country and the third largest in the world.

In 1897, the Tennessee Company began to make its own steel, using the more efficient open-hearth method rather than the Bessemer process, which, except for the Carnegie Steel Co., was still generally prevailing in Pittsburgh. Before a decade was over, the Tennessee Ensley plant in Alabama was manufacturing a large part of the open-hearth steel rails in the country; it was no wonder that in 1907 the United States Steel Corporation had to acquire such a dangerous rival, paying $35 million for all the Tennessee properties. This, of course, had nothing to do with staying the course of the panic of that year—an excuse that President Theodore Roosevelt too readily accepted from Morgan; it was simply a recognition of the power of a Southern company whose natural and financial resources had been utilized to press modernization and engage in stiff competition.

Southerners participated in and gained from the new industrialization. The workers were not the victims of outside ownership and direction; in fact, industrial wages were higher than the payments of those who were still in the handicrafts and in the semimechanized trades. And a good deal of reinvestment occurred.

Why, then, did the South continue relatively poor if it was not "colonialism" that kept it in bondage? If there was exploitation—and there was—it was because Southerners themselves held back the advance of the South on a mighty front. By 1900, probably as much as 70 per cent of the South's labor force was still agricultural; but it was an agriculture based on the cruel and inequitable sharecropping and crop-lien systems under which millions of men, women and children—white as well as black—always lived on the edge of starvation. The land reform which lay at the heart of Radical Reconstruction, once it had been abandoned in Congress, was never taken up in the South. The South, in consequence, was content to grow its cotton, corn, and tobacco through the misuse and abuse of a dependent and ignorant rural population. The crop-lien system and the store-financing of the croppers had virtually converted the former slaves and poor whites into peons; they were tied to the soil.

The hoped-for educational expansion of the South—another great dream of the Radicals—died with the failure of Reconstruction. Neither the "Redeemers" nor their successors—the leaders of the white masses— were interested in popular and higher education and the expansion of the social services, both of which would have improved the South's "human capital." The South had no counterparts to the great reforming governors of the North and West until, curiously, the appearance of Huey Long in Louisiana. The "Redeemers" were indifferent to social change and betterment, maintaining their political power by manipulation and fraud; the leaders of the white masses obtained and kept power (as many still do today) by disfranchising the Negroes and constantly keeping alive the fires of race hatred and fears and by willfully maintaining their following ignorant, prejudiced, and dependent.

It was not because of its reliance upon cotton that the South was poor. Why did Kansas do so much better with its dependence upon wheat and Iowa with its dependence upon corn? The South was poor because of its wretched land system, the bigotry and cynicism of its political leaders, and the primitive nature of its educational and welfare programs. These, combined, held down standards of living, so that the South exported the products of its enterprise instead of utilizing its coal, iron, and lumber for the further expansion of industry, and its consumer goods for the feeding and clothing of its own people. Race hatred and ignorance prevented the growth of a regional mass market and the accelerating processes of the development of local light industries and services. Not until the 1930s and 1940s—when federal funds began to pour into the South on a large scale—did per capita wealth and income begin to inch up. In 1929, the per capita annual income in the South, as a per cent of the non-South, stood at 46.7; by 1938, this had moved up to 52.3; and by 1947, to 65.3.

CHAPTER TWO

THE PUBLIC POLICIES OF GOVERNMENT

The Role of Taxation   We must now examine the leading public policies of government that emerged with the successful outcome of the Civil War. Both the central government and the States and municipalities participated in their creation; perhaps most important was their handling of fiscal policy, their shifting of the burden of taxation from business to agriculture and to consumers generally.

Well into the first fifteen years of the twentieth century, the tax systems of federal, State and local governments were openly inequitable, for the federal systems were based on consumption (tariff duties and excises), and the States' and municipalities' systems on real property ownership (for the most part the ownership of farm property and farm equipment). In consequence, taxation was regressive: the larger proportion of the population, those with small incomes, carried the tax load, while those with ability to pay (great income receivers, the inheritors of estates, companies earning profits) got off scot free or paid so little that accumulation was hardly affected.

For a brief period, in a desperate effort to open up additional sources of revenue to finance the Civil War (for reliance on paper greenback issues and on loans accelerated inflation at an alarming rate), Congress imposed modest income, inheritance, and business taxes. A mildly progressive income tax on individuals and a small inheritance tax appeared in the Revenue Act of 1862; levies were also put on bank capital and deposits and on business documents, including checks. There were taxes on the gross receipts of a small number of corporations that for the most part had to do with transportation. But these taxes amounted to relatively little and had no effect on wartime profits. On the other hand, revenues came for the greater part from customs and excises; these, including manufacturers' excises, could be and were shifted to consumers. The workers paid more than the farmers, for real wages were lower for the former while agricultural prices kept on going up.

At the end of the war, governmental debt stood at about $3 billion, of which something like $2.5 billion was in interest-paying bonds and $450 million in greenbacks. Civil War tariff duties had produced for the Treasury only $305.3 million, because rates were so high; the excises, $292 million, and the income taxes a meager $55 million.

Starting immediately with the end of the war, the slight penalties imposed on business enterprise began to be removed, and the process was completed in less than a decade; by 1883, federal financing was depending quite entirely on customs duties and the excises on liquor and tobacco. In 1866, 1867, and 1868, the wartime taxes and excises on coal and pig-iron production, corporations, cotton, advertisements, and manufactured goods generally were repealed. The inheritance tax and taxes on sales and gross receipts were dropped in 1871; the personal income tax disappeared in 1872; taxes on banks and banking and on business documents went in 1883. In the same year, Congress halved the excise on tobacco and got rid of the taxes on friction matches and patent medicines. In 1885, internal revenues were producing but $112 million and customs $182 million. Total expenditures were $260 million, with interest on debt absorbing one-fifth.

Here was a very model for all time of a developing country: tiny expenditures, a steadily contracting public debt, no outlays for the social services, and a surplus in the Treasury! Such taxes as there were were shifted to consumers. Business at the same time had its cake and could eat it. For the federal government gave it a protected and expanding domestic market due to prohibitive tariff duties, a superb railroad net and heavy immigration, a cheap labor supply and a sound currency.

The States, counties, and cities also performed heroically, for they used, almost entirely, the general property tax to obtain their revenues. The general property tax, theoretically, was a tax on personalty as well as real estate; but because the tax on personalty was hard to collect and encouraged fraud on the part of owners and collusion on the part of assessors and collectors, the general property tax ended by being a tax on farm and farm equipment and on city dwellings. Some states taxed railroads, banks, and other corporations; a handful had inheritance taxes; where income taxes had been tried they had been abandoned.

Not until the 1880s and 1890s did a small company of economists turn their attention to taxation: the important ones were Richard T. Ely, Charles J. Bullock, and Edwin R. A. Seligman. All expressed their disquiet with the American general property tax. To Bullock, it was "the most crude, inequitable, and unsatisfactory system of taxation" existing anywhere in the world. To Seligman, it was "iniquitous" because of its inequality of assessment and its inability to reach personal property; also it encouraged dishonesty, and it was regressive. All wanted taxation shifted from ownership to earnings.

Said Seligman, who had become the leading advocate of income taxation, writing in 1895:

Those who own no real estate are in most cases not taxed at all; those who possess realty bear the taxes for both. The weight of taxation really rests on the farmer, because in the rural districts the assessors add the personalty [live stock, work animals, implements] which is generally visible and tangible, and impose the tax on both. We hear a great deal about the decline of farming land. But one of its chief causes has been singularly overlooked. It is the overburdening of the agriculturist by the general property tax. . . . The farmer bears not only his share, but also that of other classes of society.

Ely, the first economist to study State and municipal taxation closely (his book on this subject was published in 1888), showed again and again how the taxes on personalty dwindled as those on real estate climbed.

Most state tax auditors and legislatures knew this; special commissions, appointed to examine tax programs, proposed changes, with varying degrees of boldness. But legislatures moved timidly and when they made attempts to strike out, the State courts held them back. A characteristic case was that of New York. Its legislature in 1866 abolished its tax on bank capital and instead sought to tax the shareholders of the stocks of national and State banks. The question was raised: What deductions for debts could shareholders make? The State Court of Appeals said none; it took the United States Supreme Court until 1880 to overrule and find that deductions were permissible—as they were for other kinds of property.

Ely in 1888 offered a program of drastic changes. He suggested that the real-estate tax be dropped by States entirely and be reserved for municipal purposes; that the taxes on personalty be abolished and that income and inheritance taxes be substituted as the basis for State revenues. Taxes on what he called "natural monopolies"—that is, railroads, bridges, canals, ferries; water, gas, and electric-lighting companies, and street car lines—should also largely be reserved for municipalities. Corporations were to pay income taxes as well. It was not until well into the next century that the criticisms and admonitions of Ely, Bullock, and Seligman were heeded. How low taxes were may be noted from the fact that, at the end of the nineteenth century, federal taxes absorbed only about 3 per cent of the national income ($6.64 per capita) and all the State and municipal taxes another 6 per cent ($13.28 per capita).

The Role of the Tariff The federal government aided business enterprise with a generous hand in still another way: dearest to the heart of Republicans was the protective tariff. To this they had been pledged in their platforms of 1856 and 1860. At the first opportunity, therefore, early in 1861, Congress enacted the Morrill Tariff. The increases were mild—the rates of the 1846 law, averaging about 25 per cent, were restored—but the outbreak of war gave the Republicans a plausible excuse to raise duties higher and higher. New revenues had to be found; on the other hand, offsets had to be created to the taxes imposed on manufacturers. Every session of Congress, from 1861 to the middle of 1864, saw new bills, pushing rates upward, introduced and passed. The Act of June 30, 1864, was rushed through the House in two days and through the Senate in one: it was protectionism without any excuses. At the war's end, the average rate on dutiable goods stood at about 47 per cent as compared with the 18.8 per cent at its beginning. Naturally, the duties produced relatively little income, as we have seen, while manufacturers needed no relief, for they were able to shift their taxes to consumers. It was small wonder that real wages for workers fell during the war years.

Tariff tinkering continued during the whole Reconstruction period. In 1867, the wool and woolen interests (this time their cause was furthered by a powerful lobbying association) got new and higher rates; in 1869, the duty on copper was increased sixfold; in 1870, steel rails (not yet being produced in the country: a typical example of an infant industry truly in its nonage) were taken under the Congressional sheltering wing.

In 1870, frightened by a Middle West beginning to feel its oats and embarrassed by a Treasury surplus, the House Ways and Means Committee brought in a bill aiming at the cutting of duties on iron, coal, wool and lumber. This was to be achieved by the general device of a horizontal reduction of 20 per cent. But the Senate refused to accede, and a compromise, leading to a halving of the cuts, was agreed upon. The horizontal reduction of 10 per cent affected manufactured goods, largely, but many raw materials were put on the free list, thus not really hurting the protected industries. In 1875, in the midst of depression and the resulting decline in governmental revenues, the 10 per cent reduction was quietly restored, while the free list remained untouched. The result was that the iron and steel, cotton goods, woolens, paper, glass, leather, and wood industries were better off than before. The tariff rates were not touched again until 1883.

From time to time, there were other attempts at so-called revision downward; but these were halfhearted and never got out of committee. There was no significant opposition from important economic, sectional or political interests. Farmers were indifferent because duties were imposed on wool, sugar, hemp, and flax, and the free list in time included molasses, coffee, and tea. Raw material producers obtained protection for coal, iron ore and pig iron. Labor was assured that tariffs were really in its interest because they raised wages and created jobs. So skilled were Republican Party efforts in connection with the last that even the American Federation of Labor permitted itself to believe that the high 1890 tariff was "The Workingman's Tariff." William McKinley, its author, campaigning for the Presidency in 1896, promised to restore its rates, which had been lowered somewhat by the Democrats in 1894, if elected: it would fill labor's dinner pails.

To offset levies on raw materials and semiprocessed goods, there were compensating duties on finished goods; woolens and iron and steel were thus safeguarded and became the special darlings of the tariff-makers. With the end of the Civil War and the resumption of foreign trade, receipts from tariffs shot up, and this led to an embarrassing consequence: surpluses began to appear in the federal Treasury. Many expedients were tried to sop these up, for the official view always was that tariffs were imposed to augment revenues. The short-term Civil War debt was funded, interest rates were reduced on the consolidated debt; bonds were redeemed before final maturity dates. At the war's close, the interest-bearing federal debt stood at $2.5 billions with the rate about 6 per cent; interest payments absorbed about 40 per cent of all expenditures. By 1883, when the surplus stood at $133 million, the interest-bearing debt was down to $1.3 billion and its servicing cost less than 20 per cent of government spending. By 1889, with the surplus at $87.8 million, the debt was down to $830 million, and in 1893, it had been reduced to $585 million. By then, the surplus had largely disappeared.

Bond redemption absorbed a large part of the surplus, with curious consequences. The Treasury bid up the bonds, frequently paying premiums for them; the dwindling amount of public debt and the high prices and low coupons prevented national banks from buying them, and thus the cover for their issue of national bank notes became smaller and harder to obtain. National banks emitted fewer and fewer notes as a result (the total stood at $124 million in 1891), and, as demands for commercial loans kept on expanding during the periods of upturns in business cycles, banks were compelled to turn increasingly to the creation of deposits.

Other expedients were resorted to for getting rid of the surplus. The federal government yielded to the clamor of Congress and expanded its public works program. It spent growing sums on oversize, unnecessary, and all too frequently ugly forts and armories, post offices, customs houses, and lighthouse stations. All sections of the country regularly received appropriations for rivers and harbors; some were usefully spent, the larger part not. In 1866, rivers and harbors had been voted a third of a million dollars, by 1893, almost $15 million. Such outlays were cynically referred to as "pork-barrel" legislation, but they served their chief purpose—they reelected Congressmen.

Another minor outlet was to be found in the modernization of the Navy. After the war, the Navy had gone into a long sleep. Its few iron and wooden ships—some had been fitted out with engines, but they all carried full complements of sail—berthed at docks or were idling long years away in the Asiatic and South American stations. Captain Alfred T. Mahan served in the China Sea after the war; when he was ordered home, he was told to sell his ship—there was no point in buying coal to fuel up his rusting engines. It was as a result of this long overland journey eastward, with a visit to Great Britain, that there took place those reflections and study out of which came Mahan's famous *Influence of Seapower Upon History*. In 1883, Congress authorized the construction of four all-steel, but unarmored, cruisers with their guns mounted in turrets instead of broadside. It was this White Squadron that Mahan proudly sailed on when it was sent to London in 1894; it was he and not the fleet's admiral who was lionized, for by then his book had been published and had badly shaken chancelleries all over Europe. American naval expenditures reached a low of $13.5 million in 1880; from thence on, they moved up, and in 1893 the appropriation was $30 million. The procession toward becoming a great seapower had begun; by 1900, the American Navy (launched, in building, or authorized) was to cost $275 million.

Nor was the merchant marine neglected. In 1891, Congress voted a subsidy to ships built and owned by Americans. Presumably this was for carrying the mails; actually, it was a construction grant, for the steamboats thus laid down were to be convertible into auxiliary naval craft in time of war.

The most impressive device of all was the pensioning off of war veterans, initially and modestly for service-connected disabilities; then for service alone for a fairish amount of time; and finally and grandly for all veterans and their survivors, whether or not the period of service had been of any consequence or the widows had been wives for some time or recent brides. This last had an interesting effect on American morals in a minor way. Young women married aging veterans and received generous pensions when widowed, and because these bounties would have terminated on remarriage, they remained in single blessedness for the rest of their lives, with devoted but unofficial consorts and growing families assuaging their grief.

The Grand Army of the Republic, the Civil War's veterans' organization, found the way to relieve the Treasury of its embarrassment—and to keep the protective and prohibitory tariffs on the statute books. Initially, it pressed for the payment of pension arrearages from the date of discharge, and this it got in 1879. On an average, Civil War veterans received $1,000 per man, and pension payments jumped from $15.6 million in 1860 to $56.8 million in 1880 and $87.6 million in 1889. In 1890, the GAR reaped the benefits of long years of agitation when it obtained its service pension for all veterans and their survivors. In return, the aging soldiers year in and year out voted Republican, for it was the Republican administration of President Harrison that showed its gratitude to the country's heroes: President Cleveland had vetoed the same bill in 1887.

The Pension Act of 1890 granted $12 monthly to all Civil War veterans who had served ninety days or more and were "unable to earn support"; survivor pensions to widows married before 1890 were also voted. Naturally, these allotments were increased as the years went by. In 1878, there were 26,000 war veterans on the pension rolls; by 1893, their numbers had jumped to 966,000, and pensions in the latter year came to $160 million. This ended the surplus; the next year, 1894, showed a federal deficit of $61 million. Too, the interest-bearing debt began to rise as a result of the Treasury's need to borrow money to replenish the country's gold reserve, which was one of the consequences of the depression of 1893-96.

In one way or another—all disingenuous, except for the great power of the protectionist lobbying interest—the tariff survived all vicissitudes. A tariff commission, appointed by President Arthur in 1882 (the surplus then stood at $146 million) reluctantly recommended reductions of 25 per cent. But Democrats stood shoulder to shoulder with Republicans and the tariff act of 1883 ended with a rise in the average duty to 46 per cent as compared with the earlier 42.5 per cent. There were small declines in the rates on pig iron, copper, wool, cheaper textiles, and steel rails, and raises for finer cottons and woolen goods.

President Cleveland finally decided to enter the lists: in his annual message of December, 1886, he attacked tariff proponents as "an army of mercenaries and monopolists with a Treasury filled by millions of dollars wrung remorselessly year by year from an overburdened, overtaxed people." The best he could get from a Democratic House in Congress was a bill reducing the over-all rate by 7 per cent; the Senate Finance Committee did not even vote out the measure.

With President Harrison's victory in 1889, and the Republicans once more in control of both Houses, the House Ways and Means Committee, chaired by William McKinley of Ohio, prepared a bill that was called "An Act to Reduce the Revenue." This was to be accomplished by two means: the elimination of the duty on raw sugar (but with a subsidy, as compensation, to domestic sugar growers); and the raising of rates so high as to affect seriously the importation of agricultural commodities and finished goods. Tin plate, as yet an unborn industry, was given the protection of a 70 per cent duty. The average ad valorem duty was in the neighborhood of 48 per cent.

But there were difficulties. Cleveland's indignation was having a delayed effect and resistance to the McKinley tariff was appearing, largely from agricultural constituencies. To buy them off, a new and more generous Silver Purchase bill was offered by the Senate as a quid pro quo; it was accepted and passed by both Houses. And so was the McKinley bill.

The Democrats won victories in the Congressional elections of 1890 and carried the Presidency and both Houses in 1892: surely, to President Cleveland, this meant a mandate for honest tariff reform. The House Wilson bill of 1894, under the Presidential prodding, sought to reduce rates generally and sharply, calling for the restoration of the duty on sugar (and the elimination of the sugar bounty) and the wiping out of the tariff on wool. The Senate, Democrats helping Republicans, amended the House bill some six hundred times, and undid much of Wilson's well-intentioned proposals. Both bills carried an income-tax provision. Despite this, Cleveland sharply attacked the Senate's work and demanded that the House reject it. It did not, and Cleveland refused to sign. The next year, the tariff act's only redeeming feature, the provision for an income tax as a permanent addition to the country's revenues, was declared unconstitutional by the Supreme Court.

Despite the fact that the Presidential campaign of 1896 was fought on the free-silver issue, and the newly elected President was pledged to strengthen the position of gold, McKinley was first and foremost a protectionist. The immediate order of the day, therefore, was tariff re-form—reform upward, amusingly enough, to replenish the dwindling Treasury receipts. The resulting Dingley tariff of 1897 turned out to be the highest ever, with the average rate 52 per cent. The duty on raw sugar was now increased (to get funds but also to give protection to the new beet-sugar growers); so was the duty on wool. But rates on woolen goods, silks, linen, and other textiles were raised; so were those on more sophisticated iron and steel products.

As a mild concession to those who called for opportunities to expand American exports of manufactured goods—Secretary of State Blaine had been the first to envision such markets in Latin America—the McKinley

Act included a "reciprocity clause." It did not provide for genuine bargaining, however; what it did was threaten Latin-American nations that the primary products which we bought from them and which were on the free list (sugar, molasses, coffee, tea, hides) would be taxed punitively if our goods suffered from unequal and unreasonable rates. The Dingley Act carried a somewhat similar clause: the President could reduce duties and even enter into treaties by which rates might be lowered as much as 20 per cent. That all this was done with tongue in cheek was revealed by the incorporation of a safety provision which declared that such treaties were to be drawn in order to "open our markets on favorable terms for what we do not ourselves produce in return for free foreign markets." President McKinley engaged in an attempt to write such treaties for he had become a genuine convert to reciprocity, but the Congress refused to ratify any of them.

Thus the United States stood, really, right up to 1934. It is true that, in 1913, the Democrats under President Woodrow Wilson cut tariff rates sharply and expanded the free list; but the outbreak of World War I made it impossible to prove the contention that the country no longer needed prohibitive duties to assure its economic stability. Despite the fact that the United States had become the world's most powerful industrial nation, it insisted upon living behind high protective tariff walls. In the process it imposed hobbles upon its own industry—whose efficiency could not be tested in competitive world markets—and it limited the expansion of world trade.

It was Alexander Hamilton who had made the classical defense of the encouragement of "infant manufacture" by tariff duties and bounties in his "Report on Manufactures" in 1791. A new nation's reliance on primary products entirely, that is to say, agriculture, was too risky: it was dependent upon the whims of foreign markets; it could not attract overseas capital or immigration; its safety and well-being were endangered in time of war. Protectionism would lead to balanced growth, for the development of manufactures and the increase of a working class would expand the domestic market for the foods and fibers the country's farmers were producing. Manufactures would encourage accumulation at home; and these savings, as a result of "parsimony," would be invested in a diversified economy exactly because it was industrialized. Hamilton was aware that protection ran the danger of leading to monopoly and a rise in prices. But only in the short run: for, said he, "The internal competition which takes place soon does away with everything like monopoly, and by degrees reduces the price of the article to the minimum of a reasonable profit on the capital employed."

Hamilton was right on all counts in the post-Civil War years. The United States, then a developing nation, was able to grow so swiftly because it protected its infant industries, notably its iron and steel. Foreign capital and European immigrants did flow into the country; domestic accumulation did take place; and an expanding home market, particularly for railroad iron and steel up to the 1880s and then for structural shapes for the industrial and commercial buildings and the public utilities of the growing cities, stimulated competition and technological and other innovational improvements. The result was that, by 1880, the United States was making more Bessemer steel rails than Great Britain; by 1890, more pig iron; and by 1895, American prices for both were lower than those of the British. The tariff had done its work, certainly, in this key industry and in the side effects for which it was responsible (an important one was a steady decline in railroad rates), exactly as Alexander Hamilton had anticipated.

Even Professor Frank W. Taussig, the leading foe of protectionism, grudgingly conceded this. In his full and authoritative study of the impact of the tariff on the iron and steel industry, he pointed out that during the years 1870-95, imports of pig iron and steel continued high and the domestic price was generally the foreign price plus the duty. The duties were being lowered, however: from $7 to $4 a ton during 1870-94 for pig iron; from $28 a ton in 1870 to about $8 a ton in 1894 for steel. But domestic prices kept on dropping from time to time below the ceiling of the added duty. Pig iron fell from $35.80 a ton in 1873 to $9.03 a ton in 1900; steel from $120 a ton to $19.58 a ton over the same period. Taussig was compelled to conclude that the tariff had worked: by 1895, the revolution "in the iron trade had been virtually accomplished." And he concluded: "Here again the protectionist will point with pride, and this time with pride more clearly justified. The object of protection to young industries—the ultimate fall in price to the foreign level—seems to have been attained." Taussig was prepared to argue that the steel industry would have grown without protection (he offered no proof, however), "but not so soon or on so great a scale. With a lower scale of iron prices, profits would have been lower, and possibly the progress of investment, the exploitation of the natural resources, even the advance of the technical arts would have been less keen and unremitting."

Taussig does not mention the Carnegie Steel Company. Certainly, by 1895, it needed no tariffs and Andrew Carnegie much later admitted this—in 1912, before the Stanley Committee of the House, which was investigating the steel industry. But the additional profits the Carnegie Company made because of the tariff, during 1895-1900, were responsible for its doing exactly what Taussig said it could: exploit the possibilities of the great Mesabi iron range of the Lake Superior country, acquire its own ore-carrying ships, improve technology and company organization, and fight competitively and successfully the new steel companies that were appearing. The United States Steel Corporation of 1901 needed no tariffs, either. But because it occupied a monopoly position for almost ten years and its management did not push innovation nearly as vigorously as Carnegie had, it kept prices up—and lost the great opportunity of invading foreign markets on a grand scale. In every real sense, the tariff now hobbled enterprise and stifled innovation.

The Role of Aid to the Railroads   Aid for railroad construction—building Pacific trunk lines that would connect the Mississippi–Missouri Valleys with the Western coast; laying out of branches and feeder lines to crisscross the Plains country and bring agricultural goods to markets— came from the federal government and from States, counties and towns. The federal government made land grants and lent money to trunk systems from 1862 to 1871. States gave lands from their public domain and underwrote bond issues. Counties and cities made grants and loans, bought stock, gave tax easements, and furnished rights of way and land for repair yards and terminal sites.

The federal government began the process in 1862 when it chartered the Union Pacific Railroad to build a trunk line from Omaha, Nebraska, to the western boundary of Utah. This was to be joined by another—the Central Pacific Railroad, a California corporation—which was to start from Sacramento, California, and build eastward until it linked up with the Union Pacific. To start the two companies off—they were to do their own financing and building—required extraordinary assistance. Previous experience had created precedents. Before the war, Congress had made land grants from the public domain to the States for the building of canals and wagon roads and other internal improvements. It had given land to Illinois, Mississippi, and Alabama in 1850 to make possible the construction of the Illinois Central, to run from Cairo, Illinois (subsequently extended to Chicago), to Mobile, Alabama. A total of almost 4 million acres was turned over and the builders were able to finance, in large part in Great Britain, the construction of the road through mortgage bonds (secured by the railroad properties, chiefly the lands thus acquired).

How federal aid succeeded in building the first link to the Pacific will be told in detail later. Similar devices—but this time entirely land grants—were authorized by Congress up to 1871 and some seventy railroads were helped. The leading beneficiaries were the trunk systems that crossed the plains, deserts, and mountains to connect the Mississippi–Missouri Valley with the Pacific: the Union Pacific obtained 12 million acres and the Central Pacific 6.3 million. The Northern Pacific—to run across the northern tier of States and Territories—got 35 million acres. The Southern Pacific and the Atlantic and Pacific, which, when joined together, were to tie the Southern California coast with Texas through the Southwest, each received 5 million acres. A total of $65.5 million in loans was voted, with the lion's share going to the Union Pacific ($27.2 million) and to the Central Pacific ($25.8 million).

To take the land grants first. Of the 155.5 million acres turned over by the federal government, 131.3 million acres were patented because the lines were actually built. This came to about one-tenth of the whole public domain. Some 18,738 miles of road were made possible in this fashion. In addition, some States, out of their own public lands, contributed 49 million acres. What was the public aid worth? At the time the federal and State governments were making the grants, public land was selling at about $1 an acre. In 1884, the Democratic Party estimated the land given away at $2 an acre, or $360 million. In 1944, a federal agency put the net proceeds of sales of the federal and State land grants, to December 31, 1941, at $434.8 million and the value of the lands still retained at $60.7 million. The average price was only $3.38 an acre.

This was so because the land-grant railroads got rid of their lands as quickly as possible and, in fact, on quite generous terms—small down payments (10 to 20 per cent), amortization over a period of years (4 to 10), moderate interest rates (2 to 10 per cent annually). Foreclosure was infrequent: working farmers who were meeting with difficulties were not pressed for unpaid balances. In short, the railroad companies made no effort to hold out lands for rises in value, nor did they act as colonization companies; they did not have the funds to engage in such activities. The general assumption that great land empires were built up by the outstanding beneficiaries—the present-day Union Pacific, Northern Pacific, Santa Fé, and Southern Pacific—simply was not true.

In all likelihood, it was the federal government that profited most. In 1898, for the original $64.6 million lent to the pioneer Pacific railroads, Washington got back $63 million of the principal and $104.7 million in interest. It was able to sell the alternate sections reserved to itself within the land-grant belts at $2.50 an acre instead of the $1.25 for pre-emption lands. And the savings it effected on carriage by the land-grant railroads of troops, public property, and the mails were very sizable. In 1945, a federal agency came to the conclusion that government deductions from the customary charges came to almost twice the value the land-grant railroads realized from their land sales. The upshot was, in 1947 Congress abolished all special rates on land-grant railroads.

This is not to say that the railroads did not engage in sharp practices as long as lax federal administration existed. But not for too long. In 1871 Congress put an end to further grants because railroads were being so slow to secure final titles, thus avoiding taxation. In 1886, it compelled companies to pay taxes on all the surveyed acreage they had earned, whether patented or not. And in 1887—because the management or mismanagement of the lieu lands had generated so much hostility—the Secretary of the Interior revoked all further lieu-land withdrawals and restored in this way 21.3 million acres to public entry. The evils about which there had been so much protest had almost all been curbed before the Populists began their general attack on the Western railroads.

In their zeal to get the Western roads built as quickly as possible—there would be quick settlement; there would be a very real rise in taxable wealth; better and competitive transportation would lower rates; towns would spring up—States, counties, and incorporated places too gave generous assistance. They bought stock and lent on bonds. They made cash donations. They furnished rights of way, materials, and labor. They gave city lots for terminals and switching yards and granted tax exemptions. Sometimes they even pledged their own credit to guarantee railroad bond issues. It is hard to estimate what all this came to; from the very beginning of railroad construction, and excluding loans and stock purchases, perhaps as much as $1.5 billion. The States, as a rule, got their money back on loans made. Municipalities and townships found their dealings with the railroads harder sledding and in the depression of the 1870s some were even thrown into bankruptcy because they could not meet charges on bonded indebtedness too sanguinely assumed. The hostility to the railroads in part came from their cavalier treatment of the lesser political subdivisions of the country, and their avoidance of taxation.

All this being said, the general conclusion must be the same. If the railroads did not bear their fair share of the tax burden, if the stocks public bodies bought did not produce the windfalls they expected, the anticipated social benefits were realized. On balance the country gained immeasurably, and the direct costs paid out were slight enough in the process of quickly converting the United States into a great industrial nation. The contribution of railroad leadership in the stimulation of investment was of outstanding importance. In the 1870s, railroad construction alone was responsible for 20 per cent of the country's gross capital formation, 15 per cent in the 1880s, and still as large as 7½ per cent in the 1890s. If to this it were possible to add investments in those industries that depended so heavily on the railroads—iron and steel fabrication, the machine-tools industry, the manufacture of locomotives, cars, and other equipment, the building of culverts and bridges, the turning out of the hand tools used to lay down the lines and in the terminals and repair yards—then the indirect effects of railroad building and operation on capital formation (**and the** creation of jobs) were probably at least as large, if not larger.

The Opening of the Public Domain   The quick disposal of the public domain played an equally significant part in the stimulation of business enterprise. During the 1840s and 1850s, a good deal of the reform thinking had to do with the settlement on the public lands of workers who sought escape from the industrialism closing in on them. In part, this was an aspect of the Utopianism that bemused middle-class intellectuals and labor spokesmen well into the 1880s and that held back the creation of a realistic and hard-bitten trade-union movement. Producers' cooperatives, whether through the creation of colonies or the ownership and management of factories by the workers themselves, would permit the bypassing of the wage system and avoid the insecurities of unemployment. So would the free settlement on the land by workers: through farming they would be able also to achieve release. Other spokesmen were troubled by the land concentration and speculation in land of the 1830s; the first was responsible for the growth of a landless tenantry; the second, for the boom and ensuing depression that set in in 1837. Inalienable tenure—vain wish!—would conquer both these evils.

The whole agitation had a curious unreality about it which the idealists and the politicians brushed aside. Establishing a farm in the public domain, apart from the fact that inadequacies of internal transportation would have made difficult the reaching of primary markets, demanded two things: agricultural skills and capital. It was idle to assume that city workers, and their wives, possessed the ingenuities and hardihood required to carve out a farm in the wilderness and to survive until paying crops were planted, grown and harvested. Sizable cash funds were necessary. Even assuming that land was to be obtained for nothing, the hopeful would-be farmer still needed a wagon and team (for initial transportation and for hauling around the farm), a full complement of tools to build a house and for farm work, food during transportation and for the first year while the crop was being made, seed, and—on the prairies—cash to hire professional plowers to turn over the tough prairie sod. Various estimates put these requirements at from $1,000 to $2,000. Only when a dwelling was erected and a crop in the soil could the pioneer farmer hope for mortgage money that would permit him to stay on.

In the 1850s, politicians, notably the new Republicans, entered the lists, and debates over a so-called Homestead bill began to fill the Congressional chambers. The Republican Party wrote such a plank into its platform of 1856 and again in 1860. Radical Republicans were concerned about the plight of urban workers and rural tenants. Horace Greeley, the influential editor of the New York *Tribune,* his mind always filled with the great possibilities of industrialization, advocated protective tariffs and free land; in this way a vast domestic market would absorb the manufactured goods of industry. Politically, the filling out of the Western prairies and plains would strengthen and make permanently safe for the Republican Party the alliance between West and East. Thus, even "squatter sovereignty"—local and not national decisions whether the territories would be slave or free—would be turned against the Northern Democrats.

,There was another important consideration: the balance of trade was against the United States; its imports exceeded its exports and this made foreign borrowings difficult. Expanding exports—of grains for foodstuffs and animal feeds and of the meat products of pork and beef, both the results of an expanding agriculture in the West—would feed an industrial England which had abandoned its own protectionist Corn Laws and was seeking new sources of plentiful and cheap food for its factory workers. From England in return—and so it happened—there would come in a richer stream of funds for short-term credits and capital investment.

Nor should one lose sight of the sincere idealistic motives of many of the egalitarian Radical Republicans. Thus George W. Julian, Congressman from Indiana, an ever-devoted advocate of homesteadism, was represented as having felt (it is his daughter writing):

Should it [the Homestead bill] become a law, the poor white laborers of the South as well as the North would flock to the territories, where labor would be respectable, our democratic theory of equality would be put in practice, closely associated communities could be established as well as a system of common schools offering to all equal educational opportunities.

A Homestead bill was passed by Congress and vetoed by the Pennsylvania Democrat James Buchanan; the rump Republican Congress of 1862—now that the Southern Democrats were gone from Washington—passed another and Lincoln signed it. It was not the heart's desire of the dreamers. Not only did it not provide for inalienability; not only was it superimposed upon an existing and complicated land law; worst of all, it created no credit machinery by which poor men and women would be aided to move out to and settle on the public domain. In consequence, land concentration was not checked; indeed, it was aided, for fraudulent entries for homesteads and the right of commutation of homesteads into pre-emptions permitted land companies to extend their holdings.

The Homestead Act provided the following. For the payment of a $10 fee, an American citizen or an alien declarant, the head of a family or an individual (male or female) twenty-one years of age or over, could file a claim on unpre-empted land for a quarter-section of 160 acres. At the conclusion of five years' settlement—and this meant the erection of a dwelling and the planting of a crop—the government would grant a final patent. The homesteader could commute his claim before the five years were over by paying the price of a pre-emption, $1.25 an acre; he could also buy a pre-emption of 160 acres for the same price.

Lax or indifferent administration of the Public Land Office permitted land companies to abuse the Homestead Act. The hopes of the reformers were not realized: between 1860 and 1900, as Fred A. Shannon proved, less than one-sixth of new farms were homesteads; possibly only one-tenth, because of the dummy entrymen hired by the land companies and the commutations sold to them. Shannon's guess was that perhaps 400,000 families, representing 2 million people, obtained free land and kept it. In the same period, the farming population in the North Central, South Central and Western States and Territories increased by more than 8 million, or approximately 1.6 million families. The great majority of the Western farmers, then, bought land—through the pre-emption system, or from land companies, or from the railroads, or from the States themselves. As far back as the beginning of the American nation, the States had been receiving lands from the public domain to encourage the establishment of public schools and the creation of internal improvements (building roads, draining swamps). In 1862, State holdings had been enormously increased through the passage of the Agricultural College Act, which gave every State setting up an agricultural and mechanical college 30,000 acres for each representative and senator it had in Congress. Out of these so-called land-grant colleges grew many of the country's magnificent State universities.

The point is this: land, when bought, was closer to the new railroads spinning their elaborate network through the whole new West; it was cheap, for both railroads and land companies sought, in fact had to have, liquidity rather than deferred profits; it was at once capable of hypothecation—mortgage money was the very life blood of agricultural survival. And the Homestead Act, by its presence on the statute books, played a great role in attracting European immigrants with farming skills to the United States. These were given real hope for flight at last from the landlordism which was generally prevalent in Great Britain, Scandinavia and Germany, and which was the basis of the unequal class society everywhere on the European continent. It is true that most of these immigrants bought land instead of entering homesteads, but they did become farmers, and thus one of the hopes for the Homestead Act was magnificently realized.

Rural settlement on a grand scale had another interesting consequence, and again we are indebted to Shannon for having said this. An increase in skilled agricultural help (but also, and Shannon does not say this, expanding mechanization on the grain farms of the West) permitted sons and daughters of American farmers to quit their rural homes and migrate to the cities. Many left because of the boredom of their daily living and were swallowed up in the vast anonymity of urban life; many were ambitious, worked hard, and became outstanding business entrepreneurs. Before the coming of good roads, automobiles, telephones, and electricity, rural America, particularly that of the great corn and wheat countries of the Middle West and Northwest, was dull, dreary, and isolated. The winters were long and bitter; chill winds swept across the plains and prairies; without mechanical appliances in the home and barns, manual labor was hard and unremitting. Youth fled, and the cities became the great safety valve of young rural Americans, as Fred A. Shannon pointed out.

Homesteadism was not the end of the governmental largess. Congress made entry easy into the timber and mineral lands for exploitation at once. Here were opportunities for profits, but also for exploration for copper, wood, lead, coal, iron and petroleum, all needed by a country on the march industrially. In 1864, the pre-emption of coal lands was made the subject of a special law. The Timber Culture Act of 1873 gave homesteaders, or others, title to quarter sections if they agreed to plant part of their property in trees. The Desert Land Act of 1877 gave away whole sections—presumably of arid land—on condition that irrigation be employed. The Timber and Stone Act of 1878 permitted the Public Land Office to sell quarter sections for $2.50 an acre, if, in its determination, such lands were unfit for cultivation. Further, at its discretion, during 1866 to 1873, it was authorized to sell other mineral lands at from $2.50 to $5 an acre and coal lands at from $10 to $20 an acre. To assist individuals and companies in exploration and development, those finding mineral lodes and petroleum pools could follow these to any depth or variation or angle, even if this led to the mining of property not owned by the pre-emptionists.

To aid in the process of rapid and successful exploration, Congress in 1879 created the Geological Survey to examine and classify the public lands and make public "their geological structure, mineral resources and products." Many States set up similar agencies and offered their services freely to all; thus industry and enterprise were served; and the foundations for some great timber and mineral fortunes were laid. The consequences of this aid and interest on the part of Congress and the States were immense. The index of physical production in mining (ten metals, plus coal and petroleum) showed a fivefold increase from 1879 to 1900. From 1860 to 1897, coal production was multiplied fourteen times and pig iron eleven times. From 1869 to 1899, the number of board feet of lumber sawed increased threefold. From 1876 to 1896, the barrels of petroleum pumped up grew sevenfold.

The Growth of the Civilian Labor Force: Impact of Immigration   A developing country cannot grow without natural resources, a labor force, capital, and entrepreneurship. Natural resources challenge all the ingenuity and skills man can command. Arable land, mineral deposits, water for transportation and power, an equable climate and adequate but not excessive rainfall are nature's gifts to him, but they are inert until men have used them efficiently. Capital must be productively and effectively employed. The working population must be trained. A society as a whole must be willing to forego immediate consumption, or the erection of monuments (the extravagant living of Rome, the pyramids of Egypt, the great cathedrals of medieval Europe) will hold back those advances by which the whole population ultimately will benefit. Natural resources and a labor supply can be bent to this purpose, given a capital fund (from savings out of profits and abstinence, from foreign investments) and an entrepreneurial class whose leadership is accepted and which is also alert to the necessity for training the working population to fit into the grand design.

The natural resources available to a fortunate America are familiar enough. The role of entrepreneurship in the United States, particularly after the Civil War, has already been discussed. Here we must look in some detail at the appearance in the United States of an adequate civilian working population. A population explosion—live births in excess of deaths leading to an increase of more than 2 per cent annually—of itself is not a basic condition for economic progress; indeed, the reverse can be the case when the methods of agricultural production, storage, and marketing do not keep ahead of the increasing mouths to be fed. This, of course, is the fundamental problem bedeviling the new nations of Africa and Asia, as well as most Latin-American countries.

In the United States, all the stars were favorable in their courses. The population grew. The number of its members of working age advanced at an even faster rate. The labor force engaged in nonfarming pursuits increased still more rapidly. There was a general commitment to education—the universal establishment of public schools for children, apprenticeship training on the job, formal technical education at higher levels, as we have seen, in the creation of the land-grant colleges. The impact of improved technology on agriculture has already been commented on in passing (more of this later) and one of its consequences has been referred to—the movement of young men and women out of the farms into the cities.

The most important reason, however, for the growth of an effective working force was immigration. Interestingly enough, at exactly those periods in American development when immigration reached peaks, so did the inflow of foreign capital, and so did capital-intensive expansion by American entrepreneurship. That is to say, those years of upturn in long business swings or cycles saw great increases in immigration, the stepping up of importation of capital from overseas, and accelerated investment by American entrepreneurship in better factories and equipment—based on automatic processes—to make possible the effective utilization of the newly arrived untrained immigrants.

Some notion of the impact of immigration upon population growth in the United States may be gained from these figures. From 1840 to 1930, the population of native American stock grew from 14.2 million to 82.7 million, less than six times the initial number. But the population of foreign stock (foreign-born and native-born of foreign or mixed parentage), grew from less than 3 million to over 40 million, or more than thirteen times the original number. By 1930, one-third of the country's total population was of foreign stock.

Immigrants thronged into the United States for many reasons. When times here were good, particularly in the construction industries, unskilled young males came by the millions to seek and find employment. (I am not overlooking the emigration out of Europe of farmers and skilled workers; but these were in the minority.) As Harry Jerome, in his pioneer *Migration and Business Cycles* (1926) has pointed out, the pull of America was immense. But there also was the push out of Europe: because of population increases; inadequate small rural holdings and famine (as in Ireland, following the disaster of the potato-crop failure in 1846); changes in public policy (the abandonment of the Corn Laws in England and the consequent fall in the need for agricultural workers); the introduction of machine techniques in textiles, the wood industries, and the fabrication of glass, which made redundant the skilled, frequently self-employed workers in these pursuits (as in England and Scotland, Germany, Scandinavia).

Aiding pull and push was an active interest in inducing immigration on the part of the American federal government and all those agencies, public and private, that had lands or transportation facilities or their services to sell—State commissioners of immigration, the American railroads and the European steamship companies, labor offices at home and abroad working directly or indirectly for American companies seeking workers. Nor should we forget the letters sent home by newly arrived immigrants who had become adjusted and could boast, in part fancifully of course, of their successes in the great land of opportunity. As compelling, if not more so, were the steamship tickets and large cash remittances immigrants sent back to take care of families left behind, and to aid younger brothers, sisters, and cousins to make the journey overseas. In the forty years from 1860 to 1900, immigration contributed fully one-third of America's population growth.

Between 1860 and 1900, the population of the United States increased 140 per cent; but men, women and children on farms, in the same years, grew only 70 per cent; while those in urban communities (having a population of 2,500 and over) quadrupled. Even more significant, to hasten economic development—and this was immigration's contribution—were the facts that the civilian population of working age (15 years and over) grew 170 per cent and the male population of working age 190 per cent. More and more, the concentration in the working population was nonfarming. (The increase, over the same forty years, in the agricultural working force was 76 per cent and in the nonagricultural 320 per cent.) And yet an ever-dwindling farming community was able at the same time to grow the foods, fibers, work and meat animals of an expanding population and economy, to produce those large agricultural surpluses for export overseas, and to create the favorable balance of trade that brought new foreign capital into the United States and paid the interest on this debt. One of the most exciting things about America's post-Civil War years, then, was that youth was on the march.

The Republican Party had promised an immigration policy; this pledge a Republican Congress proceeded to redeem when, in 1864, it established the federal office of Commissioner of Immigration and called for the naming of a superintendent of immigration at the port of New York. The law, significantly, was entitled "An Act to Encourage Immigration." Among devices set out to achieve this were the following. Contract laborers, whether recruited by agents, railroads or steamship companies, were to be permitted entry and were exempted from the military draft. That is to say, their transportation was to be paid for, and this—but no more—they were to discharge by their work. Immigrants were to be protected against fraud and their safety and comfort on ships safeguarded. On the other hand, a labor contract gave employers paying shipping costs a year's lien on wages, and contract laborers' property could also be attached. (This was a warning to homesteaders.) The Commissioner of Immigration was charged with sending copies of the law to all America's consular agents abroad and to require them to publicize as well the opportunities for immigration afforded by the Homestead Act. The fact that the federal government insisted upon control of immigration was further evidenced with its suit—and it won in the Supreme Court—against the States of New York and Massachusetts, when these commonwealths tried to place some of the responsibilities for immigration regulation on steamship companies themselves.

The Contract Labor Law, as such, probably did not bring too many immigrants; more successful abroad was the propaganda of American companies themselves. And despite the fact that such immigrants were not exploited and received going wages—they would have disappeared into the vastness of America, otherwise—a hue and cry was raised against the act. Efforts to repeal, in part, were successful in 1868 and again in 1885. Finally, in 1891, a law prohibiting the solicitation of immigration by railroads and steamship companies was put in the statute books. In order not to hinder the steady flow, Congress refused to give heed to the noisy clamor of a few that immigration be put on a selective basis: that only those of "Nordic" stock be admitted. A small number of specified classes of undesirables were ordered turned back by legislation in the 1880s and 1890s; in 1891, a modest head tax of 50 cents was imposed on all newcomers. Efforts to require a literacy test failed because of Presidential vetoes of bills when Congress passed them; such a requirement was finally put on the statute books when Congress overrode President Wilson's veto in 1917.

The Knights of Labor had been among the organizations demanding the repeal of the Contract Labor Law and it had been partially successful in 1885. The American Federation of Labor had taken up the same cause and had pressed it; as we have seen, in 1891, the encouragement of contract labor was wholly abandoned. When it came to restriction, however, the AF of L was of mixed mind. In 1896, its annual convention refused to endorse the Congressional bill for a literacy test. It did so the next year; at the same time, it attacked measures calling for sharp curtailment in the immigration flow, either by restrictive devices or temporary suspension. A resolution of that year declared:

Further restrictive measures would close the door of our great country to a great many honest, intelligent, progressive workmen who should become true and ardent trade unionists. . . . Trade unions, on account of their progressive tendencies, should be the last bodies of American citizens who advocate the turning away of fugitives from·European oppression, either political or industrial.

And to this position the AF of L adhered until the end of World War I, when it supported quota laws.

There were four great explosions of immigrants out of Europe, most of whom set out for America, and each one coincided with an upswing in a long investment cycle in the United States. These were the mass movements of 1844-54, 1863-73, 1878-88, and 1898-1907. The totals of immigrants coming to the United States in these four periods were as follows: 1844-54, 2,870,000; 1863-73, 2,915,000; 1878-88, 4,401,000; 1898-1907, 6,804,634. The pushes, or expulsions out of Europe, accompanied the pull of good times in the United States; this was clearly so in the first, third and fourth periods. In the first, the new arrivals largely came from Ireland, Germany, and the United Kingdom; in fact, more than one million were Irish and almost one million were Germans. In the third, the Germans numbered more than one million and the Scandinavians at least half a million. As has already been said, unusual increases in population, the decline of home industries, the prevalent small-farm holdings that were finding it impossible to compete with mechanized and more efficient larger farms were the outstanding reasons for the push out.

Then, in the 1890s, the character of the immigration changed: the countries of Northern and Western Europe found it possible to absorb their own increasing populations and redundant workers in their own expanding industrial plants. This does not mean that immigration from Ireland, Germany, the United Kingdom, and Scandinavia ceased entirely; but those who continued to come were older and more skilled. It was the so-called New Immigration—young people from Southern and Central Europe—who now filled out the American labor reserve as another long investment cycle started in the United States after 1897. The push out of Europe this time had the same economic reasons; along with these were the official oppression of minorities in Hungary, Russian Poland, Russia proper, and the Turkish lands, and the expansion of military establishments, through conscription, in Russia, Austria-Hungary, Italy. The heavy immigration of Eastern European Jews was due to official and unofficial anti-Semitism; but also to the decline of the handicrafts, small trading, and home industries in which they had been able to find employment. During 1898-1907, almost two million Italians came to America, as well as hundreds of thousands of Jews from Russian Poland, Russia, Austria, and Rumania, and equally large numbers of Slavic immigrants from Russia, Austria, and Hungary. There came as well Greeks, Turks, and Syrians—all young, all ready to work hard.

The Jews filled out the sweatshops of New York, Boston, Philadelphia, and Baltimore. The Italians became the day laborers—working on construction gangs—of our growing metropolises, and their women found employment in textile industries. The Poles, Croats, Slovenes, and Rumanians went to work in the stockyards of Chicago and Kansas City, the coal mines of Pennsylvania and Illinois, the textile mills of Fall River, Lowell, and Paterson, the steel mills, the iron foundries, the iron, salt, copper, and lead mines of North, South, and West. In the decade of the

1880s, the immigrants from Italy, Russia, Austria-Hungary made up 19 per cent of the total; in the decade of the 1890s, they made up 49 per cent; in the first decade of the twentieth century, the proportion was close to 70 per cent. That they were for the greater part young and males is evidenced by the figures of a representative year, that of 1906. Then, out of every 100 immigrants arriving, only 12 were under fifteen years of age and only 4.5 were over forty-five, leaving 83.5 per cent between fifteen and forty-five. (In the native-born population, only 46 per cent were between fifteen and forty-five.) The male immigrants in 1906 made up 69.4 per cent of the total. (Males constituted 50.7 per cent of the native-born population.)

It was a common—and erroneous—assumption that the Old Immigrants were for the most part skilled workers and the New Immigrants the reverse; this was one of the important reasons offered for restriction and selection. In his pioneer study, I. A. Hourwich (*Immigration and Labor,* published in 1912), proved there were no significant differences between Old and New, when each was at its peak. Table 4 shows Hourwich's figures, comparing the occupations of immigrants in the decade 1871-80 with the decade 1901-10.

TABLE 4

Occupation	1871–80, %	1901–10, %
Professional	1.4	1.5
Skilled	23.1	20.2
Agricultural pursuits	18.2	24.3
Unskilled laborers	41.9	34.8
Servants	7.7	14.1
All others	7.7	5.1

There were skilled workers among the Old Immigrants, coming in such large numbers up to the end of the 1880s: English, Cornish, and Welsh anthracite-coal, copper, and iron miners, metallurgists, potters, and glass blowers; English and Scottish carpet weavers; German and Scandinavian farmers and trained artisans in metals, wood, pottery, and the chemical industries. But there were also skilled men and women among the New Immigrants: wine growers and fruit and vegetable farmers, merchant tailors, workers in laces and embroidery, cooks, bakers and confectioners, copper and brass fabricators.

As the New Immigrants went into the hard, manual labor jobs or were readily trained for those where automatic processes supplanted handwork (mining, glass-making, iron and steel, the manufacture of clothing), two things happened during 1898-1907. First, native-born American workers and the sons and daughters of the earlier waves of the Old Immigrants moved up into the skilled occupations and also became supervisory workers in the factories and white-collar workers in factories and offices. Secondly, the Old Immigrants who continued to come—indeed were attracted to and encouraged by American industry exactly because automation required large numbers of technicians, metallurgists, chemists, tool designers—now were skilled and not unskilled workers.

The Immigration Commission, established in 1907 and publishing a voluminous report in 1911, caught this significant and complex change in the character of the American labor force. In commenting on the fact that native-born Americans, their children and the children of the Old Immigrants from Great Britain and Northern Europe were not entering the industries in which their fathers had been employed, it pointed out three important reasons for this phenomenon:

1. General or technical education has enabled a considerable number of the children of industrial workers of the passing generation to command business, professional or technical occupations more desirable than those of their fathers.

2. The conditions of work which the employment of recent immigrants has largely made possible have rendered certain industrial occupations unattractive to the native-born.

3. Occupations other than those in which Southern and Eastern Europeans are engaged are sought for the reason that popular opinion attaches to them a higher degree of respectability.

And the Commission went on to indicate, with equal understanding, that the absorption of the New Immigrants into the "mines and manufacturing plants of this country has been made possible by the invention of mechanical devices and processes which have eliminated the skill and experience formerly required in a large number of occupations." The Commission, as a consequence, did not recommend restriction of immigration; nor did the American Federation of Labor (the members of whose unions were finding increasing job opportunities in the skilled crafts) disagree.

[52]

It would be idle to assume that all was skittles and beer for the new arrivals. They collected in large cities; in 1900 half of all the foreign-born were to be found in the 160 cities of the United States having populations of 25,000 or more. Three-fourths of the Jews and two-thirds of the Irish and Italians were large city dwellers. They were crowded into great and unsanitary tenements—building construction and rapid-transit transportation simply could not catch up with the huge throngs that kept pouring in—where the death toll among the young was notably high. Sweatshops, frequently to be found in the same tenements, abounded. The absence of factory codes and inadequate inspection where primitive codes did exist; the prevalence of homework for finishing certain processes that had been begun in factories; long hours and small wages; company towns in the mining and metal industries; unemployment and hard times in periods of business recession—these were some of the prices the immigrants had to pay as they sought a foothold in the new land.

Nor should there be overlooked the failure, bitterness and corroding poverty of those who fell behind in the fast race or could never find a real place in it; this was so particularly of the parents who sometimes accompanied their youthful sons and daughters or were later sent for. Nor can the alienation of children from their parents be ignored. Some of the heavy prices the New Immigrants, with their strange tongues and customs, frequently had to pay were to see parental authority challenged by children becoming more rapidly assimilated than their elders, flight from homes, dropping out of school, rejection of religion, embarkation upon lives of crime. Yet vast numbers, both parents and children, did find secure places for themselves in a very rough and too often hostile world. (Many children of immigrants carried the scars of bloody street fights and never forgot the taunting names that were applied to them. The Irish were Micks, the Italians Wops, the Scandinavians Squareheads, the Poles, Hungarians and Czechs Hunkies, the Jews Kikes.) At the same time, because there were educational opportunities, because of the sacrifices mothers and fathers made, because of a stubborn will to succeed, millions of the young were able to escape from slums and poverty. The mobile class society of America and its great need for talents made this possible.

A final comment. The wages of the unskilled workers, whether they came from the Old Immigrants or from the New, were low. Recent analyses would seem to indicate that wages of workers in manufactures, from the end of the Civil War up to the outbreak of World War I—the years of high immigration—rose synchronously with increases in productivity. That is to say, in the aggregate, real wages improved, probably faster up to 1890, more slowly after 1890, but go up they did; and no more slowly than the advances in productivity. Such statistical examinations do not—perhaps find it impossible to—separate the skilled operatives from the unskilled laborers, an important reason being the rapidly changing nature of the kinds of tasks being performed. The operations that had required a high form of skill one year could be suddenly transformed into automatic processes the next. This, for example, had happened in the steel industry in the early 1890s, and management's demand for a reexamination of wage rates in a number of specific departments led to the tragic Homestead strike of 1892.

In any event, we may assume that the differential widened between the wages of unskilled workers and those of the skilled. One study (unfortunately, only one) of real hourly wages of the unskilled in manufacturing bears this out. (Whitney Coombs, in his *The Wages of the Unskilled in Manufacturing in the United States, 1890-1924* [1926].) The figures presented here are corrections of his money wages through the use of Albert Rees' cost-of-living index. (Albert Rees, *Real Wages in Manufacturing, 1890-1914* [1961].)

According to Rees, the real hourly wages for *all* workers in manufacturing rose 40 per cent from 1890 to 1914; they went up 17 per cent from 1890 to 1900, and 15 per cent from 1901 to 1914. According to Coombs (corrected), the real hourly wages of the *unskilled* rose 11 per cent from 1890 to 1914; but they went up 8 per cent from 1890 to 1900, and only 2 per cent from 1901 to 1914. It is apparent that not only did the differential become greater during these twenty-five years but more perceptibly so in the fourteen years 1901-14, when the "New Immigrants" flooded the country. Nevertheless, the unskilled, too, were improving their lot in the United States, although only very modestly.

The profitability of American industry, in the years of upturn of the long cycles of 1863-73, 1879-89, 1898-1907, undoubtedly in part originated in the low wages that could be paid the millions of unskilled immigrant workers. Such profits, in turn, were plowed back into the improvements of plants and machinery. These large investments in capital-saving equipment, in their turn, made possible the employment and absorption of even greater numbers of the foreign-born.

Such were the capitalist processes in America and some of the important reasons for its rapid and sensational industrial growth in less than fifty years. Table 5, giving the distribution of manufacturing production among the three leading industrial nations of the world, tells the tale quickly enough. The figures are in per cents.

TABLE 5

Year or years	World	United States	United Kingdom	Germany	Rest of world
1870	100	23.3	31.8	13.2	31.7
1881–85	100	28.6	26.6	13.9	30.9
1896–1900	100	30.1	19.5	16.6	33.8
1906–10	100	35.3	14.7	15.9	34.1
1913	100	35.8	14.0	15.7	34.5

SOURCE: League of Nations, *Industrialization and Foreign Trade*, Geneva, 1945, p. 13.

2

THE MORES

CHAPTER THREE

IN PRAISE OF THE UNITED STATES

Andrew Carnegie, Entrepreneur   Andrew Carnegie had altogether five years' schooling in Dumferline, Scotland, where his father wove damask linens in a home shop. When Carnegie was thirteen, in 1848, the family—giving up the unequal struggle, for machine looms were displacing the hand weavers—left to join relatives in Allegheny City, across the river from Pittsburgh. The elder Carnegie and his wife's brothers had been finding Scotland more and more difficult to live in. They had been Chartists engaging actively in the agitation for political reform and universal manhood suffrage, and one of the mother's brothers had led locally the Chartist left wing, which called for a general strike, and had been jailed for his pains. The young Carnegie remembered all this, and later, in *Triumphant Democracy,* he was to write: "It is not to be wondered at that, nursed amid such surroundings, I developed into a violent young Republican whose motto was 'death to privilege.' " The established Presbyterian Church with its uncompromising Calvinism affronted them (Carnegie records the fact that his mother never attended any church, either in Scotland or America). The rigid closed-class society in which they lived rejected and kept down all those democratic notions that Chartism had fostered and, at the time of the family's flight, had failed to fulfill. There was very little left when the Carnegies' meager possessions were disposed of; money had to be borrowed for the passage overseas.

The father was forty-three at the time of emigration, the mother ten years younger; Tom, the other child in the family, was five. For an immigrant, the father was too old to start anew and he drifted helplessly, first finding work as an operative in a cotton mill. It was hard, and he returned to his home hand loom, peddling his wares from door to door. The young Andrew went to work in the mill too, as a bobbin boy at $1.20 a week. The only other formal learning Andrew had was six months in night school (where he was taught double-entry bookkeeping) and some private French lessons. And yet Andrew Carnegie eventually became a highly educated man. He developed a real taste for music and the theater—he attended concerts and plays constantly—read and learned Shakespeare and poetry, was versed in the classics, and later in his life corresponded with some of the outstanding men of letters of the day. He began to collect prints and sculpture and to buy books, and it was no accident, for with learning also went taste, that his earliest benefactions were the establishment of public libraries and the Carnegie Institute, to include a library, art gallery, music hall, and a museum of natural history, in Pittsburgh.

Because of his father's failure, because of his deep devotion to a mother who kept the little family together in its early years of struggle, perhaps more because of the unequal society from which he had come and which had squandered talent so stupidly, Carnegie had a fierce desire to succeed. He had to sharpen his wits; he had to engage in self-improvement; he had to seize the main chance whenever it presented itself. How else was one like himself to emerge out of obscurity and poverty? Darwin and Spencer and William Graham Sumner expressed his yearnings and accomplishments: life was a keen, competitive struggle; the fittest survived; in the process the species, society, moved up to greater heights. It is absurd to argue—as is the current fashion—that it was the reverse: that men like Carnegie, Rockefeller, McCormick, Swift, all arrivists, interlopers, adventurers, breaking through the hard crust of custom, challenging prescription, eagerly seized upon Darwinism and Spencerism to justify their competitiveness and ruthlessness. Darwin, Spencer, and Sumner were telling the stories of their lives. To them, success needed no justification, and the mores of the America in which they lived made their achievements the basis of right conduct.

Carnegie kept on moving up, because he acquired skills as he went along and because he impressed those he worked for with his resourcefulness. He became a telegraph messenger boy; at fifteen a telegraph operator; and at eighteen, the confidential clerk of Thomas A. Scott, the superintendent of the western division of the Pennsylvania Railroad, at that time in process of building its line across the Alleghenies. Carnegie was making $40 a month (Scott was getting $125) and was the head of the household. He purchased a home for his mother and father (the price was $700, the down payment $100); he saved money; at twenty, he made his first investment—he bought ten shares of Adams Express Company. When he was twenty-one, in 1856, he was already an entrepreneur. He had met T. T. Woodruff, the inventor of the sleeping car; had persuaded Scott, now the general superintendent of the Pennsylvania, to buy two sleeping cars; Woodruff had offered Carnegie a one-third share in his company. Carnegie went to one of the local banks to finance his first payment. He got a little more than $200 on his personal note; it was the first of many similar transactions that marked the early years of his climb.

This point is worth stressing. The entrepreneur—Carnegie in this case— has ingenuity and drive; he can put together a complex of plants and technically skilled associates to turn out a unique and strategically based product; he himself has a particular aptitude—in this case, again, he knows how to get on with people, those who work with him and those to whom he wishes to sell. He needs capital, funds for plant operation, to meet payrolls and the bills of suppliers. The banks, from the beginning of Carnegie's operations—the same was true of Rockefeller, McCormick, Havemeyer—furnished the funds on personal notes. Carnegie began building up a fortune from lucky investments and from other activities which he used in part to bolster up his expanding investment in iron manufacture and then in steel; but always, right into the 1870s, he turned to the banks and received assistance from them. The capitalist and the entrepreneur, as Schumpeter pointed out fifty years ago, are two different persons and perform two different functions.

Carnegie's young manhood was spent with the railroad industry. In 1859, Scott, his mentor and friend, became vice-president of the Pennsylvania Railroad, and Carnegie succeeded him as manager of the western division. In 1861 he went with Scott to Washington: Scott in charge of military transportation for the Department of the Army, Carnegie specifically responsible for the operation of military railways and telegraphs. In 1862, Carnegie returned to the Pennsylvania and remained with it for another three years.

Carnegie went into iron manufacture at the same time only because the development and future of the railroad industry were linked with iron. With others (his brother Tom included) he set up a small wrought-iron company; then another company to make structural shapes; then one to make iron rails; and still another to make locomotives. The most important was the Keystone Bridge Company, formed in 1863, in which Carnegie had a one-fifth share. His investment was $1,250, which a bank lent him. Of the Keystone Company Carnegie wrote in his *Auto-biography:* "The Keystone works have always been my pet as being the parent of all the other works." It was the first iron-bridge company in the world; so at any rate Carnegie believed. It achieved its initial great triumph when it furnished the iron for the building of Captain J. B. Eads' splendid span of 515 feet across the Mississippi at St. Louis. Heavy iron and then steel—rails and structural shapes—constituted that strategically based product with which Carnegie's successful entrepreneurship was associated.

Was Carnegie, then, an ironmaster or a steelmaster? J. H. Bridge (who was Carnegie's editorial assistant and research man when Carnegie wrote his *Triumphant Democracy*) denied with some heat and a good deal of malice that he was either. In 1903 Bridge published his sensational *The Inside History of the Carnegie Steel Company,* whose burden was that the company was the work of technically skilled partners and employees; in fact, the dedication, naming eight men (and not Carnegie) hailed them as "The Men Who Founded it, Saved it from Early Disaster, and won its First Successes." The steel industry simply grew; it would have done so without Carnegie and his organization.

This is obviously naïve. Carnegie was no manufacturer, in the exact sense, as McCormick, Havemeyer, Westinghouse and, later, Ford were. Yet Carnegie was the heart and soul of the Carnegie companies and of steel: a man of boundless imagination and courage; quick to seize upon innovation and utilize it; early he saw the importance of accounting and chemical control in iron. He had a genius for singling out young men of talent, giving them their heads, and rewarding them generously. Incompetents, on the other hand, he could not abide, and he gave them short shrift; in the real sense of the term he was a benevolent despot. He offered to make Captain Bill Jones, the head of production of the Carnegie works, a partner; upon Jones' refusal, he paid him a salary equal to that of the President of the United States.

Of equal importance, as entrepreneur rather than manufacturer, was his access to capital and to markets. He found new uses for his products, sold them himself, and competed aggressively. He entered pools only to take the measure of other companies in the industry; he took advantage of tariffs and railroad rebates; he cut prices steeply in times of recession to keep the fires of his blast furnaces burning.

To sell his structural shapes, from the end of the Civil War and for the next five years, Carnegie played an outstanding role in making possible the construction of some of the early great iron bridges of the country. The companies seeking to span the Mississippi, Missouri, and Ohio Rivers, among others, obtained independent charters to operate toll bridges. To meet the costs of their large undertakings, first-mortgage bonds were to be issued; these Carnegie undertook to sell in Europe. He established close relations with Junius Spencer Morgan (J. Pierpont Morgan's father, who headed the firm in London), the Rothschilds, and the House of Baring; and by 1871, he had sold $30 million worth of bonds to European investors. His commissions were handsome; and he also supplied the iron to the bridge companies.

In his frequent trips abroad, Carnegie had had the opportunity to watch the iron and steel makers in Britain. By close scrutiny of their processes and through conversations with them, he had come to a number of conclusions. To continue as a maker of iron products, it was important to start by making pig iron. Iron ores were tricky—they had high or low phosphorus contents, or various degrees of iron purity; divination in running a furnace would not do—chemistry was essential. The same was true of using the Bessemer process in making steel; iron ore, limestone, coke were the basic ingredients—but in what component parts? In addition, because so many extra steps were necessary, elaborate accounting controls were required. Finally, if he was to remain in and expand his iron industries, he had to get out of everything else—his diversified security holdings, his bond promotions, his acting as an intermediary between companies needing funds and the foreign investment bankers.

In the early 1870s Carnegie made a fateful decision; it was to put all his eggs in one basket. As he explained it in his *Autobiography:* "I have tried always to hold fast to this important fact. It has been with me a cardinal doctrine that I could manage my own capital better than any other person, much better than any board of directors. . . . As for myself, my decision was taken early. I would concentrate on the manufacture of iron and steel and be master in that." In 1870, with his own capital and with bank help, he erected his first blast furnace and got out of it 100 tons daily. A second furnace was added in 1872. And in January, 1873, he organized a Bessemer steel rail company, Carnegie, McCandless & Co. His was not the initial company in the United States to do so; but his was the first successful one on a grand scale and thenceforth the industry's leader for more than a quarter century.

The panic struck in September, 1873, and for a short time the construction of the steel mill at Braddock was suspended. But Carnegie, despite the fact that the long depression of 1873-79 had set in, was determined to go on. A new company, with a new set of partners, was set up and called the Edgar Thomson Steel Co., after the president of the Pennsylvania Railroad. Carnegie poured his own funds in and again turned to the banks; they stood by, renewing his maturing paper and extending further loans. In 1874 rails were being rolled, the company was making a profit, and it continued to make steel and to make money during those difficult depression years when so many industrial enterprises were closing their gates or being thrown into bankruptcy. This was the beginning of the success story. The development of the Carnegie steel companies will be told later.

Carnegie's *Triumphant Democracy* It is against this broad background that we are to see the purpose and significance of Carnegie's *Triumphant Democracy,* which he published in 1886. The title and the covers are a kind of shout of glee and at the same time an admonition to his mother country. This is what republicanism has accomplished in the past fifty years, Carnegie is saying; this is why Britain—and the rest of Europe, as well—still enchained by monarchical and aristocratic principles, is rapidly slipping. The future of the world lies in America. The book's binding was a vivid red. On its front cover stood an inverted pyramid labeled "Monarchy"; opposite it, at a higher level, was another pyramid, on its broad base, labeled "Republic." The first was insecure, the second firmly grounded. Underneath both was a broken scepter, and on the book's backbone was an overturned crown. There are two quotations on the cover: the top one is Gladstone's famous tribute to the American Constitution; the lower one, from Lord Salisbury, acknowledges the uniqueness of the American Senate and Supreme Court as sources of strength and stability.

Carnegie was making no effort to present a balanced view as he surveyed the economic and social progress of the United States during the years 1830-80, always contrasting this with the laggard pace of Britain and the other European countries. The whole of it has the flat, shiny surface of a Byzantine mosaic, the figures exaggerated and oversize. The United States was emerging as a great urban and industrial nation. He brushed aside the heavy prices that were being paid for such a rapid pace: in insecurity and industrial conflict, in slum living and the unhappy lives of the freshly arrived immigrants and the older Americans who failed, in the inequalities of wealth and income and the same resulting fierce radicalism that he had seen in his childhood Dumferline.

Certain eternal verities had emerged; for the confident and the strong, here was the future. It was so in his case, he was saying in effect; it would be so for hundreds of thousands of others as well. Thus, Carnegie:

America is the land of equality:

There is not one shred of privilege to be met with anywhere in all the laws. One man's right is every man's right. The flag is the guarantee and symbol of equality. The people are not emasculated by being made to feel that their own country decreed their inferiority, and holds them unworthy of privileges accorded to others. No ranks, no titles, no hereditary dignities, and therefore no classes.

Public education is the great fusing element:

The free common-school system of the land is probably, after all, the greatest single power in the unifying process which is producing the new American race. Through the crucible of a good common English education, furnished free by the State, pass the various racial elements—children of Irishmen, Germans, Italians, Spaniards, and Swedes, side by side with the native American, all to be fused into one, in language, in thought, in feeling, and in patriotism. . . . There is no class so intensely patriotic, so wildly devoted to the Republic as the naturalized citizen and his child, for little does the native-born citizen know of the value of rights which have never been denied. Only the man born abroad, like myself, under institutions which insult him at his birth, can know the full meaning of Republicanism.

The immigrant is America's strength:

the majority of emigrants today are men who leave their native lands from dissatisfaction with their surroundings, and who seek here, under new conditions, the opportunity for development denied them at home. . . . The emigrant is the capable, energetic, ambitious, discontented man— the sectary, the refugee, the persecuted, the exile from despotism—who, longing to breathe the air of equality, resolves to tear himself away from the old home with its associations to found in hospitable America a new home under equal and just laws. . . .

Here, all are workers:

The Republic today is, as it ever was, a nation of workers. The idlers are few—much fewer than in any other great nation. A continent lies before the American, awaiting development. The rewards of labor are high; and prizes are to be won in every pursuit. . . . The American works much harder than the Briton. His application is greater; his hours are longer; his holidays fewer. Until recently, a leisure class has scarcely been known; and even now a man who is not engaged in some useful occupation lacks one claim to the respect of his fellows. The American must do something, even if disposed to be idle; he is forced to join the army of toilers from sheer impossibility to find suitable companions for idle hours.

Education is the key to a democracy's political stability and industrial accomplishment:

The moral to be drawn from America by every nation is this: "seek ye first the education of the people and all other political blessings will be added unto you." The quarrels of party, the game of politics, this or that measure of reform, are but surface affairs of little moment. The education of the people is the real underlying work for earnest men who could best serve their country. In this, the most creditable work of all, it cannot be denied that the Republic occupies the first place. . . . Of all its boasts, of all its triumphs, this is at once its proudest and its best.

Therefore, behold the self-reliant American:

The cause for this self-governing capacity lies in the fact that from his earliest youth the republican feels himself a man. . . . Everywhere he is ushered into a democratic system of government in which he stands upon an equal footing with his fellows, and in which he feels himself bound to exercise the rights of a citizen. . . . We can confidently claim for the Democracy that it produces a people self-reliant beyond all others; a people who depend less upon governmental aid and more upon themselves in all the complex relations of society than any people hitherto known.

One would have searched in vain for a tale like the following in *Triumphant Democracy*. The panic of 1873, which started with the failure of the banking house of Jay Cooke and Company in September, lengthened and deepened into a depression that lasted into early 1879. The usual characteristics of depression manifested themselves: business failures on an increasing scale, growing unemployment, tightness of money, cutting of wages and speed-up of work. The business exuberance of the preceding five years and easy credit available at home and abroad had led to a doubling of the country's railroad mileage from 1865 to 1873. In this, Jay Cooke had played an important role, and the failure of many of the railroads to meet the obligations on their debts involved Cooke and spread in a widening circle to stock-brokerage houses and banks. The railroads of the East—the Baltimore and Ohio, Pennsylvania, New York Central—in the face of declining revenues and to protect their shaky financial structures, embarked on programs of wage cuts and speed-ups. From 1873 to 1877, the wages for railway trackmen were decreased 37 per cent, for conductors 24 per cent, and for brakemen 23 per cent. (The wholesale price index for the same years fell 20 per cent; thus there was a decline in real wages and this was worsened by part-time employment.) At the same time, trains were lengthened, as were runs, with layoffs without pay as a result; the size of crews was also cut.

The Baltimore and Ohio's announcement in July, 1877, of a wage reduction of 10 per cent after two previous cuts, and the refusal of the road's management to treat with the workers, led to the outbreak of a series of strikes all along the line. The strikers interfered with the passage of freight trains; when derailments took place, the governor of West Virginia called out the State militia. The ineffectualness of the militia—they fraternized with the strikers—led to a request for assistance to Washington, and President Hayes sent federal troops. At the same time, the strike was spreading into Maryland, and the governor of that State ordered the militia to the troubled areas. On July 20, when strikers and sympathizers gathered around the armory in Baltimore to prevent the State troops from entraining, the militia fired into the crowds, killing twelve and wounding eighteen. The militia stayed on in Baltimore; in retaliation, the strikers set fire to the Camden railroad station. But the strike was broken because the presence of the federal troops kept the whole of the Baltimore and Ohio open to traffic.

Meanwhile the strike had spread to the Pennsylvania Railroad, where the same lengthening of trains, reduction of crews, and wage cuts had taken place. When strikers in Pittsburgh interfered with the passage of trains, and because the local militia could not be counted on, a call went out to the State capital at Harrisburg, and troops from Philadelphia appeared on July 21 to disperse the strikers and open the railroad to traffic. The soldiers tried to arrest the strike leaders; they were resisted; the troops fired and killed twenty persons and wounded twenty-nine. In retaliation, the strikers and their friends, having obtained arms, fell on the militia, which sought refuge in the roundhouse of the railroad depot. This was attacked by cannon shot and burst into flames. Happily, the militia was able to extricate itself and retreat successfully. Next, the Union Depot and the terminal of the Pennsylvania Railroad were fired and freight cars were broken into. Rioting was becoming general, a vigilance committee was organized, and a combination of armed citizens and the appearance of federal troops put an end to the violence that had seized much of the city and its outskirts. The leaders of the strike were rounded up, tried, and given prison sentences, but the federal troops stayed on for two weeks after the strike was definitely over. All of this Carnegie of course knew, and perhaps had even witnessed; none of it did he report to cloud the serene skies of the world in which he lived.

The Professional Economists Clear the Way   From two other quarters came a systematic defense of the reigning order of things, curiously enough closely conjoined right up to the end of the 1880s. These were the Protestant clergy and the professional economists; and, more frequently than not, the latter had started out by being clergymen and then held chairs in some of the leading colleges where they taught moral philosophy, or politics, or economics.

Thus the Reverend Francis Wayland, who became professor of moral philosophy and president of Brown University, published his immensely popular *The Elements of Political Economy* in 1837, which was kept in print and revised right into the 1870s. In 1878, Wayland was again revised by the Reverend Aaron L. Chapin, professor of history and civil polity and president of Beloit College, to take account of the currency disputes of the day. Chapin also wrote a widely used abbreviated text, based on Wayland, for secondary schools and businessmen.

After the Civil War, fresh texts were written by Arthur Latham Perry, a minister's son and a professor of Williams College, whose *Elements of Political Economy* appeared in 1865 and ran into twenty-two editions; and by the Reverend Francis Bowen, professor of natural religion, moral philosophy and civil polity in Harvard College, whose *American Political Economy* was published in a new edition in 1870. These were rivaled only by Amasa Walker's *Science of Wealth,* which had appeared before the Civil War but was being studied in the colleges right into the 1870s; Walker deviated from the pattern by being a successful businessman, but he lectured in economics at Oberlin and Amherst and examined in political economy at Harvard.

Wayland struck a note that was repeated in one way or another in all these books. Property, he declared, was an exclusive right which was founded on the "will of God, as made known to us by *natural conscience,* by *general consequences,* and by *revelation.*" Perry saw in the development of society's fundamental laws "the footsteps of providential intelligence"; and Walker was moved to wonder "how perfectly the laws of wealth accord with those moral and social laws which appertain to the higher nature and aspirations of man."

This providential intelligence was everywhere at work. Thus wrote Wayland, justifying the perfect laws of the market place and underscoring the penalties of sloth, in terms of natural religion:

He who refuses to labor with his mind, suffers the penalty of ignorance. . . . He who refuses to labor with his hands, suffers besides the pains of disease, all the evils of poverty, cold, hunger, and nakedness. The results which our Creator has attached to idleness are all to be considered as punishments, which He inflicts for the neglect of this established law of our being. And, on the other hand, God has assigned to industry rich and abundant rewards. . . . All that now exists of capital, of convenience, of comfort, and of intelligence, is the work of industry, and is the reward which God bestowed upon us for obedience to the law of our being.

It followed from this, "in order to accomplish the designs of our Creator . . . and thus present the strongest inducement to industry" that all property should be privately held and its rights protected and that "there should be no funds in common provided for the support of those who are not willing to labor." Those who were reduced by indolence or prodigality to extreme penury were to be relieved neither by alms nor poor relief, but through "the medium of labor." To this extent, Malthus was accepted. Otherwise the economics of these writers went back to Ricardo (with one important modification, that made all the difference, as we shall see) and to Frédéric Bastiat, whose belief that the free market place would yield a perfect harmony of interests was exactly suited to the optimistic American temper.

Said Amasa Walker, in this vein, in the 1866 edition of his book:

The union of capital and labor will be most effective when each is sure of its just reward. If the rights of man as a holder of property are sacred, and his rights of labor equally so, the greatest motive to production can be secured. If otherwise, the creation of wealth will be restricted. Men will not work or save unless sure of their reward.

And again:

The union of labor and capital is most effective where there is the greatest freedom of industry. Whenever a population is sufficiently intelligent to understand its own interests, it should be left to direct its own laborers. Its industry should never be interfered with by government. . . . No lawmaker can gather and express the desires of his people so accurately and seasonably as they are shown in the market demand; or set in train and carry on their efforts, with myriad instrumentalities, to that end, so savingly and earnestly as is done by interested, educated capitalists; or present satisfactions so happily and fully as is done by the merchant whose fortune is to answer for his appreciation of the public wants.

All these writers sang the praises of education, none more dithyrambically than Walker. Education would save the laborer from the Malthusian pit. "The more highly educated, industrially, the workman is . . . the higher will become his necessary wages" and therefore "the more reasonable his remuneration." It is imperative, in consequence, "to elevate and strengthen the humbler classes by all moral and educational influences—this is to bring comfort and leisure to every cottage, frugality and temperance to every home, to attain the perfection of the industrial state, almost to realize the dreams of Locke and Sidney."

Malthus had to be rejected. Said Walker: "The glut, famine, and death theories of Malthus have done much to impress upon political economy the shape it has today in the world's estimation. Rightly enough, if they are correct, it is called a dismal science." And Walker anticipated Carnegie by putting his finger on the same fault:

The fact is, all this British philosophy of population is perverted and diseased from its root. It comes out of social wrongs and false political institutions. . . . Prior to all consideration of such arguments, there is reason to suspect theories of subsistence and population that came from an island where holdings of land are only as one to 600 or 700 inhabitants.

And Walker ended his book—as Perry and Bowen ended theirs—on that same optimistic note we found so pervasive in Carnegie's *Triumphant Democracy*. Said Walker:

To sum up then: Although much may be produced that does not satisfy any wholesome or lawful desire of man's being; although much inequality and injustice may take place in distribution which shall so far neutralize the bounty of nature, and the industry of man; and although the greatest wealth is not logically consistent with the highest economic good—we can yet accept the former as the end and aim of our science, satisfied it is in this shape that the latter is to come to us.

Arthur Latham Perry was the most sophisticated economist of his day, and the most influential. His thinking was deeply permeated by Bastiat's conceptual analysis of the theory of value as a social science; for this freed economic reasoning from the limits Adam Smith had imposed on it through his association of value with commodities only. Human effort was at the heart of economic rewards. Said Perry: "Your man of business must be a man of brains. The field of production is no dead level of sluggish uniformity like the billowy and heavy sea"; its navigation "requires foresight, wise courage, and a power of adaptation to varying circumstances."

And Perry accepted enthusiastically Bastiat's harmony of interests, quoting with approval Bastiat's dictum that "the good of each tends to the good of all, as the good of all tends to the good of each." And he proceeded to exemplify the idea in this wise in his own words:

The presence of capital anywhere constitutes a demand for labor. The more capital there is anywhere, the stronger the demand for labor; and capital therefore is the poor man's best friend. . . . They come of necessity into a relation of mutual dependence, which God had ordained and which, though man may temporarily disturb it, he can never overthrow.

All efforts at interference—usury laws, trade unions, labor legislation, paper money, tariffs for protection—introduced those disharmonies that Bastiat and Perry were warning against.

Perry made buying and selling the key to economic activity and human progress. But he warned:

It is perfectly natural to trade. . . . Hence no law or encouragement is needed to induce any persons to trade; trade is natural . . . and on the other hand, any law or artificial obstacle that hinders two persons from trading, not only interferes with a sacred right, but destroys an inevitable gain that would otherwise accrue to two persons.

Bowen, writing in 1870, linked the providential intelligence with *laissez-faire*. Said he:

society is a complex and delicate machine, the real Author and Governor of which is divine. Men are often His agents who do His work, and know it not. . . . Men cannot interfere with His work without marring it. The attempts of legislators to turn the industry of society in one direction or another, out of its natural and self-chosen channels . . . to increase or diminish the supply of the market, to establish a maximum of price, to keep specie in the country—are almost invariably productive of harm. *Laissez-faire;* "these things regulate themselves," in common phrase, which means, of course, that God regulates them by his general laws, which means, in the long run, work to good.

Bowen, like Perry, attacked the Ricardian theory of rent, and the Malthusian theory of population, on which it was based. The two ideas were thus irrefragably linked. With improvements in agriculture, the prices of grains fall, benefiting entrepreneurs and workers. The former's rate of profit and therefore accumulation of capital rise; in the case of the latter, demand for labor, and, therefore, higher wages, result. This leads to an increase in population, and an increase in demand for more foodstuffs. Agricultural improvements can go so far; sooner or later, as population presses on the means of subsistence, inferior soils must be opened to cultivation. This raises the rents of superior lands, which raises prices—and profits fall. The worker is back where he started, living miserably at a subsistence level; the entrepreneur is thwarted in his quest for capital because of the decline in profits. Permanent economic advance is impossible.

This Bowen indignantly rejected. Such "gloomy views," he said, "appear clearly imputable to defective, unnatural, and unjust institutions of man's device and admit of remedy without shaking the pillars of social order, or impiously calling upon God to send war, inundations, or pestilence, wherewith to scourage mankind into a sense of their duty." These notions arose out of a society—Britain's—where landlordism flourished and gross inequalities inevitably sprang up.

Not so in the United States, notably in "the great valley of the Mississippi" which welcomed an expanding population, for this meant an increase "in productive power" and the growing of more grains, which after satisfying the American people "in the amplest manner" produced enough surpluses for export overseas. The United States was helping the world to escape from the Malthusian-Ricardian trap. Americans had created an open society; they had every reason to look to the future with confidence, for there was a powerful motive here to encourage frugality and saving on the part of the middle and lower classes. That was, said Bowen, "the *mobility* of society, or the ease and frequency with which the members of it change their respective social positions."

Rather than fulfilling Ricardo's prediction of a static world, the United States was on the move. And again Bowen repeated:

I find such a peculiar cause [in the United States] in the evident fact that every individual here has the power to make savings, if he will, and almost as large as he will; and has the certainty that the savings when made, the wealth when accumulated, will immediately operate in proportion to their amount, to raise the frugal person's position in life,—to give him, in fact, the only distinction that is recognized among us.

And Bowen made the point that Carnegie and Perry kept on emphasizing: "Here there are no castes, and not even an approach to a division of society by castes."

The Protestant Clergy and Capitalism The professional economists were widely read; their defense of the free market place and of the struggles and triumphs of the merchant, entrepreneur, capitalist, only buttressed the faith of the Protestant clergy. They knew that the way to salvation was through man's endless efforts to overcome his own baser nature; and that the devotion to a mundane calling in this difficult trial really and only then made the Christian God's elect. The message of work, frugality, sobriety was preached from hundreds of Protestant pulpits in the East and in the Middle West from the 1840s through the 1880s; and these sermons were collected into scores of books that contributed to that curious "cult of self-help" that was one of the hallmarks of the age. The phrase is Irvin G. Wyllie's, in his *The Self-Made Man in America: The Myth of Rags to Riches* (1954). In it he demonstrates that all Protestant sects except the Lutheran—Congregationalists, Episcopalians, Unitarians, Methodists, Baptists—contributed their spokesmen for and defenders of an austere way of life that (for the successful) had its material rewards as well.

Those who conquered the weaknesses of the flesh (sloth, intemperance, sensuality, improvidence), who overcame sternly their own impulses to stray, notably those who devoted themselves to an industrious life, would go to glory. It was an inevitable step from a life of toil to a business career, and the achievement of grace through success in the market place. Work (more subtly, not making goods but making money) demonstrated the triumph of self-discipline. Said a distinguished New England divine in the 1850s, of the merchant: he is "a moral educator, a church of Christ gone into business—a saint in trade . . . the Saint of the nineteenth century is the Good Merchant; he is wisdom for the foolish, strength for the weak, warning to the wicked, and a blessing to all. Build him a shrine in Bank and Church, in the Market and the Exchange . . . no Saint stands higher than this Saint of Trade."

The Right Reverend William Lawrence, Episcopal Bishop of Massachusetts, fifty years later—Lawrence wrote in 1901—said much the same thing, when he linked wealth and morals together. It was God's will that some men achieved great wealth; in fact, "It is only to the man of morality that wealth comes." Material prosperity is favorable to morality: it "is helping to make the national character sweeter, more joyous, more unselfish, more Christlike."

The man wholly preoccupied with his quest for personal salvation—not man's inhumanity to man, not injustice, not the absence of opportunity for the socially and economically deprived—was the true Christian. When material well-being crowned his efforts, then he knew not only that he had won, for his wealth was a sign of the divine approval, but that he was a leader of his times. Those who faltered and failed in the combat with original sin also obtained their just reward: in poverty, unemployment, the neglect of their children.

Yet wealth was a stewardship: at any rate, this was so to those who followed the teachings of Congregational ministers like Henry Ward Beecher and Lyman Abbott and Episcopalians like Bishop William Lawrence and who were prepared to accept the mediation of Jesus to soften the harshness of the Old Testament's stern justice.

The rich man must safeguard and enlarge his fortune, but he was also to use, certainly, a part of it for good works, to support his church's chapels among the poor, and foreign missions; to give to charitable organizations; to found schools for Negroes in the South. Sometimes, although far less frequently, he should create opportunities for the children of the less privileged. Said Peter Cooper, one of the very few who belonged to the last category: "I do not recognize myself as owner in fee of one dollar of the wealth which has come into my hands. I am simply responsible for the management of an estate which belongs to humanity." Cooper was a devout Christian and an active churchgoer, and it was he who created the magnificent Cooper Union in New York City, an evening technical school at the collegiate level, where instruction in engineering and architecture was free. Carnegie was neither Christian nor churchgoer, yet he came to somewhat the same conclusion in his famous article "The Gospel of Wealth," which appeared in 1889 and which met with universal plaudits and almost no derision. As late as that, most Americans were prepared to believe that the idea of self-help represented both the great and humble; the next generation began to see, as Wyllie observes wryly, that "it represented them unequally."

The Church Periodicals   Many of these success manuals, whether written by clergymen or former clergymen (Horatio Alger, the greatest of them all, had started as a Unitarian minister) were high-flown, improbable, or just plain meretricious. Church periodicals sought to get closer to the world of everyday living; and here the guidance of the technical economists is more clearly evident. The most influential of these, the weekly *The Independent,* hailed the American success story in almost every issue through the 1870s and the 1880s. Regularly, it wrote glosses on the texts of Walker, Perry, and Bowen.

There were businessmen and there were workers; but capital and labor were partners. Thus *The Independent* in 1885: "Taken as they are, their relations are not those of hostility, but of mutual assistance and cooperation." And again in 1889: "Give to both a free market without coercion or constraint on either side, and each in serving itself will, under the natural law of trade, serve the other."

There was nothing wrong about trade unions; at any rate, as long as they remained friendly societies for mutual help. Strikes were another matter, for these interfered with the right to work of other laborers. As early as 1872, *The Independent* was saying that the laws of supply and demand were as "immutable as those of gravitation or magnetism"; it must seem apparent to all that strikes could not benefit the workers because fewer hours or higher wages could only succeed in raising the cost of living, and thus upsetting the delicate mechanism of the market place. The bitter railroad strikes of 1877 plainly showed *The Independent* where labor was heading; for strikes now "substituted the law of force for the healthy operation of a natural law." And when violence broke out, *The Independent* characterized the strikers "as criminals in intent and criminals in fact."

Workers do not join trade unions voluntarily. They are not their own masters but the victims of sinister forces. Thus *The Independent* in 1886 on Terence V. Powderly and the Knights of Labor, which he headed: "Now men do not work when they want to; they work when they are ordered to, and stop when they are ordered out. We are very thankful that King Powderly rules so gently; but we must say that he has about him a number of wicked partners . . . the boycotting of railroads . . . the suppression of willing labor by force is vile and criminal, and good King Powderly might as well learn it."

The Independent followed the debates on fiscal and monetary policy closely. Taxes were to be lowered but tariffs raised; tampering with the currency (that is, raising it upward) was bad economics and worse religion—greenbackism and the silver purchase acts only proved men could follow false prophets. So, in 1883, currency tinkering had to be condemned by all good Christians, for it "has an effect on the moral feeling and the moral health of the people and tends to relax in all quarters the sense of duty and of honor in respect to pecuniary obligations."

Finally, and inevitably, there were the poor. Here *The Independent* rounded the circle, summing up the abstractions of the economists, the warnings of the clergy, and the promises of the self-help pleaders and defenders of a rich reward. For in 1889, in the midst of agrarian turmoil in the Far West and the South and rumblings in the Eastern cities, it still could say: ". . . this poverty is not due to a low rate of wages, but to the idleness, prodigality, whiskey-drinking and tobacco-chewing and smoking of those who are its victims. It is not what one earns in money value but rather what he saves from his earnings that settles the question as to his financial condition."

The early 1890s were a watershed. A new generation of economists—John Bates Clark, Richard T. Ely, Simon N. Patten, John R. Commons, Thorstein Veblen—looked at wealth and its distribution with other eyes. A new generation of Protestant clergymen—Washington Gladden, George D. Herron, W. D. P. Bliss, Walter Rauschenbusch—began to talk of the "Christian social movement." The harmonies of the free market and its automatic, evenhanded dispensing of social justice apparently either were not working or were not enough: only public intervention could maintain those balances that could prevent class warfare.

Henry Ward Beecher   Henry Ward Beecher, who accepted the call in 1847 to Brooklyn's Congregationalist Plymouth Church, which would become under his ministry the country's most important Protestant pulpit, was a representative man of his time. Beecher had been brought up in a stern Puritan home, although, as Lyman Beecher Stowe observed, the father "mitigated the austerity of Calvin's God." Beecher went to the Lane Theology Seminary in Cincinnati, which his father headed and which was one of the centers of the antislavery agitation in the Middle West. Here Beecher moved over to evangelical Protestantism, and his father's "Monarch God" became a God of Love and Service, working through Jesus. As Beecher himself declared: "I cannot pray to the father except through Christ. I pray to Christ. I must!" Beecher began contributing to *The Independent* and in 1861 he became its editor, writing that the weekly would "assume the liberty of meddling with every question which agitated the civic or Christian community." He continued much along the same lines as the editor of *The Christian Union* during 1870-81.

For almost forty years Beecher preached from the Plymouth pulpit to a doting congregation and a growing outside audience; and despite a serious personal scandal and political irregularity—a confirmed Republican, he supported President Johnson's Reconstruction program in 1866 and Grover Cleveland in 1884—he was a powerful voice in the land. No theologian, and uninterested in the higher criticism of the Bible that was beginning to come out of Germany, he was able to adjust his religion to suit the temper of an America in process of swift change. The stern Calvinism of Beecher's forebears demanded a majestic but fierce Creator knowable only because of man's fear of him, in order to support the early pioneers in their loneliness; but the United States was becoming industrialized and urbanized and middle-class in outlook if not in reality, and a sense of community was important. The Christian achieved grace within this larger world rather than in the restricted company of the Calvinist elect.

Evangelical Protestanism, to which Beecher gained so many converts, therefore accepted the rough world of the second half of the nineteenth century—private property and unlimited accumulation, individual and fierce competitive striving, success because of personal merit and failure because of want of it—but sought to build a commitment of personal responsibility into it. The Christian started out with Jesus and accepted the stewardship that Jesus had taught. Harriet Beecher Stowe wrote of her brother: "To present Jesus Christ, personally, as the friend and helper of humanity . . . the friend of each individual soul, and thus the friend of all society; this was the one thing which his soul rested on as a worthy object in entering the ministry."

The free individual, therefore—free because he had been divested of Original Sin and was capable of self-control—stood at the center of Beecher's religion. It is no wonder that he accepted Herbert Spencer, the scientific validity of evolution, and its relevance to Christianity. To him, not Darwin's "Struggle for Existence" but Spencer's the "Survival of the Fittest" held out the promise of constant improvement. Evolution was not Tennyson's "Nature red in tooth and claw," which is what modern-day Social Darwinism has made it out to be but, rather, in Beecher's words: "The more the world advanced, the more rapidly it could advance; and the glory of the blossom and the fruit lies before us yet, and it will come, not according to the speed of the ages gone by, but according to the acceleration which belongs, in the nature of things, to the advanced stages of growth."

Beecher did not need Social Darwinism to buttress his faith in the world in which he lived. He voiced the optimism of Carnegie, Perry, Walker, and Bowen. In a sermon in the 1880s he declared: {Of one thing I am certain, whatever may have been the origin, it does not change the destiny or the moral grandeur of man as he stands in the full light of civilization today."}

Beecher had been committed to this "civilization" from early manhood. He had been a Radical Republican, which meant that he was both hostile to slavery and eager for the quick industrialization of the United States. One of the reasons why he had supported President Johnson's Reconstruction program—and here he parted company with the other Radicals—was his hope that peace in the South would encourage the entry of Northern capital and thus hold out the prospects of a better life economically for whites and blacks alike. Said he at that time: "The Negro is part and parcel of Southern society. He cannot be prosperous while it is unprosperous."

Beecher hailed the immigrants. It is true their presence raised discordant notes, certainly as the newly arrived (he had in mind particularly the "Catholic Irish") made their slow adjustments. "For the rest, immigration brings strength. . . . The Dane, the Swede, the German certainly, add to the cerebral power of the nation; the Irish add to its activity." By the same token, in season and out he preached the need for the expansion of the free common-school. "Liberty of growth and equality at the start," he said, "is the law of true democratic life; and this is what the common-school gives." And: "Churches, schools, and industry are the trinity of the intelligence that is working now, here, and everywhere." And he followed Spencer in calling for the wide spread of scientific education.

Beecher, therefore, supported the capitalist system; without benefit of Spencer, he had been doing so as early as 1844. Then, in his *Seven Lectures to Young Men*, he had emphasized the value and in fact the need of private property; to this extent he had not cut himself loose from all his Calvinist moorings. It is true, it was the capitalism of his Plymouth congregation: of individual or family concerns that bought and sold in foreign trade or engaged competitively in small, highly specialized industrial enterprises. He was disquieted by the appearance of impersonal boards of directors of great corporations—in the railroads, largely; these he said "have pursued methods, which, if a single man in his private capacity should pursue, would convict him irredeemably of crime and crush him with ignominious punishment." Like Carnegie, he inveighed against stock jobbery as a way of making money.

Organized trade unionism, the unionism that engaged in bitter industrial warfare, as in 1877, and that, on its outer fringes, accepted the participation of left-wing movements, aroused his concern. Following the Haymarket Riots, in 1886, he saw the fault in the leadership. "I am very glad to see Labor organize itself" (by which he meant on a shop or on local but not on a national basis). "I am very sorry to see it so unintelligent that it involves in its interior element despotism that would dethrone the Czar of Russia himself."

Workmen, like the entrepreneurs he knew, were in transition: abstinence, hard work, austere living must lead to higher things; the individual would triumph. And if a single thought represents both Beecher's evangelical Christianity and his confidence in the future of industrialized America it is this: "You will be poor if you do not exert yourself, and at every future stage it lies with each man what his condition in society is to be." It is within this context that one must read the remark he made in 1871 for which organized labor never forgave him: "I do not say that a dollar a day is enough to support a working man, but it is enough to support a man! But the man who cannot live on bread and water is not fit to live." He was calling on Americans for greater personal effort; he was pointing, in effect, to the youthful privations of the Carnegies and the Rockefellers as the way to accomplishment in what was then a still relatively simple world. When Beecher died, in 1887, Carnegie wrote of him: "In the death of H. W. Beecher, America loses its greatest citizen, the world its greatest preacher." And the older Oliver Wendell Holmes said: "Mr. Beecher was as genuine an American as ever walked through a field of Indian corn."

The Work of the Publicists   Reaching the world of affairs more directly, and widely read because their speeches, lectures, and articles were printed in newspapers and popular journals, was a group of publicists, outstanding among whom were David A. Wells, Edward Atkinson, and William Graham Sumner. Wells for a brief period in the middle 1860s had been Special Commissioner of the Revenue; then he had turned to business, where he was successful, and to an examination of public questions, where he was respectfully heard. Atkinson was a highly competent New England textile manufacturer and a ready controversialist. And Sumner, starting out as an Episcopalian minister, had found his real platform at Yale, where in 1872 he had become professor of political and social science. All three had this in common: they regarded with suspicion any intrusion by government in the automatic processes of the market; such efforts violated the precepts of freedom, weakened popular morality, and held back the nation's economic development. Wells and Atkinson put their opposition to tariffs, fiat money, "inquisitorial, vexatious, and unnecessarily multiple taxes" in terms of the lessons they had learned from Adam Smith and the later Frédéric Bastiat and Jerome Blanqui. If these pressures could be held under control and the entrepreneur permitted to go his way unhampered, the skies would always be serene. As though he were paraphrasing Bastiat, Atkinson in 1890 was saying of the United States:

[It is a country] in which birth gives no privilege and in which all have or may have equal opportunity to attain material welfare, the working men and women . . . are steadily securing to their own use and enjoyment an increasing share of an increasing product; while, on the other hand, both the material capital which has been saved in a concrete form, and also the element which is yet more necessary to material abundance, the capital which is immaterial, i.e., the mental factor in all productions, are being placed at the service of those who do the primary work at a lessening rate of compensation or profit.

William Graham Sumner   William Graham Sumner was made of sterner stuff. He continues to intrigue us today in part because of his stubborn courage and cantankerousness (he was that rare type in America, an intellectual eccentric), in part because of his pioneer and fascinating excursion into cultural anthropology. Sumner had had an impressive education: as a youth at Yale; then in Geneva with private tutors, learning French and Hebrew; at Göttingen University, where he had acquired German, a variety of other ancient and modern languages, and a close knowledge of church history and what he called "biblical science"; and at Oxford, where he was disappointed in the university but charmed by the wide-ranging minds of his fellow students. Sumner occupied a number of Episcopal pulpits, but pastoral theology was not to his taste; by this time, as a result of his pondering over Buckle and Spencer and his decision that his metier was the study of the "science of society," he was ready for a university career. He had been a tutor at Yale before entering the ministry; he now returned to Yale where he remained until his death in 1910.

Sumner had been brought up as a churchman and had been prepared to think in terms of moral values which proved the existence of design or purpose in the world; these were final causes and religion elucidated them. Having turned scientist, first as an economist, then as a sociologist, he now rejected speculation and dogmatism. He was the complete empiricist: facts were to be ascertained by objective study; a science of society concerned itself with the consequences of men's conduct and not with purposes and motives. Theology and metaphysics were out; and so were ethical principles. Said he: "On every ground and at every point, the domain of social science must be defended against the alleged authority of ethical data, which cannot be subjected to any verification whatever."

His study of social institutions led him to believe there were laws of change and evolution; this was particularly true of the industrial society he was viewing; its character and needs permeated all societal relations. Therefore, he could say, as he scoffed at the philosophers, religionists, reformers:

It [industrial organization] creates the conditions of our existence, sets the limits of our social activity, regulates the bonds of our social relations, determines our conceptions of good and evil, suggests our life philosophy, molds our inherited political institutions, and reforms the oldest customs, like marriage and property.

These economic institutions and the societal relations that sprang from them had evolved and operated through laws. Seeking to direct society into other channels—to provide for those who dropped by the wayside; to organize the whole of living on the basis of a priori principles or dogmas presumably to overcome injustice—simply violated the "laws or rules of right living." All that the individual could do was to give his "intelligent acceptance." Said he:

There is no liberty for the intelligent man as an individual or in voluntary cooperation with others, except the intelligent obedience to the laws or rules of right living. Man must understand that what liberty properly means for the individual is intelligent acceptance of the conditions of earthly life, conformity to them, and manful efforts to make life a success under them.

Despite his rejection of his religious training, Sumner fell into the vocabulary of his stern Protestant heritage in defending the economic world in which he lived and which did dispense justice, no matter how harsh. He saw "temperance," "thrift," "savings," "above all," "work" as the instruments for achieving progress. "Industry, self-denial, and temperance are the laws of prosperity for men and state: without them advances in the arts and in wealth mean only corruption and decay through luxury and vice." This justified private property and its unequal rewards; this required that intelligent men resist the intrusion of the state and the sentimental, "humanitarian" pleas of the reformers.

Sumner was not content merely with the presentation of this theoretical model. He made his views widely known as a publicist; on every occasion he sought to demonstrate their applicability to public affairs. Therefore, he jumped into every battle—tariffs, monetary reform, the Single Tax, the habits and shortcomings of a democratic society, the threatened dangers of corporate power and monopoly practices, the too pervasive influence of theological minds in the universities, the War with Spain (which he opposed)—never impressed by authority or power, always honest and disdainful of woolly thinking, always sharp and cutting. Whether one likes today his unregenerate individualism or not, it is a mistake to call him a conservative. He was a libertarian in the tradition of Acton, Mill, and Tocqueville; and his essays today continue to delight—and infuriate.

Society was a struggle; unequal rewards, and properly so, went to those "of unequal effort and virtue." Any program to organize society and concentrate power in government or the workers—Single Tax, Socialism, trade unionism—presaged a steep drop into mediocrity. His *What Social Classes Owe to Each Other* (1883) was Sumner's first great shout of defiance against all those threats of intervention and conformity he saw already appearing.

Sumner's argument was: society, after a long period of struggle, had raised itself from the rigidity of "status" to the free flexibility of "contract." In so doing, the exceptional person had been furnished the opportunity to advance; responsibility had now shifted from the community or group to the individual. There were no classes, consequently; certainly there were no groups to whom anything was due by some other group. Individuals simply owed each other "good will, mutual respect, and mutual guarantees of liberty and security." On the other hand, legislation could not dictate good will, and justice was a matter of right, not favor.

He put the alleged leading concern of the day in these blunt, and derisive, terms.

So far as I can find out what the classes are who are respectively endowed with the rights and duties of posing and solving social problems, they are as follows: Those who are bound to solve the problems are the rich, comfortable, prosperous, virtuous, respectable, educated, and healthy; those whose right it is to set the problems are those who have been less fortunate or less successful in the struggle for existence.

And he ended up with the common-sense observation:

Instead of endeavoring to redistribute the acquisitions which have been made between the existing classes, our aim should be to *increase, multiply,* and *extend the chances.* Such is the work of civilization. Every old error or abuse which is removed opens new chances of development to all the new energy of society. Every improvement in education, science, art, or government expands the chances of man on earth.

The Forgotten Man, the solid, middle-class citizen, who minded his business, paid his bills and observed the law—and was ignored by everyone but the tax collector—was Sumner's particular concern. In an essay of that name (1883), Sumner again made a simple and, to many, uncomfortable, point. If society owed anyone a duty, it was to this Forgotten Man; and it could best fulfill its obligation by making property secure and government as cheap as might be consistent with the maintenance of such rights. The Forgotten Man, said Sumner, is the simple, honest laborer, ready to earn his living by productive work. We pass him by because he is independent, self-supporting, and asks no favors. He does not appeal to the emotions or excite the sentiments. He only wants to make a contract and fulfill it, with respect on both sides and favor on neither side. He must get his living out of the capital of the country. . . . Every particle of capital which is wasted on the vicious, the idle and the shiftless is so much taken from the capital available to reward the independent and productive laborer.

His concern about the spread of statism and the espousal of socialism (whether romantic, religious, or revolutionary) by a small but vocal company of intellectuals prompted him to make some observations on liberty and responsibility (in an article of that name, published in *The Independent* in 1889). In characteristically blunt fashion, he scoffed at the cloud-cuckoo land of the social-contract and natural-right philosophies. Liberty, he said, was the greatest civil good; but it was not a metaphysical or abstract conception. Liberty grew out of the experiences of men in the use of civil institutions; and it could flourish only under law, the greatest of these. "These facts go to constitute a status—the status of a free man in a modern jural state." And then he went on with a flourish, pointing out where liberty languished and died—in what today we would call the Big State and the Police State.

It [liberty] is unfriendly to dogmatism. It pertains to what a man shall do, have, and be. It is unfriendly to all personal control, to officialism, to administrative philanthropy and administrative vision, as much as to bureaucratic despotism or monarchical absolution. It is hostile to all absolutism, and people who are well-trained in the traditions of civil liberty are quick to detect absolutism in all its new forms. Those who have lost the traditions of civil liberty accept phrases.

CHAPTER FOUR

THE LAW WRITERS, THE LAWYERS, AND THE COURTS

How the Law Writers Protected Property   Of equal importance for the maintenance of the status quo were the mighty supports that came from the law—the writers of law textbooks, the lawyers, the State courts, and finally the United States Supreme Court itself. The original great architects of this design were two writers of law books who, interestingly enough, came from the agrarian West and not the commercial East. The first was Thomas M. Cooley, lawyer and State judge of Michigan; the second was Christopher G. Tiedeman, lawyer and law-school professor of Missouri.

Cooley's book, whose full title was *A Treatise on the Constitutional Limitations Which Rest Upon the Legislative Powers of the States of the American Union,* appeared in 1868 and went through eight editions until 1927. Tiedeman's book was called *A Treatise on the Limitations of the Police Power of the States,* appeared initially in 1886, and continued to be republished regularly and in expanded form right into the twentieth century. His second edition, printed in two volumes in 1900, he called *A Treatise on State and Federal Control of Persons and Property in the United States;* here he noted that "the first edition of the book has been quoted by the courts with approval in hundreds of cases," and gave the citations for other jurists seeking guidance.

Cooley's work was a landmark in American jurisprudence for a number of reasons. It was the first systematic commentary in the field of State constitutional law. It laid the groundwork for the defense of *laissez-faire* by expounding the idea of substantive due process; that is, the right of courts to intervene against State legislation when property rights were being threatened. It pointed the way to the imposition of limitations on the police power of the States, in other words, the broad claim that legislatures assumed they had to pass laws in the interests of health, welfare, safety, and morals. It sought the outlawing of class, or partial, legislation: those enactments that affected or benefited only a portion of the community. And it prepared the way for the much broader constitutional rule of liberty of contract.

State courts, during 1872-86, began to follow Cooley, chipping away at the police power of legislatures and giving the idea of property a broader reading: that property was not simply "possession and use" of things but more pervasively the power of the owner to full liberty of choice and action. The way was now ready for Tiedeman, who was prepared to so limit the police power and so widen the idea of freedom of contract that the only basis for State action as regards property could be the rule *sic utere tuo ut alienum non laedas* (so to use your own as not to cause injuries to others).

The year 1886, when Tiedeman's book appeared, was important for another reason: it was only then that the United States Supreme Court reversed the position it had taken in 1873 when it read the "due process" clause of the Fourteenth Amendment as assuring only procedural protections, and gave due process the same substantive meaning the State courts had begun to do as early as 1872. The legal edifice was now complete; property right and the individual's freedom of contract had full safeguards against the intrusion of State and, in fact, Congressional legislation.

What had happened was this. Before the Civil War, courts started out with the presumption that State regulations, based on the police power, were constitutional. After the Civil War they moved to the first limitation: that the police power was restricted and could be invoked only when citizens were interfering with one another under the common law of nuisances. And then they took the final step: that State regulations were presumed to be unconstitutional where restraints were imposed by statute or administrative ruling on the free and unrestricted rights of property and the relations between business and labor as regards working conditions, hours of labor, methods of paying wages, and the like.

To go back to Cooley. The general propositions that informed his exposition were these. First, there were certain "natural" rights that existed in individuals; these grew organically as society developed. They were life, liberty, the formation of family relations, the acquisition and enjoyment of property, and the making of contracts. It is true that this last right he did not expound fully until 1884, in his edition of *Blackstone's Commentaries*. Then he spelled out "liberty of contract" in this fashion:

This is the right essential to government, essential to society, essential to the acquisition of property, and to domestic relations. But here also limitations and restraints are imperative. Unenlightened nature might prompt too many contracts which would be immoral or indecent, or which would tend directly to the defeat of the purposes of government. The law must forbid these while it recognizes the right generally.

Secondly, these "natural" rights are embodied in the Constitution; and once the Constitution has been drawn up, popular sovereignty, as expressed by legislation, is bound and limited. This is what Cooley means by "implied limitations." Thus he said in his Preface: "He will not attempt to deny—what will probably be sufficiently apparent—that he has written in full sympathy with the restraints which the caution of the fathers has imposed upon the exercise of the powers of government." And, a little later, expressing his concern over popular sovereignty and legislative supremacy, he said:

the violence of public passion is quite as likely to be in the direction of oppression as in any other; and the necessity for bills of rights in our fundamental law lies mainly in the danger that the legislature will be influenced by temporal excitements and passions among people to adopt oppressive enactments.

Thirdly, an outstanding right is that of "due process," to be found in the Fifth Amendment, as a restraint on the federal authority, and in the Fourteenth Amendment, as one on the States. This is the old common-law limitation of the "law of the land"; and Cooley's most influential chapter and that most frequently cited by the State courts when they began to follow him was called "Protection to Property by 'The Law of the Land.'" In Cooley's hands, "the law of the land" or "due process" was more than a set of procedural guarantees assured the individual—a fair trial by his peers, the right of confrontation of witnesses and of appeal, protection against unreasonable searches and seizures; it was a substantive limitation to assure property full freedom of scope. So, he said: "The right to property is a sacred right." And again: "The test of unlawful interference with property is that vested rights are abridged or taken away." And more fully, when there are governmental efforts to interfere with title to enjoyment of property, then: ". . . we are to test its validity by those principles of civil liberty and constitutional protection which have become established in our system of laws, and not generally by rules that pertain to some procedure only." Cooley then defined "vested rights" in this fashion:

as a shield of protection, the term vested rights is not used in any narrow or technical sense, or as imparting a power of legal control merely, but rather as implying a vested interest which it is right and equitable that the government should recognize and protect and of which the individual could not be deprived arbitrarily without injustice.

Fourthly, an important restraint on State action was that no regulation affecting any one class of citizens, in which "their rights, privileges or legal capacities" were restricted, could be regarded as constitutional. This was the key passage—so frequently cited—that condemned so-called "class" legislation; it was from his first edition.

if the legislature should undertake to provide that persons following some specified lawful trade or employment should not have the capacity to make contracts . . . or in any other way to make use of their property as was permissible to others, it can scarcely be doubted that the act would transcend the due bounds of legislative power, even if it did not come in conflict with express constitutional provisions. The man or the class forbidden the acquisition or enjoyment of property in a manner permitted to the community at large would be deprived of liberty in particulars of primary importance to their "pursuit of happiness."

To this, he added in his second edition:

and those who should claim a right to do so ought to be able to show a specific authority therefor, instead of calling upon others to show how and where the authority is negatived.

Cooley went on with this general dictum:

Equality of rights, privileges, and capacities unquestionably should be the aim of the law; and if special privileges are granted, or special burdens or restrictions imposed in any case, it must be presumed that the legislature designed to depart as little as possible from this fundamental maxim of government.

As an important corollary drawn from these general principles was the necessity of recognizing the limitations upon the tax power, particularly upon the power to appropriate and borrow money. Taxes to do these things had to have a "public purpose." Said Cooley:

In the first place, taxation having for its legitimate purpose the raising of money for public purposes and the proper needs of government, the exaction of money from the citizens for other purposes is not a proper exercise of this power, and must therefore be unauthorized.

This "public-purpose" doctrine was seized upon at once by State courts, as we shall see; as were the others of "implied limitations upon the police power" and "liberty of contract."

Tiedeman pressed the analysis further. The heart of his position was that government could do no more "than to provide for the public order and personal security by the prevention and punishment of crimes and trespasses." In his Preface, he made his intention crystal clear. It was his purpose to show that under the democratic constitutions of the United States, and this applied to both federal and State governments, "democratic absolutism is impossible" as long as "the popular reverence for the institutions, in their restrictions upon governmental activities, is nourished." This was the peculiar responsibility of the courts: they were to safeguard "the substantial rights of the minority"; these were "free from all lawful control and interference by the majority, except so far as such control or interference may be necessary to prevent injury to others in the enjoyment of their rights."

He wanted to awaken the public, he said:

to a full appreciation of the power of constitutional limitations to protect private rights against the radical experimentations of social reformers. [If he succeeds] he will feel amply requited for his labors in the cause of social order and personal liberty.

Police regulation, when confined within their proper limits, that is to say, the maxim of *sic utere,* "should and usually would receive in a reasonably healthy community, the enthusiastic support of the entire population." But the recent "unjustifiable limitations imposed upon private rights and personal liberty" has resulted in a distrust of any exercise of police power.

In the second edition of 1900 Tiedeman expanded on his conception of the police power. Government and municipal law protect and develop, rather than create private rights, which are natural rights "existing in the law of reason." The police power, as understood in the constitutional law of the United States, is simply the power of the government to establish provisions for the enforcement of the common- as well as civil-law maxim *sic utere tuo ut alienum non laedas.* Any law which goes beyond that principle—which goes beyond regulations to provide for the public welfare and general security—is a "governmental usurpation, and violates the principles of abstract justice, as they have been developed under our republican institutions."

In his Chapter 9, which Tiedeman called "Police Regulations of Trades and Professions," he declared "No man's liberty is safe, if the legislature can deny him the right to engage in a harmless calling." And he went on:

It is always within the discretion of the legislature to institute such regulations when the proper case arises, and to determine upon the character of the regulation. But it is strictly a judicial question, whether the trade or calling is of such a nature as to require or justify police regulation. The legislature cannot declare a certain employment to be injurious to the public good, and prohibit it, when, as a matter of fact, it is a harmless occupation.

Liberty, or freedom of contract, obviously also related to transactions in the market place. Business activities were "part of the natural and civil liberty" of the individual; in consequence, the public authority had no right to interfere by "determining the conditions and terms of the contract which constitute the basis of the business relation or transaction." The fixing of price, therefore, was a private concern and no one can compel the individual to take less "although the price may be so exorbitant as to become extortionate." Therefore, freedom from State regulation of prices and charges is "a natural right" so far as the business is wholly private and is not connected with "some special privilege or franchise."

The result of freedom of contract operated equally and impartially upon workers as well as employers; workers, in short, could dispose of their labor upon such terms as they regarded most beneficial to them; and "any attempts at legislative interference are pronounced unreasonable and hence unconstitutional."

In his second edition, Tiedeman amplified his notion of liberty of contract. He agreed that the term was not to be found in any bill of rights of any American constitution; but in almost all of them the right to acquire and possess property and to pursue happiness is declared to be inalienable. This has been "rationally included" to make reasonable contracts which were under the protection of the law. To clinch his argument, Tiedeman cited rulings along these lines from the State courts of Massachusetts, Vermont, West Virginia, and Arkansas.

In his Chapter 11, "Regulation of Private Employment," Tiedeman had much to say about the conditions of the workers. It is true that more and more the nature of the wage contract was being set by the employers; they dictated the terms of employment to the "masses, who must either accept them or remain idle." The temptation, therefore, prompted by "the impulse of a generous nature," was to call "loudly for the intervention of the law to protect the poor wage-earner from the grasping cupidity of the employer." But one must go slow; and here we find once more repeated the arguments of the economists and the churchmen. Was not the suffering of the working classes due largely to their own improvidence and a desire to imitate the luxurious habits of the rich, rather than the oppression of the capitalists? On the other hand, the superior position and independence of the employer came from "the exertion of his powers; he is above, and can to some extent dictate terms to, his employees because his natural powers are greater, either intellectually or morally; and the profits which naturally flow from this superiority are just rewards of his own endeavors."

No laws can successfully cope with these natural forces, said Tiedeman. Indeed, laws that interfere in the relations of master and servant are unconstitutional. This applies to the terms of hiring and the hours of work; such efforts at regulation "interfere with one's natural liberty, in a case where there is no trespass upon private rights, and no threatening injury to the public."

Property and the State Courts Thus the text writers found "constitutional" supports—it is true, in a higher law—to buttress the arguments from other quarters. The State courts, and then the United States Supreme Court, made these doctrines the rules of conduct affecting the relations of government and business and those of employers and employees.

Almost at once, Cooley's influence was felt in the realm of taxation. In 1869 (in the so-called *Hanson* case), the Supreme Court of Iowa ruled that a statute authorizing counties and cities to lay taxes to assist private railroad corporations was not a "valid or legitimate exercise of the taxing power." The decision was written by Chief Justice John F. Dillon, and he used almost word for word Cooley's formulation when he declared that taxes were "burdens or charges imposed by the legislature upon persons or property to raise money for public purposes or to accomplish some governmental end." Said Dillon: The money demanded of the citizen was not a tax but "a coercive contribution in favor of private railway corporations." Such an act violated the due process of the State constitution: "a provision which is adequate to protect the owner from being despoiled of his property by an unauthorized tax law or alleged tax." In 1872, Dillon published his highly influential *Treatise on the Law of Municipal Corporations,* a work which went through successive editions, the fifth in 1911 containing five volumes.

Cooley himself, sitting on the Michigan Supreme bench, in 1870, in the so-called *Salem* case, in which a statute permitting townships to pledge their credit to aid railroad corporations was involved, had the opportunity to rule similarly. The tax power could not be employed for purposes not expressly specified in the State constitution. Cooley went further; he even narrowed the areas in which constitutions could vest the tax power in the hands of the legislature. One of his most interesting dicta was the statement that taxes laid by counties, townships, and cities had to satisfy two purposes: these were to be both public and local. What, then, was "public purpose"? It meant "settled usage"—that use and wont which was sanctioned by time and had the agreement of the people.

Cooley expanded these ideas in a book *A Treatise of the Law of Taxation* (1876) which was really an elaborate gloss on the key principle he had laid down on the *Salem* case. Here he had said:

By common consent also a large portion of the most urgent needs of society are relegated exclusively to the law of demand and supply. It is this in its natural operation and without the interference of government,

that gives us the proper proportion of tillers of the soil, artisans, manufacturers, merchants, and professional men, and that determines when
and where they shall give to society the benefit of their particular services.
However great the need in the direction of a particular calling, the interference of government is not tolerated, because though it might be supplying a public want, it is considered as invading the domain that belongs
exclusively to private inclination and enterprise.

From this it followed—and so the State courts began to find, ultimately
being supported by the federal courts—that public authorities could not
give financial aid (by subsidy, loan, tax exemption) to private businesses;
or to individuals or to private noncommercial associations; or to publicly
owned enterprises which had a commercial purpose.

One such case came quickly to the United States Supreme Court. It
involved the effort of the city of Topeka, Kansas, to float a bond issue to
help in the erection of a privately owned bridge. The State court declared
the law authorizing this illegal in 1874; so did the federal circuit court
of the District of Kansas (on which Dillon was now sitting); and so did
the United States Supreme Court the same year.

Mr. Justice Miller, writing the Court's opinion, in language that came
right out of Cooley, said:

The theory of our governments, State and National, is opposed to the
deposit of unlimited powers anywhere. . . . There are limitations on such
power which grow out of the essential nature of all free governments.
Implied reservations of individual rights, without which the social com-
pact could not exist, and which are respected by all governments entitled
to the name.

Clyde E. Jacobs, who has studied exhaustively the impact of these
ideas on American constitutional law in his excellent *Law Writers and
the Courts* (1954), found that, in at least forty cases involving aid to
private business (other than railroads) between 1870 and 1910 which
came before State supreme courts and the federal courts, statutes and
ordinances were invalidated in all but one because a public purpose was
not being performed. These included even efforts to use public moneys to
aid victims of disasters (fire, drought), blind people, and needy students
who could not otherwise attend a State university.

In connection with this last, the State court of Missouri in 1898 declared:

Paternalism, whether State or Federal . . . is the assumption by the government of a quasi-fatherly relation to the citizen and his family, involving excessive governmental regulation of the private affairs and business methods and interests of the people, upon the theory that the people are incapable of managing their own affairs, and is pernicious in its tendencies. In a word it minimizes the citizen and maximizes the government.

The import of these tax cases must be clear. The barriers raised against the use of public funds for everything but the barest necessities—safety, health, education—freed individuals and business enterprise from heavy tax burdens. Savings and profits in consequence could flow, virtually in their entirety, into risky ventures and innovations of all sorts. Because the tax burden was so slight for such a long time—really up to the outbreak of World War I—large private fortunes were built up which were reinvested, and the profits of companies could be plowed back into new plant, equipment, and the purchase of primary producers (mines, forests) which made industrial organizations even more efficient and lowered their costs and prices. The negligible share persons and companies had to turn over to governments out of their earnings, as much as any other single factor, contributed to the speedy transformation of the United States to the greatest and richest industrial nation of the world by 1900.

The State Courts and the Workers   Welfare legislation, to safeguard workers against the hazards of industrial employment; laws to assure them the immediate and honest payment of wages; and laws seeking to allow workers joining trade unions and protecting their rights to do so—these also were found by the State courts null and void on the grounds of the undue extension of the police power and of violation of liberty of contract.

A decision that tightly shut the door to legislation seeking to limit hours of work in industries, where the health of employees would be affected, was handed down by the New York State Court of Appeals in 1885 and was followed universally. In the case called *in re Jacobs,* which involved a statute seeking to prohibit the manufacture of cigars and the preparation of tobacco in tenement houses in the cities of Brooklyn and

New York (that is to say, where people also lived), Judge Robert Earl, speaking for a unanimous court, found the law:

interferes with the profitable and free use of his property by the owner or lessee of a tenement house who is a cigar maker, and trammels him in the application of his industry and the disposition of his labor, and thus, in a strictly legitimate sense, it arbitrarily deprives him of his property and some portion of his personal liberty.

The definition given to liberty was a sweeping one. Said Earl:

liberty, in its broadest sense as understood in this country, means . . the right of one to use his faculties in all lawful ways, to live and work where he will, to earn his livelihood in any lawful calling, and to pursue any lawful trade or avocation. All laws, therefore, which impair or trammel these rights . . . are infringements upon his fundamental rights of liberty which are under constitutional protection.

The law had been passed in the exercise of the police power—to protect the public health and secure the public comfort and safety. But the legislature's decision was not the final one in determining whether a specific act by it was a genuine use of the police power or an oppressive measure under the guise of that power. Said Earl, ". . . personal rights and private property cannot be arbitrarily invaded, and the determination of the legislature is not final or conclusive." The courts had the right to review such acts. In this instance, Earl found that the law was not a legitimate exercise of the police power but a pretended one, and one of the reasons offered was that its application was limited and not general. Even assuming that the manufacture of cigars affected the health of those making them (which Earl denied), still this did not make the statute a public health measure. If government were given the right to scrutinize trades and decide which might or might not be exercised, we would revert again to the mercantilist regulations that existed generally before the nineteenth century. And Earl said, rejecting public intervention of any sort: "Such governmental interferences disturb the normal adjustments of the social fabric, and usually derange the delicate and complicated machinery of industry and cause a score of ills while attempting the removal of one."

Similar decisions by State courts where property rights were affected (including the right to labor) followed fast within the next fifteen years.

New York's court outlawed a statute prohibiting the manufacture of butter substitutes. Michigan's court rejected a State law requiring commission merchants engaged in the sale of farm produce to post bonds. Illinois' court threw out a city ordinance which required that all work on city contracts be performed by union labor. Maryland's court found unconstitutional a statute forbidding the officers of railroads and mining corporations to have an interest in mercantile businesses. The courts of Washington and Minnesota held that regulations which limited the rights of citizens to enter into contracts with reference to their own property were illegal—unless there was some recognizable tendency to promote the public welfare.

Statutes limiting hours of work in unhealthy occupations were passed by legislatures under the police power; these the courts too struck down on the ground that they were ostensible and not real applications of police regulations. And where cities enacted ordinances fixing the eight-hour day or seeking to set minimum wages for those working for private contractors on municipal projects, State courts threw them out because they violated the worker's liberty of contract.

Nebraska's court in 1894 found a maximum-hour law in private employment unconstitutional. Illinois' court in 1895 rejected a statute prohibiting the employment of women for more than eight hours in factories making clothing. Colorado's court in 1899 invalidated an eight-hour law for workers in mines and smelters.

Efforts on the part of legislatures to regulate and standardize the payment of wages and compensation to employees—to prohibit the payment of wages in truck (merchandise) or in script or in anything but lawful money; or to prevent mining and manufacturing companies from selling their products to their employees at higher prices or profits than those obtained in the normal channels of trade; or to fine employees for defective workmanship—in a large number of States these measures were declared unconstitutional. Courts did this for a variety of reasons: the police power was not really involved; the right to pursue a calling or employment without hindrance constituted the difference between freedom and slavery; the workers had liberty of contract, which meant they could make any arrangements with employers they pleased. So, in connection with the last, the Illinois highest court declared in 1892:

[97]

Those who are entitled to exercise the elective franchise are deemed equals before the law, and it is not admissible to arbitrarily brand, by statute, one class of men, without reference to and wholly irrespective of their actual good or bad behavior, as too unscrupulous, and the other class as too imbecile or timid and weak, to exercise that freedom in contracting which is allowed to all others.

And when legislatures sought to prevent employers from requiring workers to sign "yellow-dog" contracts—that they would not join unions after having obtained employment—the State courts voided such statutes.

Professor Jacobs, who has read hundreds of cases in the State courts and has left students of the period deeply in his debt by doing so, found Cooley, Tiedeman, and Supreme Court Justice Field (in his dissents in the *Slaughter-House* and *Munn* cases) cited again and again and, as often as not, quoted with approval at great length. It is important that we examine now how Field, almost singlehanded, persuaded the United States Supreme Court to change its mind and to make the "equal-protection" clause of the Constitution's Fourteenth Amendment a shield for the safeguarding of the property of all "persons" (including corporations) and to give its "due-process" clause a substantive instead of a wholly procedural reading.

The Thinking of Justice Field of the Supreme Court   Stephen J. Field, born in Connecticut and educated at Williams College, settled in California at the age of 33, in 1849, after a *wanderjahr* in Europe, where he saw the French Revolution of 1848 at work and its abortive attempts to establish Socialist workshops. Here he read for the law, engaged in its practice, and began at once to dabble in politics. He sat in the State legislature; helped to codify California's statutes; went to its Supreme Court; and in 1859 became its chief justice. It was from this post—and because Field was a Union Democrat, supporting the war against the South—that Lincoln named him to the United States Supreme Court in 1863.

Field had started out, his two important biographers * say, on the

---

* Swisher, Carl B., *Stephen J. Field, Craftsman of the Law* (1930) and Graham, Howard Jay, "Justice Field and the Fourteenth Amendment" (*Yale Law Journal*, Vol. 52, 1943). All students are under heavy obligation to Mr. Graham for his careful and illuminating articles about the origin and early judicial history of the Fourteenth Amendment. Upon these I have drawn heavily. The leading ones are: "The 'Conspiracy

California bench and in his first years on the Supreme Court as a convinced democrat: the majority ruled; it spoke through the people's elected representatives in the legislature and in Congress; the people's choices could impose such restraints as they pleased upon business activity. The tax power was one such device that he was not disposed to tamper with, nor did he see fit to interfere with the activities of State legislatures.

Up to 1870, that is to say, as far as property rights were concerned, Field tended to side with little men as against large capital aggregations, was tolerant of legislative innovation and opposed to the expansion of judicial power, and was ready to assume that in a democratic society the open market place of ideas and discussion assured that a rough kind of equity was being served. In 1858, he said from the California bench, brushing aside the thought that oppression could become a threat to the fair world in which he lived: "Frequent elections by the people furnish the only protection under the Constitution against the abuse of acknowledged legislative power."

And then Field made a complete about-face. As Graham puts it:

The mild paternalist of the fifties became the arch-individualist of the seventies and eighties. The staunch defender of legislative power became the leader in expanding judicial review. The judge who in 1859 had given no inkling that he regarded due process as a limitation on the taxing power, in 1882 made it a limitation, not only as regards natural persons, but corporations as well.

Field had come to be suspicious of the democratic processes. Where previously he had seen, through the give and take of debate, the appearance sooner or later of balanced and reasoned judgment, now he was fearful of excess, not only on the part of minorities seizing power but also on the part of duly elected majorities riding roughshod over the rights of others. Whether minorities obtained control by revolution or majorities ran amuck, the captives of populist and demagogic leaders,

Theory' of the Fourteenth Amendment" (*Yale Law Journal*), Vol. 47, 1938); "The 'Conspiracy Theory' of the Fourteenth Amendment" (2) (*Ibid*, Vol. 48, 1938); the article above cited; "Our 'Declaratory' Fourteenth Amendment" (*Stamford Law Review*, Vol. 7, 1954); "An Innocent Abroad. The Constitutional Corporate 'Person'" (*U.C.L.A. Law Review*, Vol. 2, 1955); "'Builded Better Than They Know'" (*University of Pittsburgh Law Review*, Vol. 17, 1956).

the outcomes were the same: property and liberty were threatened and the lights all over the world were in danger of going out.

In 1897, upon his retirement from the Supreme Court, now crotchety and querulous, Field expressed his fears in these words:

As I look back over the more than a third of a century that I have sat on this bench, I am more and more impressed with the immeasurable importance of this Court. . . . It possesses the power of declaring the law, and in that is found the safeguard that keeps the whole mighty fabric of government from rushing to destruction. This negative power, the power of resistance, is the only safety of a popular government.

Three things had happened in Field's life to make him deeply apprehensive. The first was the triumph of the Radical Republicans in Congress, following Lincoln's assassination and the impeachment of President Johnson, and the imposition—so he thought—of a harsh rule on the defeated South. He recoiled particularly against the Force Act of 1871, which permitted the President to suspend habeas corpus and use the federal courts, marshals, and troops to put down the Ku Klux Klan night riders. The second was the establishment of the Commune in Paris in 1871, the effort to create a Socialist state, and the bloody excesses that followed. (He remembered the Paris of 1848.) The third was the outbreak of labor disorders in California in the same year; and the rise, in 1877, of the California Working Men's Party. This last was led by Denis Kearney, once a sailor and later a drayman in San Francisco, who had always been sympathetic to California's employers, but who now turned demagogue and, in order to obtain political power, did everything to inflame the passions of men hard hit by the great depression. Kearney had started his haranguing of street crowds in San Francisco's sand lots (his party was called the Sand-Lotters); and ended all his speeches with what became a battle cry: "The Chinese . . . The Corporations . . . The Southern Pacific Railroad . . . must go!"

Under Kearney, who was a dangerous and only too successful rabble-rouser, the Working Men's Party talked of wresting the government from the hands of the rich and placing it "in the hands of the people, where it properly belongs"; destroying land monopoly; and as well "the great money power of the rich by a system of taxation that will make great wealth impossible in the future." But what roused Kearney's following to a high emotional pitch and led to terrorization, property destruction, and personal assaults, was his condemnation of the Chinese who were originally brought into California to work on the California railroads and remained to become laborers in California's mines, small shopkeepers, and gardeners. Said the party platform: "We propose to rid the country of cheap Chinese labor as soon as possible and by all means in our power because it tends still more to degrade labor and aggrandize capital."

The Party won successes at local polls and by joining hands with the Grangers dominated the California constitutional convention of 1879. The new constitution contained a number of anticorporation clauses; created a railroad commission to set maximum rates; gave home rule to San Francisco—Kearney's bailiwick; and deprived Chinese of their civil liberties, the right to hold property, engage in certain specific occupations, or obtain employment in corporations.

According to Graham, during the whole of the 1870s, Field was becoming less and less the impartial justice and more and more a prey to "restlessness, ambition, and anxiety." (He had been hoping and, had worked hard, to get the Democratic nomination for the Presidency in 1880.) Field expressed his fears to his friends orally and in writing: of the socialism that was spreading over Europe and seemingly was gaining a foothold in his own California; of a political demagogy that could so easily pervert the democratic processes; of Granger notions and the statism these were leading to. In 1882, he literally took matters into his own hands. A powerful judiciary, at least in the United States, could erect dikes against these rising waters. Sitting as a circuit judge in the Ninth Circuit (California)—up to 1891 the justices had circuit-riding duties—Field, in the famous *San Mateo* case, made his first great move to overthrow the *Slaughter-House* and *Munn* (and other Granger) decisions.

Field, in California, even before 1882, had become associated with what disturbed commentators had come to call "The Ninth Circuit Law." One of them characterized this in 1884 as a law which is "an unwarrantable enlargement of federal jurisdiction, the erection of a general and irresponsible superintendency over the police regulations of the States, over their process of interstate extradition, and over the administration of their criminal laws." That is to say, where the decisions of circuit courts were final (one such important area was habeas corpus proceedings), the Supreme Court itself could be overridden. And Field had seized such an opportunity to enunciate constitutional law in the Ninth Circuit in 1874 when he ruled that a California law (which tried to stop Chinese immigration) was in violation of the Fourteenth Amendment because its "equal-protection" clause applied to all "persons" rather than to "citizens" alone. In 1879, in a similar case affecting the Chinese (this applied to a San Francisco ordinance permitting the police authorities to cut off the queues of Chinese petty criminals who would not or could not pay cash fines), he declared that the equal-protection clause applied to "all persons . . . native or foreign, high or low." More than this: the clause also meant protection for the enforcement of contracts, and its restraints extended to "all the instrumentalities and agencies" of State government.

Other federal California judges saw what Field meant, for in 1880, in habeas corpus proceedings, one of them held that the law passed to carry out the mandate of the new State constitution—that corporations could not employ Chinese under penalty of punishment of their officers and of loss of their charters (the officer of a mining corporation thus found guilty had petitioned for a writ of habeas corpus)—was invalid. It curtailed the economic rights of both employers and employees; for "due process" and "equal protection" under the Fourteenth Amendment included the right to pursue lawful callings. (We shall see that the *Slaughter-House* decision of 1873 had said exactly the reverse.)

The Supreme Court Before the Triumph of Justice Field   Before we discuss the *San Mateo* case (and its companion the *Santa Clara* case of 1883) we must go back to see how Field was developing his constitutional law in the *Slaughter-House* cases of 1873 and the Granger cases of 1877.

The famous *Slaughter-House* cases came before the United States Supreme Court in 1873 on appeal from a statute passed by the State legislature of Louisiana in 1869 creating a slaughter-house monopoly in the city of New Orleans. The restraints imposed, under the police power, were regarded with deep concern by business interests generally, and important members of the bar were retained for the petitioners. One of these was John A. Campbell, who had appeared in an earlier case affecting the same statute before the federal circuit court. Campbell sought relief for his clients on the basis of the Constitution's Fourteenth Amendment, specifying the "privileges-or-immunities" clause, the "due-process" clause and the "equal-protection" clause of the first article. This ran as follows:

All persons born or naturalized in the United States, and subject to the jurisdiction thereof, are citizens of the United States and of the State wherein they reside. No State shall make or enforce any law which shall abridge the privileges or immunities of citizens of the United States, nor shall any State deprive any person of life, liberty, or property without due process of law, nor deny to any person within its jurisdiction the equal protection of the laws.

Campbell placed his reliance, in questioning the validity of the Louisiana law, on the "privileges-or-immunities" clause, arguing that the Fourteenth Amendment applied not only to the recently emancipated Negroes but to laboring men as well, indeed to every class of the population. Said he: "The Amendment was designed to secure individual liberty, individual property, and individual security and honor from arbitrary, partial, proscriptive and unjust legislation of State governments." Campbell anticipated the later broad reading of the word "liberty" when he described it as the right of the person to freedom, "the power of determining by his own choice his own conduct, to have no master, no overseer put over him, to be able to employ himself without constraint of law or owner; to use his faculties of body and mind, at places and with persons chosen by himself, and on contracts made by himself."

The Court ruled against Campbell and his associates. Mr. Justice Miller, writing the opinion for the majority, declared that the Fourteenth Amendment related to the Negroes: the equal-protection clause had been designed to safeguard the civil rights of the freedmen; there was nothing in it, therefore, to warrant the assumption that States might not interfere with the activities of businesses in the furtherance of their police power. As for the arguments relating to due process, it had no relevance, while the privileges-or-immunities clause really referred to those that grew out of State citizenship and the States could control businesses as a consequence. And Miller ended with the astonishing dictum that the Fourteenth Amendment effected "no fundamental change either in the nature of national citizenship or in the sweep of Congressional power."

But there were vigorous dissents on the part of four justices, with three minority opinions being written. That by Field had the concurrence of all four, while Justices Bradley and Swayne wrote additional opinions. Field's had the greater weight and it was to it that State courts, as has been said, more and more began to refer.

Field started out by following Campbell closely; he was particularly intrigued by Campbell's reliance on the Fourteenth Amendment—that it created a new national citizenship; that all monopolies were repugnant to the beliefs and rights of American citizens. For these "encroach upon the liberty of citizens to acquire property and pursue happiness." More: all citizens enjoyed equal rights; and this meant, in the economic realm, to choose and follow lawful callings. Finally, said Field, the right to labor was one of the "most sacred and imprescriptible rights of man." At this point, he quoted from Adam Smith's identification of property with labor and his insistence that the encroachment upon the rights of the employer and employee to use that labor as they saw fit was a blow at the liberty of both. As for Miller's offhand observation about the Fourteenth Amendment, Field expressed his great annoyance and deep concern. What Miller had said was bad law and wrong historically: for he reduced the Fourteenth Amendment to a "vain and idle enactment which accomplished nothing" although at the time of its passage it had occasioned much debate and excited Congress and the people.

Professor Jacobs sees in this analysis two ideas that became part and parcel of the "due-process" contention and State court decisions. The first is that because labor, as the source of property, was property, therefore it was a basic freedom. The second is that of the identification of the interests of the employee with those of the employer; in consequence, legislation which trespassed upon the rights of workers narrowed the sphere of operations—his liberties—of the businessman.

The Supreme Court continued to stand by the Miller opinion, in 1877 again resisting Field's attempts to get it involved in the growing area of State economic legislation. Illinois, along with other Middle Western States, under pressures from the agrarian Grangers, passed laws which, among other things, established maximum rates that railroads and grain elevators could charge. The case of *Munn v. Illinois,* the first of the so-called Granger cases, arose out of a suit affecting such elevator-rate regulations in the city of Chicago. Again, the majority opinion, this time written by Chief Justice Waite, insisted upon disregarding the due-process arguments of counsel; public authority, held the Court, had always had the power to regulate businesses affected with a public interest, and grain elevators belonged in this category.

Field, this time joined by Justice Strong, again dissented. The police power was limited by the *sic-utere* maxim; and because it was not proved that the grain elevators were nuisances, the freedom of their operators, as businessmen, was being impaired. The implied limitations protected the use and income of property, as well as its title and possession; and any effort to curtail such property rights violated due process. Field ended up by describing the freedoms of businessmen in much the same language he had used in the *Slaughter-House* cases:

It means freedom to go where one may choose, and to act in such a manner, not inconsistent with the equal rights of others, as his judgment may dictate for the promotion of his happiness; that is, to pursue such callings and avocations as may be most suitable to develop his capacities, and give to them their highest enjoyment.

Field had still another opportunity to make his position clear in 1884, when the Supreme Court once more affirmed, under the police power of the state, Louisiana's right to establish a monopoly in the slaughter-house business. His opinion attacked the monopoly because of its violation of due process; repeated the assertion that the pursuit of happiness and following one's calling were irrefragably linked; so were liberty and property.

Justice Field Persuades the Supreme Court   Two years earlier, Field had handed down his decision in the *San Mateo* case in the Ninth Circuit. This came before Justice Field and Circuit Judge Sawyer in August, 1882, when the Southern Pacific Railroad sought relief from taxes imposed upon it by San Mateo County, California, on the ground that the assessments were unjust. A similar case, involving the railroad and for the same reason, was against Santa Clara County; and it was decided by the same two judges in 1883. The merits of the matter are beside the point; it is enough to note that under the new California constitution an elective board was permitted to assess the value of railroads as a whole (without deducting the mortgages on it) and prorate this among the counties for tax purposes. The result was, taxes climbed sharply; the State courts rejected the contentions of the railroad; and the

Southern Pacific turned to the federal courts for relief, hiring prominent counsel to represent it. Among these, although he did not then plead, was Roscoe Conkling, leading Republican politician, friend of Field, and recently resigned Senator from New York.

Arguments were heard in the *San Mateo* case in September, and on the twenty-fifth of that month the two judges handed down their decision, writing separate opinions; they found for the Southern Pacific. Field's opinion concerns us here; it became in effect, the law of the land. For while the *San Mateo* case was heard by the Supreme Court in 1882 (it was at this time that Conkling made his sensational argument, to which we shall return), and the *Santa Clara* case came up in 1886, in neither instance did the Supreme Court render formal opinions.

Chief Justice Waite in 1886, speaking for a unanimous bench and in an oral statement only, simply declared that all the justices understood and accepted the fact that corporations were persons within the equal-protection clause of the Fourteenth Amendment. In this offhand and somewhat cavalier fashion—despite the thunderings of Justice Miller in the 1870s and 1880s—a mighty struggle ended. The Supreme Court, having said again and again that it would never yield from its position on the *Slaughter-House* and *Munn* cases, meekly yielded. The Fourteenth Amendment protected property rights, including those of corporations, from assaults at the hands of the States; due process was assured in the federal courts. From here, the Court was to go on, step by step, until, in 1898, it became the great bastion of defense of property: judicial review, as Field so ringingly demanded in his valedictory, was to stand, like a gleaming sword, in the path of populist legislation and the too great zeal of administrative bodies.

Field's opinion in 1882 ran as follows. The circuit court could not adopt Miller's view that the Fourteenth Amendment appertained only to the freedmen. It had a much broader application. The States could legislate under the police power "to promote the health, good order, and peace of the community, to develop their resources, increase their industries, and advance their prosperity." But:

it [the Fourteenth Amendment] does require that in all such legislation, hostile and partial discrimination against any class or person shall be avoided. . . . It forbids the State to lay its hands more heavily upon one than upon another under like conditions. It stands in the Constitution as a perpetual shield against all unequal and partial legislation by the State, and the injustice which follows from it, whether directed against the most humble, or the most powerful; against the despised laborer from China, or the envied master of millions.

Field got around the difficult question of the corporate "person" by equating it with the corporators: these were natural persons, of course, and, said he, "the Courts will always look beyond the name of the artificial being to the individuals whom it represents." Therefore:

To deprive the corporation of its property, *or to burden it,* is, in fact, to deprive the corporators of their property, or *to lessen its value.* . . . Now, if a statute of the State takes the entire property, who suffers loss by the legislation? Whose property is taken? Certainly the corporation is deprived of its property; but, at the same time, in every just sense of the constitutional guaranty, the corporators are also deprived of their property.

And Field ended up:

All the guarantees and safeguards of the Constitution for the protection of property possessed by individuals, may, therefore, be invoked for the protection of the property of corporators. And as no discriminatory and partial legislation, imposing unequal burdens upon the property of individuals, would be valid under the Fourteenth Amendment, so no legislation imposing unequal burdens upon the property of corporations can be maintained. The taxation, therefore, of the property of the defendant upon an assessment of its value, without deduction of the mortgage thereon, is to that extent invalid.

This called, in other words, for the substantive protection, under due process, of corporate property against discriminatory and partial legislation.

The So-called "Conspiracy Theory" of the Fourteenth Amendment
Roscoe Conkling, in his appearance before the Supreme Court in 1882, in the *San Mateo* case, offered a curious argument. It was nothing less than the fact that the writers of the Fourteenth Amendment, the Congressional Joint Committee of Fifteen in 1866—of which he had been a member, and hence party to all the discussions—in drafting its first article, had had a double purpose. In introducing the ambiguous term "person"

rather than "citizen" in the "due-process" and "equal-protection" clauses, the Committee's intention was to protect the rights of corporate property as well as those of the newly emancipated slaves. Out of his statement has arisen the so-called "conspiracy theory" of the Fourteenth Amendment: that the Radical Republicans, among them Conkling, who dominated the Committee, were already aware of the fact that corporations—insurance companies, express companies, railroads—were under fire from State legislatures, which were threatening their charters and seeking to encumber their activities in a variety of ways; and that they worked secretly in this fashion to afford such corporations relief. Said Conkling, at this point in his argument, implying that such knowledge was a prime concern of the Committee: "At the time the Fourteenth Amendment was ratified, as the records of the two houses will show, individuals and joint stock companies were appealing for Congressional and administrative protection against invidious and discriminating State and local taxes."

Conkling's contention was impressive. He came before the Court with the manuscript Journal of the Committee and purportedly read from it (he misquoted at one point and changed the meaning of a key sentence at another by the introduction of a comma which had not been there); and sought, as Graham says, by "surmise, conjecture and hypothesis"—never clear-cut proof—to persuade the Court of a plain purpose. The Committee, in all its discussions, again and again distinguished between "citizens" and "persons," using the first, in the "privileges-or-immunities" clause, to safeguard the political rights of Negroes; and the second, in the "due-process" and "equal-protection" clauses, to defend property. (At no point, however, did Conkling say that corporations were being talked of explicitly; he hinted at it, by reference to the petitions.) He then drew the obvious inference. Could anyone now suggest that Americans, drafters and ratifiers alike, "when engrafting the Fourteenth Amendment upon the Constitution, omitted, only because they forgot it, to say that citizens might be stripped of their possessions without due process of law; provided only the spoliation should be under the pretense of taxation and the victims robed in a corporate name?"

Whether the Supreme Court gave any weight to these startling assertions, there is no way of telling. Had the Court read the Journal it would have seen that Conkling was trying—by misquotations and innuendo—to lead it up the garden path. It never spoke, as we have seen; and only in an oral dictum, in 1886, it accepted Field's rulings, never considering the important matter of original intention.

Despite all this, and dismissing at once the idea of "conspiracy"—and here we follow the acute and careful studies and conclusions of Graham—was there anything in what Conkling said? We must remember that the Republicans on the Committee were largely Radicals: that they were truly and deeply devoted to the cause of safeguarding Negro rights and, at the same time, were committed to greater freedom for capital and the rapid industrialization of the United States. The States, certainly, by seeking to impose heavy burdens on property, were slowing up, if not making too difficult, the accomplishment of this grand purpose. The drafter of Article One of the Fourteenth Amendment was John A. Bingham of Ohio, a railroad lawyer, aware of the difficulties some of the railroads were already encountering at the hands of the States. Conkling came from New York, where he knew there were foreign insurance companies already in the toils and confronted by discriminatory State laws relating to licenses, taxes, and the deposit of large cash bonds. They were appearing in the State courts: one such suit had been started in New York in 1854, and their lawyers were arguing violation of due process.

All this was in the air. And Graham's studies also indicate that at least one member of the Committee knew that the idea of corporate personality had already appeared in the State courts. Nevertheless, Graham is convinced there was no "plot." He cites two reasons as compelling. First, that Bingham, who was so wholly absorbed in Negro rights, simply repeated in his 1866 drafts and in speeches on the floor of the House what he had been saying earlier, and here, all his allusions were to "natural persons." Secondly, there were no corroborating statements supporting Conkling from other members of the Committee, although his remarks had been widely reported in 1882 and had become a kind of *cause célèbre;* too, Conkling had remained silent for sixteen years, until his appearance as advocate for the Southern Pacific Railroad. Graham therefore is moved to say: "From a study of the evolution of the phraseology in the Joint Committee, the writer feels confident that Section One [of the Fourteenth Amendment] was not *designed* [his italics] to aid corporations, nor was the distinction between 'citizens' and 'persons' conceived for their benefit."

Graham concludes—whatever may have been the original purposes of the framers of the Fourteenth Amendment—that it was the Civil War itself which "consummated a marriage of idealistic and economic elements in American constitutional theory." He wrote this in 1938. The author of this book came to the same conclusion simultaneously and independently in the same year. The Republican Party—particularly its Radical wing—was committed to such a purpose. The forebodings of Justice Field, and his perseverance, in season and out of season, finally triumphed—as far as property rights were concerned—in 1886. By that time, one notes wryly, the Supreme Court had long forgotten about Negro rights.

Property Triumphant in the Supreme Court The way was now clear for the Supreme Court to act on a number of constitutional issues that previously it had regarded as outside its purview. In 1887, in *Mugler v. Kansas,* Justice Harlan, in a dictum only, accepted the doctrine of substantive due process, as a limitation upon the police power of the States, when he said: "[The Courts] are at liberty—indeed are under a solemn duty—to look at the substance of things, whenever they enter upon the inquiry whether the legislature has transcended the limits of its authority." In another dictum, the next year, in *Powell v. Pennsylvania,* Harlan extended the idea to complete equality in the choice of a calling or trade. Said he:

The main proposition advanced by the defendant is that his enjoyment upon terms of equality with all others in similar circumstances of the privilege of pursuing an ordinary calling or trade, and of acquiring, holding, and selling property, is an essential part of his rights of liberty and property, as guaranteed by the Fourteenth Amendment. The Court assents to this general proposition as embodying a sound principle of constitutional law.

In both these cases, State laws had been upheld. But in 1897, in *Allgeyer v. Louisiana,* the Court reaffirmed Harlan's dicta and found a Louisiana law—it sought by fines, and otherwise, to prevent citizens of the State from dealing with foreign marine-insurance companies—unconstitutional as a violation of liberty of contract. Justice Peckham now spoke for a unanimous court when he declared:

In the privilege of pursuing an ordinary calling or trade and of acquiring, holding, and selling property must be embraced the right to make all proper contracts in relation thereto. . . . the power [of States] does not and cannot extend to prohibiting a citizen from making contracts of the nature involved in this case outside of the limits and jurisdiction of the State, and which are also to be performed outside of such jurisdiction.

And then, making specific reference to the Fourteenth Amendment, Peckham laid out the broad general rules applying to the contractual rights of individuals.

The liberty mentioned in that Amendment means not only the right of the citizen to be free from the mere physical restraint of his person, as by incarceration, but the term is deemed to embrace the right of the citizen to be free in the enjoyment of all his faculties; to be free to use them in all lawful ways; to live and work where he will; to earn his livelihood by any lawful calling; to pursue any livelihood or avocation, and for that purpose to enter into all contracts which may be proper, necessary and essential to his carrying out to a successful conclusion the purposes above mentioned.

Peckham once more spoke for the Court in *Lochner v. New York* in 1905. The New York legislature had passed a statute limiting the hours of work in bakeries on the ground that this was a legitimate exercise of its police power: excessive labor in such an occupation was deleterious to health. The State's Court of Appeals—reversing the earlier Earl decision in *in re Jacobs*—upheld the legislature. On appeal to the Supreme Court, the decision was reversed; and Cooley's thesis of class legislation and the right of workers to engage in any occupations they sought fit were made constitutional law. Said Peckham:

Statutes of the nature of that under review, limiting the hours in which grown and intelligent men may labor to earn their living, are mere meddlesome interferences with the rights of the individual, and they are not saved from condemnation by the claim that they are passed in the exercise of the police power and upon the subject of the health of the individual whose rights are interfered with, unless there be some fair ground, reasonable in and of itself, to say that there is material danger to the public health or to the health of the employees, if the hours of labor are not curtailed.

It was this decision that drew the outraged and celebrated dissent of Justice Oliver Wendell Holmes. At the beginning of his career on the

Supreme Court, he asserted the position he steadfastly adhered to in a long and useful life. His own private feelings were irrelevant as regards suits coming before the Court; his agreement or disagreement with any particular economic theory had "nothing to do with the right of a majority to embody their opinions in law." And then:

The Fourteenth Amendment does not enact Mr. Herbert Spencer's *Social Statics*. . . . A constitution is not intended to embody a particular economic theory, whether of paternalism and the organic relation of the citizen to the state or of laissez-faire. It is made for people of fundamentally differing views, and the accident of our finding certain opinions natural and familiar, or novel, and even shocking, ought not to conclude our judgment upon the question whether statutes embodying them conflict with the Constitution of the United States.

Similarly, the dikes went down as regards the property rights of corporations; the Granger cases were overthrown. In 1890, a Minnesota law, which had established a State railway commission empowered to fix rates and had denied judicial review, was challenged by the Chicago, Milwaukee and St. Paul Railroad: the rates were confiscatory; the railroad was being denied its rights under the "due-process" and "equal-protection" clauses of the Fourteenth Amendment. The Supreme Court agreed, declared Minnesota's law unconstitutional, and said: "This power to regulate is not the power to destroy, and limitation is not the equivalent of confiscation." Judicial review was affirmed; the reasonableness of a railroad rate was "eminently a question for judicial investigation, requiring due process of law for its determination."

In *Reagan v. Farmer's Loan and Trust Co.* (1894), affecting the establishment of rates by the Texas railway commission; in *Missouri Pacific Railroad v. Nebraska* in 1896, where the same issue was involved; in other cases having to do with a Kentucky statute in 1896 and a Texas statute in 1897—the Supreme Court reasserted its broad right to scrutinize the activities of the States and their agencies and pass upon the reasonableness of the rates they sought to fix.

In 1893, Nebraska, seeking to overcome some of these adverse decisions, passed a law which fixed "reasonable maximum" rates for the carriage of freight. But it allowed the railroads to test their reasonableness in the State Supreme Court; if the court found such rates unreasonable and unjust, it could order the State's board of transportation to raise them. Foreign (non-Nebraskan) stockholders of a number of the railroads—disregarding the further relief available in the State court—sued in the federal courts against the establishment of a rate structure by statute alone. This proceeding came to the Supreme Court in the celebrated and very influential *Smyth v. Ames* case in 1898.

The restraints of Article One of the Fourteenth Amendment were now and for the first time fully enunciated. Corporations were persons. Rates were to be "reasonable." The federal courts had the power to examine, that is to say, employ judicial review, in the whole procedure of rate-fixing, whether by State law or commission. The Court therefore declared the Nebraska statute unconstitutional, among other things saying: "One [foreign stockholders and foreign corporations] who is entitled to sue in the Federal Circuit Court may invoke its jurisdiction in equity whenever the established principles and rules of equity permit such a suit in that court; and he cannot be deprived of that right by reason of his being allowed to sue at law in a State court on the same cause of action."

The Supreme Court went much further; it defined all the elements that legislatures and commissions were to consider in setting rates based on "the fair value of the property." What were the factors entering into fair value? These, said the Court: (1) the original cost of construction; (2) the amounts expended in permanent improvements; (3) the amount and market value of the outstanding stocks and bonds; (4) the reproduction cost new; (5) the probable earning capacity of the property under the rate fixed; (6) the sum required to meet operation expenses.

In the 1870s and 1880s, the great American architect Henry Hobson Richardson, returned from studies in France and much taken by French Romanesque buildings, began to spread over the land—in Chicago, Cleveland, Cinncinnati, St. Louis, Pittsburgh, all the rapidly growing cities where American business was showing such vitality—his own, imaginative conception of Romanesque design. His buildings, shorn of delicate and useless ornamentation, employing materials that suited the climate and conditions of the places they were to serve, caught exactly the meaning of this new world. In their mass and proportion, they celebrated and saluted the new city fathers and the new captains of industry: for they were simple, stable, and formidable. They were to last forever—and almost all still stand, even the courthouse and jail of Pittsburgh.

The Supreme Court built such another edifice in its interpretation of Article One of the Fourteenth Amendment. Right up to the 1940s, the greater part of the decisions here recorded were the law of the land.

CHAPTER FIVE

LABOR ORGANIZATIONS, RADICALISM, AND CAPITALISM

Labor Strengthens the Hand of Capitalism   To speed American capitalism on its way, perhaps the greatest assistance of all was rendered by American labor. The workers' obsession with Utopian ideas—appearing first in the 1840s and 1850s, and continuing after the Civil War right into the 1880s—prevented the organization of all the manual workers into effective and fighting bodies. Utopianism had many facets. To bypass industrialization and the factory system, before the Civil War, it advocated the creation of self-sufficing and self-contained communities or colonies or associations, where, by the cultivation of the land and the maintenance of the handicrafts, a nonprofit and nonmarket economy would be maintained.

After the Civil War, under the lead of the short-lived National Labor Union and later the Knights of Labor, the tactics of Utopianism changed somewhat. Workers were to be banded together in local units regardless of the particular craft or industries with which they happened to be associated. They were to have a central direction and be under a central discipline: in the case of the Knights of Labor particularly, a hierarchical structure was built up where local assemblies, so-called, were combined into district assemblies, and these in turn sent delegates to a general assembly, which formulated policy for the whole organization.

Neither the Knights of Labor nor the National Labor Union before it picked the strike and the boycott as the strategic weapons of the working class. Industrial disputes were to be settled by discussion and arbitration.

The well-being of workers was to be improved by self-help and by political reform. The first placed its whole reliance upon producers' cooperation; but here, unlike the Utopians of the ante-bellum decades, the financing initially of these cooperatives was to come from the workers themselves through their own assemblies. Mines would be bought, mills and factories erected, and these would produce better and cheaper for the market because they were worker-owned and -managed and because they were not tied in to the wage-and-profit nexus.

Political reform—by pressure on the existing legislative processes, but more and more through the formation of independent workers' parties—was to achieve the eight-hour day, the termination of undesirable, competitive immigration (the Chinese, contract laborers), mechanics lien laws; most important of all, monetary reform. More and more, as the result of the failure of producers' cooperatives and the inability of workers to win strikes (in part because of the refusal of the central organizations to support them), Utopianism in America after the Civil War was bemused by the presumable hopes held out by an elastic currency and then by a constantly expanding one. Consequently, the leaders of the National Labor Union and the Knights of Labor espoused the ideas of Edward Kellogg and Alexander Campbell. Later, in the 1870s, the Knights of Labor supported Greenbackism and joined hands with the Greenback-Labor movement. In the 1880s, the Knights of Labor were silverites and allies of the Farmers' Alliances, whose ideas of augmenting the money supply by the creation of the so-called Sub-Treasuries reverted to the notions of Kelloggism.

Why money? Why more money? In the Jacksonian period of the 1830s (and continuing into the next two decades) the American workers had been hard-money men, hostile to banks and bank notes and partial only to the circulation of specie and a fractional currency. Banks were monopolies: through their creation of credit they dominated and directed enterprise; their multiplication of bank notes was inflationary, and workers knew that wages lagged behind prices when the money supply increased.

In the post-Civil War years, the organized workers—those who followed the lead of the National Labor Union and the Knights of Labor—continued their opposition to banks and bank notes; but now they wanted more money and a money supply that was to be tied to the interest rate. Only the federal government could furnish this money, however. This was because both reform labor organizations encouraged the workers to believe that breaking loose out of the tightening net of industrialism and wage-labor could be accomplished only through easy credit. With lots of money available and low interest rates, workers could establish themselves independently or in concert (through cooperation) in small shops or in the handicrafts. Thus they could isolate and possibly even supplant the factory systems; a classless society would be achieved and the money monopoly shattered; and the class war that the radicals were talking of—true, they were European immigrants almost entirely— would be spared Americans.

Edward Kellogg was a New York merchant who, because of his own reverses, began to cast about for the reasons for the existence of an unequal society and his own misfortunes. In 1848 he published his *Labour and Other Capital* which got its basic notions from the so-called Ricardian Socialists and from John Law, and the colonial land banks, and Robert Owen and Pierre-Joseph Proudhon. Labor was the source of all value. But labor was robbed of the fruits of its toil because production, for its financing, paid an interest rate in excess of the labor cost of the banking business. The physical wealth of the country, said Kellogg, was growing at the rate of $1\frac{1}{4}$ per cent a year; but money, the "representation of wealth," on the other hand, was increasing at an annual rate of 12 per cent. If money's interest could be kept at around 1 per cent, then, as Kellogg said in the subtitle of his book, the rights of both labor and capital would be secured and the wrongs of both eradicated, "without infringing the rights of property" and at the same time giving labor its "just reward."

How to do it? By using government, said Kellogg. And he declared: ". . . if excessive interest rates deprived labor of its just reward and diverted its savings to the capitalists, and if accumulation by interest is a necessary function of money delegated to it by law, the evil lies in existing monetary laws and can be remedied only by legislation." The Kellogg proposal ran as follows. The federal government was to issue paper legal-tender currency to individuals upon real-estate security (obviously, for the workers, as skilled artisans and mechanics, this also meant their shops and tools) at an interest rate uniform throughout the nation, a rate which reflected labor's "natural power of production." This rate was to be 1.1 per cent. To keep the rate around 1 per cent, the currency was to be made "interconvertible" with government bonds, the government changing the currency into bonds if the interest rate fell below 1 per cent and the bonds back into currency if the rate went up.

Alexander Campbell, a delegate to the National Labor Union, revived Kelloggism in 1864 in a pamphlet which, in a reprinting in 1868, bore the title "The True Greenback, or the Way to Pay the National Debt Without Taxes and Emancipate Labor." It was Kellogg-cum-Campbell that the National Labor Union accepted. There now already existed a federal paper currency, the Greenbacks. This was to be the only money in circulation, and a full legal tender. The Civil War debt—of long-term bonds and short-term notes—was to be turned into interconvertible bonds, and the magical point about which bonds and paper currency was to revolve was an interest rate of 3 per cent. Loans were to be made in the same security Kellogg had proposed.

The Declaration of Principles—a typical reformist document filled with the fuzzy language and thinking of the times—of the National Labor Union in 1868 called upon American workers to create a national labor party; they were to fight against land monopoly and for the eight-hour day, cooperation, better housing, and the establishment of mechanics' institutes. The unemployed were advised to "proceed to the public lands and become actual settlers." Workers were warned not to strike. But the Declaration's concentrated fire was directed against banks and their money monopoly. It said: ". . . this money monopoly is the parent of all monopolies—the very root and essence of slavery—railroad, warehouse and all other monopolies of whatever kind or nature are the outgrowth of and subservient to this power." The remedy was to be found in interconvertible bonds and legal-tender Greenbacks.

The vagaries of Greenbackism need not be followed here. An expanding currency would produce inflation—and hurt the workers qua workers; but more money would cheapen credit and push up prices—and, it was hoped, help the workers metamorphose into independent producers. By 1872, interconvertibility (and public loans) was dropped. Greenbackism now meant simply more paper money. The fortunes of the Greenback-Labor Party and the Sub-Treasury scheme of the Farmers' Alliances will be discussed later. It is enough here to observe that the workers who followed these banners were now the captives of manufacturers and farmers who, too, magically, were to find their lot easier by cheap money.

For cheap money alone—without the illusion now of the creation of a vast and happy company of independent producers—had nothing to offer the workers as workers. Unhappily, the great mass, who were not skilled, simply had nowhere else to go.

The skilled workers were quickly disenchanted with the National Labor Union and the Knights of Labor and sought to survive independently, but with varying fortunes. They combined their locals together into national unions; they talked strike and used it to obtain the eight-hour day and higher wages; they gave politics a wide berth; they did not follow the lead of the radicals who inveighed against the capitalist system. They wanted higher wages and job security. Organized labor—always the skilled workers—was to be a countervailing force to the power of the capitalists.

The national unions grew in numbers and in combined membership, but they had their ups and downs and many disappeared during the severe depression of 1873-79. In the 1850s these national unions had first made their appearance among the printers, the stonecutters, the hat finishers, the iron molders, the machinists. Subsequently, there emerged such bodies among the building-trade workers, the railway workers, the cigar makers, the coal miners. The depression took such a heavy toll that there were not more than 50,000 such skilled workers surviving in unions in 1878.

It was in the American Federation of Labor, appearing in its new and final form in 1886, under the tough leadership of Samuel Gompers and Adolph Strasser of the cigarmakers and Peter J. McGuire of the carpenters, that the national unions found a safe haven. Gompers and Strasser had had their experiences with the Socialists; all three had been in and out of the Knights of Labor; by the late 1880s they were disillusioned with radicalism, reform, cooperation, money nostrums, the idle dream of one big unionism. The large and floating body of the unskilled—and this included the Negroes—was too uncertain and too treacherous a foundation on which to build a trade-union movement. The national unions, consequently, grew in numbers and strength—and survived. Nevertheless, in 1897, there were not more than $\frac{1}{4}$ million workers in national unions affiliated with the AF of L; and in 1904 (the high point until 1911) only 1.7 million. These were concentrated in transportation, the building trades, the metal and machinery trades, and in mining. If national unions not members of the AF of L are included—the totals were ½ million in 1897 and 2 million in 1904—these reached only 2 per cent of the country's labor force in the earlier year and only 7 per cent in the later year.

Enough has been said about the incapacity of Utopianism to extract concessions for the whole working class from capitalism and from public authority. The national craft unions, either independently or when banded together under the leadership of the American Federation of Labor, were no more successful. Their limited purposes were achieved; but all they ended in doing was to segregate a small group of the total labor force and create it into an aristocracy of workers who obtained job security and higher relative wages for themselves at the expense of the great mass of the unorganized.

It can be argued—and it was so maintained by the neoclassical economists who were confronted by a legalized and recognized trade unionism—that labor organization as such led to no relative increase in the distributive share wages received from the total national income. As a result of the competition (imperfect, it is true) at work in the market place of an expanding economy—increased productivity, from time to time dearth in the existence of skilled workers, incomplete mobility of labor—total wages go up automatically; but they rise secularly not much more than the rises in productivity. (Today, with strong labor movements everywhere in the nations of the Western world, increases in wages are tied to the growth of the Gross National Product—which can be higher than increases in productivity.)

F. W. Taussig, the outstanding neoclassical economist in the United States, could say as late as 1928 he sided

with those who contend that the mere matter of wages is not likely to be greatly affected one way or another by the presence or absence of unions. . . . Economists would agree in saying that for the material prosperity of the great mass of workingmen it makes no great difference in the long run whether there is a closed shop or an open shop, militant union or peaceful company union. . . .

Thus, in America, in the post-Civil War period, when labor organization and trade unionism were ineffectual, the average annual growth of productivity was in the neighborhood of 3 per cent and so was the wage increase. Real wages and earnings, consequently, rose: for workers in manufacturing, they were 50 per cent higher in 1890 than they had been in 1860; and they were 40 per cent higher in 1914 than they had been in 1890. The total working population was better off, thanks to the ingenuity of capitalism and the improving skills of the workers themselves. (For increases in productivity come from both labor and capital inputs.)

Professor C. D. Long in his *Wages and Earnings in the United States, 1860-1890* (1960) thus links wage improvements and productivity: "Our own tentative suggestions indicate that the net increases in real wages and earnings of manufacturing workers between 1860 and 1890 are not inconsistent with increases in productivity, when measured by manufacturing value added per worker in constant dollars." And Professor Albert Rees does similarly in his *Real Wages in Manufacturing, 1890-1914* (1961): "The rate of growth of real wages was the same as the rate of growth of output per weighted unit of labor and capital combined for the domestic economy. . . ."

This being so, trade unionism nevertheless can affect wages as they exist relatively among industries and relatively among different kinds of workers (the skilled and the unskilled): it can, that is, if it has organized the greater part of the civilian labor force in all industries and among all kinds of workers. The national unions before and later under the American Federation of Labor did neither. Up to 1917, as has been said, the AF of L unions' strength was to be found in a few industries; up to the 1930s, they failed to organize the unskilled. Given aggregate increases in the wages of labor, at the same time there were marked differentials among industries and between the skilled and the unskilled. But when a total labor movement exists—and it did not in the United States— unions organized on industrial lines, unions of unskilled workers bargaining side by side with unions of skilled workers, will end by narrowing occupational differentials. The skilled will get relatively less, the unskilled relatively more. This occurs because bargaining for all the workers in an industry or a plant is for "across-the-board" wage increases; only so can the unskilled be prevented from acting as strike-breakers when the skilled (usually in the minority) threaten to shut down plants.

Thus, the AF of L unions engaged in discrimination: by disregarding the unskilled, by failing to organize those industries where women were largely employed (textiles is the leading example), and by debasing the status of Negro workers. Unions of the skilled crafts, in those communities where a Negro labor force existed, refused to admit Negroes to apprenticeship training, thereby permanently barring them from membership. Samuel Gompers, the president of the American Federation of Labor, was hostile to such practices, spoke repeatedly against them, but he was compelled to yield. The constitution of the AF of L was therefore amended in 1900 to accept this exclusionist and discriminatory policy; it permitted the chartering of separate colored central labor councils, local unions, and federal local unions. The wage rates of such Negro workers— even when fully skilled—were lower than those of the whites. But most of the Negro workers were not organized, even at these lower levels.

Because the national unions and the leaders of the AF of L looked upon voluntarism as the basic principle of their organization and survival, they kept cabined, cribbed, and confined the impact of unionism upon the economy and upon public policy. Voluntarism's coin had two sides. On its face was the promise that organized labor would take care of its own: that it was an agency for bargaining for wage-and-hour improvement and it was a friendly society. Member dues and contributions built up strike funds; but they also created financial resources out of which the unions' unemployed, the sick, and the superannuated could be taken care of, even to the erection of hospitals for the chronically ill and homes for the aged.

On the obverse side, voluntarism opposed public outlays for such purposes. The demand that the state concern itself with the welfare of its working population—provide for protection against ill health, old age, and unemployment, eradicate child labor, and pass and enforce safety legislation in mines and factories—was the basis of the strength of the total labor organizations of Germany as early as the 1860s under the leadership of Ferdinand Lasalle, and of Great Britain beginning with the 1890s under the leadership of Keir Hardie and others. Such unions had economic and political programs. Independent labor parties inevitably developed out of the latter to extract concessions from the state, as in Germany, or to compel middle-of-the-road parties (the Liberals in Great Britain, the Progressive Party under Theodore Roosevelt and the Democratic Party under Franklin D. Roosevelt) to take up the same causes.

The reformism of the AF of L unions, because of their suspicion of state interventionism and their fear that a politicalized trade union movement would subordinate industrial demands to Utopianism or revolution, was narrowly limited. The AF of L counseled its member unions in election campaigns to support their political friends and oppose their political enemies; to this extent it was neutral as between Republicans and Democrats and neutral about capitalism itself. So, in 1895, the annual meeting of the AF of L adopted a resolution which declared flatly "that party politics whether they be democratic, republican, socialistic, populistic, prohibition or any other, should have no place in the conventions of the American Federation of Labor."

As for its own legislative programs, these too were confined to a very small number of aims. Leading its agenda was the demand for the outlawing of court injunctions in labor disputes; their use, even when only temporarily issued, could cripple or break strikes. Next came the request that labor unions be exempt from the antitrust laws. The antitrust laws could be used against boycotts—organized labor's second great weapon—on the ground that they were conspiracies, and criminal and civil penalties could be imposed on their participants. There were a few others: the legalizing of the eight-hour day for workers in the public services and those on public contracts, the abolition of child labor, minimum wages for women, factory safety legislation and laws recognizing workers' compensation for industrial accidents. Even if these had been realized, and generally they were not right into the 1930s, the burdens imposed upon capitalism and the state would have been slight.

The AF of L unions were not opposed to capitalism. They knew they had to live with the American commitments to private property and to private decision-making in business enterprise. All they sought in return was industry's recognition of the unions' control over the jobs in which their members were involved: to make trade agreements for hours and wages, to fix working rules (which inevitably led to featherbedding), to regulate apprenticeship, to establish the closed shop so that only union members in good standing could obtain employment. Of course its leaders from time to time engaged in talk that would seem to indicate they had a wider vision. Gompers spoke often of "the amelioration of the conditions of the workers and their final emancipation." In 1893, in addressing himself to the query put to him by a legislative committee, What did labor want? he declared: "It wants the earth and the fulness thereof. There is nothing too precious, there is nothing too beautiful, too lofty, too ennobling, unless it is within the scope and comprehension of labor aspirations and wants."

In 1899, Gompers pointed out it was futile for government—the Sherman Antitrust Law was what he had in mind—to fight against "the legitimate development or natural concentration of industry." The trusts were evil because they corrupted the political processes; they had to be abided until "the toilers are organized and educated to the degree that they shall know that the state is by right theirs, and finally and justly shall come into their own while never relaxing in their efforts to secure the very best economic, social, and material improvements in their conditions." Did this mean the take-over of the state by political action or revolution? Not at all. It meant that organized labor was to be a second force growing as powerful as private industry, powerful enough to affect policy by the pressures of collective bargaining. This looks a little bit like the corporative state about which honest reformers were speculating in the Europe after World War I: the British Guild Socialists and the German Walter Rathenau are cases in point. We know, however, how quickly this corporativism was corrupted by Mussolini: organized labor became a creature of the state instead of an equal partner.

In commenting on these observations of Gompers, Daniel Bell says shrewdly: "If one regards unionism as a social force which by its own position in an industrial hierarchy becomes a challenge to managerial power and changes the locus of power in capitalism, then Gompers' strategy of focusing on the day-to-day issues was undeniably correct." However, the American unions in Gompers' day never became such a second force; nor have they today.

It was in line with such thinking that Gompers was willing to associate himself with the National Civic Federation, formed by a group of industrialists of which Mark Hanna—coal and iron tycoon of Ohio, mentor of President William McKinley, Senator from Ohio—was the leader and president. The purpose of the Federation was the maintenance of industrial peace; this could best be furthered by trade-union recognition. Gompers consented to become the Federation's vice president. In 1901, Gompers wrote: "There is a substantial trend toward agreement between the laborers and the capitalists, employed and employer, for the uninterrupted production and distribution of wealth, and, too, with ethical consideration for the *common interests* of all the people." (Italics in original.) And in the same year, in addressing the National Civic Federation, Gompers could say: "There is in our time, if not a harmony of interests . . . yet certainly a community of interests, to the end that industrial peace shall be maintained."

There was not a powerful enough radical movement in the United States—at any rate, before the first decade of the twentieth century—to offer threats to the stability of capitalism or to wring concessions from public authority or the dominant political parties. Radicalism in the post-Civil War period, such as existed—whether it was the radicalism of Lasalle or Marx or Bakunin, all of which had their adherents in America—never reached the working classes in any measurable numbers. The preachments of European radicalism—of a permanently stratified class society and of class war—fell on deaf ears. The facts were plain: there were no ruling castes, no prescription whether political or economic, no limited suffrage or limited educational opportunities in America. Besides, most such radicals were Europeans who spoke and published their newspapers in foreign tongues. Moreover, these movements tended to break off into splinters because of obscure doctrinal differences, so that the cohesion which a radical movement requires to have any impact never was maintained for long. And when radicalism became important enough to form dual or their own unions—and thus challenge the AF of L—organized labor had to disown it.

Such cohesion, ideologically, did not appear until the turn of the twentieth century. The creation of the Socialist Party—following the gradualist line of the German Eduard Bernstein and the British Labor Party—was threatened by no fragmentation and could move ahead steadily; the Socialists were opposed to dual unionism and therefore were able to penetrate significantly into the AF of L unions. Side by side with socialism there sprang up the anarchosyndicalism of the Industrial Workers of the World, which had an American leadership and was orientated to American conditions. Its greatest threats lay in its ability to organize the unskilled and to preach industrial turmoil, disorganization and sabotage as the way of bringing capitalism to its knees. The *coup de grâce* would be delivered by the general strike.

Radicalism, both gradualist and revolutionary, was clearly on the march in the United States for the decade or so from 1905 to 1917. It was no accident that Progressivism should appear at the same time, advocating middle-class reform of the political processes, ameliorative legislation for the workers, the close regulation of industry by government to some, and the break up of big business into small atomistic units, to others. Progressivism in America wanted to have the best of both worlds: a system of private ownership and decision-making with a contented working population whose major insecurities—ill-health, superannuation, unemployment—might, in part, be charmed away. Progressivism was characteristically American. Its outstanding political leaders—Theodore Roosevelt from 1910 to 1916; Franklin D. Roosevelt in the 1930s—were wellborn and educated, and possessed independent financial means; yet neither Roosevelt was a traitor to his class. Their intention was wholly to make America safe for capitalism: somewhat cleaned up, true, but capitalism nevertheless.

The Role of Utopian or Reform Unionism Before the Civil War
Utopianism held the stage in the 1840s and 1850s and, despite its failures, was picked up again by reformers in the 1860s, 1870s, and 1880s. In the ante-bellum period, the leading note that was struck was association: workers would escape from the rigors and insecurities of the industrial system by forming communities of their own and engaging in agriculture and the handicrafts. There was only the vaguest kind of notion of how such activities would fit into a market society. It was hoped that benevolently inclined capitalists would come to their assistance—for Utopianism refused to accept the fundamental Marxist assumption of class war—and would provide the needed funds to establish the producers' cooperatives which would sustain the colonies in the new Canaan.

These really were not workers' movements but the fads and fancies of the intellectuals. They were aware of the ferment going on in Europe among what Marx bitingly characterized as the Utopian Socialists: of activities of the successful textile manufacturer Robert Owen; of the appeal of Count Claude de Saint-Simon to French industrialists to do something toward social amelioration; of the flaming attacks on property by Pierre-Joseph Proudhon, who nevertheless preached class collaboration; and of the "scientism" of Charles Fourier, who had "discovered" a new social psychology and new principles of efficient and happy labor. New England and New York humanitarians, transcendentalists and reformers (all members of the middle class, all vaguely troubled by their inability to find places for themselves in a swiftly changing world) seized with avidity upon these new ideas coming out of England and France.

There was Robert Owen, the wealthy New Lanark, Scotland, textile manufacturer, with his notion of a society made up of cooperative communities financed by labor-exchange banks. Labor exchanges would be established where commodities, their value based on labor costs, would be traded for "labor notes"; these in turn were to be used to acquire other kinds of goods similarly deposited. What if goods did not move and surpluses piled up in the exchanges? There would be suspended in circulation accumulating "labor notes" whose values obviously were bound to depreciate. Owen set up such an "Equitable Labor Exchange" in London in 1832; it quickly failed. Nevertheless the idea kept popping up; Louis Blanc, in 1848 in Paris, had a somewhat similar notion; and probably the Sub-Treasuries of the Farmers' Alliances in the United States went back to the same Utopian source.

Owen himself financed one such community of the kind he was talking of in Indiana, which he called New Harmony and which he left in the charge of his son Robert Dale Owen. A varied host descended upon the new Utopia: well-intentioned but unskilled men and women, petty sharpers, the lazy and ineffectual, and some really distinguished people with sound ideas about education and agronomy. But the scheme could not work—it ate up the greater part of Owen's fortune—and had to be abandoned; the heritage it left to America was in the persons of Owen's four sons, who remained in the country to become useful citizens.

Most influential of all was the Frenchman Charles Fourier. In the grand mood of the eighteenth-century philosopher, Fourier devised a psychology based on the human "passions"; from this he spun out broad theories of social behavior; and, using both, he formulated systems of education and societal arrangements through which men would be free and contented in their labor. The social unit for the new society was to be the so-called Phalanstery, where work would be "attractive," waste eliminated, and labor discord charmed away. The members of a Phalanstery were to divide themselves into groups and series; all were to find useful work conforming to their particular "passions." There was a place for small children: Fourier, a bachelor who loved cats and hated children, saw that youngsters liked to mess around in dirt. Such a "passion" had its usefulness; children were to be organized as Little Hordes to clean streets and sewers and spread manure.

This kind of pretentious silliness attracted the attention of a band of lofty, middle-class New England transcendentalists who established their famous Brook Farm outside of Boston in 1841. Initially, Brook Farm was a community, with a good school, based on a "system of brotherly cooperation" in place of "selfish competition." It got nowhere; in 1844, the Brook Farmers turned to Fourier as their inspiration, divided themselves into groups and series, and struggled as agriculturists and educators until the building which was to house all the business of the Phalanstery, burned down.

Brook Farm itself was finished but its influence was pervasive, in part as a result of the launching of *The Harbinger,* a journal for the dissemination of Fourier's ideas to which, among others, Henry James (the elder), John Greenleaf Whittier, James Russell Lowell contributed. There were other Phalansteries, but none survived beyond the 1850s.

The land reformers constituted still another company. Their inspiration came from the Englishman George Henry Evans, who migrated to America and began at once to broadcast his message of equal property for all. Evans' ideas underwent a number of transformations. At first he preached the necessity for destroying industrialism and replacing it with "rural republican townships" where land would be held only by the cultivators themselves in an inalienable tenure; industrial production, on the basis of the handicrafts entirely, would be wholly for use. But, in time, Evans was compelled to bow before the inevitable: his program came to stand simply for free lands from the public domain for all actual settlers.

Evans found a patron in Horace Greeley, who threw open the columns of his New York *Tribune* to the Englishman's strange and somewhat hysterical notions. Evans talked of getting rid of the "hoary iniquities of Norman land pirates" and subduing capitalism by pulling away its chief prop—feudal landholding! The escape for the worker (who had no funds) was free entry into the public lands. For, then, said Evans: "Tens of thousands who are now languishing in hopeless poverty, will find a certain and speedy independence." It is difficult to understand what Horace Greeley—high-tariff protectionist and foe of trade unionism—was doing in this gallery. In any event, the only outcome of Evans' preachments was their absorption in the form of Homesteadism by the new Republican Party; and it was in the Republican Party, too, that Greeley found a sheltering harbor.

Finally, we are to note the revival of the cooperation agitation, both on the consumer and producer sides, with the real goal the latter. The consumer cooperative societies were to hoard their savings and open small workshops: by this device they were to extricate themselves from the iron jaws of the wage-labor system. Small groups of workers listened to the earnest middle-class intellectuals and formed such societies during the years 1847-52: iron molders in Cincinnati, tailors in Boston and New York, printers in Philadelphia became cooperators. But they quickly failed, as had the more pretentious communities of the Owenites and the Fourierists.

Out of this wreckage there did emerge a toughened but severely limited labor movement; one that was to eschew political reforms and involve itself only in day-to-day gains. It was based on craft lines formed into national organizations. It concerned itself only with the skilled workers, and saw as its one purpose the "creation of combinations for mutual agreement in determining rates of wages and for concert of action in maintaining them." So spoke the National Typographical Society, the first of the new national craft unions to appear, in 1850. And it laid down a line that has been followed by American trade unionism ever since; for the address of the printers went on to say: "Indeed, while the present wage system continues in operation, as an immediate protection from calamities it [unionism] is clearly the only effective means which labor can adopt. So far as it extends it destroys competition in the labor market, unites the working people and produces a sort of equilibrium in the power of the conflicting classes. . . ."

The stonecutters did similarly in 1853, the hat finishers in 1854, and the iron molders and machinists in 1859, combining into national craft bodies with programs of business, or job monopoly, or pure-and-simple trade unionism—these were the scornful terms flung by Socialists at the same unions in the 1890s. What they sought were collective bargaining agreements with employers, the weapons they used were the strike and the boycott. They were to train their own skilled workers through the apprenticeship system. But these national unions constituted a tiny proportion of the country's manual workers. The rest continued to

[129]

wander in the wilderness, from time to time—again led by the reformers—believing they saw in sight the Promised Land where they would find safety and security at last.

The Role of Utopian or Reform Unionism After the Civil War   The National Labor Union—its leading spirit was William H. Sylvis, an iron molder—appeared in 1866 and lasted only until 1872. Presumably basing its strength on the new national unions, it was in reality a loose association, functioning almost entirely through annual conventions where grandiose schemes were evolved in resolutions. To these conventions came some workingmen but largely the delegates were made up of spokesmen for eight-hour leagues, anti-monopoly societies, land reform bodies, and currency faddists. Professor Norman T. Ware characterized the National Labor Union in this fashion: "It was a typical American politico-reform organization, led by labor leaders without organizations, politicians without parties, women without husbands, and cranks, visionaries, and agitators without jobs."

Sylvis, the head of the Iron Molders International Union, was a typical Utopian: he was opposed to strikes and for the joining of hands with capitalists to abolish the wage system and establish a nonprofit cooperative America. Sylvis' death and the drift of the Union toward monetary reform and political action alienated the few trade unionists still associated with it; by 1872 it had disappeared from the scene.

Centering in Philadelphia, another effort to unite the workers for economic and legislative action and mutual aid was also making its appearance. This was the Noble Order of the Knights of Labor, which was founded in 1869 when a small company of garment cutters banded together as a secret society. The original intention was the creation of so-called local assemblies on craft lines; before very long, however, because the Knights were meeting with success in smaller rather than larger communities, the "mixed" assembly became the norm. Thus, almost from the start, the pattern became fixed: all who were engaged in productive activity—whether owners of small shops or farmers or workers, whether men or women or whites or black—were enrolled. Where resistance to the dilution of the membership occurred, the Knights were perfectly willing to create special mixed assemblies, made up of women or of Negroes exclusively. Only lawyers, bankers, saloonkeepers, professional gamblers and stockbrokers were denied membership. The organization consequently was not a labor union in the traditional sense, and not even a few basic industrial demands could be formulated or gain general adherence. Mixed assemblies and district assemblies turned out to be no more than debating societies; and because the Knights opened its doors so widely, it was easily penetrated by middle-class reformers who sought—and succeeded—in committing it to the popular agitational programs of the day.

Its vows of secrecy made the organization suspect to the Catholic hierarchy; and only when it came out into the open as a result of a threatened ban by the Papacy, did the Knights begin to grow. This was in 1878; this was the year, too, of the emergence in its councils of Terence V. Powderly, who dominated the Knights as the so-called Grand Master Workman until 1893. Powderly, a talkative, flamboyant Irish Catholic, had been apprenticed as a machinist, had become a member of the Machinists and Blacksmiths International Union, and had dabbled in the local politics of his native Scranton, Pennsylvania, whose mayor he had succeeded in becoming under the banner of the Greenback Labor Party during 1872-82.

Powderly made it clear that the Order was not to be a class organization. Neither Socialism nor industrial warfare was to cure society's ills; the first was to be fought, the second avoided. The collaboration of all, bosses and workers alike, was to make each man his own employer toward the day when a cooperative commonwealth would put an end to the wage system.

The first General Assembly, to which were elected delegates from District Assemblies, met in 1878 and drew up the Order's constitution. Like all statements of its kind it was grandiloquent, filled with alarums and excursions—and vague. Thus, its preamble proclaimed:

The alarming development and aggressiveness of great capitalists and corporations, unless checked, will inevitably lead to the pauperization and hopeless degradation of the toiling masses. It is imperative, if we desire to enjoy the full blessings of life, that a check be placed upon unjust accumulation and the power for evil of aggregated wealth. This much-desired object can be accomplished only by the united efforts of those who obey the divine injunction: "In the sweat of thy face thou shalt eat bread."

And the following were the Order's aims, among others:

To bring within the folds of organization every department of productive industry, making knowledge a standpoint for action, and industrial and moral worth, not wealth, the true standard of individual and national greatness.

To secure for the workers a proper share of the wealth they create; more of leisure that belongs to them; more societary advantages; more of the benefits, privileges and emoluments of the world.

But how? And here the answers were typically reformist. Tactics were to follow two lines of direction: the establishment of producers' cooperatives (usually to be financed by local or district assemblies) and participation in local and national independent political activity. The political program of the Knights—as announced from time to time by the General Assembly—was also the typical reformist mixed bag. The public domain was to be reserved to actual settlers only. All laws which did not bear equally upon capital and labor were to be abrogated. Workers were to be paid weekly in lawful money. The contract system for government work was to be abolished. The eight-hour day was to be established. (But workers were not to strike for it, or for anything else. Employers and workers could conciliate their differences through the good offices of friendly arbitration.) The program included safety and public-health codes; mechanics lien laws; the abolition of child and convict labor; an end to immigrant contract labor—and monetary reform. In connection with the last, this:

a purely national circulating medium, based upon the faith and resources of the nation, and issued directly to the people, without the intervention of any system of banking corporations, which money shall be legal tender in payment of all debts, public and private.

Producers' cooperatives were attempted—and sooner or later were shut down because of unskilled management and inadequate financing. In 1887, or so it was claimed, there were more than a hundred such groups functioning, distributed in the following kinds of enterprises: one bank, fifty-one grocery stores, eleven retail stores, eleven newspapers, fifty-five workshops and factories. Most of these were located in rural communities and small towns. And here is to be found one of the reasons for the Knights' weakness: the greater part of its membership was native-born

American, most were not skilled craftsmen but rather small proprietors or farmers or unskilled workers. This kind of membership also is reflected by the attitude of the Order toward strikes.

Craft unions did appear in the Knights in trade rather than in mixed assemblies; they were to be found in cities and, in the Southwest, among the railroad workers in the new railways appearing in that region in such large numbers, particularly in the 1880s. Efforts had been made to organize the trade assemblies into separate district assemblies—Samuel Gompers, a member of the Order, had pushed this idea—but Powderly was adamant in his opposition. These craft unionists understood that the strike was their leading weapon. They used it to seek union recognition and wage increases—as was done against the Gould railroads, the Wabash, the Missouri Pacific, and others. Appeals were made to the central organization for support: to accept openly the role of a collective bargaining agency, to amass a strike defense fund. To this Powderly would never yield; in fact, speaking of strikes in 1880, the General Assembly declared: "[They] are as a rule productive of more injury than benefit to working people [and] consequently all attempts to foment strikes will be discouraged." When the Order's executive board had to yield and finally sought to accumulate a defense fund, the rural assemblies refused to pay their assessments and the effort petered out.

The same was true of strikes to obtain the eight-hour day. The Federation of Organized Trades and Labor Unions of United States and Canada (the predecessor of the AF of L) in 1885 issued a general call for such a strike on May 1, 1886. The collaboration of the Knights was sought; after a good deal of hemming and hawing, Powderly promised it—and then issued a secret order to the Order's assemblies withdrawing his approval.

In 1889, in his *Thirty Years of Labor*, Powderly explained (and further compounded) his confusions in this fashion:

To talk of reducing the hours of labor without reducing the power of machinery to oppress instead of to benefit is a waste of energy. What men gain through a reduction of hours will be taken from them in another way while the age of iron continues. . . . The advocates of the eight-hour system must go beyond a reduction of the number of hours a man must work and [must] labor for the establishment of a just and humane system of land ownership, control of machinery, railroads and telegraphs, as well as an equitable system of currency before he will be able to retain

[133]

the vantage ground gained when the hours of labor are reduced to eight per day.

Despite all these evidences of a befuddled leadership, the Order's membership grew spectacularly in the 1880s. By the end of 1883, it claimed 52,000; in 1886, 730,000. And then it as sensationally declined. The year 1886 is critical in its history. The eight-hour strikes met with many successes for craft unions in cities, when something like 350,000 workers struck. The tragic Haymarket affair in Chicago on May 4, 1886, grew out of the eight-hour demonstrations and strikes involving the Chicago stockyards and the McCormick harvester works; the anarchists particularly had played an important part in organizing the Chicago workers for these activities. The Haymarket was popularly linked with the growth of the Knights and its presumed support. The year also saw strikes again on Gould's Southwest roads. Powderly refused to support his own assemblies involved and took occasion to issue a general circular to all the Order's members condemning strikes. The strikes against Gould ended in failure. Craft unionists began to give up their assembly charters, and it was as a result of these desertions and because of Powderly's refusal to work out a *modus operandi* with the national craft unions that the leadership of the Federation of Organized Trades and Labor Unions was prompted to change its role and take on the form and purposes of the present AF of L. This was also in 1886.

At its first annual convention in December, 1886, the AF of L refused to seat delegates from the Knights (they had been accepted as members of the earlier FOTLU) and declared open war in a resolution:

The Knights of Labor have persistently attempted to undermine and disrupt well established Trades' Unions, organized and encouraged men who have proven themselves untrue to their trade, false to the obligations of their union, embezzlers of moneys, and expelled by many of their unions, and conspiring to pull down the Trades' Unions, which it has cost years of work and sacrifice to build. . . . We condemn the acts above recited, and call upon all workingmen to join the unions of their respective trades, and urge the formation of National and International Unions, and the centralization of all under one head, the American Federation of Labor.

From then on, the Knights really became an adjunct of the farmer parties of the Far West. It participated in the creation of the National

Union Labor Party—really, a farmer organization—in 1887. It sent delegates to the St. Louis convention of the farmer Northern Alliance in 1889. It supported General James B. Weaver, the Populist Party presidential candidate, in 1892. By 1890, the Order's membership had fallen to 100,000. And in 1893 Powderly was ousted as a result of an intrigue in which that restless revolutionary spirit Daniel De Leon of New York—as an intellectual he had been permitted to become a member of a mixed assembly—and James R. Sovereign of Iowa joined hands. De Leon almost captured the moribund Knights; but Sovereign finally won and De Leon was thrown out in 1895. The Order, now almost entirely made up of western farmers and small town handicraftsmen, drifted quickly into its final decline. Ever true to reformism, it backed Bryan and free silver; this was its last appearance in the national political arena.

The American Federation of Labor   Increasingly aware of the threats to the survival of trade unionism from so many quarters—the law courts, business depression, the use of the militia, the beguiling and lulling admonitions of the reformers; the fact that unions were isolated from one another—the leaders of national craft unions sought to devise ways and means of protecting themselves. Their first effort, the Federation of Organized Trades and Labor Unions started in 1881, was unsuccessful. It had no central authority or leadership; it had no revenues; it could not appeal for the support of strikes by a tightly knit working class. It contented itself with passing resolutions and from time to time calling for the enactment of legislation. By 1884 it was faltering. The events of 1886 indicated where its true destiny lay. Those who had emerged in the activities of the FOTLU and in the struggles with the Knights of Labor saw the need for a new kind of organization. As a result of discussions taking place in 1886 among the leaders of national trade unions, a convention assembled in December, 1886, which gave birth to the American Federation of Labor.

Twenty delegates from some twenty-five national unions, whose combined membership was about 316,000, absorbed the FOTLU and promulgated a constitution. The purpose of this American Federation of Labor was to be:

the encouragement and formation of local trades and labor unions, and the closer federation of such societies; the establishment of national and international trade unions, based upon a strict recognition of the autonomy of each trade; the federation of all national and international trade unions, to aid and assist each other . . . and to secure national legislation in the interests of the people.

Only wage workers who were "favorable to trade unions" were to be members. The Federation as such was to avoid political activity. An executive council was to be set up with the following functions: to watch legislation, to organize national unions and new locals where nationals did not yet exist; to secure the unification of all labor organizations while recognizing "the right of each trade to manage its own affairs"; to pass upon boycotts when inaugurated by the affiliated nationals; when strikes and lockouts occurred, to issue appeals for voluntary financial assistance for the unions involved. The Federation itself was to have an independent treasury derived from charter fees and a per capita tax on each member in good standing. Regular officers, to be elected annually, were provided for and salaries assured them. The AF of L was on its way. Unlike previous efforts to bind organized labor together, the AF of L thenceforth survived every vicissitude and continued to grow steadily—at any rate, until 1904. Samuel Gompers was elected the AF of L president and was re-elected annually (except once, in 1894) until his death in 1924.

Within the first decade of its existence, the AF of L successfully met a series of tests. The challenge of the Socialists came first. At the 1893 convention a so-called "Political Programme" was adopted which in effect sought to commit the AF of L to independent politics, for it called for the nationalization of telegraphs, telephones, railroads and mines, an eight-hour day legally established, and a so-called Plank 10 which demanded "the collective ownership by the people of all means of production and distribution." This whole program was to be submitted to the affiliated nationals, State federations and city councils in a referendum. Other resolutions sought to pledge the AF of L to an alliance with the farmers and supported free silver.

It was Plank 10 that aroused Gompers, Strasser and McGuire; the referendum was having widespread support; but clever parliamentary maneuvering on the floor of the 1894 convention obtained, first, the defeat of the preamble of the Programme (favoring independent political action) and then Plank 10 itself. A resolution for free silver was again carried. In revenge, the Socialists refused to support the reelection of Gompers to the presidency—but he returned to office the next year. The Socialists tried again in 1895; this time they were decisively routed and the threat of radical capture was finally stayed. Instead, a resolution was passed which called upon workers to participate in politics, but "the class interests of labor demand measures in preference to party measures and, we, therefore, recommend to the workers more independent voting outside of party lines."

Bryan's nomination in 1896 and the full commitment of the Democratic Party to free silver presented another challenge. Three times the AF of L had endorsed free silver. In July, 1896, Gompers once more took over, and issued a circular letter to the affiliated unions warning their members against being taken in by "the partisan zealot, the political mounteback . . . the effervescent, the bucolic political party, cure-all sophist and fakir." Labor organizations before had foundered on the rock of politics. There was no official endorsement of Bryan and Gompers noted his defeat with satisfaction when he wrote: "[The unions] had weathered the storm successfully and will now have a clear field to work upon."

Dual unionism was the third test. In 1895, the AF of L took a decisive step when it decided that member unions could not be affiliated with both itself and the Knights of Labor. That stormy petrel, that truly committed revolutionist, Daniel De Leon, launched another effort after his failure to penetrate and take over the Knights and the defeat of the Socialists in the AF of L. In late 1895 he created the Socialist Trade and Labor Alliance, as a challenge to both the Knights and the AF of L, and met with momentary successes when the central labor federations of New York, Brooklyn, and Newark and the United Hebrew Trades of New York joined him. Gompers immediately sprang to the alert. The dissidents were barred from the AF of L; and Gompers poured out his wrath on De Leon and on dual unionism in these words:

We note . . . that the work of union wrecking is being taken up by a wing of the so-called Socialist Party of New York headed by a professor without a professorship, a shyster lawyer without a brief, and a statistician who furnished figures to the republican, democratic, and socialist parties. These three mountebanks, aided by a few unthinking but duped workers, recently launched from a beer saloon a brand new national organization with the avowed purpose of crushing every trade union in the country.

Thus the AF of L under Gompers. It plowed a straight and narrow furrow. It was dedicated only to "unions, pure and simple" (Gompers' phrase). Day-to-day demands should be the unions' only concern: "The way out of the wage system is through higher wages," said Gompers in 1890 in the same declaration. Reformism—cooperation, third-party politics, an independent labor party, collaboration with all "the producing classes"—diverted unionism from its aim and its purpose. And this was equal partnership with capital in an industrialized society.

Toward the time when a powerful labor movement could claim its share of power, it had to go its own way; voluntarism was the key. Government itself was suspect: the unions had learned bitter lessons when the United States Attorney General in 1894 smashed the Pullman strike by using the Sherman Antitrust Law against the strikers and when other attorneys and other courts employed injunctions to hobble labor's efforts to organize and use the boycott.

Dual unionism had to be suppressed. Maintaining the job monopolies of the crafts was the way to survival. The basic tactic was the closed shop—control by the union itself of the job. To achieve this, using strikes and boycotts, was through the writing of trade agreements with employers. The trade agreement was to recognize collective bargaining, the agency of the union as the representative of the workers, and the right of the union to debar from work (if the closed shop was granted) all who were not in good standing as union members. With such recognition, the unions also pressed for, and usually obtained, understandings about seniority and control over apprenticeship, overtime, the displacement of workers by machinery, and the speedup—all those so-called working rules which could be used to freeze union members in jobs whether or not they continued productive. These work rules, in reality incorporating restrictive practices, leading to redundancy, or featherbedding, constituted organized labor's greatest threat to that continuing expansion of the industrial processes under private ownership to which labor itself was not averse.

Radicalism   There were radical voices raised in post-Civil War America, but their impact upon both the workers and the state was slight. The winds of doctrine sweeping over Europe after 1850 quickly reached America: the "Scientific Socialism" of Marx and Engels, the democratic centralism of Ferdinand Lasalle, the terroristic anarchism of Michael Bakunin, all had their American votaries who formed little circles, published newspapers (usually in foreign languages), occasionally and briefly penetrated trade unions—and quarreled among themselves, splintering off into fragments over obscure doctrinal questions and suddenly disappearing. Unlike the Europeans whom they so sedulously aped, they made no contribution to the theory and tactics of the labor movement or revolutionary action; none, that is to say, except for the work of one man. That was Daniel De Leon; but more of him later.

The first International had made its appearance in London in 1864; originally a congress and organization speaking for trade unions, intellectuals before long took over, using its platform and pronouncements to air their revolutionary ideas. Marx dominated the First International from 1867 on, and here he collided head on with Bakunin. Marx was for revolution, but it had to wait upon the full development of a class-conscious, disciplined, industrialized working class; to Bakunin, revolution could be achieved—and at once—by conspiratorial, terroristic activity against the holders of power. The bitter wrangling of two highly intelligent, dogmatic and implacable antagonists diverted the energies of trade-union leaders, split them into warring camps—and destroyed the International. Marx had Bakunin expelled in 1872, but the International was already dying. Its headquarters were moved to New York, of all places, and by 1876 it was finished.

The First International got to America at once. William H. Sylvis, speaking for the National Labor Union, expressed sympathy with the International's aims and sent a delegate to the 1869 convention. Sylvis even employed the characteristic Marxian vocabulary, while half of him was still involved in Utopian dreaming and planning. Thus in a letter to the general council of the International, Sylvis said:

Our recent war has led to the foundation of the most infamous money aristocracy of the earth. The money power saps the very life of the people. We have declared war against it and we are determined to conquer—by means of the ballot, if possible—if not, we shall resort to more serious means. A little bloodletting is necessary in desperate cases.

A number of sections of the International made their appearance. One was the so-called "Section 1 of New York," made up of German working-men, writing and holding their meetings in German. They were dedicated and doctrinaire Marxians; they were able to create branches—among Germans in other cities—they gave their support to strikes, but gained no adherents for Marxism itself. And there was that curiosity, Section 12. The International, because it seemed to promise all sorts of new and exciting ideas, attracted the same sort of men and women—partially educated, at loose ends, ineffectually trying to do something about a world in which they had no secure places—who a generation earlier had been Utopian Socialists. One of these was Stephen Pearl Andrews, once a philosophical anarchist, more latterly, a Swedenborgian, then an exponent of women's rights and free love. A little group of devoted followers, which called itself the "Pantarchy," applied for and was admitted into the First International because it also talked vaguely of Socialism.

Section 12 came to be dominated by two sisters, Victoria Woodhull and Tennessee Claflin, young women of obscure origin who worked their way from the Middle West to New York as magnetic healers, fortunetellers, and spiritualists. In New York they set themselves up as "lady brokers"; that they were engaged in a promiscuous business can be seen from the fact that the aged and ailing Commodore Vanderbilt became the lover of Tennessee. It was Vanderbilt who financed the brokerage house of Wood-hull, Claflin and Co. In turn, Victoria backed Andrews, and the two ladies started a paper called *Woodhull and Claflin's Weekly,* whose masthead bore the fighting slogan "Progress! Free Thought! Untrammeled Lives." Among other things—it was adept at scandalmongering, it exhorted women suffragists to revolt, it printed tips on the stock market—the *Weekly* published the complete text of the Communism Manifesto in English.

Section 1 and Section 12—the sedate German Socialists and the American Pantarchists who talked of woman suffrage, free love and a universal language—soon became embroiled in controversy. The Germans and the Pantarchists took their quarrel to the International's general council, which expelled Section 12. Nothing daunted, Victoria Woodhull and Andrews organized the "Equal Rights Party," which in 1872 nominated Woodhull for the Presidency of the United States and the Negro Frederick Douglass for the Vice Presidency. What was left of American Marxian socialism, under the impressive name of the North American Federation of the International Workingmen's Association, never got over the shock of its exposure to Andrews and Woodhull, and disappeared along with the International itself.

Ferdinand Lasalle had worked with Marx in Germany as early as 1848, when together they had founded the *Neue Rheinishe Zeitung*. But they had soon parted, for personal as well as ideological reasons. Lasalle was a dashing figure: a persuasive and eloquent speaker, a great lover, a friend and correspondent of the powerful in Germany, Bismarck among them. Marx was none of these, and had gone into exile as a revolutionist, while Lasalle stayed at home and built up his reputation among the politically great and the workers themselves. He founded the German Workers Party and preached the ideas of the peaceful capture of power by parliamentary means rather than trade-union action solely. There a democratic, centralized state—pursuing nationalist purposes as opposed to Marx's internationalism—would inaugurate widesweeping programs of social amelioration, the inevitable first step to Socialism itself. The German Socialism of the last quarter of the nineteenth century—gradualist and not revolutionary, nurturing its strong trade unions, engaged in party politics and parliamentary speech-making, obtaining from the state universal education and public programs for the care of the sick and the aged was the creation of Ferdinand Lasalle and not Karl Marx. For these reasons, Marx pursued Lasalle implacably, even calling him that "Jewish nigger" (because of Lasalle's swarthy complexion): and both were Jews!

Lasallian clubs appeared in the United States in the large cities. There were many such small groups in New York, and Chicago became an important center. The depression spread Lasallian ideas among American trade unionists with the result that the Social Democratic Party of North America made its appearance. In 1876 its name was changed to the Workingmen's Party, in 1877 to the Socialist Labor Party; and then—so characteristically American and so quickly diluted by reformism—it endorsed James B. Weaver, the presidential nominee of the Greenback Labor Party. In 1879, the Lasallian Socialist Labor Party claimed 10,000 members in a hundred locals in twenty-five cities. At the end of the depression, most of the membership had melted away and those who remained were almost entirely foreign-born and foreign-language speakers.

In 1880, the Socialist Labor Party split in two, one segment joining hands with Bakunin's anarchistic International Working People's Association. The other continued barely alive until De Leon moved into its destinies in 1890. Bakunin's anarchism was more than terror through conspiratorial societies: the "propaganda of the dead" that he preached was to symbolize the total revolt of anarchists against society itself. Anarchism was notably powerful among the workers in those parts of the world—Russia, Italy, Spain, Latin America—where state repression outlawed trade unions and used savage political reprisals against the workers. Thus said the anarchists of Romagna in 1878 in a manifesto:

Let us arise, let us arise against the oppressors of humanity; all kings, emperors, presidents of republics, priests of all religions are the true enemies of the people; let us destroy along with them all juridical, political, civic and religious institutions.

But anarchism had an ideology that, in part, leaned on the ideas of William Godwin and Pierre-Joseph Proudhon—the abolition of authority and property; in part, on the mutualism of Bakunin and Kropotkin. Because authority—state, church, military, police power—was suspect; because the institutions authority created could be captured by reactionary forces politically, anarchists rejected any kind of political participation. To Bakunin, Marx stood for "authoritarian communism." But the way to freedom was by the establishment of independent communes, made up of the workers only, in which all capital—factories, tools, land, raw materials—would belong to those who created it. These communes would be bound together in a free federation. The tight, dictatorial, dogmatic discipline of Marx' Communist Party threatened liberty; anarchism, said Bakunin, offered "the voluntary and considered agreement of individual efforts toward a common aim." And Bakunin went on:

At the moment of action, in the midst of struggle, there is a natural division of roles according to the aptitude of each, assessed and judged by the collective whole: some direct and command, others execute orders. But no function must be allowed to petrify or become fixed, and it will not remain irrevocably attached to any one person.

It was this anarchism that Johann Most brought to America in 1882. In and out of the jails of Europe for political activity, in and out of all the shades of European radicalism, Most finally lit on the terroristic element of Bakuninism to release mankind from oppression. Most was not an eccentric; he probably was unbalanced, a state brought on by the ignominy of his illegitimate birth, a badly disfigured face, and the cruelties he suffered at the hands of the police. Most resumed publication of his *Freiheit* (suspended by the London police); he toured the United States, creating anarchist clubs as he went; he published a manual on the tactics of terror. Its title gives its intention: "Science of Revolutionary Warfare: A Manual of Instructions in the Use and Preparation of Nitroglycerine, Dynamite, Gun-Cotton, Fulminating Mercury, Bombs, Fuses, Poisons, Etc., Etc." These were to be used to "Extirpate the miserable brood! Extirpate the wretches!"

Most cut a wide swath at the formation of the American section of the International Working People's Association in Pittsburgh in 1883. (It came to be known as the Black International.) Here were gathered delegates from all kinds of radical clubs, some speaking for left-wing trade unions, some for anarchist societies. The preamble of the so-called Pittsburgh Manifesto there drawn up was largely Most's work. The body of this statement did incorporate Bakunin's ideas about an anarchist society; nothing, on the other hand, was said about trade unions. To this extent, syndicalism was not yet linked to anarchism. The Industrial Workers of the World were to accomplish that in 1905.

Said this address "To the Workingmen of America":

We could show by scores of illustrations that all attempts in the past to reform this monstrous system [capitalism] by peaceable means, such as the ballot, have been futile, and all efforts in the future must necessarily be so. . . . The political institutions of our time are the agencies of the propertied class; their mission is the unfolding of the privileges of their masters; any reform in your behalf would curtail these privileges. . . . That they will not resign these privileges voluntarily we know. . . . Since we must then rely upon the kindness of our masters for whatever redress we have, and knowing that from them no good may be expected, there remains but one recourse—FORCE! . . .

By force have our ancestors liberated themselves from political oppression, by force their children will have to liberate themselves from economic bondage. "It is therefore your right, it is your duty," says Jefferson—"to arms."

What we would achieve is, therefore, plainly and simply:

First:—Destruction of the existing rule, by all means, i.e., energetic, relentless, revolutionary, and international action.

Second:—Establishment of a free society based upon cooperative organization of production.

Third:—Free exchange of equivalent products by and between the productive organizations without commerce and profit-mongering.

Fourth:—Organization of education on a secular, scientific and equal basis for both sexes.

Fifth:—Equal rights for all without distinction of sex or race.

Sixth:—Regulation of all public affairs by free contracts between the autonomous communes and associations, resting on a federalistic basis.

Among the radicals, anarchism held the stage for almost a decade. It was the Chicago group that became involved in the disastrous Haymarket affair. Its leaders, August Spies and Albert R. Parsons, understood the role of trade unionism in holding the workers together: it was within the unions, as the workers moved from strike to strike, that the processes of radicalization could take place; the unions were educational forums by which its members could be prepared for revolution. But the unions—rather than clubs or cooperatives—were also to be the basis of the future society of autonomous communes. This was the heart of the later syndicalism (taken from the French for trade unions, *les syndicats ouvriers*); and when for political terror, as the device of direct action, there were substituted the ideas of sabotage and the general strike, then the twentieth-century anarcho-syndicalism was fully formed.

At the same time, Spies and Parsons were speaking the Bakunin-Most language of violence against the rulers of society. Thus in the *Alarm* (and similar sentiments were being voiced in the German *Verbote*) Parsons could write:

Dynamite! Of all good stuff, that is the stuff! Stuff several pounds of this sublime stuff into an inch pipe (gas or water), plug up both ends, insert a cap with a fuse attached, place this in the immediate vicinity of a lot of rich loafers, who live by the sweat of other people's brows, and light the fuse. A most cheerful and gratifying result will follow. In giving dynamite to the downtrodden millions of the globe science has done its best work. The dear stuff can be carried in the pocket without danger, while it is a formidable weapon against any force of militia, police, or detectives that may want to stifle the cry for justice that goes forth from the plundered slaves. . . . A pound of this good stuff beats a bushel of ballots all hollow—and don't you forget it!

And Spies—after the Chicago police had fired into a group of strikers in front of the McCormick plant on May 3, 1886, killing six—could say in his famous "Revenge" circular, of which 5,000 were distributed:

REVENGE!
Workingmen to Arms!!!
If you are men, if you are the sons of your grandsires, who have shed their blood to free you, then you will rise in your might, Hercules, and destroy the hideous monster that seeks to destroy you. To arms. We call you, to arms!

Did Parsons and Spies mean this? This was the vocabulary of advocacy. Was it also being used for direct incitement and did it, in fact, lead to violence? It is hard to say, for when a meeting to protest the conduct of the police assembled on the evening of May 4 in Haymarket Square, the speakers—Parsons, Spies, Samuel Fielden, all anarchists—said nothing about dynamite, or arms, or a march on the police station. They spoke reasonably and without heat. The meeting was about to break up when a large company of police descended on it. Suddenly a bomb was thrown, killing one of the policemen and wounding several. The police fired into the crowd (and at each other); shots were fired back. Seven officers were killed and some sixty wounded; how many the police killed and wounded among the participants of the meeting was never fully ascertained. It was never proved that the bomb was thrown by an anarchist, nor was it demonstrated that the gunfire first came from the meeting. In an atmosphere of violent emotion, stirred up by the local newspapers and vigilante groups, a grand jury brought in indictments against nine men, of whom seven were anarchists and two were not. Eight men were brought to trial (one had fled the country), and a packed jury and a highly prejudiced judge found all eight guilty of murder. For seven, the jury fixed the penalty at death; these were Spies, Parsons, and Fielden, and also Michael Schwab, George Engel, Louis Lingg, and Adolph Fischer. In the case of Oscar Neebe, the sentence was fifteen years in the penitentiary. The governor of Illinois commuted to life imprisonment Fielden and Schwab; Lingg committed suicide in jail; and on November

11, 1887, Parsons, Spies, Fischer, and Engel were hanged. In 1893, Governor John P. Altgeld gave the three in prison, Neebe, Fielden, and Schwab, full pardons because of the unfairness of the trial—and suffered political and financial ruin as a consequence. The Haymarket affair at the same time put an end to the Black International in the United States.

Daniel De Leon   In another time, another place, Daniel De Leon might have had the same shattering impact upon the world of a Lénin or a Mao Tse-tung. Like the Russian and Chinese revolutionaries, De Leon contributed nothing to the theory of communism itself; like them, he accepted, without a hair's breadth of difference, the whole vast Marxian schema of dialectical and historical materialism, the class struggle, the polarization of society with the increasing immiserization of the working classes, and capitalism's inevitable collapse as a result of its own internal contradictions. De Leon came to Marx later in life than had Lenin and Mao; once having done so, with the same single-mindedness, he devoted all his energies, like Lenin and Mao, to analyzing and sharpening the tactical tools that would turn the workers into the revolutionary vanguard of the oppressed. That the United States continued to advance economically with giant strides; that the real wages of workers kept on rising; that there was no landlordism, no despoiled peasantry, no economic or political prescription, no suppression of unions or political parties—none of those conditions which bred unrest and were the seedbed for revolution—all this was beside the point to De Leon.

De Leon was born in 1852 on the Dutch island of Curaçao in the Caribbean. His father's name was Solomon and his mother's Sara Jesurun—Jewish names, obviously, although curiously De Leon later was reported to have said his origins were Catholic and his family Venezuelan and rich. The father had been a surgeon in the Dutch colonial army and had died when De Leon was twelve; the family must have been well off, for the young De Leon studied at a gymnasium in Germany and later at the University in Amsterdam. Here he acquired Latin and Greek and mastered Spanish, French, German and English. He came to the United States when he was twenty-two and settled in New York, where he tried his hand at a variety of pursuits available to a young man with a European classical education. He was the associate editor of a Spanish newspaper devoted to the cause of Cuban liberation; he taught Latin,

Greek, and mathematics in a school in Westchester. In 1876 De Leon entered Columbia Law School, specializing in constitutional and international law, and practiced law after his graduation, in New York and perhaps in Texas as well.

When DeLeon was thirty-one, in 1883, he was appointed to a prize lectureship in international law at Columbia University. This post he held for six years, and then he left, not because he had begun to identify himself with labor causes but probably because he was not appointed to the permanent tenure of a professorship. From thence on he lived modestly and somewhat precariously, using his language skills to translate books, among them seventeen of the nineteen volumes of Eugene Sue's popular historical romances called "The Mysteries of the People; or History of a Proletarian Family Across the Ages," and many of the writings of Marx, Engels, Lasalle, Bebel, and Kautsky, the great leaders of Socialism: all this while he lectured and edited *The People* (the organ of the Socialist Labor Party), writing most of it himself, for which he received $30 a week.

In 1886, De Leon threw in his lot with the United Labor Party, a mélange of Socialists, reformers and trade unionists, which was formed to enter the New York mayoral election and which named Henry George as its candidate. (The other two in the contest were Abram S. Hewitt, wealthy ironmaster and son-in-law of Peter Cooper, picked by the Democrats, and Theodore Roosevelt, by the Republicans.) George was no radical. The whole purpose of his famous *Progress and Poverty* was to preserve private enterprise and business initiative; it was land monopoly that was the devil of the piece, for speculative land ownership burdened enterprise and labor with all those inequities, said George, that were becoming the hallmark of the modern world. A single tax on land values would free entrepreneurs, farmers and workers and re-establish those balances and just rewards among all the productive forces of an economy and polity out of joint because of the expanding power of monopoly. The Single Tax, in consequence, became the slogan of the United Labor Party, and with George's defeat (the Catholic Church attacked him; the Republicans gave Roosevelt little support; Hewitt was elected) the uneasy alliance broke up. De Leon sought other pastures.

He joined the Knights of Labor in 1888: as an intellectual he could become the member of a mixed assembly. He became affiliated with the

Nationalist movement—that curious crusade for the establishment of the "principle of association" that swept middle-class America in the wake of Edward Bellamy's sensationally successful Utopian novel *Looking Backward* published in 1888. Bellamy's pleasant—and (today, to us) dull—romance suited the middle-class temper of the times. Why not escape into a never-never land where cultivated people talked of and sought to establish a rational society based on work that suited the individual tastes of all, where there were no greed, ambition, political corruption, property accumulation, wealth or poverty? There was a modern note: Bellamy and his followers, unlike the Utopians of forty years earlier, accepted industrialism; and the many Nationalist clubs spread the word and prepared for political action (without political organization). The flavor of the movement may be caught from this statement of principles:

We advocate no sudden or ill-considered change; we make no war upon individuals; we do not censure those who have accumulated immense fortunes simply by carrying to a logical end the false principles on which business is now based. The combinations, trusts and syndicates, of which the people complain, demonstrate the practicability of our basic principle of association. We merely seek to push this principle a little further and to have all industries operated in the interest of all by the nation. . . .

It was all sweetly reasonable, and permitted earnest young men and women to have a mild fling. Nationalism got nowhere; in 1890, De Leon was out of it—he had joined the moribund Socialist Labor Party and made it a personal instrument for the development of his techniques of Marxian revolution. For the SLP was used by De Leon to penetrate and seek to capture the Knights of Labor and the American Federation of Labor; having failed, he worked to disrupt and confuse these labor movements by dual unionism—his Socialist Trade and Labor Alliance. His brand of socialism was rejected by the Socialist Party, which, in part, appeared in 1900 as a result of a split in the ranks of his own SLP. In 1905, De Leon was in at the birth of the Industrial Workers of the World, taking his now paper organization the ST-and-LA into it. The IWW, in true anarcho-syndicalist fashion, was opposed to any sort of political activity; this did not prevent De Leon from maintaining his SLP. He was at war with society; and with the Socialists, the trade unionists, and, before too long, the IWW itself. In characteristic fashion, after having been ousted by the main group in 1908, he formed a schismatic one. In characteristic fashion—by this time he had developed vituperation to a high art (like Marx, like Lenin)—he called his once comrades in revolution "slum proletarians" and "beggars."

This strange little man—he was short and slight with a massive head, sharp black eyes, an elegantly trimmed beard and mustache—lived his life surrounded by a tiny coterie of devoted disciples, and distrusted and disliked by many, many more, notably those in the labor movement. His friends and admirers wrote of him in dithyrambs that bordered on idolatry; his enemies with a distaste—a compound of grudging respect for his gifts, fear of his methods—that could not be shaken off years after he was dead. Thus, his disciple and biographer, Arnold Petersen:

De Leon ranks as one of the great social architects of all time, as one of the great social master builders of the ages, taking his place with Solon and Cleisthenes, with Morgan and Marx, and towering above the social architects of our own American Revolution.

On the other hand, Morris Hillquit, one of the founders of the twentieth-century Socialist Party, in his autobiography *Loose Leaves from a Busy Life* (1934), wrote:

Daniel De Leon was a fanatic. A keen thinker and merciless logician, he was carried beyond the realm of reality by the process of his own abstract and somewhat talmudistic logic. . . .

He was a trenchant writer, fluent speaker, and sharp debater. For his opponents he had neither courtesy nor mercy. . . . [He] was not a social democrat with the emphasis on the "democrat." He was strongly influenced by the Blanquist conception of the "capture of power" and placed organization ahead of education, politics above economic struggles, and leadership above the rank and file of the movement. He was the perfect American prototype of Russian Bolshevism.

And thus, Samuel Gompers in his autobiography *Seventy Years of Life and Labor* (1925):

No more sinister force ever appeared among the Socialists than Daniel Loeb, or Daniel De Leon as he later called himself. [This nasty reference to "Loeb" is typical of the anti-Semitism some Jews practice against other Jews.] He was first a single taxer and then embraced Socialism which became a fetish with him. . . . He infused vitriol into Socialist propaganda. It was De Leon who invented the epithet "labor fakers" for application to trade union officials. He used his intellectual ability to train and embitter the differences between Socialists and trade unions. De Leon gathered around him a group devoted to warfare on trade unions. They could not content themselves with efforts to capture the labor movement, or with the Socialist Labor Party but determined to create a labor movement of their own. . . . This Socialist Union [The Socialist Trade and Labor Alliance] was to be a general hodge-podge of perversion of the industrial union. . . . It was a movement that imperiled the American Trade Union movement. . . .

De Leon had started the implacable war. In 1893, in an editorial in *The People,* he had written of the trade-union leaders:

The "pure and simple" has been found out. Some are ignorant, others are corrupt, all are unfit for leadership in the labor movement. To civilize and unite them is out of the question. The social revolution must march on the bodies of each and all. . . . Clear the way. Kick the rascals out.

And in 1895, in *The People,* after he had failed in the Knights of Labor and the American Federation of Labor:

The American Federation of Labor has become the football of two political crooks. Its fate and that of the order is the fate that ever awaits pure and simpledom. The workers will no longer seesaw backwards and forwards from the Knights to the Federation and back again. The two have now become a stench in the nostrils of the American proletariat. They have been the buffers of capitalism against which every move of progressive organization has spent its forces. Let us reorganize upon that higher plane that sooner or later the labor organizations are bound to take . . . the plane of identity of economic and political efforts, consolidated, inspired, guided and purified by the class consciousness of the wage slave, who, having nothing to lose but his chains, and a world to win, is ready to devote himself to nothing less than to his complete emancipation.

The same note—that the industrial proletariat was being misled and betrayed by the "labor fakers"—was repeated again and again: notably in his important pamphlets "What Means This Strike?" (1898) and "Two Pages from Roman History" (1902). Lenin undoubtedly knew De Leon's broad position, and in particular these two statements underscoring the fact that unionism without a political, revolutionary leadership ended up and was lost in arguments and compromises over wages, hours, and security, for the same ideas are repeated in Lenin's "What Is To Be Done?" (1903).

And the same is true of De Leon's basic conception of unionism: it should be organized only on broad, industrial lines, as a weapon and as the preparation for the future Socialist society. As early as 1904, in a lecture called "The Burning Question of Trade Unionism"—anticipating the Industrial Workers of the World and also Lenin's theory of Sovietism—De Leon said:

The trade union has a supreme mission. The mission is nothing short of organizing by uniting, and uniting by organizing, the whole working class industrially—not merely those for whom there are jobs, accordingly not only those who can pay dues. That unification of organization is essential in order to save the eventual and possible victory from bankruptcy, by enabling the working class to assume and conduct production the moment the guns of the public powers fall into its hands—or before, if need be, if capitalist political chicanery pollutes the ballot box. The mission is important also in that the industrial organization forecasts the future constituencies of the parliaments of the Socialist Republic.

And, specifically, in 1906—after the IWW had been formed—in *The People:*

Industrialism is that system of economic organization of the working class that denies that Labor and the Capitalist Class are brothers; that recognizes the irrepressible nature of the conflict between the two; that perceives that the struggle will not . . . end until the Capitalist Class is thrown off Labor's back; that recognizes that an injury to one workingman is an injury to all; and that consequently . . . organizes the WHOLE WORKING CLASS into ONE UNION, the same subdivided only into such bodies as their respective craft-tools demand, in order to wrestle as ONE BODY for the immediate amelioration of its membership, and for their eventual emancipation by the total overthrowing of the Capitalist Class, its economic and political rule."

It was the political party—De Leon's Socialist Labor Party, Lenin's Bolshevik, later Communist, Party—tightly controlled, kept pure ideologically by throwing out deviationists and schismatics and unendingly warring against revisionist or gradualist Socialists, that was to lead and instruct this industrially organized working class. Said De Leon about such a revolutionary political party: "A political party that sets up 'immediate demands' by so much blurs its 'constant demand' or goal. The presence of 'immediate demands' in a Socialist platform reveals pure and simple politicianism—corruption, or the invitation to corruption."

It was not to be a mass proletarian party; it was to be small, cohesive, disciplined. So De Leon wrote in 1896 (long before Lenin):

In all revolutionary movements, the thing depends upon the head of the column—upon that minority that is so intense in its convictions, so soundly based on its principles, so determined in its action, that it carries the masses with it. . . . Such a head of the column must be our Socialist organization.

To keep the party unsullied in its dedication to the Marxian Word, to maintain control in his own hands, De Leon embarked upon purge upon purge—again anticipating and showing the way to Lenin. As early as 1896, De Leon had said about party discipline:

No organization will inspire the outside masses with respect that will not insist upon and enforce discipline within its own ranks. If you allow your own members to play monkeyshines with the party, the lookers-on, who belong in this camp, will justly believe that you will at some critical moment allow capitalism to play monkeyshines with you.

Whose discipline? His own. It was small wonder that a company of the party faithful raised the cry of "Robespierre!"—and left him.

De Leon let those in the SLP, who wanted to join hands with the revisionist Social Democrats, go; good riddance—for Social Democracy, said De Leon, stood for "reformism, Utopianism, fakerism, opportunism." But when New York secessionists (led by Morris A. Hillquit) sought to take *The People* along with them, De Leon went to the courts and won out. Because they would not accept his reading of Marx, he expelled from the SLP his closest friends and collaborators—the editors of *The People,* the German *Vorwärts,* and the Yiddish *Abenblatt.* Even his eldest son Solon he was prepared to part with forever because Solon De Leon had the temerity to question the Marxian theory of surplus value. But the quarrel had wider implications, as Arnold Petersen, De Leon's panagyrist, saw. "The fact is [wrote Petersen] that young De Leon's challenge of Marxian economics inescapably raised the question of the moral right, and logical justification, for maintaining the Socialist

Labor Party as a political party." It was to maintain this revolutionary party, as we have seen, that De Leon was willing to split the IWW even to the point of surrendering his influence upon it.

De Leon died in 1914, three years before Lenin's arrival at the Finland Station in Petrograd after crossing Germany in a railroad train which the Germans had given a safe conduct. Had De Leon lived, in all likelihood—like Trotsky—he too by one device or another would have made his way to Russia to help in creating that Socialist Republic that alone could be Mecca or Jerusalem. And unlike other American radicals who later made the pilgrimage—Bill Haywood, the leader of the IWW, who jumped his bail; Emma Goldman, the anarchist, by deportation—he would not have been saddened or disillusioned. What had been a world of fantasy in America had suddenly become reality in Russia; and the "dictatorship of the proletariat" (really, the iron domination of the Communist Party) would have exactly suited De Leon's tastes.

3

THE STRUCTURE OF AMERICAN CAPITALISM

CHAPTER SIX

AGRICULTURE

Did the Farmers Pay for the Country's Industrialization?   I have sought to point out that if a developing country is going to move upward to maturity, someone has to pay the price. This is not the same as the Marxian theory of exploitation: that the surplus value produced by workers and farmers is absorbed by the profits of the industrial capitalists, leading to an absolute fall in wages and the bankruptcy of small farm owners. The fact is, in the United States from 1865 to 1900, the real wages of workers, in the aggregate, went up. So did the real income of farmers, in the aggregate. Workers and farmers, as a whole, contributed a disproportionate share, largely because of the regressive taxes on consumption (tariffs, exises) and the general property tax, which turned out to be a tax on realty. Also, the very limited development of public welfare programs—for health, child care, old age, education—which could have been borne only by taxation on earnings gave workers and farmers little additional imputed income from social services. In addition, the unskilled workers paid a larger share than did the skilled workers because of wide wage differentials; and the poor farmers of the South throughout the whole period and the poorer farmers of the Far West in the years 1886-1896 similarly paid a larger share than did the prospering farmers of the East and Middle West.

This having been said, we must note that the benefits of industrialization—of the processes of change from developing to developed—were spread throughout the nation, albeit with an uneven hand. Real wages for all workers, skilled and unskilled, were higher in the United States than anywhere else in the world: at least twice as high as those of the

United Kingdom and Scandinavia, more when compared with the real wages of France and Germany. And the mobility of American society, plus its educational opportunities, permitted many more workers, because they were younger, to move upward into the technical and supervisory jobs and independent trades and businesses, than was possible in the Old World.

A similar observation can be made in the case of the farmers. Always excepting the South, where the tenancy of white and black sharecroppers was permanent, land ownership was the general status of the American farmers. There was tenancy in the East, the Middle West, and the Far West: but for the greater part this was in reality ladder tenancy. Farm laborers could and did become tenants; as a result of hard work and the availability of mortgage credit, a great many tenants became farm owners. A part of the tenancy reported by the censuses consisted of the sons and sons-in-law of owning farmers who were tenants during the lifetime of their parents and became owners with their death. In any event, because of the constant improvement of agricultural properties—the plowing back of part of income into the erection of farm structures, mechanization, drainage and irrigation, the purchase of livestock—the owning farmers of the United States reaped their reward when more and more they were able to serve a domestic market. This was so from 1897 to 1922 or 1923, for during this period of two decades and a half, farm real-estate values went up as did real farm income when measured by the ratio of prices received for agricultural commodities to prices paid (which included interest, taxes, and wages as well as the purchases the farmers had to make to keep their agricultural properties going concerns). In other words, owning farmers were able to cash in on deferred income, despite the fact that, in the period of rapid industrialization, they were paying a disproportionate share for the country's growth. Again, as in the case of the workers, this scarcely jibes with the Marxian theory of exploitation.

Alvin S. Tostlebe, who is responsible for the latest analysis of farm capital in his *Capital in Agriculture: Its Formation and Financing Since 1870* (1957) points out these interesting facts. First, between 1870 and 1900, when farm prices were declining, agriculture's real capital formation (in constant dollars) in these years proceeded faster than during any subsequent years. Secondly, farmers got their land cheap or for nothing.

Thirdly, railroad rates kept on dropping, while the urban market kept on growing relatively and absolutely and the foreign market absolutely. The result was that farmers were encouraged to expand and diversify their operations, and they plowed back their earnings into farm improvements. Tostlebe estimates that for 1900-09 (he has no earlier figures; but the ratio for self-financing probably was higher before the turn of the century) loans and bank credit contributed $2.7 billion to the financing of new farm capital as contrasted with the $6.6 billion that came from farm income and savings. It was no wonder that the steady rise in agricultural output, or productivity, which make possible the relative reduction in the number of agricultural workers, was matched by the simultaneous rise in capital per farm worker. In 1870, it was $2,900 (in 1910-14 dollars); in 1920, it was $4,400. The increase was 10 per cent per decade.

A more detailed look at what was happening to agricultural capital and Farm Gross Product will make us less certain about agricultural discontent; we shall have to deny, unlike many historians today, that farming was unprofitable, and deny as well that the farmer was the victim of and paid the price for the country's industrialization.

In terms of constant dollars (1910-14), the value of America's farm plant—land, buildings, implements and machinery, work animals and livestock, and crop inventories, during the years 1870-1900—increased 104 per cent as compared with 24 per cent for the years 1900-1920. In the cotton Southeast, for the earlier period, the rise was 60 per cent as compared with 38 per cent later; in the Corn Belt, the figures were 63 per cent and 7 per cent; and in the wheat-growing Great Plains, the figures were 1,259 per cent and 52 per cent. On a per capita basis, measuring the value of farm physical assets in the same constant dollars, and for every person in farming, the increase during 1870-1900 was 28 per cent in the whole United States. For the Great Plains, the increase was 130 per cent and in the Corn Belt it was 23 per cent.

Marvin W. Towne and Wayne O. Rasmussen have measured Farm Gross Product during the nineteenth century; this including sales, improvements of plants, home manufacture and consumption. In terms of 1910-14 dollars the increase was from $2.2 million in 1860 to $5.8 million in 1900, or 164 per cent. The greatest decade of advance was that of the 1870s, when the increase was 50 per cent; yet it was also 13 per cent in the 1880s and 26 per cent in the 1890s, which were the decades of Farmers' Alliances organization and activity. The Farm Gross Product per farm worker increased 60 per cent during the same forty years. For the decades of the 1870s, 1880s, and 1890s, the increases were respectively 49 per cent, 4 per cent, and 15 per cent. From 1860 to 1900 the farm population grew from 20.1 million to 31.2 million, or 55 per cent; in short, the Farm Gross Product grew three times as rapidly as did the farming population.

The Role of Farm Exports   Farm technology was keeping abreast of industrial technology, and therefore making possible the feeding of an expanding urban population and the sale abroad of great surpluses of cotton, wheat, and meat products, to balance the country's international payments. The American agricultural revolution—setting in in the 1860s— thus had two parts: its roles abroad and at home.

The abandonment by England of its Corn Laws in 1849 (under which it had been protecting an inefficient farm plant) threw open its markets to the importation of foreign foodstuffs. This speeded the English industrial revolution (cheaper food made possible lower costs; farm workers were diverted into industry), but it also had profound effects on the processes of American industrialization. For the United States, during 1860-90, was the basic supplier of Britain's food requirements: its wheat, pork products, and animal feeds. At the same time, America's agricultural exports (cotton, wheat, corn, pork products, beef) made possible the country's change-over to a favorable balance of trade.

Up to 1873, American imports exceeded exports, and because of low tariff policies existing until 1864, imports had been made up in greater part of finished and semiprocessed manufacturing goods (65 per cent of value of total imports, annual average, 1850-59). But the United States, like all underdeveloped countries, was a capital borrower, and obviously had to pay interest on the long-term loans incurred to finance state improvement projects (the Erie Canal is an outstanding example) and on the short-term obligations of American merchants financed by the great English private banks. How were imports surpluses and interest payments met? By the invisible services of the freight earnings and the sales of ships of America's magnificent wooden merchant marine, up to about 1850: and by the export of gold from the California mines, from 1850 to

1875, when more than one billion dollars in gold went overseas to pay American balances.

By 1875, these splendid supports of the American economy were gone. At the same time, the country was committed to a high protective tariff policy which, in many instances, placed prohibitive tariffs on exactly those commodities which the country had been importing (iron and steel products and wool and woolen textiles were the American industries having the particular attention of the tariff makers). The American wooden ships yielded before superior British technology—iron, steam, the screw propeller, regular packet services for passengers and fast freight. The California gold mines were played out. As for American imports, manufactured and semiprocessed manufactured goods dropped to 40 per cent of the total value, annual average 1890-99.

What made all the difference? How could the United States pay for the increasing importation of crude materials for use in manufacturing (these goods moved up from 8.55 per cent of total imports during the 1850s to 24.66 per cent of total imports during the 1890s) and for continued foreign borrowings, largely to finance the construction of trunk railroad systems? This was the key role of American agricultural surpluses: cotton, which began to come back in the 1870s; and even more important, American foodstuffs. From 1852-56 (annual averages) to 1897-1901 (annual averages) exports of wheat and wheat flour increased from 19 million to 197 million bushels; corn and corn meal, from 7 million to 192.5 million bushels; pork products, from 103.9 million to 1,528 million pounds; beef products from 26 million to 357.9 million pounds; and cattle from 1,400 to 415,500 head.

The effect on the balance of payments was immediately evident. For the period 1874-95, American exports totaled $17.2 billion against imports of $14.7 billion. The surplus made possible *our* payment of freight charges, tourist expenditures abroad, immigrants' remittances, and a good part of the interest earned by foreign investors in the United States. Our currency was sound; public debt was being steadily reduced; there was a continuing demand for American cotton and farm products—so that foreign investments in the United States kept on mounting. By the end of the nineteenth century the United States was a net debtor on capital account by almost $3 billion: this represented British, German, and Dutch investments in American rails and mines, land and mortgage companies, public utilities, and (although only slightly) manufacturing enterprises.

Europeans and Americans were aware of what was taking place and of the impact of American agricultural surpluses on the European world. An Austrian writing in the late 1870s declared that "hereafter England's wheat fields will lie in America." And commenting on the flood of American foodstuffs into European markets, he said:

In the sixteenth century American competition ruined the mining industries of Europe, changed the direction of world commerce, brought about by the increased amount of precious metals a revolution in prices, transformed the social conditions and prepared the terrible civil war of the seventeenth century—the Thirty Years War. May the competition of America in the nineteenth century lead to more happy results. No doubt it is the greatest economic event of modern times.

And a New York Congressman, at about the same time, was saying: "By the repeal of the Corn Laws, England enlarged the area of her agricultural resources. Free interchange annexed the food-growing acres of other nations. . . . The United States became practically a part of England."

Farm Technology Many factors contributed to the expansion of American agriculture. The federal government and the States made enormous land grants to railroads and a good part of these were quickly sold at low prices. The Homestead Act of 1862—under which a quarter section of 160 acres could be acquired for nothing after an improvement had been erected and a five-year settlement had been completed and another quarter-section obtained as a pre-emption at the knock-down price of $1.25 an acre—played a part although, up to 1900, only about one-ninth of the lands entered were through Homesteadism. So did the vast and competitive railroad net which was spun up and down and across the trans-Mississippi West. These trunk lines and their feeders opened up the virgin Great Plains to cattle and sheepherders and to wheat growers, forced down railroad rates, and made possible the shipment of live cattle to the feeding bins of Iowa and the Middle West and to the stockyards of Omaha, Kansas City, and Chicago; wheat to the flour mills of Minneapolis and Buffalo; and the dressed-meat products (thanks to refrigerated railroad cars and ships which appeared in the 1880s) to the cities of the Eastern seaboard and the markets of Europe.

AGRICULTURE

Most important was the appearance and improvement in new farm implements and machinery. Up to the 1880s, again thanks to competition, basic machines were constantly being changed and added to: the productivity of farmers sharply increased and machine prices dropped, so that investment in machines and tools became an important part of farm physical plant. Some key figures tell the story. In 1910-14 dollars, the value of implements and machinery rose from $300 million in 1870 to $800 million in 1900. Farm machine prices (100 = 1910-14) fell from an index of 251 in 1870 to 94 in 1900, a decline of more than 60 per cent. And agricultural productivity including both labor and capital inputs, from 1869 to 1899, went up 40 per cent; in fact, the gross output per agricultural worker showed an increase of 46 per cent.

Up to 1850, a good deal of tinkering had taken place with agricultural tools and machines—harrows, seed drills, corn planters, plows, mowers and reapers, and threshers. Few, however, had been manufactured and sold commercially. The improved plow in which the moldboard, share, and landside were made of cast steel—the chief innovator being John Deere of Grand Detour and then Moline, Illinois, in the 1840s—was able to break the tough sod of the prairies. And the mechanical horse-drawn reaper which cut the grain—the inventions of Obed Hussey in 1833 and Cyrus H. McCormick in 1834—opened up the Great Plains to wheat. The second important breakthrough in the improvement of the plow came with the use of chilled iron (a soft-center steel) which was more durable and cheaper and was the work of John Oliver, in 1868. A few years later, the sulky plow (a riding implement with one bottom) and the sulky gang plow (with a number of bottoms) were in common use. Riding machines made the horse important; the agricultural revolution was as much associated with the horse, and therefore the growth of hay, as it was with the improved plow and the mechanical reaper.

McCormick had moved his plant to Chicago in 1847; he was an alert and aggressive businessman; in fact, after his invention, his chief contributions to the industry lay in his merchandising methods. It was McCormick more than anyone else who made machine harvesting generally known and who, therefore, did so much for the spread of wheat-growing in the North during the Civil War years. (In 1865, it was estimated, there were 250,000 mowing and reaping machines in use in the United States, as compared with about 70,000 in 1858.) McCormick, instead of licensing his patent like Hussey, manufactured. He advertised widely; he was among the first merchandisers to sell at a fixed price and to offer a guarantee; his agents were carefully trained so that they were ready to give instruction in maintenance and repairs; and he sold on credit. As much as anything that publicized the effectiveness of his machines was his entry into all the contests and trials of the county fairs and the international exhibitions held periodically in the great European cities. In the latter, he won prizes (but sold no machines); but the splendor of these awards had their effect on the farmer buying public. By 1880, the McCormick company, a family partnership, was valued at $3.5 million, although its net profits for the year were $1 million, and McCormick himself, when he died three years later, left a fortune of $10 million.

If McCormick did not lead in the improvements of the reaper, he quickly followed, so that sharp competition continued to play its part, encouraging further invention and lower product prices. The self-rake reaper, which mechanically distributed the cut grain in a swath at the side of the machine, first appeared in 1854. (McCormick followed seven years later.) The harvester, a reaping machine which carried a man on a platform who bound the cut grain, was being sold on a small scale in 1864; it was not until 1870 that production reached 1,000 machines. (McCormick followed in 1875.)

The first mechanical wire-binder on the harvester was being sold in 1874: it presented problems, for the cut wire remained in the straw and thus was eaten by cows and horses, and in the grain, causing havoc to the milling machines. A twine-binder, which eliminated these problems and was also cheaper, followed in 1880.

At this point innovation ceased, the number of companies began to decline (from 100 before the twine-binder's appearance to 22 after), and a group of giants took over, seeking to eliminate the cutthroat competition which was paring down profits margins. There were no pools, but undoubtedly there were other informal agreements affecting prices, rebates, the bribing of competitors' employees and the judges of field trials. By 1900, five large harvester companies had emerged, with the McCormick interests representing more than 40 per cent of their total capital worth. In 1902 these were combined by J. P. Morgan and Co. into the International Harvester Co., with a capitalization of $120 million. None of this was water—the purpose of the merger was to check the undesirable competition that kept on flaring up. The new organization was responsible for the manufacture and sale of some 90 per cent of the mowers and grain-binders.

The combine, which joined together the harvester and thresher in a single operation right on the field, made its appearance in the 1890s; but it was practicable only on the very large bonanza farms of California and was not widely used until later. Steam engines for threshing purposes also were being employed in California on the field before the end of the century. Further mechanical advances, however, had to await the development and its application to agriculture of the internal combustion engine.

The so-called bonanza farms of the 1880s and 1890s of California and the Red River Valley of North Dakota—where 4,000 to 6,000 acres were planted in wheat and hay and much of the land was rented—were operated almost entirely by machinery. One of these farms included in its inventory 67 plows (eleven were gang plows), 64 harrows, 32 seeders, 6 mowers, 34 self-binding harvesters, 7 steam engines and threshers, 50 wagons, and 125 work animals.

Leo Rogin in his *Introduction of Farm Machinery in Its Relation to the Productivity of Labor in the Agriculture of the United States During the Nineteenth Century* (1931) presented a series of examples, from actual records, to show how sharply reduced was the amount of labor time employed in putting in and securing an acre of wheat.

Giving figures for a bonanza farm in the Red River Valley, Table 6 shows the man-labor time necessary to work one acre of spring wheat in 1893.

TABLE 6

Implement or operation	Motive power	Number of hands	Acres per day	Man-labor time per acre	
				Hr.	*Min.*
Gang plow	4 horses	1	4	2	30
Drill	4 horses	1	20	0	30
Binder	3 horses	1	10	1	00
Shocking	Hand	1	6	1	40
Threshing (from shock)		31	100	3	6
Total				8	46

And Table 7 shows a characteristic amount of labor, by hand method entirely, necessary in connection with the operation of one acre of winter wheat during 1829-30.

TABLE 7

Implement or operation	Motive power	Number of hands	Man-labor time per acre	
			Hr.	Min.
Plow	2 oxen	1	6	40
Sowing	Hand	1	1	15
Brush harrow	2 oxen	1	2	30
Reap (sickle, bind, and shock)	Hand	2	20	00
Haul sheaves to barn	2 oxen	2	4	00
Thresh (flail)	Hand	4	13	20
Winnow (with sheet)	Hand	3	10	00
Measure and sack grain	Hand	1	3	20
Total			61	5

What Rural America Was Like   Again and again efforts have been made to penetrate through the romantic glow that envelopes the farmer movements of the 1870s and 1880s. Actually, their political platforms and proclamations furnish only occasional clues to the underlying reasons for farmer discontent in the Middle West in the 1870s and in the Far West in the 1880s. One must piece out, in part from their achievements when they were in power in some of the States, in part from a wholly subjective analysis, what really was at the heart of the so-called agrarian malaise.

There is no doubt that there were stirrings and that these took the form of third-party movements. In the 1870s a number of States were captured by the Grangers, and legislation, usually affecting the railroads, was written. Beginning with the late 1880s and continuing to 1896, the two Farmers' Alliances of the South and the Northwest also entered State politics and then, beginning with 1890, national politics. One must observe, however, that the first movement centered in the Middle West. Within a decade or so, the zeal, enthusiasm, and evangelism of this region had largely burnt itself out; now the uncompromising hostility to the East and its ways (and, by that token, to banking and industry—in brief, to business) shifted over to the cotton South and the wheat Great Plains.

With this reservation: the Populism of the South was tied in with the internal struggle for the control of the Democratic Party in that section. In many instances the newly risen leaders of the Southern "white masses"—those yeoman farmers and small-town businessmen who had played no role in the determination of the South's course before the Civil War and who had again been disregarded when the political "redemption" of the Southern States was beginning to take place in the 1870s—were determined to use every means to achieve control of the Democratic Party. The activities of the Southern Alliance, which began to reach the rural white South, was one opportunity that could be employed to undermine the so-called Confederate Brigadiers, or Bourbons. The other was the disfranchisement of the Negroes. Populism in the South, in consequence, became part of a bitter internal political contest: the "white masses" won, and ever since the South has been dominated by these spokesmen for the smaller farmers and the lawyers, professional men, and shopkeepers of the back country.

Here is one clue, then. Grangerism and Populism were hopeless efforts to continue the domination in the United States of the rural America of the family farm, the crossroads merchant, the county-seat lawyer in the face of the growing importance of urbanization and industrialization, the increasingly heterogeneous nature of the American population (because of the new immigration), the closer and closer ties with international banking and trade. The rural world was the heartland of America: its pristine virtues—independence, self-sufficiency, sturdiness—were born and nurtured here. In part, then, this was a struggle against submergence, not only political but spiritual.

That the small town was isolated from the new major currents; that it bred, as a result, a crankiness and hostility to ways that it regarded as alien; that it was quick to assume it was the victim of plots and conspiracies ("The Crime of 1873," "The Money Power," "The Anglo-American Gold Trust," "The International Bankers," "The Jews") when times were out of joint for it—these were manifestations of an uneasiness and growing sense of decline of status and leadership. The younger people, both boys and girls, were leaving rural America to seek the hazards of new fortunes—and a more exciting life—in the booming larger cities. Older people, the misfits and the unsuccessful, were left: to speak, to shout, to organize, to demonstrate, to write the newspapers and manifestoes of these agrarian hosts.

Their spokesmen made up a motley and curious company. Ben Tillman, unsuccessful farmer and land speculator of South Carolina; Thomas E. Watson, author of small talents and newspaperman of Georgia; C. W. Macune of Texas, wanderer and dabbler in many things, law, medicine, business, manager of a farmer's exchange, who had lived in California, Kansas, and Texas, and succeeded in none of them; General James B. Weaver, in and out of every third-party movement of Iowa, whose Civil War laurels were becoming more and more faded; Ignatius Donnelly of Minnesota, whose failures in business, the law, and politics kept on mounting to an amazing total; William Jennings Bryan of Nebraska, small-town lawyer without a practice and politician without office. These were scarcely the successors of those who had spoken for the earlier, rural, small-town, self-contained America—those who had come out of Monticello, Quincy, Concord; these were not the ones to assume the mantle of a Jefferson or John Adams or Emerson. It was small wonder that Greenbackers, Grangers, and Populists (as well as the Knights of Labor) had nothing to offer except confusion about money, escape from industrialism, and bitter and vicious hostility to a rapidly changing, quickly growing world that was leaving them stranded in rural backwaters and country small towns. They fed on their grievances (many imagined); their failures (all real) only made them the more defiant and unreasonable and easy prey to fantasy.

Here are three characteristic statements coming out of this rural America, made to an army with tattered banners and calling out to one another outworn shibboleths. Ignatius Donnelly wrote the preamble to the Populist platform of 1892 (when the United States was in the midst of boom times); he said in it:

The conditions which surround us best justify our cooperation; we meet in the midst of moral, political, and material ruin. Corruption dominates the ballot-box, the legislatures, the Congress, and touches even the ermine of the bench. . . . The newspapers are largely subsidized or muzzled, public opinion silenced, business prostrated, our homes covered with mortgages, labor impoverished, and the land concentrating in the hands of the capitalists. The urban workmen are denied the right of organization for self-protection, imported pauperized labor beats down their wages, a hireling standing army, unrecognized by our laws, is established to shoot them down, and they are rapidly degenerating into

European conditions. The fruits of the toil of millions are boldly stolen to build up colossal fortunes for a few, unprecedented in the history of mankind; and the possessors of these, in turn, despise the Republic and endanger liberty. From the same prolific womb of governmental injustice we bred the two great classes—tramps and millionaires.

And thus spoke "Editor" William A. Peffer for an embittered Kansas, growing wheat by machine methods on mortgaged farms: an expansion which the farmers themselves had pushed. What follows is from Peffer's *The Farmer's Side* (1891); his editorials had helped elect him to the United States Senate in 1890.

We see plainly that behind all the commercial villainies of the time this power [of Wall Street] rests in placid security while the robbing of the toiler proceeds. These men of Wall Street, posing as missionaries conquering deserts and building republics, men piously assuming universal dominion, religiously dictating the financial policies of nations, moving in an atmosphere of radiant morals, self-appointed philosophers teaching honor and honesty to an ignorant world, these men of fabulous fortunes, built upon the ruins of their fellows, are in fact the most audacious gamblers in Christendom. . . . Touch any spring along the keyboard of commercial gambling and a Wall Street sign appears. This dangerous power which money gives is fast undermining the liberties of the people. . . . This is the power we have to deal with. It is the great evil of the time. Money is the great issue—all others fade into insignificance before this, the father of them.

And in another place, Peffer said: "Money is a necessary instrument of commerce and ought not to be freighted with any charges beyond the mere cost of United States issuance. Interest is wrong in principle."

And here is William Jennings Bryan speaking before—and sweeping off its feet—the Democratic convention held at Chicago, on July 8, 1896. This is the defiance and the autointoxication of rural America:

You come to us and tell us that the great cities are in favor of the gold standard; we reply that the great cities rest upon our broad and fertile plains. Burn down your cities and leave our farms, and your cities will spring up again as if by magic; but destroy our farms and the grass will grow in the streets of every city in the country.

And here is another clue. The loneliness, the drudgery, the early loss of youth: these too fed the springs of agrarian resentment. In the rural

America of the Dakotas, Kansas, Iowa—where the summers were blazing hot and the winters bitter cold—there were no hard-surfaced roads, no telephones, no movies, no television or radio, no automobiles, no consolidated schools, no public libraries, no rural free delivery, no popular magazines, no electricity, no household appliances for washing and cleaning: there was nothing to relieve tedium, lighten toil, make possible escape into the worlds of romance, adventure, and derring-do. The life was bleak, unadorned, of continuous toil for father, mother, even small children. Religious revivalism again and again swept over the prairies and Great Plains; and after it had spent itself, left the "converted" exhausted—and unredeemed.

One need turn only to the bitter tales of Hamlin Garland's *Main-travelled Roads* (he is writing in the late 1880s of his boyhood's rural Wisconsin, Dakota, and Iowa) or to Ed Howe's saturnine *The Story of a Country Town* (the scene is eastern Kansas in the early 1880s, while Howe was living there) to see the countryside drained of the sentiment and claptrap with which its political prophets invested it.

Here is Garland describing one of his farmer women:

It was a pitifully worn, almost tragic face—long, thin, sallow, hollow-eyed. The mouth had long since lost the power to shape itself into a kiss, and had a droop at the corners which seemed to announce a breaking-down at any moment into a despairing wail. The collarless neck and sharp shoulders showed painfully.

And here is a young school teacher, in one of the tales, talking of her husband:

You must remember that such toil brutalizes a man, it makes him callous, selfish, unfeeling, necessarily. A fine nature must either adapt itself to its hard surroundings or die. Men who toil terribly in filthy garments day after day and year after year cannot easily keep gentle; the frost and grime, the heat and cold will soon or late enter into their souls. The case is not all in favor of the suffering wives and against the brutal husbands. If the farmer's wife is dulled and crazed by her routine, the farmer himself is degraded and brutalized.

Howe's novel is of sad, discontented, lonely, unfulfilled people: of boys and girls and men and women who labor long and bitterly and take no pleasure in their toil. Husbands and wives, when the day's work is finished, spend long hours in silence together; there is nothing to talk about, nothing to do. Even the young narrator, who has mastered the printing trade and become the successful owner of the town's paper, speaks of himself of turning into a "Fairview man, miserable and silent, without hope or ambition." And this of the women:

I was brought up in a community where the women were overworked, imposed upon, and unhappy. . . .
The pale, fretful women of Fairview, who talked in the church of the heavy crosses to bear, and sat down crying, passed before me in procession. . . .

And this of the men; young Ned is passing them in review:

I never formed a good opinion of a man there that I was not finally told something to his discredit by another citizen, causing me to regard him with great suspicion. And if I said a good word for any of them, it was proved beyond question immediately that he was a very unscrupulous, a very ridiculous, a very weak, and a very worthless man. There were no friendships among them, and they all hated each other in secret, there being much quiet satisfaction when one of them failed.

The Grange, the Farmers' Alliances, and the Populists   As early as 1867, when the Patrons of Husbandry (later the Grange) appeared, the farmers were stirring and meeting in conventions, their chief focus of concern being railroad malpractices—high rates; rebates to favored shippers; combinations with warehouse men and granary owners. In the early 1870s, local parties appeared in Illinois, Minnesota, Wisconsin, Michigan, Indiana, Missouri, to demand railroad legislation and to talk of money. For the most part, they were deflationists; on banking they were of mixed minds. The Wisconsin farmers wanted the national debt "honestly paid"; those of Indiana called for public paper money without the intervention of any system of banking corporations, but that the principal and interest of the national debt were to be paid in coin; those of Michigan and Missouri wanted a speedy return to the hard money and free banking; in Nebraska, they were also for the resumption of specie payments.

Haynes, in his discussion of the third-party movements in the West during 1873-75, points out that the farmers were so-called anti-monopolists (in most of these states Granger laws were passed for the regulation of railroad rates and practices either by statute or by state commissions) but that a majority of them demanded a return to specie payments as soon as possible.

By 1875, however, these same farmers had become Greenbackers. The idea of an expanding and irredeemable paper currency had been floating in the air as early as 1867: the National Labor Union had advocated it; Pendleton's "Ohio Idea" had bemused many politicians and had got into the Democratic Party platform in 1868; a National Labor Reform Party named candidates on such a program (it got only 30,000 votes). But the labor movement fell apart, and the farmers took over. Under various names (National Independent Party, National Labor Reform Party, Greenback Labor Party), Greenbackism played a small and unsuccessful role in national politics during 1875-1880. In the election of 1876, Peter Cooper, nominated by the National Greenback Convention, polled only 81,000 votes; these showed that the Greenback sentiment prevailed largely in Illinois, Indiana, Iowa, Kansas, Michigan, and Missouri. (How uninterested labor was is indicated by the fact that only 251 votes for Cooper were cast in Chicago, 21 in Cincinnati, 93 in Pittsburgh, 289 in New York and 50 in Brooklyn.)

The high-water mark was reached in the Congressional elections of 1878, when more than one million votes were cast for candidates of the Greenback Labor Party. The election manifesto called for the national government to assume the exclusive functions of coining money, regulating its value, and making it a legal tender; there was to be the free and unlimited coinage of silver; money was to be adequate and a minimum amount was to be fixed on a per capita basis. The platform, for the first time, took a hard look at taxation and among other things came out for the taxation of all forms of private property as well as a graduated income tax. The heaviest votes were polled in the West: one-half of the total came from Iowa, Michigan, Missouri, Illinois, Indiana, California, Wisconsin, Kansas, Minnesota, and Nebraska. Fourteen Congressmen were elected. But by 1880, with General Weaver of Iowa as the standard bearer, and the appeal largely directed to the farmers, the vote had dropped off to 308,000 and came from the Far West; the Middle West was no longer interested. And thus Greenbackism waned and it disappeared formally after the election of 1888 when its candidate polled 144,800 votes.

Then the Farmers' Alliances of the South and the Northwest appeared on the stage. Editors of farm journals, lawyers, men seeking to form farm cooperatives and farmer social clubs—as the Granger movement began to disintegrate—were talking organization as early as 1880. What they offered was a mixed bag: social clubs were to carry on also educational programs (books like Bellamy's *Looking Backward,* Donnelly's *Caesar's Column,* Peffer's *Farmer's Side,* Weaver's *A Call to Action,* Powderly's *Thirty Years of Labor* were to be read and discussed); cooperatives and so-called exchanges were to be created for purchasing, marketing, insurance; picnics were to be held, forums conducted, eleemosynary programs developed. In the South, the talk centered in what was being called a "strictly white man's non-political secret business association."

In connection with the last, all the efforts died quickly. The most ambitious was the Farmers' Alliance Exchange of Texas, which Macune managed. It set out to market cotton and grain on a commission basis; buy farm implements, dry goods and groceries for resale to farmers; and extend credit to farmers (all for the purpose of breaking the crop-lien system). But banks would not discount the Exchange's notes, and it quit in twenty months. Similar experiences and failures and the inability of cooperatives to get off the ground (refinancing was once more the problem) inevitably turned these Alliancemen to politics and the fabrication of paper programs.

By the end of the 1880s these local organizations were fused into two great bodies—the Farmers' and Laborer's Union of America (which came to be known as the Southern Alliance) and the National Farmers' Alliance (which came to be known as Northern Alliance). A third group, the Colored Farmers' National Alliance and Cooperative Union, was organized independently but worked closely with the other two.

Efforts at union—this time to formulate legislative programs and to enter into politics—immediately were pressed. The first set of meetings looking to this end took place in St. Louis in December, 1889, where delegates gathered from the three farmer bodies and where there also converged representatives of the now rapidly failing Knights of Labor and a miscellany of zealots, eccentrics, and torchbearers for Greenbackism, Prohibition, Union Labor, and the old soldiers (who wanted service pensions). The American Federation of Labor disdained an invitation to send representatives; farmers, it said, were employers and therefore the foes of workers. There were independent meetings, but no union—

for the two main farmer organizations would not agree on a common program.

Both Southern and Northern Alliancemen wanted government ownership of railways and telegraphs and the end of landholding by aliens. The Southern Alliance delegates talked money; the Northern Alliance delegates were more interested in such railroad abuses as avoidance of taxation, withholding of lieu lands from settlement. On money and banking, the Southern Alliance advocated the abolition of national banks; the issuance of legal-tender Treasury notes in sufficient volume to permit the business of the country to operate on a cash basis (this meant a per capita formula); and the free and unlimited coinage of silver. The Northern Alliance said much the same things about national banks (close them down) and Treasury notes (issue them). About silver they were silent, and they pressed for tax reform—a "graded" income tax and a tax on real-estate mortgages and all other sorts of real and personal property. Here was where the shoe really pinched.

It was at the Southern Alliance meeting in St. Louis that Macune unveiled his famous Sub-Treasury plan: Macune was now in Washington as the editor of the Alliance's official journal *The National Economist*. It was this scheme that captured the attention and fired the fancy of the Southern men and became the heart of their agitation; for it promised escape from the crop-lien system; was a way of financing farm surpluses; and at the same time offered a virtually unlimited amount of government money as legal tenders.

Thus Macune proposed: The national banks were to be abolished. They were to be replaced by government Sub-Treasury offices in every county producing $500,000 or more in nonperishable farm products (grain, cotton, tobacco, sugar, wool); these offices also were to be warehouses and elevators. The Sub-Treasuries were to lend against certificates of deposit up to 80 per cent of the local current value of the produce; issue legal-tender Treasury notes against them; charge an interest rate of 1 per cent; and hold the commodities off the market for a year. These were then to be sold at public auction, with charges for storage being made against the borrowers. The certificates of deposit were negotiable and anyone holding them might receive a loan in the legal-tender notes at any time. Those who did not negotiate loans and simply held the certificates of deposit could redeem the commodities—if prices went up;

the same was true for those who paid off their loans to get their certificates back.

Otherwise, the Treasury notes remained in circulation; their numbers being constantly increased with each harvest if agricultural prices did not suit the borrowers, and with the national government paying storage costs and having the responsibility of disposing of the crop surpluses. (Obviously, prices would go down, as more and more farmers expanded acreage to take advantage of government price supports and surpluses were dumped on the market.) The inflation of the whole economy as a result of this pumping of enormous sums of paper money into it yearly did not trouble—if they ever gave a thought to it—the Southern Alliance. (One may note, in passing, that the broad general lineaments of this intriguing notion reappeared in 1933 in the Agricultural Adjustment Act.)

Soon, trouble broke loose in the farther West, as a result of a succession of drought-caused bad crops, the collapse of the real estate boom, and mortgage foreclosures. Local farmer political parties began to appear in early 1890 in Kansas, Nebraska, and South Dakota; and, in the South, Alliancemen joined hands with Wool Hat Boys and Red Necks and raised havoc with, and began the capture of, the Democratic Party. The farther West was caught up—this was so particularly of Kansas—in another revivalist fever, with excited and unruly meetings taking place everywhere in schoolhouses, churches, town halls, open squares, and meadows; this time it was not the Devil or Demon Rum that was to be cast out but the moneylenders (national banks, mortgage companies, international bankers, the Jews). In Kansas, the exhorters and the tub thumpers carried not the banners of the Lord but those of the new party, the People's Party; and Mary E. Lease—one of the more prominant tub thumpers told her listeners: "What you farmers need to do is raise less corn and more Hell!" And another Kansan wrote:

We want money, land, and transportation. We want the abolition of the National Banks, and we want the power to make loans direct from the government. We want the accursed foreclosure system wiped out. . . . Kansas suffers from two great robbers, the Santa Fe Railroad and the loan companies. . . . The people are at bay, let the bloodhounds of money who have dogged us thus far beware!

In 1890, Kansas alone elected five Populist Congressmen, a majority in the lower house of the state legislature, and sent Editor Peffer to the United States Senate. South Dakota also elected to the Senate the Reverend J. H. Kyle. As for the South, Alliancemen helped send Tillman as governor to the South Carolina State capital, to begin his dirty work of disfranchising the Negroes; and similar although lesser triumphs were achieved with sooner or later the same results in Georgia, Virginia, North Carolina, Mississippi, Kentucky, and Missouri. (There is no point in trying to conjecture that perhaps Southern Alliancemen were taken in by the young Southern segregationists who were beginning to rise—Ben Tillman of South Carolina, Cole Blease of North Carolina, Jeff Davis of Arkansas, James Vardaman of Mississippi. After all, the Alliance had started out by being a white man's secret organization: Negro farmers could join with them in action, but only as members of their own segregated Alliance.)

Flushed with these victories, the Southern Alliance met once more, this time at Ocala, Florida, in December 1890. The manifesto (not yet political, however) largely repeated the demands set forth in the St. Louis statement, with these changes: tariff revision was demanded; government control of railroads was substituted for government ownership; and Macune's Sub-Treasury scheme was formally endorsed. To catch the Northern Alliancemen, who did not want to talk easy credit so much as mortgage relief, the Sub-Treasury plan had one addition: the national government was to set up in effect a land bank (a bureau of the Treasury) to lend on farm real estate, and issue more Treasury notes, at 1 per cent interest.

With the way thus prepared, the third party, the People's Party, was finally announced at Cincinnati in May, 1891; although the delegates attending were largely from the Northern Alliance. (We must not forget that the new Southern politicians wanted to capture and remake in their image the Democratic party.) This is what the call for organization had to say about money:

The right to make and issue money is a sovereign power to be maintained by the people for the common benefit. Hence we demand the abolition of national banks as banks of issue, and as a substitute for national bank notes we demand that legal-tender Treasury notes be issued in sufficient volume to transact the business of the country on a cash basis without damage or especial advantage to any class or calling, such notes to be legal tender in payment of all debts, public and private, and such notes, when demanded by the people, shall be loaned to them at not more than 2 per cent per annum upon non-perishable products, as indicated in the Sub-Treasury plan, and also upon real estate, with proper limitation upon the quantity of land and amount of money.

The free and unlimited coinage of silver was also called for, as well as the prohibition of alien land ownership, the seizure of lands held by railroads and other corporations "in excess of such as is actually used"; and it was demanded that all taxation be so devised that it "not be used to build up one interest or class at the expense of another." To catch the eye of labor and other dissidents, there were planks for an eight-hour day, universal suffrage, and the election of the President, Vice President, and Senators by direct vote.

At St. Louis, on February 22, 1892, the People's Party was formally launched with a gathering of all those who had shown their ability to carry the fight in local elections. All the farmer leaders of the South and West were now assembled: Senator Peffer of Kansas, Senator Kyle of South Dakota, General Weaver of Iowa, Ignatius Donnelly of Minnesota, Thomas E. Watson of Georgia and the "big five" of the Southern Alliance—Polk, Macune, Livingston, Tillman, and Terrell, for the Southern Alliance and the Southern politicians had yielded to persuasion and the South was committed to the cause. The platform started off with Donnelly's flamboyant preamble and largely repeated what had been said at Cincinnati—with some significant changes about money. Disenchantment with Macune, who had been found engaging in shady business and political ventures, led to a watering down of the Sub-Treasury scheme (it was approved with the reservation "or some better system"); Treasury notes were also demanded to pay for public improvements; and here appeared the mystical formula—"We demand that the amount of circulating medium be speedily increased to not less than $50 per capita."

The nominating convention met on July 4, 1892, at Omaha; Donnelly's preamble was repeated; so was the money plank; so was the free-silver plank, except that it now wanted the free and unlimited coinage of silver "at the present legal ratio of sixteen to one." It was apparent that the silverites were making inroads and that the Sub-Treasury idea was losing its appeal; in fact, in another half year it was no longer to be found at the heart of the Alliance's money talk.

In the 1892 election the Populists made the most impressive advances a third party had up to then achieved in America: General Weaver, the Presidential candidate, obtained 22 electoral votes; ten Congressmen and five Senators were sent to Washington. And the South was being shaken, for in a number of states Populists joined with Republicans to unseat Democratic administrations; while in South Carolina, Governor Tillman was openly defying his party, characterizing Cleveland's candidacy "as a prostitution of the principles of Democracy, as a repudiation of the demands of the Farmers' Alliance, which embody the true principles of Democracy, and a surrender of the rights of the people to the financial kings of the country."

The same tale was repeated in 1894: the popular vote increased 42 per cent over that of the preceding election; seven Congressmen and six Senators were sent to Washington, including Tillman as Senator, breathing fire to bring Cleveland low (and to save the South from the Negroes). For again, fusion between Populists and Republicans met with success in North Carolina, Texas, and Alabama. This fact and the heavy barrage of free-silver propaganda (intensified manyfold as a result of Cleveland's forcing the repeal of the Sherman Silver Purchase Act in 1893)—plus the onset of depression—were responsible for the capture of the Democratic party in 1896 by the silverites and the nomination of Bryan.

The Populists committed a strategic blunder: they decided to meet in convention after the Republicans and Democrats, probably anticipating only halfhearted gestures toward reform on the part of the two major parties. And then their cause was lost. The Democratic platform satisfied in greater rather than lesser degree the Alliancemen's demands for more money.

Said the platform:

[The] money question is paramount to all others at this time. . . .
We are unalterably opposed to monometalism which has locked fast the prosperity of an industrial people in the paralysis of hard times. Gold monometalism is a British policy, and its adoption has brought other nations into financial servitude to London. It is not only un-American but anti-American. . . .
We demand the free and unlimited coinage of both silver and gold at

the present legal ratio of 16 to 1 without waiting for the aid or consent of any other nation. We demand that the standard silver dollar shall be a full legal tender, equally with gold, for all debts public and private. . . .

We are opposed to the issuing of interest-bearing bonds of the United States in time of peace and condemn the trafficking with banking syndicates. . . .

We . . . denounce the issuance of notes intended to circulate as money by national banks as in derogation of the Constitution, and we demand that all paper which is made a legal tender for public and private debts, or which is receivable for dues to the United States, shall be issued by the United States and shall be redeemable in coin.

And this was all; the Populist hopes for an expanding currency based on public loans for agricultural products and land went aglimmering. And as for taxation (without specific reference to railroad properties and other forms of real and personal property), the Democratic platform condemned the Supreme Court's outlawing of the income-tax provision in 1895 and simply said that "it is the duty of Congress to use all the Constitutional power . . . so that the burden of taxation may be equally and impartially laid, to the end that wealth may bear its due proportion of the expense of the Government."

The Populists had been outmaneuvered; with much grumbling on the part of many, Bryan—and "success in our time" was accepted. The Populists drew up their own platform, again subordinating silver to their other financial ideas; but their fortunes were tied to Bryan's and with Bryan's defeat, they were finished.

That Populism had been cozened was plain to the left-wingers in its midst; the espousal of the free-silver doctrine was the poisoned cup. Thus, Henry Demarest Lloyd, who had labored hard to prevent the endorsement of Bryan, wrote in October, 1896, in the midst of the campaign:

The People's Party convention at St. Louis was the most discouraging experience of my life. It was not so much that the leaders were tricked and bulldozed and betrayed, but that the people submitted. The craze for success "this time" had full possession of them. . . . The free silver movement is a fake. Free silver is the cowbird of the reform movement. It waited until the nest had been laid by the sacrifices and labors of others, and then it laid its eggs in it, pushing out the others which lie smashed on the ground.

Ignatius Donnelly Ignatius Donnelly, born and brought up in Phila-delphia—where he practiced law and sought to enter into Democratic politics and where he dabbled in real estate, all unsuccessfully—migrated to Minnesota in 1856 at the age of twenty-five to make his fortune. He was no luckier there; a grandiose land-development scheme collapsed with the panic of 1857—and Donnelly was again in politics, this time as a Republican. He was elected to Congress for three terms and, as always, followed the main chance: an ultra-Radical, he was hostile to Lincoln and supported the Congressional Reconstruction program; he blew hot and cold on the tariff question, finally coming out for high tariffs; anxious to get a transcontinental railroad for the Northwest, he helped the Northern Pacific obtain its huge land grants—and acted as an open lobbyist for railroads, receiving stock in some dubious ventures. The last did not help him in 1868, and despite his avowal that "If I am returned to Congress I shall go there as a firm friend and advocate of the Northern Pacific Railroad Company," he was refused Republican nomination, ran independently, and was defeated.

For a brief period Donnelly returned to his farms to grow wheat, but he could not remain for long out of politics, off the hustings, or away from the lecture platform. He was witty, fluent—and turbulent: all this fitted in with the temper of the growing Northwest. Donnelly was sud-denly converted to low tariffs; had become what he called an anti-monopolist (the railroads were now the enemy); and joined the ranks of the Liberal Republicans in 1872. At the same time, he was a hard-money man, supporting the resumption of specie payments. He became a Granger, once more seeking to ingratiate himself with all factions, both supporting farmers' cooperatives and trying to push the Grange into politics. He was successful; an Anti-Monopoly Party was formed in Minnesota in 1873 and Donnelly once more was in public office—he had been elected a State Senator. To establish his control over the Anti-Monopoly Party, and to force the Democrats to join hands with it, Donnelly needed a newspaper and he succeeded in establishing a weekly, the *Anti-Monopolist,* which he largely wrote himself and which a rival paper described in this fashion (exactly hitting off Donnelly as well): "[It is a] singular newspaper, as unlike other journals as Donnelly is unlike other men. . . . It is brimful of fight and fun, and bristles all over with invective . . . and is as dangerous a plaything as a porcupine."

But the sands were running out for the Grange in Minnesota; the Democrats deserted the coalition with the Anti-Monopolists, and two years later Donnelly was in the camp of the Greenbackers reversing himself on money as he had already on the tariff and railroading. To no avail; he failed in his bid for a Congressional seat and in 1880 was out of politics and back on his farms—where his achievements were no greater than they had been in politics. Most of the next decade he spent writing a group of books and these sold, giving him money, leisure, and a curious kind of acclaim. With no real knowledge of the careful work being done in the new sciences, depending as much on magic and old wives' tales as he did on Darwin and Fiske (it is a mistake to call his writings "science fiction"; they were "pseudo-science") Donnelly wrote at hot speed *Atlantis: The Antediluvian World* (1882) and *Ragnarok: The Age of Fire and Gravel* (1883). *Atlantis* was filled with the kind of undigested learning that delighted the last half of the nineteenth century. With impressive quotations from all the natural sciences and most of the ancient and modern languages and literature, citing Lettish folktales and Chaldean and Amerind myths, Donnelly proved to his rural neighbors (and to W. E. Gladstone!) the existence of that fabled island in the middle Atlantic from which had indubitably sprung the civilizations and religions of the Western world. To an age awed by the fresh discoveries of archaeology, geology, and biology, but yet unfamiliar with the rigorous methods of science, this farrago of nonsense was accepted as scholarship. *Ragnarok* was even more fantastic: its idea was that the earth's geological structures were the result of a collision with a great comet, which had sprinkled its debris all over it; all of this represented some sort of divine judgment and was tied in with Original Sin.

From these, Donnelly moved to Shakespeare, for quite early he had become convinced not only of Bacon's authorship but that the 1623 Shakespeare folio contained an internal arithmetical cipher which revealed its real origins and even told in great detail Bacon's life and the villainies of Shakespeare. Donnelly had reached this conclusion in 1882 and he set to work writing *The Great Cryptogram,* which appeared in 1888. One thousand pages long, its first half was filled with the same mishmash of learning that characterized his earlier books: Shakespeare did not (but Bacon did) have the broad sweep of knowledge and experience necessary for the writing of the plays. The second half unfolded the discovery and the application of the cipher to the plays (largely, however, *Henry IV*) and to a defense of Bacon himself.

The book was a failure; it did not make money and in fact was received with derision. One wag, applying the same arithmetical cipher to *Don Quixote,* proved that that had been written by Bacon, too. Another foray into Minnesota politics ended similarly (this time he was seeking to use the Minnesota Farmers' Alliance to obtain election to the United States Senate). Minnesota knew its Donnelly, for said a local newspaper at the time:

He is brilliant, but vain and impractical. He has some good ideas but ruins all by attempting to carry everything to the extreme and riding rough-shod over all opposition. He has tired and sickened the legislature with his verbosity, and has lost his following by the continued advocacy of impractical measures.

Thus Donnelly, like all inadequate, rejected and therefore embittered men before and after him, turned against the world which had refused to recognize his merits and his proffers of leadership. His *Caesar's Column* (published pseudonymously in 1889) and *The Golden Bottle* (1892) were not, although they seemed to be, in the then popular genre of Utopian fiction, where escapists envisioned a simpler and hence happier life for all mankind.

Caesar's Column is Utopia-in-reverse. Its *mise en scène* is the United States of 1988 (filled with all of Jules Verne's wonderful gadgets), which has inexorably moved into the degradation that its acceptance of Herbert Spencer, Christianity, capitalism, and free democratic institutions had prepared it for. A plutocratic dictatorship, largely made up of Jews, governs cruelly and evilly, using a police force of "Demons" to terrorize workers and "serfs" who themselves have become brutalized. The "Demons" patrol the country with dirigibles from which they drop explosive bombs and "a subtle poison which rolls steadily forward, killing all who breathe it." An uprising takes place, led by the secret "Brotherhood of Destruction"; the "Demons" are subverted; and after a wild orgy of lootings and killings, the erstwhile masters are compelled to build their own pyre on which they are burned. The last monument of Western civilization is "Caesar's Column," a huge pyramid of the heads of the plutocrats, severed and sheathed in a concrete shell. A handful of survivors—a great fire wipes out the leading city—flee to Africa, where, at last, they are able to set up a true Utopia, a Christian Socialist state based on the principles of the Farmers' Alliance and the Knights of Labor.

The Golden Bottle has for its hero a Kansas farm youth, Ephraim Benezet, whose appeal to heaven—his father has become the victim of the money changers—is answered with a magic vial; its liquid can turn iron into gold. Thus fortified, Benezet saves his father's farm and his Kansas county from the usurious mortgage owners. His fame spreads and he becomes President of the United States. And high time! For the country has been debased and debauched as a result of the ruin of its independent yeomanry and the filling up of its cities by the ignorant hordes from Europe who are the easy dupes of America's capitalist masters—and responsible for its vice and crime. Benezet's inaugural address promises to free America by giving it plenty of money, and by banging the doors shut to immigration. Says he, "Our country was the safety-valve which permitted the discontents of the Old World to escape. If that vent was closed, every throne in Europe would be blown up in twenty years. . . . For the people of the Old World, having to choose between death by starvation and resistance to tyrants, would turn upon their oppressors and tear them to pieces." And so it turns out, with Benezet declaring war on Europe and himself leading an army of liberation. Accompanied by the usual looting and carnage, the autocratic heads of Europe are overthrown—the Russian Czar is assassinated by the Nihilists—and a United States of Europe is set up to be followed by a Universal Republic. Thereafter, peace, plenty, low interest, and the green-belt town prevail and man achieves Utopia.

In this way, unconsciously, Donnelly was having his revenge. The Minnesota Farmers' Alliance listened enrapt to Donnelly's flamboyant oratory, it helped elect him to the state senate once again in 1890 and made him Alliance President; but it did not assist him to climb. Donnelly led the Minnesota delegation to the National Alliance Convention in Cincinnati in 1891, and because his authorship of *Caesar's Column* was now generally known, he was made chairman of its resolutions committee. From the start, Donnelly talked third-party, thereby infuriating both Southern and Northern Alliance leaders. But he had his way, and it was his preamble to the St. Louis platform of 1892, with its rodomontade about tramps and millionaires, that swept the convention and committed the farmers to independent action at the polls.

The results of the elections of 1892, while impressive, were unequal—in Minnesota, for example, where farmers were cool to the Sub-Treasury scheme, Donnelly, who was the People's Party candidate for governor, ran a poor third. Donnelly became more irresponsible as a consequence. He now became the chief advocate of the charge of "The Crime of 1873"; he linked it with an international conspiracy of bankers, whom he called the "European Rothschilds," and he openly identified himself with the silver-mining interests by becoming vice-president of the American Bimetallic League. (It was at the 1893 conference of this curious association that Colorado's Populist Governor, Davis H. Waite, shouted: "If it [violence] is forced upon us . . . it is better, infinitely better, rather than that our liberties should be destroyed by tyranny . . . that we should wade through seas of blood—yea, blood to the horses' bridles.")

Donnelly kept on insisting that he was first and foremost for fiat money; yet he allowed, without demur, the deep penetration of the silverites into the People's Party. And in 1895, he wrote the *American People's Money*: fiat money, ran its burden, was the ideal remedy; it had to wait, however, for as long as a metallic currency was generally used silver had to be the equal partner of gold, as it had always been. Here were two characteristic passages:

. . . just as the sun and moon moved together through the heavens, so these, their typical metals, move side by side, for hundreds of centuries, in the affairs of mankind; and that it would be as great an invasion of the orderly arrangements of nature to seek to pluck the money from its orbit as it was to tear the white metal from the commercial firmament.

[And yet this was exactly done by "The Crime of 1873"] . . . silver was not the victim of an open and public war; it was secretly slain by the stilettos of hired bandits, in the darkness of the night.

What to do in 1896? The Populists had postponed their nominating convention; the silver Republicans had seceded from their party; Bryan, with his silver plank, had captured the Democratic Party and been named its standard-bearer. Publicly, Donnelly was opposed to Populist fusion with the Democrats; privately, he sent out feelers to the Democrats (and at the same time entered the Populist convention as a candidate). Donnelly ended by seconding Bryan's nomination at the Populist convention and accepting the submergence of the People's Party platform.

From then on, Donnelly's light became dimmer and dimmer. In 1898, he was still able to say: "Scientific paper money, irredeemable, based on the credit and wealth of the nation, issued and its volume controlled by the nation without the intervention of banks is the Populist ideal money." He drifted toward Socialism but in 1900 ran as the People's Party—the poor remnant that remained—vice-presidential candidate. He died in 1901.

What Banks Were Charging for Interest   If there had been a dearth of money in the United States, interest rates would have gone up; but the reverse happened. During the 1880s and 1890s, interest rates declined steadily, not only for long-term government, corporation, and municipal bonds, but for short-term commercial paper as well. Government bonds yielded, after 1880, only 2 or 3 per cent; New England municipals fell from an average of 5.67 per cent in 1873 to 4.15 per cent in 1879, and 3.07 in 1899; railroad bonds fell from 6.5 per cent in 1873 to 4.66 per cent in 1879, and 3.07 per cent in 1899.

New York City banks progressively dropped their interest rates for choice commercial paper (60-90 days) from 8.49 per cent during 1850-59 (10-year average) to 6.46 per cent during 1870-79, 5.14 per cent during 1880-89, and 4.51 per cent during 1890-99. As for the South and the Plains country, the fragmentary data available to us would indicate two things: that during the height of the money agitation in the South and the Plains country (1888-96), the average rate of interest earned by national banks in non-reserve cities, that is, the smaller cities, was falling; and that the differential between Eastern cities and those of the South and the Plains was narrowing.

The figures in Table 8, in per cents, give average gross rates of return of national banks in non-reserve cities.

In the Northwest, during the turbulent years of the farmer agitation, local State parties were talking of things other than money. In Minnesota, for example, where Donnelly cut such a wide swath, however slight his effect on the State's legislature, attention concentrated on these matters: Grain inspection and elevator charges were too high—therefore establish state-owned elevators. Insurance rates, against hail and fire,

TABLE 8

	Region II[1]	Region III[2]	Region IV[3]	Region V[4]
1888	5.80	8.57	7.24	9.83
1896	5.48	7.68	6.47	8.90

[1] Region II: New York, New Jersey, Pennsylvania, Delaware, Maryland, and District of Columbia.

[2] Region III: Virginia, West Virginia, North Carolina, South Carolina, Georgia, Florida, Alabama, Mississippi, Louisiana, Texas, Arkansas, Kentucky, and Tennessee.

[3] Region IV: Ohio, Indiana, Illinois, Michigan, Wisconsin, Minnesota, Iowa, and Missouri.

[4] Region V: North Dakota, South Dakota, Nebraska, Kansas, Montana, Wyoming, Colorado, New Mexico, and Oklahoma.

SOURCE: Lance E. Davis, "The Investment Market, 1870–1914: The Evolution of a National Market," *The Journal of Economic History*, XXV (1965).

were burdensome—therefore the Alliance was to set up its own companies. The prices of binder twine and agricultural machines had to be regulated. Overshadowing all other concerns were the derelictions of the railroads ("the robberies of the railroad corporations"): they were avoiding or escaping taxation; rates were too high because of excessive capitalization; the lieu lands were a source of deep vexation. As late as 1893, the Minnesota Alliance wanted no part of the Sub-Treasury plan.

The Plains Country   It is to the Great Plains themselves that we are to look for an explanation of the real basis of Western farm discontent. Starting at about the 98th meridian and running through western and southern Kansas, northeast Colorado, northwest Nebraska, southwest South Dakota, and much of central and western North Dakota is the Plains country. To the east, the prairies have an annual rainfall in excess of twenty inches a year and are covered with tall grass. In some areas, stands of trees are to be found. Once the tough prairie sod was plowed, it was easy to plant wheat; and, when the land became too expensive, corn—because of the regularity of rainfall and the warm humid nights.

The Great Plains are something else again. They are covered by short-grass vegetation; the rainfall averages less than twenty inches a year, and in fact shifts unpredictably with no recognizable pattern. When rain does come to the Plains it is often concentrated in violent cloudbursts of short duration, causing most of the rainfall to be ineffective. The region is also characterized by higher than average winds and great variation in extreme temperature. The Plains can be cultivated either by a regular rotation of the small grains with fallow, to permit moisture and nitrates to accumulate in the soil, or by irrigation. Otherwise, when the dust storms come, the light topsoil is blown away.

Before the Civil War—indeed, for the whole period 1830-60—there was relatively little rainfall on the Plains, so that the entire region, in meteorological terms, took on the aspect of a semiarid rather than a dry subhumid zone. To early Americans this vast area stretching west of the Missouri River to the foothills of the Rocky Mountains came to be known as "The Great American Desert." The rains came again in the 1870s and continued with some regularity until 1887, but John W. Powell, formerly of the U. S. Army, now turned geologist, was not fooled. He had begun his famous explorations of the Far West in 1867 and the more he continued his penetration of the area the more disturbed he became.

In 1879 Powell wrote for the Secretary of the Interior his epoch-making paper, "Lands of the Arid Region of the United States," in which he argued for a complete change in the land-use pattern of the Plains country. His suggestions revolved about these three points. First, all arid lands were to be classified as mineral, forest, pasture, or irrigable, with no cultivation outside the irrigation districts. Secondly, there should be a change in the system of land survey to conform with the available water supply; that is, the artificial geometrical pattern (which did well enough for the prairies) should be abandoned. Thirdly, the land system of the Plains was to be adapted to the needs of irrigators and cattlemen who were the only settlers capable of using the land efficiently. Irrigation districts of not less than nine settlers were to be established, each farmer receiving 80 acres of land; cattlemen were to be organized in similar units of nine or more with each to receive 2,500 acres of grazing land in those sections where water was available.

Powell's admonitions fell on deaf ears. Lulled into security by the adequate rainfall of almost two decades legislators, farmers, and the railroads were prepared to believe that prairie and Plain were much the same. The result was, settlers pressed farther and farther westward, coming from eastern Kansas, Iowa, Illinois, and Minnesota; that is to say, from areas that had been settled twenty to forty years previously. In 1900, the home State of the largest number of North Dakota settlers had been Minnesota; the largest number of western Kansas settlers came from eastern Kansas and Iowa. Indeed, Iowa, which was the richest agricultural State in the Union, lost population during the decade of the 1880s.

Why this large internal movement—which lasted until 1887 and then dropped off so drastically within the next eight years? There were four reasons for the first and only one for the second.

Many of the homesteaders were speculators. As land values shot up in eastern Kansas and Nebraska and in Iowa, homesteaders sold out and took up claims or bought land in the western regions. Credit for land purchase was easy, either from the railroads or from land mortgage companies. Those who moved west had every reason to assume that their land values would rise, too. Said a contemporary Dakotan of the earlier settlers of the Territory:

Even the homesteader in most cases seems to be a land speculator. In one county homesteaded eight years ago, four-fifths of the homesteaders have now quit the land. They either sold outright or borrowed on a mortgage and abandoned their claim. In other words, most of the homesteaders were not seeking a home but a speculation in land. . . . The average farmer is one third farmer and two thirds speculator.

Secondly, the new settlers were wheatgrowers; and wheat must be planted on lands of low cost. The steady improvement in farm machinery—sulky plows, harvesters, and threshers—and their declining costs made it possible for a family to plant and harvest at least two quarter sections, if not more. There was no human labor required other than for the plowing, heading, and threshing. Land costs were low and so were overhead costs. Also, in the 1870s, two improvements in the milling industry furthered the great expansion of so-called hard wheat, to which the area is adapted. The introduction of the middlings purifier permitted the saving of the glutinous portion of the wheat which had previously been boiled out with the bran. And the wider use of rollers (brought over from Europe) permitted the elimination of the excessive heat characteristic of the earlier millstones and therefore the production of a high-grade flour. What happened in the Dakota Territory was also occurring in other sections of the Plains country. Dakota's population in 1880 was 36,000 and its wheat harvest less than 3 million bushels; in 1885, population had climbed to 152,000 and the wheat crop was 38 million bushels.

Thirdly, railroads—encouraged by States and counties with all sorts of assistance, including the financial help of railroad-bond purchases and cash grants—pushed their feeder lines into every part of the region. In Kansas, railroad mileage in the 1880s grew from 3,100 to 8,800; in Nebraska, from 1,600 to 5,600; in Dakota, in 1888, there were 4,400 miles of track, with new building going in at the rate of 800 miles a year. In this open country, railroad construction costs were low; in western Kansas, where the railroad fever was highest, public subsidies were so generous that they frequently paid the whole cost of building. Too, the lines (those of the Missouri Pacific, the Burlington, the Atchison, and the Rock Island) were parallel and competing; so that, when the boom was over—in 1887—the state of Kansas had only a few points where a farmer could not find a station within from 10 to 15 miles of his home to market his produce. Kansas, with its sparse population and no industry other than agriculture, had a railroad mileage in excess of New York's and more than all of New England's!

The railroads did everything they could to promote settlement. They established land departments and sold land on easy credit terms. Thus the Burlington and Missouri (later the Chicago, Burlington, and Quincy), which had large land grants, sold land on either short-term credit (3 years) or long-term (10 years) with the interest rate in the neighborhood of 6 per cent. The average price for its Nebraska land was as little as $5.14 an acre. They offered to donate land for the establishment of academies and denominational colleges, as well as for town sites. Agents were established in Europe and ministers were sent abroad to interest fellow religionists in migrating to America. Henry Villard, the president of the Northern Pacific, set up a general European agency in Liverpool with more than seven hundred subagencies in the British Isles, Norway, Sweden, Holland, Switzerland, and Germany. James J. Hill's Great Northern Railroad, which pushed its fingers into every mile of the Dakota wheat country, thus sang the praises of Dakota's Red River Valley in a publication which flooded the Middle West and Europe:

Let mythology tell of the Gardens of the Hesperides, the mystical Elysiums; let poets rave of their vale of Tempe and Cashmire; let Egypt boast of her wonderous God-watered valley of the Nile, Italy of her olive-crowned slopes, and France of her vine clad hills, but in our glorious northwest there is a valley fairer and more fruitful than them all—the Red River Valley.

And in the fourth place, mortgage money was plentiful and rates were low. The land boom started in the mid-1870s and continued until 1887, when it reached its height—and then collapsed and disappeared for a whole decade. Land mortgage companies for the most part were organized in the West but obtained their capital by the sale of bonds in the East or in Europe, and from local bank loans. How numerous such companies were and how keen the competition among them may be noted from the fact that more than 150 such companies came under the supervision of the banking authorities of the states of Connecticut, Massachusetts, New York, and Vermont alone. Rates were quite moderate, considering the heavy risks involved with mortgaged farms so widely scattered that supervision of them by the companies was difficult. Rates kept on falling. In central Kansas, before the boom was swept away, a farmer with well-improved land could get mortgage money for 6 or 7 per cent; the commission, which went to the agent who wrote the loan, added another 2 per cent a year. In southwest Kansas, where the land was less well developed, by 1887, the maximum rate (including the commission) was about 11 per cent. Ten years earlier, the mortgage rate was 16 to 17 per cent—12 per cent for the interest and 4 to 5 per cent for the commission. The commission—of which Populists made so much—started by being 12 to 15 per cent and then dropped off to 10 per cent. It was the common practice to spread it over three years, which was usually the life of the mortgage. If the mortgagee found difficulty in making his mortgage payments, he had no trouble in getting a chattel mortgage—on his equipment and livestock—as well; this he obtained from local bankers.

When the bubble burst in 1887—due to the cessation of rain, a series of very severe winters, and low prices for wheat—bankruptcy followed for farmers and for most of the land mortgage companies. Beginning with 1887, and continuing for ten years, rainfall became a trickle; during this decade there were only two years in which the Great Plains farmers were able to produce full crops. For five of the ten years there were virtually no crops at all. During 1886-87, in particular, blizzards decimated the herds on the open ranges.

AGRICULTURE

One of the greatest of the land mortgage companies, the J. B. Watkins Land Mortgage Company of Kansas, had been founded in 1873; had opened offices in New York and London in 1876; and in the eighties had pushed its activities into Nebraska and Dakota. By 1893, it had supervised the sale of obligations totalling $18 million, of which $5 million had been in debenture bonds. On these latter it paid an annual dividend of 10 per cent. But as a result of foreclosures (with taxes still to be paid) and no takers for the abandoned land, the Watkins Company was forced into bankruptcy in 1894.

Panic swept over Dakota, Kansas, and Nebraska—and people streamed out of the blighted areas. In six counties in southwest Kansas alone, population dropped from 6,872 in 1890 to 2,633 in 1900. In the whole of Kansas, during 1889-93, 11,122 farms were foreclosed. In 1895, in fifteen Kansas counties, 75 to 90 per cent of the land was owned by land companies, which themselves were in receivership. Not only farms but the new boom towns were affected; those who fled left behind heavy tax burdens incurred as a result of local improvements and aid so lavishly granted to the railroads.

TABLE 9

Average for	Wheat		Silver per oz.
	s.	d.	s.
1867–77	54	6	58½
1878–87	40	–	50 –
1885–94	30	6	42½
1885	32	10	50¹¹⁄₁₆
1890	31	11	47¹¹⁄₁₆
1894	22	11	28¹¹⁄₁₆

SOURCE: *The Economist, 1843-1894*, 1943, pp. 138-54.

The collapse in the Great Plains was due to prolonged drought—and, strangely enough, to a fall in wheat prices. Liverpool was the world's clearing house for wheat and because Britain was the largest single purchaser, the British import price set the world price (and not the skulduggeries of American bankers and grain dealers in the Chicago exchange, as the Populists wished to believe). As Table 9 shows, Sauerbeck, the English statistician, recorded the drop in wheat prices over the period 1867-1894. The figures are in shillings and pence per quarter, or 8 bushels. They are compared with the price of silver.

It will be observed that the price of wheat dropped more sharply than the price of silver, or prices generally. Sauerbeck's index of 45 commodities (largely representing British imports) showed that from 1867-77 (average) to 1894, prices fell 37 per cent. That of corn declined 39 per cent; the price of beef 26 per cent; of pork 15 per cent; and of bacon, 20 per cent. (These were important Middle West exports to Britain—and their prices help to explain why the Middle West was not interested in Populism.) On the other hand, the wheat price from 1867-77 to 1894 declined 49 per cent.

The explanation for what was happening to wheat prices is twofold. Transportation rates from Chicago to New York and from New York to Liverpool declined steeply. During the years 1873-75, the carriage of a bushel of wheat from Chicago to New York fell from 34 cents to 17 cents; the movement downward continued steadily until by 1905 the rate was as low as 8 cents. During 1879-85, the ocean freight rate from New York to Liverpool dropped from 12 cents to 5 cents a bushel and fluctuated around 5 cents for the next 15 years.

More important was the opening up of new areas of wheat-growing so that, beginning with 1885, American wheat surpluses no longer controlled the world market. Two great areas expanded their supplies and exports and at a greater rate than did the United States. The first was the freshly opened up countries of Canada, Australia, and Argentina—due to easy land laws, railroad-building, and the encouragement of European immigration. The second was the great central and eastern European plain, made up of the Danube Basin (present-day Bulgaria, Hungary, Rumania, Yugoslavia) and Poland and Russia. Here, railroad construction and easier credit made possible greater wheat surpluses. Acreage expanded, production increased, and lower-cost wheat for the whole world resulted.

Expressed in five-year averages, Argentina's wheat acreage grew from 2 million acres during 1885-89 to 8.87 million acres during 1899-1904; Australia's, in the same period, from 3.31 million acres to 5.43 million acres; Canada's, from 2.58 million acres to 4.14 million acres; the six European exporting countries expanded from 57.26 million acres to 75.48 million acres. The American increase was considerably smaller— from 48.55 million acres to 59 million acres. In consequence, whereas American wheat acreage represented 86 per cent of the growing land of the four overseas exporting countries during 1885-89, it stood at 76 per cent during 1899-1904.

A similar story can be told of cotton. Larger American supplies beginning with 1870 (acreage increased from 9.2 million acres in that year to 21.9 million acres in 1894 and 30 million acres in 1904), plus new cotton lands opened up in Egypt, India, and Russia, depressed world prices.

Nevertheless, to the Populist leaders of the late 1880s and the early 1890s, the reason for Western and Southern malaise was "a conspiracy against the people"—made up of the organized money power, the railroads, the local grain and cotton dealers, and the terminal elevator operators.

A word about the last. The commercial organization of the grain trade—the assembling, handling, inspecting, grading, financing, transporting in bulk—plus the vast railroad net, made the American wheat trade the most efficient in the world and helps account for its leadership in world markets during the 1870s, 1880s, and 1890s. American methods were closely studied by foreign observers; they sang their praises and sought to emulate them. Curiously enough, one of America's triumphs was the establishment of the futures market: an institution that came under such bitter condemnation from the Populists and their sympathizers. (Note, for example, Frank Norris' novel *The Pit*.) Futures trading, linked with the financial resources traders could command, made possible the orderly carry-over of surpluses; and, on the other side of the shield, their movement into markets when prices rose. The traders, as Morton Rothstein points out (*Mississippi Valley Historical Review*, December, 1960), by "protecting millers, dealers, and exporters from losses . . . helped to narrow the difference between the average price paid to farmers and the average price charged to the ultimate consumer."

Nevertheless, "People's Money, People's Land, People's Transportation" would solve all the problems that beset the two regions. Escape from the money power lay in the creation of a greater money supply through either the Sub-Treasury loans of the Southern Alliance or the free and unlimited coinage of silver. All prices, of course, would go up in consequence: the prices the farmers paid as well as the prices they received. Monetary inflation, in any event, could not affect favorably the world prices for wheat and cotton—unless American surpluses were entirely segregated from world markets. The last the New Deal tried during the 1930s in the interests of restoring American farm purchasing power. Its successes were no greater than the Populists' could have been.

From 1897 on, the skies began to brighten: as more and more intensive farming replaced extensive; as reliance upon the domestic market replaced the foreign; as devices of self-help—farm cooperatives—made for improved and orderly marketing, the utilization of surpluses, mass purchasing of supplies and implements parts. Up to the 1920s demands for reform and currency tinkering became small, still voices.

CHAPTER SEVEN

THE RAILROADS

The Most Important American Industry   The most important industry that gave spur to America's impressive economic advance in the post-Civil War period was the railroad. The railroad opened the trans-Mississippi West and made possible the quick settlement of the wheat and cattle countries. It hastened the development of iron and steel. It was a key factor in encouraging immigration—of families of men, women and children who came to take up farms in the Western country and of young men attracted by employment opportunities on the railroad construction gangs. (In the 1880s as many as 200,000 men were working at any given date building the railroads; the greater number were recently arrived immigrants.) It bound the country together politically and economically. It absorbed a growing part of domestic savings and the greater proportion of foreign capital flowing into the United States because of the country's political stability and the higher rate of interest such investments offered.

The railroad industry produced a whole new generation of entrepreneurs and innovators: a company of men who were at once alert to the possibilities of building fortunes out of the creation and financing of railway companies, and who worked, with varying degrees of ingenuity and success, to make these companies profitable by constructing, or buying or leasing, branch and feeder lines and by the constant improvements of the original properties: double-tracking roads, re-laying rights of way, eliminating curves and grades, throwing bridges over rivers and digging tunnels through mountains, substituting steel for iron rails, acquiring better-built and heavier locomotives and cars.

These men, particularly those associated with the Western roads, were innovators and risk-takers in the real sense; starting as they did in the 1860s, when domestic savings were still not adequate, they had to develop imaginative (and, by our reading today, suspect) devices to obtain the necessary funds. They saw opportunity writ large in linking the Pacific coast with the Mississippi River, and they spun out their intricate network in anticipation of traffic and in fact even before settlement. They accepted the competitive market structure; roads were built to compete with each other. Survival and growth were possible, therefore, only as a result of the lowering of rates, the improvement of management and services, and the reduction of costs.

Here, the railroad construction in the United States during the three decades of the 1860s, 1870s and 1880s sharply departed from the pattern that had appeared in the Eastern section of the country during 1830-60. Railroads, certainly up to the 1850s, had been built—promoted by city merchants and in part financed by them and their municipalities—initially to serve already settled country, to open hinterlands and connect them with seacoast ports and the cities and towns on water systems or on canals. They were necessarily short lines. The gauges that were used varied from region to region. They were employed as a rule to carry less-than-carload freight; the bulky traffic—wheat and flour, cotton, coal, timber—was to move on the flatboats and barges of the rivers and canals. Hence, no trunk systems were conceived of or designed. Those trunk railroads that emerged in the East—the New York Central, the Erie, the Pennsylvania, the Baltimore and Ohio, the Albany and Maine—were put together later from bits and pieces as the possibilities of through traffic and the inadequacies of the rivers and canals (because they could not be kept open during the whole year) came to be understood. The railroads, then, in the beginning, did not open unsettled country and they did not compete with each other.

The same was true of Great Britain and, when the railroads came to be built on the European continent, of France, Germany, Austria, Russia. Another important difference must be observed. Except for Great Britain, where railroads, as in the United States, were privately owned, the European nations built their railroads almost entirely out of public funds and generally continued to operate them as public monopolies. The result was that, after the Civil War, railroads were constructed faster in the United States; in time they were built better; and by the

1890s—when the American railroad net was finished—they served literally every city and good-sized town with more than one connection. Communities of 10,000 to 20,000 inhabitants could boast of at least two railroads from which to choose for passenger or freight service. And as for New York and Chicago, on them converged railroads from every section of the country and from countless interior districts.

There can be no question that the United States paid a price for this kind of dog-eat-dog entrepreneurship. The process was ruthless and wasteful. The depression of the 1870s, the sharp recession of 1883-84, and the depression of the 1890s undoubtedly originated from railroad overbuilding and at the same time took a heavy toll, in the form of bankruptcy, in railroad failures. There was widespread corruption: the bribery of public officials, members of legislatures, judges, to obtain charters, public assistance, tax exemptions, the flotation of additional stock issues. Stock-watering, largely for the purposes of obtaining additional capital but frequently also to line the pockets of promoters, speculators, and their political henchmen, was the rule. Because there was a bitter struggle over through traffic and the chief weapons were rate-cutting and rebates to large shippers, interior communities and the smaller men (farmers, little factory owners) not in a position to benefit from this sort of competition had to pay higher for short hauls and for less-than-carload shipments.

Had the federal government been willing, which it never was, to build the Western railroad itself, these evils might have been avoided. It would not have built so rapidly or so imaginatively; it probably (considering the timid, procrastinating nature of public functionaries) would not have pushed modernization so swiftly, taking the chances, as the private entrepreneurs did, that earnings would eventually catch up with the constant fresh injections of capital that railroad modernization required.

J. A. Schumpeter, who studied the American rails and their revolutionary impact on the whole economy more closely than anyone else, in *Business Circles* (1939), came to this conclusion, and the writer agrees:

My conviction is that had it been politically feasible to entrust an ideal civil servant with the dictatorial power over all railroad matters and all land, this individual would have produced the same ultimate results at incomparably smaller economic and moral costs. But the point is that no such individual was possible in the milieu of those times and that had he been possible, he would have been lynched immediately by the very people whose pocketbooks and cultural attitudes he would have been protecting.

As early as 1850, William H. Seward, then Senator from New York, called for large land grants to the company seeking to build the Illinois Central, even at the risk of foregoing federal earnings from land sales. He declared that

the best and highest interests of the people of the United States in regard to this domain is not to derive from it the highest amount of current revenue, but it is to bring them into cultivation and settlement in the shortest space of time and under the most favorable circumstances.

The *Commercial and Financial Chronicle,* in 1873, after the first great post-Civil War building spurt had been completed, said:

Our new railroads increase the value of farms and open new markets for their products. They lessen the time and cost of travel. They give a value to commodities otherwise almost worthless. They concentrate population, stimulate production, and raise wages by making labor more efficient.

And so spoke Senator S. M. Cullom of Illinois in 1886, recommending Congressional passage of the bill that became the Interstate Commerce Act:

Had the railroads grown up under systematic regulation, the commercial relations of the railroad to the community would doubtless have been more satisfactory, but on the other hand it cannot be doubted that expansion would not have been so rapid. A method of uniform regulation adopted at the outset might have prevented a needless waste of capital and obviated or mitigated certain existing evils, but it would assuredly have retarded the building up of the country in comparison with the progress attained under freedom from legislative restrictions.

Two further contemporary witnesses may be cited. James Bryce, that wise and discerning foreign visitor, wrote of the railroad "Kings" (so he called them) of the United States and their methods in his first edition of *The American Commonwealth* in 1888.

War is the natural state of an American railway towards all other authorities and its own fellows, just as war was the natural state of cities towards one another in the ancient world. . . . The president of a great railroad needs gifts for strategical combinations scarcely inferior to those, if not of a great general, yet of a great war minister. . . . If his line extends into a new country, he must be quick to seize the best routes,—the best physically, because they will be cheaper to operate, the best in agricultural or mineral resources, because they will offer a greater prospect of traffic. He must so throw out his branches as not only to occupy promising tracts, but keep his competing enemies at a distance; he must annex small lines when he sees a chance, first "bearing" their stocks so as to get them cheaper; he must make a close alliance with at least one other great line, which completes his communications with the East or the farther West, and be prepared to join this ally in a conflict with some threatening competitor. . . .

And thus wrote S. F. Van Oss, another Englishman, in his authoritative work, originally published in Britain, *American Railroads as Investments,* in 1893. He is speaking of the part competition played in the rapid construction of the American rail net:

One of the most prominent among its salutary effects was that it contributed substantially to the growth of the country. . . . Without low rates, the result of competition, agriculture would be impossible in many regions flourishing with low transportation charges; and thus competition actually made business. . . . Further, competition improved trains and passenger as well as goods service. . . . It also perfected the Americans in the art of moving freights cheaply, an art in which they are unexcelled.

Van Oss then proceeded to give some examples of what competition was doing to serve the American economy. First he contrasted Liverpool and Manchester, on the one side, with Chicago and St. Louis, on the other. The two English cities had between them a population of 1.6 million and a country tributary to the railways serving them of 4 million people. Between these two great centers there were only three direct and different railway connections. Chicago and St. Louis had between them a population of 1.75 million and a hinterland in Illinois alone of 4 million. Seven different railways ran and competed between these two cities. He pointed out, in further exemplification of his argument, that there were four direct lines between Omaha and Denver, five between Chicago and Cincinnati, six between St. Paul and Kansas City, and seven between Chicago and Des Moines. The best, and most extreme, example he found of this kind of intense rivalry was the services available to shippers between New York and New Orleans. There were 106 railway lines that could be used between the two points, varying in length from 1,180 to 2,053 miles; but rates were the same on all of them for through shipments.

Building the Railroads   It was not until 1835 that the railroad pattern took shape in the United States: steam locomotives fired by wood and then anthracite coal were to haul cars for passengers and freight using flanged wheels, on tracks covered with iron over fixed roadbeds. The railroads grew slowly for almost a decade and a half. In 1830 there were only 23 miles of line; in 1840 2,818 miles (as against 3,326 miles of canal); and in 1850, 8,929 miles (as against 3,700 miles of canal). From 1850 to 1855, the miles of track more than doubled; and from 1855 to 1860 (really up to 1857) almost doubled again, so that in 1860, mileage totaled 30,626. In the decade of the 1850s, the new construction largely took place in the Middle Atlantic, Middle Western and Southern States. But short lines were running West of the Mississippi River into Iowa and Missouri, and a little building had already been begun in California and Oregon. Trunk systems had appeared in the Erie and the Baltimore and Ohio. The Illinois Central, from Chicago to Mobile, was operated as a single company. In 1853, nine small companies between Albany and Buffalo were combined to form the New York Central Railroad. The Pennsylvania, operating from Philadelphia to Harrisburg, was pushing across the Alleghenies to reach Pittsburgh before the decade was over.

Yet, when the Civil War ended, it could scarcely be claimed that even the Eastern United States had an integrated or an efficient railway system. It is true, to the enthusiast, and Albert Fishlow is one such (see his *American Railroads and the Transformation of the Ante-Bellum Economy,* 1965), there seemed to be what he calls an "articulated national network." It was possible to travel from New York to Chicago or St. Louis or Dubuque, Iowa, by an all-rail route, but not by a single trunk system. The then so-called West (the Middle Western States and Iowa) had almost 10,000 miles of road, and Chicago, by 1860, saw ten different lines entering the city and, with twenty branch and feeder roads, was reaching 4,000 miles. But in the South, where there had been a good deal of building in the late 1850s, the railroads fed the ocean and gulf ports rather than running east and west or north and south; and even here, water transportation continued to be the preferred, and cheaper, form of carriage.

Given the great spurt in building from 1855 to 1860 and the linking of roads together, Fishlow admits, to quote him (and this belies the title of his book):

What the railroads did *not* do before the Civil War was to forge a national market. The primitive state of physical integration not only prevented it, but probably also testifies to its unimportance. There were too few economies of scale in production, or distribution, to be reaped from direct rail contact and that is one reason why overtures in that direction were so limited. This was still a period before interchange of parts was universal, before standard products were marketed, before the full effects of industrialization were apparent, let alone realized.

In addition, before the Civil War, there were no important bridges over wide rivers. The diversity of gauges, especially in the South, made costly and slow the cross-country shipment of freight. Wooden bridges, iron rails, light locomotives, small-capacity cars, manual braking and coupling kept down the volume and speed of freight movements—and costs were high. Water transportation still competed successfully with the rails: in fact, wheat, corn, timber and a good deal of coal moved eastward on riverboats and canal barges. As late as 1860, all the New York canals carried more freight tonnage than did the two Erie and New York Central through-systems.

What were still to come were the great Western railroads, and technological innovations—in steel rails, heavier and more efficient locomotives, larger cars of steel, the safety coupler and automatic air brakes, and iron bridges to span America's mighty rivers.

There were three great railroad construction booms: from 1866 to 1873; from 1879 to 1883; and from 1886 to 1892. In the first, total mileage in the United States was doubled, and the country's first Pacific Railroad, from Omaha, Nebraska, to Sacramento, California, was completed. In the single year 1871, 7,400 miles of track were laid down. In the second boom, total construction was 40,000 track-miles. In 1881 alone, building was almost 10,000 miles and in 1882, 11,600 miles. In the third boom, total construction was almost 50,000 miles. In 1887, building reached its zenith with 13,000 miles of track laid. By 1893, the job was virtually finished; then the United States had 176,500 miles of track.

The Transcontinental Railroads   As early as 1845, Americans began to consider seriously the building of a transcontinental railway and, in fact, eight years later Congress authorized government engineers to make surveys of the Western regions for likely routes. They suggested five. At this point, Congress became deadlocked because Southern spokesmen refused to give their assent to any route to the Pacific other than one that ran through the South and Southwest; with this veto, planning but not discussion ceased. The outbreak of the Civil War and the departure of Southern men from Washington united Congress. In 1862, Congress passed (and amended in 1864) the Pacific Railway Act and chartered a private company, the Union Pacific Railroad, which was to build a railroad from Omaha, Nebraska, to the western boundary of Utah. This was to be joined by another, the Central Pacific Railroad (a California corporation), that was to start from Sacramento, California, and build eastward until it met the Union Pacific. These were through lines, using what came to be known as the standard gauge of 4 feet 8½ inches; thus the Western plains and the Rocky Mountains were to be crossed and the whole of California linked with the rest of the United States.

Congress, for the most part, and many ordinary citizens as well, were not convinced that such a road, traversing unsettled territory (as far as whites were concerned), would be profitable. But the possibilities offered were compelling. The road would bind California to the Union and open her markets to the Middle West. It would make practicable the orderly settlement of the Plains and protect farmers and herders from the roaming Plains Indians. It would facilitate the movement of troops and military supplies for the defense of the long Pacific coastline against foreign penetration and perhaps even attack. There would be immense social gains (in the language of the economist, "external economies") to the whole nation: this was the greater vision and one that was magnificently realized in less than a single generation. Thus, one of the senators voiced the same sanguine hope that had prompted Seward to support the construction of the Illinois Central. He said:

Our population would be increased, our resources developed, and the continent covered with people and states from the Atlantic to the Pacific. Our wealth would be more than doubled; so would our products. A new impulse would be given to our agriculture, manufacturing, mining, commercial, and navigating interests.

To realize this, the two companies, which would do their own financing and building, needed help of a massive kind. This was made available through land grants and mortgage loans. The Union Pacific and the Central Pacific were to receive free the rights of way and the timber, earth and stone they needed from the public lands. They were to get ten alternate sections (a section was 640 acres, or a square mile) on each side of the right of way for each mile of track laid down. (The alternations between railroad land grants and government—or settled—sections made a checkerboard pattern.) Beyond the 10 miles on each side of the right of way was established another belt of indemnity land from which the roads could compensate themselves if the alternate sections granted them had already been entered by settlers. (These were the so-called lieu lands, over which much controversy later raged because all the land-grant railroads dragged their feet about surveying or releasing this region to private settlement.) Finally, the railroads were to receive government loans (subordinated to a railroad first mortgage in 1864) as soon as every 20-mile stretch was completed and approved. The railroad builders were to be lent $16,000 for every mile completed in level country, $32,000 for every mile built in the foothills, and $48,000 for every mile in mountainous territory. In return—using the example of the earlier wagon roads—the railroads were to "be and remain a public highway for the use of the government of the United States, free from toll or other charge upon the transportation of any property or troops of the United States." (The Supreme Court, later, because the railroads furnished the equipment, fixed the rates for the government at 50 per cent of the ordinary charges; and mail carriage was set at 80 per cent of the regular mail rate.)

It was anticipated that the moneys realized from the sale of the public lands and the loans made available would provide one-half of the necessary capital. This turned out to be wholly illusory. Neither the backers of the Union Pacific (Thomas C. Durant and Oakes and Oliver Ames) nor those of the Central Pacific (Collis P. Huntington, Leland Stanford, Mark Hopkins, and Charles Crocker) had the necessary funds themselves, nor could they command enough from the sale of stock or borrowings from banks. The result was that building lagged—and here we shall follow only the fortunes of the Union Pacific, although the Central Pacific was confronted by the same problems and used the same expedients to resolve them; workers could not be obtained, contractors paid, necessary equipment acquired. By July, 1866, the Union Pacific had laid down only some 300 miles of track. But the subordination of the government mortgage did open the door for further financing.

Thus appeared the Credit Mobilier (charted in Pennsylvania and owned by some seven persons who also owned most of the Union Pacific stock), which was to build the rest of the railroad—meaning that it was to raise the necessary capital. The Credit Mobilier was capitalized at $4 million and, of course, most of this had to be raised. The career of the Credit Mobilier (the same was true of the Crocker Construction Company in connection with the Central Pacific) was devious and shady: public officials were bribed; labor was sweated (the Chinese who built the Central Pacific lived in virtual slavery); extravagant profits were made by the insiders. In any event—exactly because capital was obtained quickly— the roads were built.

In 1867, construction could now be resumed in earnest. Discharged soldiers, Irish immigrants, and Chinese coolies (on the Central Pacific) filled the work camps and labored in a veritable frenzy to complete the task. Marauding Indians, the parching heat of the deserts, the rigors of mountain winter, the absence of creature comforts of the most elementary kind—none of these was permitted to interfere in the task of spanning the continent. To spur the builders on, the Central Pacific was to be allowed to go east beyond the California border; the Union Pacific, too, could go as far west as its resources would permit. Throughout the winter of 1868 men toiled in the mountains, in one day laying down as much as 8 miles of track. That winter saw 20,000 men engaged in railroad building. By the spring of 1869, both gangs were in western Utah; on May 10 of that year their work was finished when locomotive head touched locomotive head at Promontory, Utah, 30 miles west of Brigham, and the last spike was driven into the ties.

What did the Union Pacific cost? What profits did the trustees of the Credit Mobilier make? What was the road capitalized at when it was running—that is, how much stock-watering took place?

Professor R. W. Fogel, in the latest study of the financing of the Union Pacific, comes to the conclusion that the road cost $59 million to build. To do this the company (for the most part through the Credit Mobilier) sold or borrowed against the $27.2 million it got in government bonds; the $27.2 million of its own first mortgage bonds; the $10.4 million of its own land-grant bonds; and the $9.3 million of its own income bonds. It also sold stock, for which it got $11 million. Its own securities were, of course, not sold at their face value; the land-grant bonds, for example, were discounted at at least 40 per cent. At the same time the Credit Mobilier was compelled to pay from 1 to 1½ per cent monthly for the money it had to borrow to turn over to subcontractors and suppliers.

At the end of 1872, the promoters, who also controlled the Credit Mobilier, thereby getting the contracts and letting them out, had for themselves $9 million in cash and the Union Pacific stock they had voted themselves, which was then worth in cash $11 million. This came to $20 million; and by another calculation, Professor Fogel reduces the profit to $11.1 million; either sum is considerably less than the $44 million the Congressional Committee, investigating the scandals, charged the insiders with having obtained.

Having in mind the risky nature of the enterprise Durant and the Ameses were embarking on, it is the considered opinion of Professor Fogel that the profits obtained from construction were not too high. they were trying to raise money to build a road whose immediate prospects, if any, were highly dubious, they were taking chances with their own funds, and they were gambling that the Union Pacific's securities would rise high enough to permit them to pull out their own investments and also make a profit.

Ironically, the original promoters, D. C. Durant and Oakes Ames, who risked their personal fortunes, were not among the beneficiaries. Ames went bankrupt and Durant was hard hit financially as a result of the heavy personal loans he had incurred which had been secured by the bonds of the railroad; in 1870, these had dropped so sharply in value that he had been sold out by the banks. Three other persons in the group had also suffered the same fate and by January, 1871, all these men were out of the Union Pacific. At that time the land-grant bonds were selling at 53, the income bonds at 32, and the common stock at 9.

By 1879, the book value of the Union Pacific's obligations was $114 million (against the real cost of construction of $59 million). The excessive capitalization the railroad had to carry—it has been said here that the issue of watered securities was one way of monetizing the future economic earnings of the railroads and making the entire country assume the burden of the capital creation that resulted—got the Union Pacific into difficulties repeatedly. This, plus mismanagement. If the government had built the road it might have done so at a lesser cost, but it would have taken longer. There was not, however—the debates in Congress in 1862 clearly proved this—the slightest chance that any one was disposed to have the government embark on so chancy an undertaking. In any event, in this youthful period of risky private enterprise, the bold and unscrupulous, when successful, made a good deal of money; stockholders sometimes gained and sometimes lost; and the American nation, in a generation, realized large social returns from increases in the national income, savings to private shippers, and significant benefits to the federal government itself in the cheap carriage of its troops, property, and the mails.

The Effects of Competition Because of the help so quickly and generously given by federal, State, county and city governments to so many of the Western railroads—as we have already seen—it was inevitable that overbuilding should take place. The railroads had to scramble for the traffic in the fierce competitive race, sending out branches and leasing short lines in order to push their fingers into every area where pay freight could be picked up. Thus, the so-called Granger Roads of the livestock and grain country crossed and recrossed one another. Out of Chicago and running westward were the Chicago and Northwestern, the Chicago, Rock Island and Pacific, the Chicago and Alton, the Chicago, Milwaukee and St. Paul, and the Chicago, Burlington, and Quincy. Even the Union Pacific's monopoly was a brief one, for the Northern Pacific was completed in 1883 and the Great Northern in 1893. In the East, there were five great trunk lines—the Grand Trunk (for the most part Canadian, but dipping into the United States), the New York Central, the Pennsylvania, the Erie, and the Baltimore and Ohio. By 1880, there were already twenty competitive routes from St. Louis to Atlanta, available to shippers, their lengths varying from 526 miles to 1855 miles.

To mitigate the rigors of this competitive strife, all sorts of devices were attempted with varying degrees of success. The anthracite-coal railroads of the Middle Atlantic States—the Philadelphia and Reading, Lehigh Valley, Delaware and Hudson, Delaware, Lackawanna and Western, Central of New Jersey—bought coal lands and became coal operators. Boards of directors of bituminous coal companies and those of the railroads carrying their coal became interlocked and tying agreements followed. Rebates were granted large customers. Where traffic involved a particular commodity and heavy competition for it existed (petroleum, meat products), so-called evener devices were set up to apportion the business on a pro-rata basis among the roads. The South Improvement Company, a creation of the Rockefeller interests, was an effort in this direction. It failed, because of public protest—and because such under-standings could not be enforced in the law courts.

The same was true of railroad pools. These sought to apportion terri-tories, or divide traffic, or divide or even earnings. Hundreds of such agreements were entered into and did not survive for long, for rather obvious reasons. They were in violation of the common law and there-fore not enforceable. Participants in pools, having learned something of the methods and financial position of rivals, took advantage to reduce their own costs, and either cheated or demanded reapportionment and larger prorations. Leaks occurred, and public hostility forced the aban-donment of pools. We shall see in greater detail, in our examination of the Western railroads, how efforts at the establishment of pools really got nowhere.

This competition had brought economic effects, all salutary to the country at large. It forced the lowering of rates, and therefore more efficient railroading. Classifications of commodities were constantly being changed, and rates were dropped in the process; as a result, the roads found it possible to compete with water transport for the carriage of heavy goods. Discounts were offered for carload lots; and this stimulated the appearance of independent freight companies which could assemble small shipments for common destinations.

In Table 10, Kirkland demonstrates how changes in all classifications fell in the westward movement from New York to Chicago, from May, 1865, to December, 1888. The prices shown are in cents per 100 pounds.

TABLE 10

	First class	Second class	Third class	Fourth class
May, 1865	215	180	106	96
December, 1888	75	65	50	35

SOURCE: E. C. Kirkland, *Industry Comes of Age,* 1961, p. 94.

The case of Western products moving eastward from Chicago to New York was similar. The prices again are in cents per 100 pounds. During the years 1866-1897, the price for the carriage of wheat fell from 65 cents to 20 cents, or 70 per cent. (In the same period, wholesale prices dropped 60 per cent.) During the years 1870-1899, the price for the carriage of dressed beef fell from 90 cents to 40 cents, or 55 per cent. (In the same period, wholesale prices dropped 43 per cent.) The railroads could afford to do this because of declines in the prices they had to pay for steel rails and coal; and because—as we shall see—of technological and operational innovations and therefore greater efficiency.

In time, the railroads became the butt of farmer discontent. Rates were higher in the West than in the East (yet, there was a point here: for there was no two-way traffic; the freight cars shipped the cattle and grain eastward, and returned westward virtually empty); short hauls carried higher charges than did long ones; rebating was common; so were favors to larger shippers, particularly warehousemen and elevator operators, at the expense of smaller ones. Much was made of the excessive capitalization of railroads and hence a heavy rate structure on a fraudulent valuation. Yet if all this was so, how was it that freight rates went steadily downward? In 1885, Charles Francis Adams, at that time president of the Union Pacific, as he viewed the profitable shipment of cattle 2,000 miles or more, and grains 1,500 to 1,800 miles, could say that this was done at rates which would have been considered in other countries "incredibly low."

Even the commonly voiced complaint that Western farmers were at the mercy of monopoly roads, which could charge all the traffic would bear, has little validity. The case of Jay Gould—the alleged wrecker of so many railroads—is an interesting one. During 1879-82, alone, he was responsible for the construction of more than 4,000 miles in the Northwest and Southwest, adding extensions and feeders to the Texas Pacific and the Union Pacific, but as well to the Wabash, the Missouri Pacific, and the Missouri, Kansas, and Texas. He cut rates, broke up rate structures and territorial agreements and traffic pools; and he forced competing lines to rebuild and extend and to meet his freight charges. During 1879-82 and 1886-87 there was a vast amount of building by the Burlington, the Rock Island, the Northwest, and the St. Paul, from all of which the Northern Alliance country benefited. There followed a general and permanent drop in the cost and a rise in the improvement of services.

Julius Grodinsky, in his *Transcontinental Railway Strategy, 1869-1893*, gives a painstaking analysis of the enormous amount of construction taking place in the Northwest and the Southwest during the great era of railroad building of 1879-89. Trunk lines were put together; feeder lines penetrating deep into pioneering country were built: much of this was highly competitive in terms of lines, rates, and services. Pools from time to time were set up and quickly failed, as railroad entrepreneurs engaged in life-and-death struggles (bankruptcy was frequent) for greater shares of the business.

The upshot was sharp rate reductions, exactly in the country where the complaints against the railroads and charges against their exactions were loudest.

Comparing 1879 with 1889, Table 11 shows the changes in miles of

TABLE 11

		1879	1889	Per cent changes
Atchison, Topeka and Santa Fe	Miles of road	996.9	7,110.2	+613.2
	Rate per ton-mile ..	2.122¢	1.228¢	− 42.1
Chicago, Burlington and Quincy	Miles of road	1,857.2	5,140	+176.8
	Rate per ton-mile ..	3.15¢	1.60¢	− 49.2
Chicago, Milwaukee and St. Paul	Miles of road	1,996	5,678	+184.5
	Rate per ton-mile ..	1.72¢	.99¢	− 42.5
Chicago and North-western	Miles of road	2,798	4,250	+ 51.9
	Rate per ton-mile ..	1.49¢	.98¢	− 34.2
Chicago, Rock Island and Pacific	Miles of road	1,257	3,266	+156.6
	Rate per ton-mile ..	1.21¢	1.02¢	− 15.7
Denver and Rio Grande	Miles of road	337	1,493	+343.0
	Rate per ton-mile ..	3.62¢	2.10¢	− 42.0
Missouri Pacific	Miles of road	421.5	5,019	+1,090.5
	Rate per ton-mile ..	1.19¢	1.13¢	− 5.1
Northern Pacific	Miles of road	1,193	3,778	+216.7
	Rate per ton-mile ..	2.59¢	1.40¢	− 46.0
St. Paul, Minneapolis and Manitoba (Great Northern)	Miles of road	656	3,006	+358.2
	Rate per ton-mile ..	2.88¢	1.27¢	− 55.9
Southern Pacific	Miles of road	2,360	6,052.4	+156.5
	Rate per ton-mile ..	2.75¢	1.77¢	− 35.6
Union Pacific	Miles of road	1,042	6,996	+571.4
	Rate per ton-mile ..	1.99¢	1.37¢	− 31.2

SOURCE: Julius Grodinsky, *Transcontinental Railway Strategy, 1869-1893: A Study of Businessmen,* 1962, pp. 414-17.

road operated and in rate charges per ton-mile, for the outstanding Western railway systems.

It will be seen that drops in rates per ton-mile were in the neighborhood of 40 per cent, with James J. Hill's road, the Great Northern, decreasing its rates by 55.9 per cent. (Gould's Missouri Pacific reduced its rates by only 5.1 per cent and his Union Pacific by 31.2 per cent—but his rates in 1879 had started out by being much lower than those of his competitors.) That these declines were *greater* than those of agricultural prices may be noted from the fact that the prices farmers received for wheat fell 37 per cent and for corn 25 per cent between the two years.

Yet there was one charge made against the railroads that was wholly valid, and again this had to do with their avoidance of taxation. The transcontinental railroads had been granted great areas of land, as a stimulus to construction, by the federal government and by many of the Western and Southern states. In 1872, the Commissioner of the General Land Office estimated, this had come to 150,000,000 acres. Some of it was not taken up because of failure to build—possibly 20 million acres. But of the rest, the railroads were slow (or failed entirely) to certify and patent more than two-thirds of their lands; because of uncertain ownership, in consequence, taxation was impossible. And the courts upheld the railroads. Thus, of the 12 million acres the Union Pacific received during 1871-96, it had patented only 4 million; the Central Pacific, out of 8 million acres, had patented only 2 million; the Northern Pacific, out of 47 million acres, only 20.5 million; the Kansas Pacific, out of 6 million acres, 2.5 million; the Southern Pacific, out of 6.7 million acres, only 2.6 million. It was not until 1886 that Congress finally declared that all railroad lands were to be taxed, whether or not formal patents had been issued.

Equally vexatious was the handling of lieu lands. Land-grant railroads had received alternate sections stretching variously 10 to 20 miles on each side of their rights of way; but some of these lands had already been entered by squatters; railroads were therefore permitted to take other lands in lieu of those pre-empted by settlers. These, too, they were in no hurry to patent. Much of this land was in forest or contained coal, iron, copper and other minerals. It took many years for these grievances to be satisfied.

Where the Capital Came From It has already been pointed out how railroad construction and initially operation as well were financed. It was done through loans: a series of mortgage bonds in some form of priority, bonds which were mortgages on equipment, on land grants, on income. Efforts were made to sell stock; but usually stock went gratis to promoters (and to politicians), to suppliers and contractors, and to the purchasers of junior bond issues. Bonds and stock were sold at discounts. In any event, these securities—whether held by promoters, railroad operators, contractors, or the public at large—were used as collateral for bank loans; in this fashion American banking played a significant role in the creation of railway capital.

The Western railroads could not have been built so swiftly nor the Eastern and Southern railroads modernized had not foreign capital been readily available. In the money markets of London, Amsterdam, and Berlin, American railway bonds were regarded as good risks: because of the faith and credit of the American government itself (it had always honored its obligations), because of the favorable American balance of payments (which permitted therefore the free flow of earnings out of the United States), and because of the high railway coupons. Foreigners could hope for from 5 to 6 per cent on American railway investments (with stock thrown in frequently) as against about 3 per cent on their money at home. Thus, A. K. Cairncross in his *Home and Foreign Investment, 1870-1913* (1953) indicates that during the decade of the 1870s, British investors were getting an annual yield on their American rail securities of 5.7 per cent and a capital appreciation of 3.6 per cent. (At the same time, the return on British Consols, or public debt, was 3.26 per cent and capital appreciation 0.58 per cent.) There were risks, naturally. On balance, however, the immediate large returns on bonds, the real hopes of capital appreciation, the ultimate expectation that sound management and the country's growth would also bring dividends on common stock, justified the foreign interest. The investments of foreigners paid out directly and indirectly, in social gains, to their own countries, and helped the United States immeasurably.

Foreign ownership of American railway securities grew in consequence. In 1853, perhaps one-tenth of the value of American rails was held abroad; by 1870, this had increased to about one-fifth; in 1890, to about one-third; and in 1899 stood at between one-fourth and one-third. It was estimated that in 1899, something like $3 billion in American securities were owned abroad, for the greater part in American rails. British investors held $2.5 billion of this amount, Dutch $240 million; German $200 million, Swiss $75 million, and French $50 million. Many American railroads might almost be considered foreign-controlled; at any rate, concentration of stock ownership abroad gave the British, German and Dutch investors voices on boards of directors. Thus, during 1890-96, according to William Z. Ripley, an early and very good student of American railroading, 75 per cent of the Louisville and Nashville's securities were in foreign portfolios, 65 per cent of the Illinois Central's, 58 per cent of the New York, Ontario and Western's, 52 per cent of the Pennsylvania's, 52 per cent of the Reading's, 37 per cent of the New York Central's, 33 per cent of the Great Northern's, 21 per cent of the Baltimore and Ohio's, and 21 per cent of the Chicago, Milwaukee and St. Paul's. Almost all of these were first-class railroads; in fact, only two went into receivership during the depression of 1893-96.

The British appeared in American rails on a large scale with the financing of the construction of the Illinois Central in the 1850s, and their interest continued up to the outbreak of World War I. Jay Cooke, the Philadelphia banker, who had performed such yeoman service in the sale of American Civil War bonds abroad, went to the European continent during 1870-73 to dispose of the securities of the Northern Pacific and Oregon Navigation Company, among others. Cooke failed in 1873 because his banking house had become so heavily involved in the extension of loans backed by railway securities; and both the Northern Pacific and the Oregon Navigation Company were in trouble. Germans were caught in these difficulties: to protect their interests they sent Henry Villard to the United States, and he, before long, came to dominate the Oregon Railway and Navigation Company, the Oregon and California Railroad, and the Northern Pacific. Bond issues for other Western railroads were floated in Germany: the Chicago, Burlington, and Quincy, the Kansas Pacific, the Davenport and St. Louis, and the Union Pacific. The same was true of the Dutch, who bought bonds issued by the Atchison, Topeka and Santa Fe, the Missouri Pacific, the Central Pacific, and the St. Paul and Pacific. (This last became one of the integral parts of the great railway empire the Canadian-born James J. Hill was to build in the Northwest in the form of the Great Northern.)

Capital and the Western Railroads   It was in building the Western railroads that the raising of the necessary capital funds presented the greatest difficulties. The men responsible were not railroad men in the conventional sense. They were not managers or operators, laying out lines carefully as traffic opportunities presented themselves, watchful of profit-and-loss statements and balance sheets, assuming obligations toward customers, labor, equity owners. They were, rather, promoters, financiers—and speculators. They cultivated the money markets at home and abroad, seeking to obtain capital by whatever means, cajoling (and often bribing) State legislatures into obtaining charters and tax exemptions that would give them some special, sometimes only fleeting, advantage over rivals. As Julius Grodinsky, who has re-examined this problem with more understanding than any other scholar, has put it: "They led, they built, they merged, largely because of their ability to raise capital."

Stock was next to impossible to sell. Loans at banks had to be obtained at high rates of interest. Frequently small sums—to meet interest on bonds—could not be had at any price. But they persisted: building the original pioneer lines; acquiring short independent companies; laying out branches; crossing and recrossing one another's territories. They engaged in bitter traffic and rate wars, cutting prices—which were never raised when uneasy peace descended from time to time. They were innovators, as we have defined the term here: imaginative and bold, conjuring up great visions and the successful ones realizing them.

These men did not always triumph. In the depression of the 1870s, Thomas A. Scott of the Pennsylvania, who tried to move into the Southwest, failed; so did Jay Cooke in the Northwest. Henry Villard suffered heavy reverses in the recession of 1884. Collis P. Huntington's three partners in the Central Pacific—Stanford, Hopkins, Crocker—fell out of the swift race (with fortunes) and left California railroading to Huntington alone. He survived because of his close connections with New York banking. There was only one man who did not use these methods, and that was James J. Hill, who entered the cockpit with railroad experience. He pursued his plan of pushing his line from St. Paul through the wilderness of the Northwest unrelentingly: initially making profits—which could be plowed back—by opening up the rich wheat Red Valley of Dakota and, surviving every vicissitude, reached the Pacific in 1893 and made the Great Northern one of the impressive properties of America.

Who were these promoters and financiers that built the pioneer lines and put together the great systems of the West? They were Jay Gould, who moved in and out fitfully—a dark genius—in the destinies of the Union Pacific, but who was responsible for the Missouri Pacific. Huntington continued as the guiding hand of the Central Pacific and laid out the Southern Pacific. Villard, starting with the Oregon Railway and Navigation Company, ended up by being largely the builder of the Northern Pacific. By 1883 the Great Lakes were connected with the Pacific Coast. Thomas Nickerson began the Atchison, Topeka and Santa Fe, which in time became one of the greatest and soundest, in terms of its financial position and operating successes, of the Western roads. J. M. Forbes shaped the career of the Chicago, Burlington, and Quincy; Albert Keep built up the Chicago and Northwestern. Some of these roads, as we shall see, went down in the depression of 1893-96. They were rescued, as we shall also see, by the bold, innovational leadership of the banking houses of Morgan and Schiff.

Were they Robber Barons? They were, in that some of them used fraud, chicanery, and deceit to accomplish their purposes. They pursued their game of war on each other with zest and without mercy. They acted with boldness and a high degree of recklessness in their operations in and manipulations of the stock market. They issued securities with no regard for the fictitious capital values they were creating. (If one seeks a gloss on the role of monetary inflation in the development of a new country, here is an interesting and curious example. The inflation came from private businessmen: the railroad financers who issued the securities and the commercial banks which accepted them as collateral, thus expanding their demand deposits.) They sold stocks short to throw into difficulties independent lines they wished to acquire and bought them up for a song. In times of recession they bought the securities of their own companies; in upturns of the business cycle, they sold. They made great fortunes—sometimes lost them.

On balance, the fortunes were made from the capital gains they acquired. This was so because the railroad builders had from the start an abiding, passionate conviction that the country's growth—the settlement of the Western States, the opening up of the great agricultural, mining,

[214]

timbering industries—would justify their confidence and great expectations in the risks they were taking.

Julius Grodinsky, in his book *Transcontinental Railway Strategy* (1962), gives an example (in Table 12) of the price the pioneering railroads had to pay to acquire funds during 1869-73, the first period of great Western construction. These were bond issues; the stocks could not be sold.

TABLE 12

Railroad	Name of bond	Interest rate, %	Sales price
Atchison	Second mortgage	7 (gold)	50
Atchison	Land-grant	7 (currency)	73
Denver & Rio Grande	First mortgage	7 (gold)	66
California & Oregon	First mortgage	6 (gold)	79½
Northern Pacific	First mortgage	7.3 (gold)	83
St. Paul & Pacific	First mortgage	7 (gold)	65

SOURCE: Julius Grodinsky, *op. cit.*, p. 11.

Money was made and lost. Many bond issues were defaulted in the depression of 1873-79. Money was made during 1879-83, when another upsurge of building took place and confidence ran high; lost in 1884; made again during 1885-92, the greatest single period of building; lost again in the great depression of 1893-96. Stockholders, although they paid little, got little or nothing on their investments. Nothing on Southern Pacific and Texas and Pacific stock; nothing on Central Pacific stock; dividends on Union Pacific stock during 1880-84, and then no dividends for twenty years. Of all the Western roads, only the Atchison paid regularly every year, but even it had to suspend payments during the depression years 1893-96.

Who, then, gained? The railroad promoters and speculators in their own company securities and those of the lines they bought out, who made their killings out of capital appreciation. Yet even here, one must note, a good deal of such profits were plowed back—Gould and Huntington are interesting examples—into further railroad construction and into modernization. Thus profits, however gained, added to the country's capital. Not all did so, of course. As Grodinsky puts it:

All this was accomplished by sharp and almost continuous reduction in selling prices [rates]. Some investors secured reasonable returns—others lost. Some speculators received substantial, even exorbitant profits—and many, particularly the very early pioneers, lost much more. Whoever gained, and whoever lost, the public was the gainer. Some of the roads were efficiently operated and gave good service; others gave poor service. This outcome was the essence of competition. Competition served the public well.

That is to say, the American people and the American economy were the real gainers. By the end of 1892, the major building programs of the Western railroads were largely finished. In the processes of struggle in the arena and the bitter competitive feuding, the United States was provided with a number of alternative transcontinental routes all equipped with extensive branch systems. The roads had been built quickly, at low cost, and were being run efficiently, cheaply, and fast as the result of the introduction of many technological devices. Above all, and most important of all, rates were low and continued low, even after the era of stabilization set in—that is, after 1897. All this before the Interstate Commerce Commission, created in 1887, had the real power to regulate services and rates. The building, financing, management, and operation of the American railroads demonstrated how a competitive market system was able to assume and complete a task of gargantuan proportions, despite the absence of a large pool of domestic savings, whether individual or private, and without massive government intervention.

How much overcapitalization was there before the depression of 1893-96, as a consequence of which and through the work of the Morgans and Schiffs, a good deal of the water was squeezed out? Van Oss, very well-informed because he was acting as an adviser to British investors, writing at the end of 1892, put the real worth of the 171,000 miles of road at $6.8 billion (on the basis of a knowledgeable estimate of cost of construction plus improvements) as against the claimed worth of $10.1 billion. H. V. Poor, the outstanding American railway authority of the day, insisted that the bona fide investment in the rails did not exceed the total of their funded and floating debt (bonds); a large part of the stock, as investment ($8.4 billion), he was prepared to write off. Therefore, the amount of water in rail securities was $4.6 billion.

Despite this, Van Oss thought American rails constituted an excellent investment. He pointed out that the average return on all American railroad bonds was 4.36 per cent; that the first investors had bought them around 67; and that the return on real investment averaged about 6.5 per cent. Many of the great trunk systems were paying much more than the average on their bonds in 1890; for example, New York Central 6.09 per cent; Erie, 6.73 per cent; Atchison, 4.6 per cent; Burlington, 5.2 per cent; Union Pacific, 6.6 per cent. And what was the stock—there was a total of $4.6 billion in existence in 1892—worth? They were paying on the average 1.8 per cent. At a high estimate, the original investor did not pay more than 10 per cent of the then claimed value, or $465 million; he was getting then 18 per cent upon actual value.

In the face of the overcapitalization, Van Oss was able to write as follows (he could not anticipate the depression that soon set in, of course, or that the drastic reorganization that took place as a result of the ensuing bankruptcies, would force a writing down of claimed capital worth):

Perhaps in no respect have changes been so healthy as in the relations between the [railroad] corporations and their shareholders. The era of "railroad rascals" has gone, and men of integrity are filling the places they have vacated. The American railway has ceased to be chiefly a gambling implement for Wall Street, and properties are no longer wrecked for speculative purposes. . . .

On the whole, then, there has been a great improvement, and which says more, it continues. This has, of course, enhanced the value of American securities as investments, and there can be little doubt that this value will rise further still; returns, perhaps, may not advance much, but their safety and regularity surely will.

Van Oss' confidence was justified—after 1897. Up to and even beyond 1914 the railroads became sound and secure investments, bonds frequently selling at premiums. Institutional savers, particularly the life insurance companies of the country, had a large part of their portfolios in rail bonds. The gamble of the pioneer railroad promoters and financiers paid off before too long; the country's gains were achieved in even a briefer period.

The Great Railroad Builders   At the age of sixty-six years, with a fortune he had made in operating steamboats, Cornelius Vanderbilt in 1860 went actively into the railroad business, for he saw the great opportunity of linking New York City with Buffalo and the Middle West. In 1853, he had helped to unite the nine short lines along the route from Albany to Buffalo under the name of the New York Central. But New York could be reached only by way of the New York and Harlem or the Hudson River Railroad; and both were on the east side of the river. Vanderbilt began to buy into the New York and Harlem and by 1864 controlled it; he carried on the same operations in connection with the Hudson River Railroad and the New York Central and three years later he dominated these too, consolidating them into the New York Central and Hudson River Railroad. In 1873, the New York and Harlem, with its valuable entrance into New York, was leased (it always continued to be a family property of the Vanderbilts), and thus began one of America's great trunk systems. The elder Vanderbilt was a shrewd Wall Street speculator, although he met his match in Daniel Drew and Jay Gould in his unsuccessful effort to acquire the Erie. He doubled the capitalization of the New York Central and then justified what he did by double-tracking his lines, substituting steel rails for iron, throwing modern bridges across embankments and rivers, and acquiring for his railroad the Grand Central Terminal in New York City.

Vanderbilt's work was not finished with his death in 1877. His son, W. H. Vanderbilt, continued the process of expansion and consolidation. By 1885, the New York Central system had acquired control of the Lake Shore and Michigan Southern (linking Buffalo and Chicago), the Michigan Central (linking Detroit and Chicago), the Canadian Southern (linking Detroit and Toronto), as well as 800 miles of other lines in Ohio, Indiana, Michigan, and Pennsylvania. It had bought up the competing West Shore and was figuring prominently in the competing Nickel Plate. In 1885, the House of Morgan began to shape the destinies of the New York Central when it sold $25 million in New York Central stock to English investors. With this additional capital, the growth of the system went on unchecked. Allied with it were the Chicago and Northwestern, the Cleveland, Cincinnati, Chicago and St. Louis, and the Boston and Albany; thus the New York Central was at the gateways of the Northwest and the Southwest and reached across New England. In all, by 1893, the Vanderbilt lines—owned, leased, or tied together by communities of interest—controlled 15,476 miles of first track. They were well run; had a splendid roadbed and modern equipment; and were able to survive the depression of 1893-96, paying dividends throughout these difficult years.

The Pennsylvania system was similarly well put together, well run, and financially sound. Its stock was never inflated, nor was it ever manipulated on Wall Street; expansion came in large measure from plowed-back earnings and from leased lines whose floating debt the Pennsylvania assumed and met. Van Oss, writing in 1892, when he reported that the Pennsylvania controlled 7,950 miles of railway and canal, gave it the accolade: it was the first and foremost railroad of the United States; and while it controlled only one-twentieth of the country's mileage, its gross earnings amounted to one-ninth of those of all the American railroads. Its founders saw, as did Vanderbilt, the importance of bringing the Middle West to the Atlantic seaboard, with the result that by 1858 they had a through line running from Philadelphia across the Alleghanies to Pittsburgh. Under J. Edgar Thomson and T. A. Scott (Carnegie was a friend of both) and under B. B. Roberts, the Pennsylvania spread its network into the most important Middle Atlantic and North Central industrial centers. By 1869, the railroad was operating 1000 miles in Pennsylvania and was reaching Lake Erie through New York State; the next year, by lease of the Pittsburgh, Fort Wayne and Chicago, it was in the Middle Western metropolis; in 1871, by a similar alliance with the Pittsburgh, Chicago, Cincinnati and St. Louis, it was at the Ohio and the Missouri Rivers. In the 1880s it also spread south, reaching into Wilmington, Baltimore, and Washington, and north, to Lake Michigan and Lake Ontario.

The Pennsylvania was a pioneer in the use of technological innovation: it was the first to lay Bessemer steel rails; to use the steel firebox under the locomotive boiler; and to experiment with the airbrake and the block-signal system. From 1860 on, the Pennsylvania never failed to pay a dividend. It survived the depression of the 1890s so well that when it launched on a great improvement program under A. J. Cassatt—beginning with 1899 and costing one-half billion dollars; this included tunneling under the Hudson River and the erection of the great Pennsylvania Station in New York City, which was finally demolished in 1966—it was able to obtain all its necessary capital from the sale of bonds at low interest rates and stock at a premium. Despite this new financing, it did not have to change its dividend rate.

[219]

The Erie, never recovering from the manipulations, overexpansion and overfinancing, first of Daniel Drew and then of Jay Gould and Jim Fiske, was one of the first railroads to go under in 1893. Chartered in 1832, it was operating 460 miles of line from the Hudson River to Lake Erie by 1851. In 1859, it was in the bankruptcy courts. After being reorganized, it fell into the hands of Daniel Drew, a stock-market operator, who loaded the company down with a heavy floating debt which the road's run-down property found it impossible to carry.

Drew sold his own stock short, at one time depressing the price from 90 to 50. To thwart Vanderbilt, who was trying to get control of the Erie to join it with the New York Central, he twice issued convertible bonds, which were turned into 100,000 shares of stock and sold—in the face of court injunctions to the contrary. As a result he was forcing Vanderbilt to the wall.

Working with Drew was Jay Gould—then, in 1867, only thirty-one, and already the possesser of a fortune as a stockbroker and speculator. It was Gould who was sent to Albany and the State legislature to have the convertible bond issues legalized. He took with him a sum variously estimated at from $300,000 to $1,000,000, distributed it where it could do the most good, and returned with a law which not only made the bonds and stock legal but also forbade interlocking directorates among Vanderbilt's railroads and the Erie. Vanderbilt discovered he had met his match, settled with Gould (who had now become the master and was soon the president of the road), received a million dollars as a sweetener, and left the Erie to Gould's devices.

The machinations of Gould are too complex to detail. He was at the controls of the railroad until 1872, embarked on an expansion campaign to the West that was doomed to failure, loaded the company down with debt, and left it a physical wreck. It went into bankruptcy in 1875 (Gould was always able to extricate himself: he sold Erie short before the bankruptcy was announced and made a killing on the stock exchange), and because it was in such bad shape it failed again in 1893. Then it owned or leased almost 2,000 miles.

Jay Gould now moved his activities to the Far West and Southwest, continuing to finance himself by bold stock-market speculations, which were frequently associated with the railroads he sought to dominate. He would be a "bear"—depressing the values of the feeder lines and independent companies he wanted to acquire; and then would turn "bull"—

forcing up the prices of the trunk systems to which he had added the newly gained lines. Frequently, he and his followers bought securities in recession and depression and then sold when recovery had fully returned. He made his large fortune out of capital gains in this fashion, but it should be said in his defense that a good part he reinvested in the railroads themselves, building additions and improving the physical properties, if not the services. In any event, and here his social contributions were considerable—even if stockholders and bondholders, who bought for investment and not speculation, made little—Gould was the leader in drastically pushing down railroad rates in the regions in which he operated.

Gould entered the destinies of the Union Pacific in 1875, buying control at depression prices. He began to build as soon as the depression was over in 1879 and by 1882 had added more than 1,200 miles of line, as branches and feeders, to the Union Pacific. He absorbed independent lines—the Kansas Pacific (running from Kansas City to Denver), the Denver Pacific (from Denver to Cheyenne), the Oregon Short Line and the Oregon Railway and Navigation Company. The Union Pacific had started out with 1,042 miles of line; by 1890, it was controlling, by ownership, proprietary interest and leases, 8,100 miles.

Gould's appearance here and in the Southwest (as a result of his acquisition of the Missouri Pacific and its great expansion) was a highly disturbing element. For almost a decade—until the end of the great railroad boom in 1887—he literally terrorized his competitors and rivals. He broke up rate structures and traffic pools; he forced down rates; he was highly competitive—and compelled the other large trunk systems to build their extensions to meet his offer of services throughout the Southwest and the Far West. The record construction of 1879-81 and again of 1886-87—by the Atchison, the Burlington, the Rock Island, the Chicago and Northwestern, the St. Paul—and the reduction of rates were efforts by Gould's rivals to match his policies. The railroads paid a heavy price in the depression of 1893, as did their security owners. But—the gains to the country were immense.

Gould's latest and in fact only good biographer, Julius Grodinsky, ends up his full and careful study with this judgment:

. . . the public benefited from his activities as a man of business in the railroad industry and in the field of speculative capital. As a leader in the railroad industry he built many new roads; he broke down local territorial monopolies, destroyed traffic pools, and wrecked railroad rate structures. As a leader in the arena of speculative capital, he transformed millions of dollars of paper profits into productive wealth in the form of new railroads. Gould made fortunes for many of his followers, and produced losses for others. . . . The public did gain permanently. . . . To Gould, as much as to any other single business leader, goes the credit for that far-reaching reduction in rates that characterized the growth of the American economy in the generation after the Civil War.

If Gould moved in and out of many railroads all over the country (buying into them during the depression of the 1870s and then selling out for large profits on the upturn) there was one which had his abiding interest and which he retained until he died, and that was the Missouri Pacific. (By 1881, Gould controlled almost 16,000 miles of line, which included, in the East, the Central of New Jersey and the Delaware, Lackawanna and Western; in the Middle West, the Wabash; in the Far West, the Union Pacific; and in the Southwest, the Missouri Pacific.)

The Missouri Pacific, to run from St. Louis to Kansas City, was completed in 1865, having received financial aid and a large land grant from the state of Missouri. In 1875, it had defaulted on its bonds and Jay Gould picked up the railway for a song. Gould began to buy independent lines, lease, push out the main line in all directions, and construct feeders. The original road had been only 283 miles long. In not much more than six years, by 1881, the Missouri Pacific system was controlling 5,000 miles of road. It went south to Laredo, Texas on the border; southeast to New Orleans; southwest to El Paso, Texas. It was also in Arkansas, the Indian Territory (Oklahoma), southern Kansas, and eastern Colorado. And this is what Gould built in the Southwest alone during 1879-82; these were additions to roads that were part of his Missouri Pacific system:

Texas Pacific	1,010	miles
International Great Northern	256.71	miles
Missouri, Kansas and Texas	588.2	miles
Missouri Pacific	466.5	miles
St. Louis, Iron Mountain and Southern	198.0	miles
	2,519.41	miles

At an average cost of $20,000 a mile (which was low), the total value of new capital created in this region alone by Gould was in excess of $50 million. In the light of such performances, it is too ingenuous to dismiss Jay Gould as the "Robber Baron" par excellence of his era. When Gould died in 1892, he left to his family the highly profitable integrated Missouri Pacific, the Western Union Telegraph Company, and the Manhattan Elevated Railroad in New York City.

At the time of the completion of the Union Pacific-Central Pacific in 1869, and in 1870, plans were already under way for the building of three other transcontinental railways to the Pacific. On the north, the Northern Pacific, started by the Philadelphia banker, Jay Cooke, was projected to run from Duluth on the Great Lakes to Puget Sound. Another—beginning in St. Louis—was to run along the 35th parallel and cross the Colorado River in northern Arizona. To do this, Congress in 1866 chartered the Atlantic and Pacific Railroad, awarded it land grants, and gave its approval to the Southern Pacific to build out of San Francisco and join with the Atlantic and Pacific near the Arizona–California boundary. The third, following an extreme southern route, was to originate in the lower Mississippi Valley, run parallel to the Mexican border, and end in Los Angeles and San Diego. After a number of false starts, a company emerged called the Texas and Pacific Railway in which T. A. Scott and J. Edgar Thomson of the Pennsylvania Railroad were the guiding geniuses.

Only the Northern Pacific, as originally projected, was realized. The Atlantic and Pacific did not become a trunk system; it was built from Los Angeles eastward to Albuquerque in New Mexico and at this point became part of the Atchison, Topeka and Santa Fe, which had absorbed the line running westward from St. Louis. The Texas and Pacific did start at New Orleans but ran through Central Texas to El Paso on the western border of Texas. It was the Southern Pacific (joined with the Central Pacific, and therefore a Huntington property) which began at San Francisco, went south to Los Angeles, and then eastward along the southern edge of Arizona into Texas at El Paso and then south along the Rio Grande to Houston and New Orleans. These were the Pacific trunk systems—to be joined in time by the St. Paul and Pacific, which was destined to become the Great Northern under the magic hand of James J. Hill.

It is James J. Hill among the railroad men who deserves our admiration most. He was innovator, builder, operator, and skillful—and sound—financier all rolled into one. The Great Northern Railway Company—which was his creation and with which he opened up the northernmost portion of the Northwest to wheat, cattle, timber, and mining—became one of the country's great systems. Hill was Canadian-born, quit his schooling at fourteen, and at eighteen, in 1856, came to St. Paul—then a frontier trading post—where he worked for a company operating steamboat packets on the Mississippi River. He made money in the coal business, among his customers being the primitive railroads of the region, and he followed their activities—and shortcomings—with growing interest. One such railroad, the Minnesota and Pacific, had been chartered by Minnesota in 1857 and given State lands that came to total 4 million acres, as well as financial assistance. The road defaulted in its obligations; Minnesota took over; and two years later, in 1862, the franchise became the property of the St. Paul and Pacific. Building out of St. Paul, the road began to construct westward into the Red River Valley of Dakota and northward to Winnipeg in Canada. But it too fell on hard times, and in 1873 was bankrupt.

It was at this point that Hill, thirty-five years old, moved. He wanted the St. Paul and Pacific, but his own capital resources were slender. He turned for financing, therefore, to fellow Canadians—Donald A. Smith (later Lord Strathcona and Mount Royal) of the Hudson Bay Company and his cousin George Stephen (later Lord Mount Stephen) of the Montreal Bank; both were to build the Canadian Pacific. Among them they were able to buy out the interests of the Dutch bondholders in 1878 and a year later set up the St. Paul, Minneapolis and Manitoba. Hill became vice-president and two years later president, a post which he held until 1907.

With the benevolent interest and support of his Canadian backers, Hill began to build west and north along the northern edge of the United States, steadily advancing toward Puget Sound. In 1879, the original line had only 560 miles, but it was in the country's richest wheatlands and it at once began to accumulate surpluses. These earnings—always paying a dividend of 6 per cent on the common stock—

were plowed back into expansion. In 1884, the company's mileage was 1,378; by 1891, it was 2,800. In 1890, a holding company, the Great Northern Railway Company, was established, and in 1893 Puget Sound was reached at Tacoma. A branch was built southward to Portland and another in the east, from St. Paul northward to Duluth. It added proprietary lines (representing stock ownership of independent companies) and leased lines. It obtained additional capital from its own equity shareholders, to whom it sold stock and bonds.

Hill was the railroad man par excellence and the Great Northern was the best run—and its rates the cheapest—of all the Western railways. Hill was able to compete successfully with the Northern Pacific—which the Great Northern paralleled—and his railway's services were vastly superior because the Northern Pacific was carrying a heavy debt burden. Van Oss points out that the Great Northern's costs-of-operations-to-earnings ratio was perhaps the lowest in the country: this stood around 50 per cent as contrasted with the usual railway experiences of 67-69 per cent.

Hill knew that his railroad was not worth one penny more than the Northwest: that the prosperity of both was indissolubly joined. The settlers of the Northwest—the wheatgrowers, cattlemen, timber cutters—therefore had his real concern; and he followed their progress with the interest of an enlightened eighteenth-century English landlord. Hill helped in the building of communities; he guided agricultural projects, bred blooded cattle, taught crop rotation, and the uses of irrigation and fertilizers; he opened banks and made possible the creation of churches and schools. Ever with an eye open to business, Hill sensed the importance of Far Eastern markets for the products of the new American industrialism. (E. G. Harriman was to follow in his footsteps a decade later.) He built steamers and made one unbroken bridge from the Great Lakes and the upper Mississippi to Japan and China, and soon Minnesota flour and Ohio nails, shipped by way of the Great Northern, were being landed in Hong Kong, and Mississippi cotton and Pennsylvania rails were reaching Yokohama. On the other hand, Iowa barns were being built from the timber of the forest lands of the Washington and Oregon country which the Great Northern tapped.

In 1893 the Northern Pacific was once more in receiver's hands; Hill and his partners, with approval of the road's bondholders, were prepared to guarantee interest and principal on the funded debt, upon receipt of the capital stock. The state of Minnesota disapproved, but Hill, Strathcona and Mount Stephen achieved virtually the same end by furnishing part of the funds needed for the Northern Pacific's reorganization and buying stock in the market. There was thus a community of interest existing between the old rivals, and it was because of this that J. P. Morgan, acting for both railways, in 1901 was able to buy most of the stock of the Chicago, Burlington and Quincy (it reached into both Chicago and St. Louis), obtaining the funds from the sale of a bond issue which was guaranteed jointly by the Great Northern and the . Northern Pacific. Harriman's insistence that he and the Union Pacific be made party to the acquisition of the Burlington led to the creation of the Northern Securities Company, a grandiose though short-lived, venture, for in 1904 the company was ordered dissolved by the Supreme Court.

Technology and the Railroads   There were a number of reasons why innovation in the railroad industry took place. New capital was regularly being obtained—from increases in funded or floating debt; from the reinvesting of profits made by railroad promoters in stock-market manipulations—to make improvements possible. Competitive rate wars and the driving down of rates forced cost reductions. The leadership of well-run roads—the New York Central, the Pennsylvania, the Atchison—had to be followed. The period saw, in consequence, all sorts of devices and methods being introduced that, as Van Oss pointed out, made American railroading the most advanced in the world.

The introduction of Bessemer steel speeded up the whole process of change and improvement. Steel rails could be substituted for iron. Faster and more powerful locomotives and stronger and larger cars could be built. Longer and heavier trains could be run. The appearance of block signaling (1864), air brakes (1869), automatic couplers (1873) made for greater safety, speed, and the more efficient use of yards and track facilities. Work was pushed ahead to standardize gauges. It was possible to synchronize railroad operations all over the country as a result of the adoption, by the railroads themselves, of four standard time zones (1883). Railroad associations worked out uniform freight classifications so that by 1890 three major classification systems had emerged: one for the Northeast, one for the South, and one for the West. A through bill of lading was devised and was being generally used. Fast freight lines—to assemble shipments for common destinations and route them over the country's vast and intricate network—crisscrossed the United States and, because they too were competitive, offered the benefit of the low rates to smaller shippers. Either independent bridge companies, charging tolls, or the railroads themselves were throwing iron bridges across the wide rivers: over the Monongahela at Pittsburgh in 1865, over the Ohio at Cincinnati in 1867 and at Parkersburgh in 1871, over the Mississippi at St. Louis (Eads' great triumph) in 1874.

The United States had been obtaining its railroad iron from England; even as late as the years 1866-70, rail imports from England were as high as 50 per cent of American production. Tariff protection (as we have seen) for American steel rails and the vast expansion of the domestic steel industry (Carnegie was the first to see steel's opportunities in the rapidly growing railroad industry) pushed English imports into the background and gave steel primacy over iron. Immediately after the Civil War, steel rails began to be made and continued to be turned out during the depression years of the 1870s. The fact is, in the half decade 1876-80, steel-rail production exceeded iron-rail (613,000 tons to 409,000 tons, with all rail imports 134,000 tons). By 1881-85, iron-rail production had almost entirely disappeared (164,000 tons to 1,284,000 tons of steel rail). During 1886-90, the ratios of iron rails to steel rails was 86,000 tons to 1,921,000 tons, with all rail imports 56,000 tons.

Replacement of iron track and the laying of new steel track went ahead rapidly. In 1880, only 29 per cent of total track was steel; but by 1884, the proportion was 58 per cent; by 1890, 80 per cent; and by 1897, 89 per cent.

The more effective use of tracking—in addition to the fact that steel could carry greater loads—was further achieved by the introduction of so-called "lap-sidings": instead of double-tracking throughout, single tracks could be split into two tracks—to permit two trains to pass without stopping—and then narrowed down again. During the 1860s, too, track tanks were installed which allowed locomotives to take on water without slacking speed. Also, as track substitutions and gauge changes took place, railroads cut their maximum gradients from 1 per cent to ½ of 1 per cent, and this too made for greater efficiency in the use of locomotive power and for lower costs.

Steel revolutionized the character of the railroad locomotive and the freight car. Constant experiment with design made them heavier and reduced operation costs. The weight of locomotives had been limited previously because of the lesser reliability of iron track. Steel track and steel locomotives permitted more pressure, weight and wear on all parts of the engine. In 1850, a locomotive of 50,000 pounds was considered unusual; in 1900, one of 300,000 pounds was not uncommon. The introduction of the compound locomotive—in which passing steam out of the boiler into the exhaust by two clyinders in succession was effected—made for greater power and a saving in fuel. Better tracks and locomotives enormously increased the carrying load of trains: from 200 tons in 1865 to 2500 tons in 1900; at the same time, speed was advanced from 25 miles an hour in the earlier year to 65 miles in the later.

The use of steel for freight-car construction made possible the reduction of the unladen weight of the car and the increase of the car's loading capacity. In 1865, the weight of a car was 60 per cent of its total laden weight; by 1900, the ratio had dropped to 26 per cent. In 1865, a freight car's capacity was 10,000 pounds; at the end of the century, 110,000 pounds. Van Oss marveled at American railroad efficiency, constantly comparing American experiences with England's to the disadvantage of the latter. He pointed out that the average English freight car carried 8 tons and weighed 5 tons, or a ratio of 1.6 to 1; while the American freight car carried 30 tons and weighed 12 tons, or a ratio of 2.5 to 1. As rates fell drastically, declines in the cost of transportation had to take place—for survival. He cited the case of the New York Central, whose drop in rates was 60 per cent during 1870-89 but which succeeded in almost compensating for this by pushing down the cost of transportation 52 per cent. On the Pennsylvania, the experiences were even better: in the same twenty years, the cost of moving freight per ton-mile was reduced from 1 cent to two-fifths of a cent. Because of these economies, American transportation charges were 50 per cent lower than in England.

One of the railroad industry's greatest accomplishments was the universal installation of the standard gauge, that is to say, a width of 4 feet 8½ inches as the inside distance between the two rails on which the trains moved. Originally, because the early railroads were built as short lines and for different purposes, there was no concern about the moving of through traffic. The standard gauge had been adopted in England in

1846; by 1860, only one-half of American trackage was following the English example. Some roads employed a gauge as wide as 6 feet. The decision to use the standard gauge on the Union Pacific hastened uniformity in the North and West in the 1870s, and by 1880, 80 per cent of trackage was standard. Only the South—where the 5-foot gauge was common—was, to a certain extent, cut off from the rest of the country.

There were all sorts of expedients used to overcome differences, but these were expensive and time-consuming. The most successful was the interchangeable truck: cars were lifted at transfer points with an elevating machine and trucks with the proper widths replaced the ones used on narrower or wider gauges. Heroic measures were necessary to change the Southern wider gauge to the standard one; and these were taken during two days, Monday, May 31 and Tuesday, June 1, 1886. Previously, all the Southern railroads had been converting their rolling stock and setting new inside spikes. On the two days agreed upon, all traffic was stopped and some 40,000 men set to work pushing the rails of some 13,000 miles of track into position and driving the new outer spikes. By 1890, say G. R. Taylor and I. Neu, in their *The American Railroad Network* (1956), the American railway system had been integrated, for

trackage breaks at rivers and in cities had been all but eliminated. Most of the great streams had been repeatedly bridged. Tracks had been joined in the towns; belt lines had been built through and around the great cities; terminals had been improved; and many lines had been double-tracked.

Two important services had been developed to facilitate the movement of through freight over the many existing lines. The first had been the so-called fast-freight lines; before the Civil War these were independent of the railroads and owned their own cars. Beginning with 1866, there appeared the "cooperative lines"—owned by the railroads and performing the same kind of function. Competition quickly sprang up: thus, before long, Boston, New York, and Chicago were being served by four such companies. In 1891, Chicago, the country's great rail center, was housing the offices of twenty fast-freight lines prepared to move traffic in every direction. It was these companies that introduced the second significant reform: the through bill of lading, a commercial instrument which was unknown before 1860.

[229]

Bankruptcy and Reorganization Of equal weight, in putting American railroading on a sound and profitable basis, was the wholesale reorganization that took place following the disastrous failures of the 1893-96 depression. At the end of the first twelve months of the collapse, on June 30, 1894, the Interstate Commerce Commission reported that 192 railways—operating 40,818 miles of track—were in the hands of receivers. The total capitalization of the bankrupt roads was $2.5 billion: this represented one-fourth of the country's railway worth. The Richmond Terminal System, controlling some 6,000 miles of track in the South, had been the first to go; among other early failures—many of these had been in difficulties previously, some again and again—were the Philadelphia and Reading, the Erie, the Northern Pacific, the Union Pacific. Before the depression had run its course, the Atchison and the Baltimore and Ohio, two well-run roads, had joined the list of casualties. The reasons for the difficulties of the roads were familiar enough: overbuilding, the construction of competitive lines, the leasing of unprofitable independent lines to round out trunk systems, and—in many cases—earlier mismanagement as a result of which an enormous debt had been accumulated. Bankruptcy affected stockholders, who were liable to assessment, and bondholders, who stood in danger of having their claims written down or subordinated. What was equally ironical, as far as equity owners were concerned, was the fact that several years before the depression hit, 60 per cent of the capital stock of American rails had been paying no dividends.

The broad process of reorganization was the work of private banking firms which, like their English prototypes, also engaged in the investment banking business. They had entered into rail financing as soon as the Civil War was over, had helped in the raising of capital for many of the pioneer Western roads; and their connections with foreign money markets made it possible for them to bring European investors into these activities. The reorganizations were the largest tasks they had assumed to that time, and the ingenuity, boldness, and success with which they carried out their operations put them at the very center of the American business complex. Here was another example of highly skilled entrepreneurship, this time in the area of financial management. These investment bankers went on to create the American industrial mergers and holding companies of the next half decade; and they continued to sit on the boards of the reorganized railroads and the new giant corporations to wield great power. The greatest of these investment banking houses was Drexel, Morgan & Company (whose senior partner was J. P. Morgan), which was closely associated with English banking; next in importance was Kuhn, Loeb & Co. (whose senior partner was Jacob H. Schiff), which had many ties with German banking.

The processes of the reorganization of the bankrupt railroads were broadly as follows. Called in by the trustees, the investment bankers acquired the property on behalf of the equity owners; these were assessed for the purposes of obtaining cash in order to fund the floating debt, which was also reduced; bondholders agreed to lower interest rates; and new preferred stock was issued and given to stockholders and bondholders for their cooperation. And these were the consequences: the floating debt was paid or funded—in any case it was reduced. Fixed charges were lowered. New working capital was provided. The weak and unprofitable parts of the road—whether extensions built or independent lines leased—were abandoned or consolidated. To assure the success of the program a voting trust which the bankers controlled was usually created for a limited period. Two such reorganizations will be examined: that of the Richmond Terminal (which also included the Richmond and Danville and the East Tennessee Railroads), the work of Morgan; and that of the Union Pacific, the work of Schiff.

The Richmond Terminal Company had failed in 1892 and Morgan was called in in February, 1893, having received carte blanche from the stockholders. In about fifteen months, the work of reorganization was completed; and in another year—that is, by November, 1895, when the country was still in the midst of deep depression—the newly organized Southern Railway was a working and healthy system. Stockholders in the Terminal Company were called upon to pay an assessment of $12.50 a share, with lesser amounts from the shareholders of the East Tennessee (but the value of common and preferred stocks was diminished). New common stock was to be sold, and new bonds as well. The total in cash thus to be realized—some $23.25 million—was to be used toward paying off part of the floating debt, expenses incurred by the receiver and the reorganization, and new construction on the two allied railways. The new company, to be called the Southern Railway, was to refund the bonded and floating debt at a reduced coupon for a total of $140 million;

and to issue new noncumulative preferred stock ($75 million) and new common stock ($160 million) to replace the old at lower dividend rates. The old debt had been $153.8 million; the new, as issued was $104.6 million. Fixed charges, also, were lowered from $9.5 million to $6.8 million. (These were further reduced in 1894 and 1895 by funding the interest on some junior bond issues.)

In September, 1894, the new Southern Railway found itself operating only 4,500 miles as against the earlier 6,000. Some leased companies were dropped; the rest gave up their leases, and their property and financial obligations and management were absorbed into a single, consolidated organization. Before, there had been as many as thirty-five different corporations, most of them semiautonomous and exacting a heavy toll from the parent company, which had guaranteed their debts and paid excessively for the leases. New management added to the mileage of the system by building and by the absorption of the Central of Georgia Railway, so that by the end of the century the Southern Railway was operating 7,500 miles of track, was well run, and had not increased its rates. The prediction of a contemporary that the Southern Railway Company, as the great trunk line of the South, would set the pace for other railway systems of the region, was quickly realized.

There were these caveats: dividends on common stock were not paid for twenty years, and the temporary voting trust, controlled by the House of Morgan, became permanent. The character of the Morgan accomplishment was thus summed up by a railway authority in 1904 (the quotation is from E. G. Campbell's pioneer study, *The Reorganization of the American Railroad System, 1893-1900* [1938]):

For a management to succeed in doing anything with such unpromising railway material, to take a collection, or rather a congeries of poorly constructed, over-bonded roads, built to sell rather than to operate, and located in the most unpromising territory, from a traffic standpoint, in the United States and to weld this material into a great railway system which is not only solvent, but which holds out a reasonable prospect of dividends to its common shareholders, is one of the noteworthy achievements of American railroad history.

The Union Pacific had expanded during the 1880s, acquiring among other roads the Denver Pacific, the Kansas Pacific, the Oregon Short

Line, the Utah Northern and the Oregon Railway and Navigation Company. It had constructed too many branch lines; it had paid too much for companies it had absorbed or leased; it had built up no adequate sinking fund to meet the principal and unpaid interest due the federal government in full in 1899 for the advances made to speed original construction. When the company failed in 1893—it was virtually bankrupt in 1890—its total capitalization was $192.6 million, of which $131.7 million consisted of bonds and $60.9 million the par value of its stock.

After a good deal of backing and filling and the appearance and disappearance of earlier reorganization committees, one was formed in 1895—Jacob H. Schiff was on it as the prospective underwriter—that met with the approval of stockholders and with which the federal government (because of the debt owed it) was prepared to deal. Stocks were to be assessed $15 a share; new bonds and new preferred stock and common stock were to be issued—to obtain cash in order to discharge the government debt in full, to exchange for the old securities, and for the expenses of the receivership and other immediate requirements. The bond issue came to $80 million (the government was paid $74.6 million); the preferred stock issue to $75 million; the common stock issue to $61 million. Interest on bonds and dividends on the preferred were reduced, so that the annual charges on these were to be $6.4 million; this could be met out of the net earnings. The underwriters proceeded to reorganize the subsidiaries and to divest themselves of much dead wood, and on January 1, 1898, the new Union Pacific emerged.

Almost at once the last of the great railroad tycoons, E. H. Harriman, appeared in the destinies of the Union Pacific. The alliance of Schiff and Harriman, the one a bold and imaginative banker, the other a successful railroad financier and operator who had gained his spurs in the management of the Illinois Central, rehabilitated the Union Pacific almost overnight. Harriman went on the board's executive committee, in a year became the board's chairman, and from then until his death (in 1909) ran the company. He brought the Oregon Short Line and the Oregon Railway and Navigation Company into the new organization, began rebuilding and modernizing lines and equipment, and in a short period increased carrying capacity by 75 per cent. Harriman had large dreams: of a single, unified Atlantic-Pacific system; even of one that circumscribed the globe. With the help of Schiff he moved methodically to accomplish his purpose. He gained control of the Southern Pacific (and with it the Central Pacific), sought to link the Illinois Central with the Union Pacific, and with James J. Hill organized the Northern Securities Company to tie the Chicago, Burlington and Quincy into his Union Pacific and Hill's Great Northern–Northern Pacific combination. The Supreme Court dissolved the last; and Harriman turned his attention eastward. He acquired the Baltimore and Ohio and bought into the Reading and the Central of Georgia. His network reached into Oregon and California, Chicago, St. Louis, New Orleans, Atlanta, and Savannah. But the system could not hold together for long. The Union Pacific was ordered severed from the Southern Pacific by the Attorney General; the control of the Baltimore and Ohio was relinquished in a special stock dividend to the Union Pacific stockholders; and not long after Harriman's death, the Union Pacific was again where Harriman found it when he appeared in its affairs in 1898. But instead of a bankrupt and inefficient railroad, he left it rich and secure.

Railroad Regulation   The first State law for the general regulation of the railroads was enacted in Massachusetts in 1869. Under it there was set up a board of commissioners with powers to investigate railroad methods, listen to complaints, and report all discriminatory practices to the legislature or the State Attorney General. In fact, the commission's powers were only supervisory; its chief weapon was the creation of an articulate public opinion. Here it was eminently successful, largely because C. F. Adams—who became in time an outstanding railway authority and the nemesis of Gould—guided the commission in its formative years. The example of Massachusetts was followed generally in the East, and in New York and the remaining New England States similar commissions were soon at work.

The states of the Middle West and the West required stronger fare before they could be satisfied, and with the entry of the farmer in these regions into politics, the first mandatory railroad laws were written into American constitutions and placed on statute books. The Patrons of Husbandry—which came to be popularly known as the Grange—had appeared in 1868, as a nonpolitical organization initially interested in the establishment of farmer-producer cooperatives. These had largely failed because of want of capital and skills, and more and more the Grange concentrated its attention on railroad abuses, more particularly the high rates being charged. With the outset of depression in 1873, the Grange supported local farmer parties, and these met with growing successes, although it should be held in mind that local shippers and merchants, also smarting from inequitable railroad practices, joined hands with the farmers. The upshot was that between 1871 and 1875, regulatory laws, usually calling for the creation of railroad or railroad-and-warehouse commissions, were passed in Illinois, Iowa, Michigan, Minnesota, Missouri, and Wisconsin. By 1885, such commissions were in operation in twenty-four States and one Territory out of the thirty-eight States and eight Territories in the Union.

The mandates frequently came from newly written state constitutions. (This was so in Illinois, Missouri, Nebraska, and California, and in a number of the Southern States.) Thus, the Illinois constitution of 1870 declared railroads to be "public highways and free to all persons for the transportation of their persons and property thereon, under such regulations as may be prescribed by law." The State's legislature was instructed to pass laws establishing reasonable maximum rates and to prohibit unjust discrimination and extortion; parallel or competing lines were to be forbidden to consolidate. The legislature acted at once and in 1871 created a railroad-and-warehouse commission. In 1873 and subsequently these prohibitions ("unjust discrimination and distortion") were spelled out, to include: the drawing up by the commission of a schedule of reasonable maximum rates; the declaration that discrimination between persons and places—rebates, drawbacks, passes—was illegal; and another declaration that the commission's rulings were to be regarded as prima-facie evidence of reasonableness. Other States outlawed railroad pools as well, and sought to overcome higher charges for short hauls than for long ones, when these had initiated in the same place and were over the same road. It may be noted, in passing, that the federal Interstate Commerce Act, when adopted in 1887, was anticipated in every one of its sections by the Granger laws.

By 1875, it was plain that the Granger laws were not working. The Minnesota law was repealed in 1875; the Iowa law remained but one year on the statute books; the Wisconsin law was in operation for only two years; the injunctions of the Southern constitutions upon their State legislatures were never really obeyed. The Granger laws failed for the following reasons. There was a complete lack of technical skill on the part of the persons invested with the job of regulating the roads. The hostility and the ingenuity of the railroad managers (and their lawyers) more than offset the untutored zeal of the farmer-commissioners. The depression of the seventies checked railroad construction and made the agrarian West apprehensive lest its drastic action put a stop to new building altogether. The rate wars of the middle and late 1870s resulted in a permanent lowering of rates; these were pushed even lower when new and competitive building was resumed in 1879. The decline of the Grange and the farmer parties it had supported (by 1880, the Patrons of Husbandry had become only a fraternal organization) removed the pressure of public opinion from law-making bodies.

In the face of all this, the Supreme Court in 1876 found the Granger laws constitutional; even more, it declared that, until Congress might see fit to act, the States had the power to regulate interstate commerce insofar as the welfare of their own particular citizens were concerned. These so-called Granger cases arose out of appeals from the laws of Illinois, Iowa, Minnesota, and Wisconsin (the leading ones were *Munn v. Illinois* and *Chicago, Burlington, and Quincy Railway v. Iowa*). The decisions laid down the following principles of State action: under its police power, a State might regulate a business of a public nature. The right to regulate had not been contracted away unless the legislature had specifically so declared. Powers of regulation rested with the legislature and not the judiciary; hence the courts could not pass in review the exercise of the regulatory power of the legislature. In other words, the courts were not competent to review the question of the reasonableness of rates fixed by the legislatures or their agencies. If there were legislative abuses, said Chief Justice Waite, in writing the majority opinion in *Munn v. Illinois,* then the polls were the refuge of the people, and not the courts.

Because the State laws and State commissions were quickly proving their incapacity to cope with "discrimination and distortion" and because there existed a large no man's land where no laws were to be found at all, Congress was being pressed to legislate. From 1868 on, resolutions and bills in increasing numbers were recorded on the journals of both houses. A Senate Committee made a formal report in 1874. (It opposed regulation; only competition would drive down railroad rates, and the committee recommended that this come from waterway transportation, which should have Congressional help.) The House passed a bill in 1874, again in 1878, and once more in 1885. The Senate took no action, but growing pressures from all over the country—from Eastern legislatures, from the boards of trade of large cities, from big shippers as well as small, and from, of course, Western farmers and communities—could not be gainsaid. Senator S. M. Cullom of Illinois (in his home State he had been a stalwart friend of regulation) introduced a bill in 1884; this having failed, he prevailed upon the Senate to conduct another inquiry, with himself at the committee's head.

The Cullom Committee began its hearings in the latter part of 1885 and did so with great energy, moving through a good part of the country. It listened to railroad presidents, State commissioners, economists, farmers, merchants, manufacturers, packers, and millers. It was therefore able to report in 1886: "It is the deliberate judgment of the Committee that upon no public question are the people so nearly unanimous as upon the proposition that Congress should undertake in some way the regulation of interstate commerce." And the report put its finger on the source of disaffection in these words (it will be observed that it was concerned with commercial rather than agrarian grievances):

The policy which has been pursued [no federal regulation] has given us the most efficient railway service and the lowest rates known in the world; but its recognized benefits have been attained at the cost of the most unwarranted discriminations, and its effect has been to build up the strong at the expense of the weak, to give the large dealer an advantage over the small trader, to make capital count for more than the individual, credit and enterprise, to concentrate business at great commercial centers, and to necessitate combinations and aggregations of capital, to foster monopoly, to encourage the growth and extend the influence of corporate power and to throw the control of the commerce of the country more and more into the hands of the few.

Meanwhile Cullom introduced his bill again, as did Congressman J. H. Reagan of Texas his in the House. (Reagan had been responsible for the successful House measures of 1878 and 1885.) Both bills recognized that the center of the railroad problem had moved from where it had been in the early 1870s; the key question was no longer rates but discrimination. There were differences in the two bills, but their reconciliation was only a matter of time.

It was in the midst of this Congressional debate—in October, 1886—that the Supreme Court once more moved; this time to reverse itself completely and to repudiate the *Munn* decision. The case (*Wabash, St. Louis and Pacific Railway v. Illinois*) arose out of the Illinois railroad law's long-and-short-haul clause, which made it unfair discrimination for a road to charge the same or more for the transportation of freight of the same class over a shorter distance than it did for a longer one. The Court held the Illinois statute unconstitutional: the States had no right to regulate interstate commerce or to interfere with traffic moving across their borders. Their jurisdiction extended solely and exclusively over intrastate commerce; relief could come only through Congress in legislation of a national character. And thus were swept away nine-tenths of the State railroad-rate laws.

In January, 1887, Senate and House accepted a conference committee's report—the Senate yielded to the House and adopted its clause against pools and its wording of the long-short-haul prohibition—and President Cleveland signed the bill on February 4. Although, as we shall see, accomplishment fell far short of the intention of its makers, it was path-breaking in this sense: the federal government, using an administrative agency with quasi-judicial powers—the first of a company that later was to grow and flourish—intruded itself into the economic process. The walls of the citadel of private decision-making and *laissez-faire* had been breached; and, by the same token, the railroad industry became a monopoly enterprise, not only regulated but assured in time (for the Supreme Court had to follow through the logic of "reasonableness" of rates) of a "reasonable" return on investment.

The first three sections of the Interstate Commerce Act were largely based on the English law of 1854. They provided that all charges made by carriers should be "reasonable and just"; that special rates, rebates and drawbacks were illegal; and discrimination between persons, places, and commodities was to be proceeded against. Section 4 was the long-short-haul prohibition which made it unlawful for a carrier to charge more for transportation or carriage for a short haul than for a long one, when the conditions were substantially the same, when the same line was doing the hauling, and when the shorter distance was included in the longer. Section 5 made pools illegal. Section 6 called upon the railroads to file schedules of rates with a commission. And thus the Interstate Commerce Commission was set up: appointed by the President with the advice and consent of the Senate, the ICC was to have the authority to look into the management of interstate carriers, summon witnesses, and invoke the aid of the federal courts. After inquiry and hearings where violations had been charged and examined, its "findings shall thereafter in all judicial proceeds be deemed prima facie evidence as to each and every fact found." The first chairman of the ICC was Judge Thomas M. Cooley, the author of *Constitutional Limitations*.

The Interstate Commerce Commission did not find its work easy sledding. It was compelled to go to the courts again and again, and the judicial process moved slowly. Not until 1894 did the Supreme Court give its assent to the Commission's judicial powers; not until 1896 were witnesses compelled to appear and testify. Appeals from adverse rulings went to the federal courts; cases went back to the ICC for the filing of a new order and might be appealed again. It took four years as a rule for this procedure to unwind itself; the upshot was that by 1900 only nineteen petitions for relief against discriminations had been filed. The law was obscure; and the Supreme Court—in its conservative temper after 1886—ruled against the ICC in fifteen out of the sixteen cases that came to it out of the Commission from 1887 to 1905.

Two of these were almost fatal. In 1897, in the so-called *Maximum Freight Rate* case (the Interstate Commerce Commission had entered an order against a railroad in 1894) the court ruled that the ICC had no authority to set a maximum rate. The Commission had never claimed the rate-making power; it had, however, repeatedly said that it might prescribe a modification of rates if discrimination had been established. This the Court denied. In its decision it declared that the power to fix rates was a legislative and not an administrative or a judicial function; that the Congress had not transferred this right to the Commission; and that the Commission had not been given the power of prescribing rates and therefore could not seek aid from the courts to compel carriers to accept its schedules. What was left for it to do? It could collect statistics; it could compel the railroads to publish their rate schedules; it could move against discrimination.

The very same year, in the *Alabama Midland* case, the Supreme Court declared that the Commission was not empowered to render arbitrary judgment in the matter of long and short hauls unless it had considered every conditioning factor in the situation. It ruled that the "substantially similar circumstances" of the law were to be literally interpreted: Were the conditions of competition the same? By water? By rail? Were the two places involved affording the same kind of market outlets? Unless the Commission could prove these and other factors to be exactly similar, then it had no right to declare a rate unreasonable even if it involved a shorter haul.

As a consequence, the Interstate Commerce Commission fell into desuetude. It was not revived until 1906, when, as a result of President Theodore Roosevelt's campaign in the interest of railroad regulation, Congress passed the Hepburn Act. This law gave the Commission the right to reduce rates when complaints had shown them to be unreasonable or discriminatory. In 1910, Congress eliminated the "substantially similar circumstances" from the original act, and the long-and-short-haul clause began to have some meaning. And in 1913 the Interstate Commerce Commission was given the right to make a physical valuation of railroad properties as the first step toward arriving at a scientific basis of rate-making. Reasonableness of rates was to be tied to reasonableness of return on investment. By this time the railroads had become rich and powerful, and the hopes of the original innovators had been realized even beyond their most fanciful plans, plots, and stratagems.

CHAPTER EIGHT

MONEY AND BANKING

The General Role of Money "What is money?" "Is there an adequate stock of money?" were questions that roiled the waters of the post-Civil War period. Discontent on the fringes—affecting from the start the organized working-class movement, including until about 1875 new small manufacturers, and becoming a major issue in the late 1880s and early 1890s with the farmers growing wheat in the Far West and cotton in the South—had its inevitable impact on politics. There was, as a consequence, much tinkering (although of a minor sort) with the National Banking Act, first passed in 1863, and with the amount of greenbacks in circulation, first issued in 1862 to help finance the Civil War. A small addition to the currency came with the purchase of silver under the Bland-Allison Act of 1878 and a somewhat greater one with the Sherman Silver Purchase Act of 1890-93. The storm over money did not blow up to large proportions until the early 1890s, when the Populists advocated their Sub-Treasury scheme, and then really became portentous when the Democrats under Bryan came out flatly for the free and unlimited coinage of silver.

All of this, in greater part, was due to a general failure to understand what money really was. The fact is, given the broader definition universally accepted today, for the country at large there was an adequacy of money for the whole period. (Except, of course, during the later years of the depressions of 1873-79 and 1893-96. Today, with a more knowledgeable manipulation of the monetary system of central banking, money can be pumped into the economic stream to soften the rigors of recession and prevent business downturns from becoming the calamities they were in the nineteenth century.)

It has been commonly assumed that wholesale prices fell so sharply during 1873-96—the overall figure was 50 per cent—because the money supply was insufficient; it was the farmers particularly who made the charge. It should be observed, however, that, during the same years, the wholesale prices of farm products declined 45 per cent, while those of metals and metal products dropped 66 per cent, those of house furnishings 50 per cent, and those of textiles 56 per cent. A number of observations are therefore in order. The price fall was not unique to agricultural products. In all likelihood, the prices of the things the farmer bought fell more sharply than the things he sold, so that his relative position was better rather than worse. More important, America's great industrial advances took place during a period of sharp deflation. (So much for the contentions that growth and development are basically affected not only by inflation but that a creeping inflation is both a *sine qua non* of economic change-over and also desirable public policy.)

Why then did prices drop—if the money supply was adequate—during these years? One may propose these reasons. The free market, fully competitive even to the point of ruinous competition, generally prevailed. (Nothing demonstrates this more conclusively than the falls in railroad rates and the price of steel rails—both areas which were capital-intensive and where one might suppose the assumptions of managed prices would be substantiated.) Again, the virtual absence of business taxation permitted the wholesale plowing back of profits into technology, so that production and productivity sharply increased. This was particularly so in most industrial enterprises which were still noncorporate and nonpublic; profits did not have to be distributed and could be used for all sorts of purposes—vertical integration was one, development another—to lower costs and speed mass production. And, thirdly, the vast expansion of the domestic market, as a result of population growth and urbanization, permitted the passing on of lower costs into lower prices. The aggregate real income of farmers and the real wages of workers went up; the more successful among them—the general farmers of the Middle West and the East, the skilled craftsmen—were able to buy more; this in turn encouraged further technological improvements (through capital investments) and hence lower costs. True, wheat prices fell below the general average; but it was exactly in wheat-growing, among the major staple crops, that the greatest triumphs of productivity were accomplished. One must, in short, seek other reasons for the obsessions with money (and the hostilities to banking) on the part of some of the workers and some of the farmers.

What Money Is The simplest definition of "money" will suit our purposes best. Albert G. Hart says money is "property with which the owner can pay off a definite amount of debt with certainty and without delay"; and then he even broadens the definition by saying: "Money is property that community custom treats as if it were legal tender." (Albert G. Hart and Peter B. Kenen, *Money, Common Debt and Economic Activity*, 1961.)

This being so, and having in mind the role of custom (and the stability and proper debt management of governments), money is more than currency alone. Jefferson and Jackson assumed money was only currency in the most limited sense; that is, gold and silver; the workers and farmers of the post-Civil War period wanted to add to this only irredeemable government-issued paper bills (but not bank notes). But money also includes checking accounts based on bank deposits; and, with the greater and almost instantaneous ease of withdrawal, time or savings deposits. And, as near-money, in a descending scale—depending upon the two additional criteria we have suggested of stability and public debt management—are public short-term debt and public long-term debt. Finally, we should include as near-money savings-and-loan shares and the net cash values of life insurance.

The general reader may be interested in seeing how the money supply is made up at a given point of time by what Hart calls degree of "moneyness" (that is, degrees of certainty and length of delay). The figures represent the liquid assets of the nonbank public at the end of 1959; they were compiled by Hart. Metallic small change $2 billion and paper bills $26 billion, making up $28 billion of currency. Checking deposits $112.5 billion and time deposits $101.2 billion—so that the first four categories total $241.7 billion; and these Hart calls "cash assets." In addition are these other "liquid assets" in order of convertibility: U.S. government securities, $132.1 billion; savings and loan shares $53.4 billion; and net cash value of life insurance, $92 billion. The whole comes to $519.2 billion.

One cannot offer a similarly close analysis of the nature of the money supply during 1865-1896, simply because the reporting of banks was not good enough; but certain educated guesses have, in recent years, been made, and these will be used here as our discussion develops.

Some Historical Conceptions of Money   Alexander Hamilton—that extraordinary young man, whose impressive labors (in the face of the hostility of Jefferson and Madison) started off the young American Republic on the right track—knew as much about what constitutes money as any modern sophisticated American today. In the first place, he was aware that bank deposits were money. Thus, he said in his *Report on the Bank* in 1790:

Every loan which a bank makes is, in its shape, a credit given to the borrower in its books, the amount of which it stands ready to pay, either in its own notes, or in gold or silver, at his option. But in a greater number of cases, no actual payment is made in either. The borrower, frequently by check or order, transfers his credit to some other person . . . ; who, in turn, is as often content with a similar credit, because he is satisfied that he can, whenever he pleases, either convert into cash or pass it to some other hand, as an equivalent for it. And in this manner the credit keeps on circulating, performing in every stage the office of money. . . .

Secondly, he knew that U.S. government obligations were "near-money," assuming proper debt management by the setting up of a sinking fund for extinguishment and for open-market purchases. Thus, stability of value and general acceptance would be assured. And in this way—and this is why Hamilton argued for the funding of the whole Revolutionary debt—more "active capital" would be created (that is to say, using our modern terminology, the economy's liquidity would be increased) and the narrow fluctuation in the value of the government bonds (the term then used was "stock") would make them sound security for bank loans and also add them to the money supply.

Thirdly, Hamilton recognized the role of velocity as a force in determining prices and volumes of trade. As early as 1780, in a letter to Robert Morris, when he proposed the creation of a national bank, Hamilton put his finger unerringly on the reasons for the depreciation of the Continental currency. Its quantity was rising; but the complete collapse of confidence in the financing of the Continental Congress led to the more rapid circulation of the paper simply because people would not hold it. It entered into trade; and because goods were scarce, prices rose and a decline in the real value of money took place.

But given confidence in government (and when production is below full plant capacity), even if the quantity of money is increased and its velocity stays constant or rises (Hamilton called this money's "circulation"), the increase in the volume of goods produced or traded will be far greater than the increase in prices. Also, the interest rate will fall because of the greater amount of money available for the creation of bank deposits.

And Hamilton said: "Public utility is more truly the object of public banks than private profit," thus sensing the key role of central banking, so finally, a national bank as opposed to wholly private banks could both furnish needed financial assistance for government and maintain a proper level of sound money. This last would be achieved by requiring, when necessary, the redemption of State bank notes in coin and by acting as a bankers' bank, rediscounting their commercial paper. All of these ideas tied in with Hamilton's conception of the need for an energetic central government—certainly while the young America was still friendless, economically immature, and ringed around by great and hostile foreign powers.

These lessons were forgotten exactly when they had the same relevance as when Hamilton spoke. In the earlier period, the major concern was the establishment of the full faith and credit of the American republic; in the post-Civil War period, it was the creation of confidence in the business community. Nothing was more imperative than a stable and uniformly accepted money supply.

Yet it was then that the economists, like the monetary cranks of the period, wandered in strange pastures. Thus in 1877 Prof. Francis A. Walker of Yale University, the doyen of American economists, in his treatise called *Money* (and the book was republished unchanged as late as 1891), said flatly: "[Bank] deposits, like every other form of credit, save the use of money; they do not perform the function of money." And because he believed this, Walker, with his impressive influence, advocated both the expansion of greenbacks and the monetization of silver.

It was widely assumed, therefore, that there was a shrinkage of money; and all sorts of calculations were made to demonstrate this to account for the fall in prices. The most commonly accepted was linked with a per capita distribution. Thus a popular writer in 1887—and his book had wide currency—demonstrated the sharp contraction that had taken place in this fashion. Of course, he ruled out deposits as money, but, curiously enough, he included U.S. government obligations (as well as the greenbacks and bank notes). Therefore, in 1865, the money supply was $1,651 million and the per capita distribution $47.42; in 1873, the money supply (due to the funding of U.S. short-term certificates, bills, and notes, the increasing redemption of U.S. long-term bonds, and the disappearance of State bank notes) was $738.3 million and the per capita distribution $17.48; while in 1877, the money supply was as low as $696.4 million and the per capita distribution $14.60.

A per capita distribution (with no correction, of course, for prices) of $50 became the magical figure that the money reformers aimed at. This did not include deposits and, because banks also became the centers of attack, did not include bank notes. It was being said widely of the national banks that their practices were usurious, for they were charging excessive rates of interest; they discounted checks; they contracted their loans in time of stress; they favored industrial and commercial businessmen as against the farmers; they were—declared the farmer spokesmen notably—the agents and pawns of the international bankers. Money, then, was to be made up of coin (gold and silver), the greenbacks, and government notes having full legal tender with varying degrees of redeemability. Money reformers and the leaders of the workers demanded irredeemability, as we have already seen; the Populists called for a certain measure of redeemability—as we also have seen.

When it was already too late to stay the growing popular clamor, economists began to raise their voices about the role of deposits as money. It was not until 1887 that the influential Charles F. Dunbar, professor of political economy at Harvard, declared in a learned journal (and he repeated substantially the same observations in his popularly written *Theory and History of Banking* in 1891):

It [deposits] adapts itself to the demand of the moment without visible effort. . . . From the figures indeed the conclusion is irresistible that if, for any reason, the credit of a deposit currency through the agency of the national banks is hindered or limited, it will make its growth by means of State banks; and if not by these, then by a system of private banking, which no legislation can touch. . . .

And Dunbar denied contraction, linking stability with the return to the gold standard in 1879, for he said:

In fact, so soon as specie payments were firmly established and the value of credit currency was settled by its assured conversion at pleasure into a solid medium, contraction ceased to be any proper object of dread.

Money up to 1863 Thus, a developing economy seeking to transform itself into an industrial nation requires an expanding money supply uniform in value, responsive to the needs of business, and at the same time possessing real elements of stability. Shall government provide the money supply? Shall it be done by banks? Or shall it be done by banks and government together?

Up to the outbreak of the Civil War, there was general agreement that government was to play no active role in the creation of money. Not only did the Constitution deprive the States of the right to coin money or issue "bills of credit," but it was silent on Congress's power to do anything other than "coin money" and "regulate the value thereof." Indeed, as late as 1870, when the Supreme Court, after blowing hot and cold, decided that the Civil War U.S. notes (the so-called greenbacks) were legal tender, George Bancroft—who had always been a Jeffersonian and who had supported the Jacksonians—cried out in protest: "Our federal Constitution was designed to end forever the issue of bills of credit as legal tender in payment of debts, alike by the individual states and the United States."

Under Alexander Hamilton, it is true, a national bank was chartered and was given limited functions in the issuance of bank notes, but one of its most significant roles was as a regulator of the notes issued by State banks—that is to say, by insisting upon redemption in coin and holding their specie reserves, it could assure the uniformity and stability of the money supply. To this extent, the First Bank of the United States and its successor, the Second Bank, particularly under the presidency of Nicholas Biddle after 1823, played the role of a central bank. Hamilton also was aware, as we have seen, of the part to be assumed by the consolidated public debt in connection with the money supply. At the same time, he called for the creation of devices for debt retirement. He was wise enough to know that this could not be pushed without regard to particular circumstances. Thus, in his *Report on Manufactures,* in 1791, he said:

[247]

There ought to be in every government, a perpetual, anxious, and unceasing effort to reduce that [debt] which at any time exists, as fast as shall be practicable, consistent with integrity and good faith. [But:] It is, therefore, highly important, when an appearance of necessity seems to press upon the public councils, that they should examine well its reality, and be perfectly assured that there is no method of escaping from it, before they yield to its suggestions.

These wise admonitions went by the board in the administrations of Andrew Jackson and his successors. Jackson took pride in extinguishing entirely the public debt (thus depriving business of an important device for augmenting credit); and his successful attack on the Second Bank of the United States and its abolition deprived the country of its only agency for the regulation of its currency. Jackson and his followers in the Democratic Party charged that the Second Bank was a monopoly and notably that it was disregardful of the monetary (and credit) needs of the agrarian South and West. Actually, the Jacksonians were hostile to all banks and suspicious of any sort of money other than coin. This principle was written into the Independent Treasury Act (1840), which made that federal agency the exclusive one for handling government transactions, all of which were to be in gold and silver; also its funds were to be held in its own vaults in Washington and in sub-treasuries in cities throughout the country. That is, no bank notes were acceptable as legal tender as far as the national government itself was concerned; to this extent, therefore, as a regulator of the currency, central banking was abandoned altogether.

Ironically, despite their hostility to banks (an antagonism which was to continue until the end of the nineteenth century) and their suspicion of all currency other than gold and silver, Democrats and Western and Southern agrarians needed money and credit. There followed, in consequence, an extraordinary and, in many states, uncontrolled burgeoning of State banks. Except for New England, New York, and Louisiana, and in the 1850s, Indiana, Missouri, and Iowa, the virtually unchecked chartering of State banks by legislatures—with no real requirements for adequate capitalization, and maintenance of cash reserves, note redemption, and supervision by State authorities—led to monetary confusion in the 1840s and more particularly the 1850s. In the words of Bray Hammond in his authoritative *Banks and Politics in America* (1957): "The results of this Jacksonian revolution were obvious in monetary inflation, in speculation, in wasted labor, in business failures, in abandonment of an efficient means of credit control, and in corruption of a sound monetary system."

True to their hard-money principles (or prejudices), a number of Southern and Western States sought to ban banks altogether; a few set up a single monopolistic bank, with branches, with the State itself furnishing a part of the capital. Two of them, the Bank of Indiana and the Bank of Missouri, did very well; on the other hand, the Bank of Illinois, involved in public improvement schemes, quickly failed. Texas, Arkansas, and Iowa, in their State constitutions, absolutely banned any kind of banking; in the last, the agrarians, discussing the prohibition, were convinced that banking was a "withering and blighting curse," and that nothing else "ever devised by mortal man was so successful to swindle the people." It was inevitable, of course, that Iowa should become the happy hunting ground of out-of-State banks and in Iowa City alone there were circulating the notes of more than three hundred banks, many of them at discounts because of the absence of all real possibilities of redemption. As well, counterfeiting was rampant.

In the 1850s, however, need as against prejudice (or speculative interest as against conservatism) prevailed; and free banking was installed in Ohio, Illinois, Wisconsin, Tennessee, and Indiana—only to repeat all the errors as well as the deceits of the free banking of Michigan, which had become notorious in the 1840s as the exemplar of wildcat banking. These free banks monetized State debts (usually the bonds of Southern States selling at discounts of 10 to 20 per cent); issued bank notes against them; and made redemption—even if it could have been achieved—difficult or impossible by locating their offices in inaccessible places. Most of them failed in the panic of 1857.

Hugh McCulloch, president of the Bank of Indiana—which survived fraud and mismanagement—and later Secretary of the Treasury under President Andrew Johnson, thus described the free-banking of Indiana, installed in 1852, as a rival to the sound Bank of Indiana: "Anybody who could command two or three thousand dollars of money could buy on a margin the bonds necessary to establish a bank, to be paid for in its notes after its organization had been completed." And he gave as an example the history of three men who, with $10,000, among them bought "mostly on credit, $50,000 of the bonds of one of the Southern States." These were placed in the hands of the treasurer of the State; the circulating notes which were issued against them were then used to pay for the bonds. McCulloch went on:

This transaction having been completed, more bonds were bought and paid for in the same manner; and the operation was continued until the financial crisis of 1857 occurred; at which time, this bank, which had started with a capital of $10,000, had a circulation of $600,000, secured by State bonds, on which the bank had for two or three years been receiving the interest.

Bray Hammond seeks to exculpate the farmers themselves from such flimflam. The wildcat banks, he insists, "lent no money to farmers and served no farmer interest. They arose to meet the credit demands not of farmers but of States engaged in public improvements." Whether they lent directly or not to farmers, the banks did increase the circulation and this process eased credit. And certainly, the farmers clamored for public improvements—how, otherwise, were they going to get their products to market?—as loudly and persistently as any other interest. Farmers dominated the legislatures of the Western States in the 1850s, when free banking was authorized, as much as they did in the post-Civil War era—when they became easy money advocates—and as indeed they still do today in many of these States.

The commercialization of agriculture—and the need for reapers and other mechanical devices, and blooded livestock, plus the farmers' insatiable demand (or greed) for more land—required an increase in circulation and constantly expanding credit facilities. Only for a short period, in the years just after the end of the Civil War, when the farmers' prosperity in the West was unexampled and they therefore were silent in the bitter debate over expansion or contraction of the greenbacks, did agrarian interests express indifference to the money question; but during the late 1880s and early 1890s they made themselves heard. The Populist crusade articulated at every point agrarian resentments and yearnings. The Populists attacked banks—as agrarians had as far back as Thomas Jefferson, John Taylor of Caroline, and Andrew Jackson—but they wanted an expansion of "lawful" money to ease credit and to pay for their earlier follies when limited markets and high prices had encouraged them to overextend themselves in the purchase of land, equipment, and stock.

In any case, when Senator John Sherman of Ohio, who really was the father—and the outstanding defender—of the National Banking Act of 1863, arose to make his famous speech on the floor of the Senate on February 10, 1863, he offered, among others, the following reasons for the creation of a national banking system with the right of note issue:

This currency will be uniform. It will be printed by the United States. It will be of uniform size, shape and form; so that a bank bill issued in the State of Maine will be current in California; a bank bill issued in Ohio will be current wherever our government currency goes at all. . . . There is no limit to its convertibility. . . .

As a matter of course, now [under State banks], when a note is issued in Ohio, if it struggles as far as Washington, it is discounted two per cent, although it is just as good as any other note, and is driven back by the very fact that it is at a discount. If that note has the similitude of the United States of America, and the stamp and the guarantee which the United States gives it, it would go everywhere; a note-holder would not care whether it were issued in Ohio, Connecticut or California. That very similitude would give it a broader circulation, and, consequently, a more profitable circulation to the bank; it would not be returned so quickly. . . .

There is another important advantage which the banks would derive from this system. They would be guarded against all frauds and alterations. There would be but five or six kinds of notes in the United States, instead of the great diversity that there now is.

Money During the Civil War and Reconstruction Periods   As soon as it became apparent that the Civil War was going to be long and sanguinary, awesome tasks confronted the government. Not the least of these was the size and nature of the money supply, and this had to be expanded for many and compelling reasons. There were the requirements of government itself, as federal revenues dropped, as well as the needs of businessmen if wartime production was to be speeded up. There was the heavy outflow of gold to pay for imports and the hoarding of gold at home as confidence in easy victory disappeared. And the reluctance of both the Treasury and Congress to sell U.S. government obligations at a discount and an equal fear of expanding tax revenues, lest business take alarm and fail to engage in new wartime ventures, also played their parts in the decision to issue fiat money which could be used as legal tender and to charter national banks which could issue notes, against the purchase and security of war bonds.

To check the drain of gold, specie payments were suspended at the end of 1861—but a free market was permitted to exist. The price of gold naturally went up—the premium on gold was as high as 103 per cent in 1864—and even at the end of fiscal 1865 the premium was as high as 57 per cent.

Three legal-tender acts were passed—the first in 1862, the second and third in 1863—authorizing the Treasury to emit a total of $450 million in so-called United States notes (these came to be called greenbacks) which were legal tender for both public and private debts. Only the interest on the public debt and import duties—the latter constituting a fund out of which the former was to be met—were to be paid in coin. Also, the third legal-tender act permitted the Treasury to sell up to $400 million in short-term Treasury notes, and these constituted a further addition to the money supply. At the end of the War, there were in circulation $378 million in greenbacks and $205 million in Treasury notes.

Two changes in fiscal policy halted the emission of greenbacks: the marketing of government securities was put in the hands of the Philadelphia banker Jay Cooke, and he and his associates were highly successful in selling them at home and abroad; and in 1862 and more particularly in 1864 Congress took the plunge and vastly expanded the internal tax system (including the imposition of a federal income tax) so that revenues from internal sources mounted from $10 million in fiscal 1863-64 to $209 million in fiscal 1864-65.

The legal-tender program, during the War, was generally supported in Congress by the Republicans. They favored a cheap money policy and protective tariffs—the first, because an expansion of the money supply made for easier credit and the possibility therefore of inaugurating new business ventures, while a mounting premium on gold diminished imports; the second, because the encouragement of "infant manufacture" which Hamilton, and later Clay, had advocated could occur only behind the sheltering walls of high tariffs. On the other hand, easy money was opposed by the Democrats, who continued to be loyal to the

Jacksonian ideas of hard money. By the same token, and for the same reasons, the Republicans backed Secretary of the Treasury Salmon P. Chase, and his most stalwart supporter Senator John Sherman, in the establishment of a National Banking System which would increase the money supply and make it uniform. And the Democrats—again equating "lawful" money wholly with coin—were in opposition.

By 1869, important shifts had taken place. The Republican Party— with the Old Radicals, who consistently had been inflationists and protectionists, gone from its councils—now began to demand, in the interests of price stability, the contraction of the legal tenders and the resumption of specie payments, with the retention of protectionism, of course. If duties were left very high and new schedules were constantly being added, it no longer was necessary to maintain a premium on gold in order to check imports. Monetary stability, too, would encourage the return to the United States of the foreign investments which were so badly needed if railroad construction and modernization were to take place on a vast scale.

The Democrats, on their part, became monetary expansionists, foresaking their long-held loyalties to coin as the only kind of "lawful" money that was acceptable and calling for additional emissions of legal tenders, because these were government issues and because their continued suspicion of banks and bank notes made it imperative that public money be increased.

The position of the economist Henry C. Carey of Philadelphia, during the war years and those immediately following, is illuminating. (He died in 1879; he had the widest influence of the economists of his day.) He was the spokesman par excellence for protectionism; and he was for easy money, because this would defend American manufacturers, farmers, and workers from the financial, or banking, "monopolists" of the Eastern seaboard who were allied with the trading or importing interests and hence hostile to domestic industrial enterprise. By combining manufacturers, farmers, and workers in a common cause—in a "union of all producing classes," Carey sought to reinvoke that "harmony of interests" of which Hamilton had spoken as early as 1791. Carey, too, held that money was made up of currency entirely; bank deposits to him, as to Francis A. Walker in the 1880s, as we have seen, did not augment the money supply.

Certainly, the iron manufacturers of Pennsylvania (and of New York and the Ohio Valley as well) followed Carey closely, as did the Pennsylvania Old Radicals in the House of Representatives, Thaddeus Stevens and William D. ("Pig-Iron") Kelley. The ironmasters were the most powerful element in the creation of the American Industry League in 1867, which chose Peter Cooper, the country's outstanding iron manufacturer, as its first president. Speaking before the League in 1868, Cooper raised the flag of defiance when he attacked those "whose pecuniary interests, as importers, agents, and merchants are directly and deeply identified with those of the manufacturers of Great Britain and Continental Europe." It was this clamor that halted Secretary of the Treasury McCulloch's efforts to contract the greenbacks in 1868. In another year, however, the short-time postwar recession of 1866-68 being over, the ironmasters were ready to settle for monetary stability; and even though the country was in the midst of a serious depression beginning with 1873, they refused to continue following Peter Cooper, who, true to his soft-money views, had accepted in 1876 the nomination for the Presidency of the Greenback Party.

The workers, too, had become converts to soft-money ideas, and this in the face of their earlier adherence to Jacksonian hard-money notions and the fact that, because of wartime inflation, their real wages had fallen. The obsession of the organized workers with money—under the leadership of the National Labor Union in the late 1860s and of the Knights of Labor in the 1870s and 1880s—we have discussed in an earlier chapter.

As for the farmers, during the Civil War, and in the immediate postwar years, they seemed indifferent to the whole money question. The war produced agricultural prosperity—the prices of wheat and corn were particularly high—and this continued into the recession years 1866-68. As a result, farmers as such took no part in the discussions about the contraction or expansion of the legal tenders, nor did they support the so-called Pendleton Plan or the Democratic Party in 1868, when it went inflationist. Indeed, agriculture was only mildly interested in money during the 1870s, when the Greenbackers were carrying on their agitation. To the farmers, the bankers and Eastern financial "monopolists" were not so much the enemies as were the railroads and granaries and warehousemen; the Granger Acts of this decade were directed at the control of these agencies and the elimination of their abuses. We have earlier discussed the farmers and money; and more later.

The bankers were of mixed minds. Those of New York and New England, as early as 1866, were already committed to "sound" money. They were for the contraction of the legal tenders and the resumption of specie payments. In part, they had been the direct beneficiaries of the wartime inflation that had come from national banknote issues, for, as Carey pointed out again and again, the apportionment of notes that had been set up had favored heavily the banks of these two Eastern sections. In part, their alliances continued to be—again noting Carey's insistence—with merchants, traders and importers, rather than with manufacturers. It should be observed further that an inflationary period is likely to be much more favorable to farmers and industrial enterprisers than to banks; certainly during the Civil War, as Wesley Clair Mitchell demonstrated so cogently in his *History of the Greenbacks* (1903), interest (and rents) lagged even behind wages (and, of course, far behind profits) in returns on capital. Mitchell showed that the call-money rates ranged between 5 and 7 per cent and 60-day loans never went higher than 9.3 per cent during 1863 and 1864. This scarcely compensated for the sharp decline in the purchasing power of money; those who held mortgages were even worse hit, for principal was affected. Even the high dividends banks were able to pay (in New York they were highest in 1865, averaging 11.88 per cent) did not make up for the price inflations of 1864 and 1865. By 1866, prices were beginning to move down steadily, and interest and bank-stock dividends, therefore, were bringing in a relatively much more satisfactory return. In the light of these circumstances it is not difficult to see why Eastern bankers so openly fought the anticontractionists of 1866 and the expansionists of 1868 and later.

Western bankers, on the other hand—at any rate, during the immediate postwar years—were opposed to contraction. Robert P. Sharkey, in his closely reasoned and highly informing *Money, Class, and Party: An Economic Study of Civil War and Reconstruction* (1959), quotes a Western banker writing to the *Bankers' Magazine* in 1866:

Let the currency alone! Lay no violent hands upon it. Do not disturb its equilibrium by experiments. After such an unprecedented struggle the country needs all the rest it can obtain; and every facility for its recuperation should be resolutely preserved intact, until its prostrate energies are again brought into action, its immense resources developed, and its industry established upon a solid and permanent foundation. . . . For these purposes, we need all the currency we have; its diminution to any considerable extent would immediately put a stop to the recuperative efforts of the country . . . and plunge it into a deeper abyss of financial calamity.

Within three years, although the Congressional debate was a bitter one, the issue was decided. Hugh McCulloch, the Secretary of the Treasury, in 1866, sought a limited contraction of the greenbacks; and he had his way over the objections of Old Radicals in the House like Stevens and Kelley of Pennsylvania, Bingham and Hayes of Ohio, and Julian of Indiana, and in the Senate of Wade of Ohio and Chandler and Howard of Michigan. The recession of 1866-68 and the growing (and alarming) popularity of the "Ohio rag-baby" idea—which was translated into a Congressional proposal by Congressman Pendleton of Ohio in 1867—gave Congress pause in pursuing McCulloch's policy further. For the Pendleton Plan demanded the abolition of national bank notes and their replacement by an augmented greenback supply; in this way, argued Pendleton, the interest being paid the banks on the bonds they held (as security for their bank notes) could be saved, in fact diverted into a sinking fund for the redemption of the wartime bond issues. At one and the same time, consequently, bank notes would be eliminated, bonds exchanged for greenbacks, and what was left could be ultimately redeemed—to the lightening of the tax burden.

But the Democratic Party—which in the Presidential contest of 1868 had swallowed whole the inflationary notions of the Pendleton supporters—was soundly defeated by the Republicans having as their standard-bearer the war hero U. S. Grant; too, the recession was over at the end of 1868. In 1869 Congress laid down monetary policy as regards the greenbacks once and for all in this wise (Stevens was now dead; Sumner was gone from the Senate; the New Radicals dominated the Republican Party and in the House voted for the so-called Public Credit Bill of 1869, 108 for to 36 against): The existing volume of greenbacks in circulation was to remain substantially untouched; the government pledged itself to pay all its obligations—greenbacks and interest-bearing bonds and notes—in coin; and it solemnly promised to resume specie payments "at the earliest practicable moment." The Republican

Party, despite its initial Radical antecedents, was now, and continued to be during the later renewal of the soft-money agitation, the party of sound money. And manufacturers and bankers agreed.

The amount of United States notes (greenbacks) in circulation fluctuated narrowly: at the end of fiscal 1866, the total was $327.8 million; fiscal 1869, $314.7 million; fiscal 1874, $371.4 million; and then the course was downward, getting as low as $256.1 million at the end of fiscal 1896.

In the midst of prolonged depression in 1875, a Republican Congress took the plunge: it voted that on Jan. 1, 1879, the legal-tender greenbacks (to be reduced to $300 million) were to be made redeemable at par, in gold or silver, at the discretion of the Treasury. Obviously, the most important reason for the step was to bring American prices into harmony with those prevailing in gold-standard countries; these had been moving downward, so that American price declines were simply part of a universal phenomenon. To conciliate those interests still concerned about the continued fall in prices—and the return to specie payments seemed like a deflationary measure—the National Banking Act was amended in two important particulars. The old regulation for banknote apportionment, which had discriminated against the Western and Southern States, was rescinded; and the absolute limitation upon the issue of bank notes ($300 million) was dropped. In the latter connection it may be observed that this presumably liberalizing gesture turned out to be of no significance, for the rise in the price of government bonds discouraged banks from purchasing additional quantities as a cover for note issue. The fact is, as we shall see, banks were turning away more and more from note circulation as the basis of the country's money supply.

The fall in the price of gold (in 1876 it was at 107, and at the end of 1877 at 102½) helped banks and the Treasury in accumulating gold toward the day when resumption would take place. American agricultural surpluses contributed significantly, for the constantly growing demand of Europe for American foodstuffs led to a dramatic change in the country's balance of trade. Beginning with 1873, exports began to exceed imports, by 1878 the balance in America's favor being $257.8 million. A sizable part of this was being paid in gold.

On Jan. 1, 1879, the Treasury possessed $135.4 million in gold coin and bullion, $167 million in silver dollars, and $15.5 million in fractional silver coin. The net amount of gold thus available for redemption of the legal tenders was 40 per cent of the notes outstanding; also, more than one-half of the remainder of the notes was being held by the national banks themselves. As a result, the critical day passed without moment, and very few notes were presented for redemption in gold. Indeed, by the end of the year, so fully in accord were Americans with the step taken and so confident were they in the solvency of the government that the holders of coin obligations of the Treasury accepted more than $250 million in notes in payment.

At this point, an observation may be made that has relevance to the heated discussions over government monetary policy that took place later. Did greenback contraction, the return to the gold standard, and the limited purchases of silver precipitate the fall in prices (which, from 1873 to 1896, continued downward steadily) and therefore to agricultural distress? What is interesting in this connection is this: despite the drop in circulation and the decrease in the currency supply, the industrial and agricultural advances of the country went ahead on seven-league boots. Increases in output and significant changes in the nature of output (the mounting shift-over from agricultural to industrial production) were unexampled in our history; the rate of growth of 1865-1900 far exceeded that of 1900-1929, for example. In other words, improving productivity and market expansion, in the United States and in the whole Western world, and the highly competitive nature of the market, were responsible for the general price decline. Prosperity and economic progress, in short, were possible and realizable independently of the position of commodity prices and could take place even when prices were falling.

Another observation: the fall in circulation did not necessarily mean monetary stringency, for the steady increase of bank deposits and of the substitution of checks for notes kept the total money supply at a high level. One will have to look for other reasons than those put forth by the embattled agrarians of the 1880s and 1890s—that monetary dearth was responsible for agricultural distress and intransigency—to account for the alarms and excursions of Populism and free silver.

The Role of Silver   The demands for additions to the money supply did not cease with the final decisions taken by Congress concerning the greenbacks. The focus of agitation now shifted over to silver: it was charged that silver had been demonetized illegally and surreptitiously, that it ought to be coined freely at the ratio of 16 to 1 to gold.

In 1873, after having debated the question on and off and without too much interest for two years, Congress passed an act revising and amending the laws relating to the mints and the coinage of money. Hidden away in the verbiage of a long and involved piece of legislation was a clause which, in effect, permitted the suspension of the minting of silver: the silver dollar, in other words, was omitted from the list of coins. This superseded the legislation of 1834 and 1837, which had authorized the minting of gold and silver at assay offices at a ratio which changed from time to time, being generally fixed at 16 to 1.

Congress, in 1873, was simply recognizing realities; for thirty-five years previously, little silver had been offered for minting because its market price had been rising. In 1870, the market value of silver was in the ratio of 15.57 to 1; in 1873, 15.92 to 1. In other words, in 1873 the silver dollar was worth $1.02. A few years later the silver production of the world began to increase with the discovery of new lodes in Colorado, Nevada, and later Utah. Silver now was no longer at a premium but was worth less than gold (at 16 to 1). In 1874, the ratio fell to 17.94 to 1; in 1879, 18.39 to 1. Then it became profitable to mint silver dollars; but when the possessors of silver bullion took their stock to assay offices, they found that the law of 1873 had demonetized silver.

Thus arose the cry of the "Crime of 1873." To silverites, the law had been born out of a conspiracy the American money monopolists had entered into with British bankers! Their purpose was to force the single gold standard on the world for the benefit of creditors and in the interests of a dearer dollar. This charge of a "conspiracy" has no merit, for there is no evidence in the Congressional debates of any intent other than a recognition on the part of Congress that the silver dollar, up to that time, was no longer being minted at the request of the holders of bullion. But plausibility was given to this talk of a conspiracy, which now apparently had become international, when the rest of the European countries began to follow Britain in abandoning silver. Germany did so in 1871, as did also in 1873 the Latin Monetary Union (France, Switzerland, Belgium, Italy, and Greece); the Scandinavian countries, Spain, and Holland followed suit by 1875. This, rather than giving the free-silver advocates pause, only led to a redoubling of effort—the silver-mining interests naturally had a large stake in the agitation.

Legislation, therefore, was regularly introduced; the Bland-Allison Act of 1878 was finally passed; it was less than even half a loaf. The Treasury was authorized to buy and mint $2 million to $4 million silver bullion monthly, making its purchases at the market. Against this, silver certificates of not less than $10 were to be issued (in 1886, Congress authorized silver certificates of $1, $2, and $5). During 1878-1890—the years when the law was on the statute books—only 378 million silver dollars (at a cost of $308 million) were added to the money supply. It is doubtful if more than 35 per cent of them circulated: because they were heavy and unwieldy and because the banks frowned on their use, they were quickly retired to Sub-Treasury offices.

On the one hand, efforts to withdraw the silver altogether, on the other, to expand its quantity, engaged their proponents in a wordy debate. Entirely for reasons of political expediency, the latter won. The McKinley tariff bill of 1890 was before the House and had little chance of passage without the support of Western Congressmen. To win them over, a new silver-purchase act was agreed on; and the tariff bill became law.

The so-called Sherman Silver Purchase Act of 1890 in important particulars departed from the lines laid down in the act of 1878. The Treasury was now to buy 4.5 million ounces of silver monthly for coinage (this was virtually the total American production; by this time, the ratio had dropped to 19.77 to 1); against this were to be issued Treasury notes which, of course, had full legal tender. These notes could be redeemed either in gold or silver at the discretion of the Secretary of the Treasury; after July 1, 1891, silver dollars were to be coined only as they were necessary for redemption.

Between 1890 and 1893, when the law was repealed, a total of $153 million was expended for silver—and issued as Treasury notes, thus by this amount expanding the money supply. (But as the Treasury purchases were made in ounces, and because the price of silver continued to fall, there was a limit and a contracting one to the issuance of Treasury notes. To this extent, "unlimited" coinage did not occur; and this is why, beginning with about 1893, the demand from the silverites came to be the "unlimited coinage of silver at a rate of 16 to 1.") The law was repealed, as has been said, in 1893 at the insistence of President Cleveland; to him and his supporters the depression of 1893, which had then set in, was closely linked with the purchase of silver, which, in turn, caused a want of confidence in America's fiscal integrity on the part of both American and foreign bankers. The former curtailed their loans and also sought redemption of Treasury notes in gold. The latter began to withdraw bank deposits in gold. The sharp drop in the Treasury gold reserves forced an unwilling Senate to yield to Presidential pressures, and repeal took place on Oct. 30, 1893. Thus ended the experiment with bimetallism; but not the popular outcry. To silver supporters and farmers the continued depression only proved their contention that inadequate money was at the root of all the evil that had befallen America.

The National Banking Act   We must now tell the story of the National Banking Act—to which allusion has been made in passing— in systematic form. The proposal for the creation of a network of national banks originally came from Secretary of the Treasury Chase, who found his model in New York State's free-banking scheme. (The heart of that plan had been the issuance of notes against the deposits of securities, which were not necessarily public obligations.) Chase was both hostile to the idea of greenbacks and convinced that the notes of the State banks were inadequate and uncertain for the additional monetary needs of the country. In the first place, there were only $200 million of them in 1861; secondly, many, perhaps most, were emitted against a miscellany of securities frequently of a dubious nature; thirdly, there were not adequate specie reserves to protect their circulation and assure redemption; and fourthly—because of the prohibitions under which the Independent Treasury operated—State bank notes were not acceptable as legal tender for government transactions.

When Chase first put the idea before Congress, in 1861, he stressed, however, two additional considerations: bank-note issues based on government bonds would create a market for these securities; again, they would provide an expanded currency which would possess "uniformity in security" and furnish an "effectual safeguard, if effectual safeguard is possible, against depreciation." Senator Sherman, in his speech of February 10, 1863, echoed these sentiments and furnished additional arguments for the enactment of such a measure. He made much of the need for monetary uniformity, as we have seen. The new national banks would be depositories for public funds and would facilitate tax collection. They would be an important link in binding the country together. Said he:

It will promote a sentiment of nationality. ↞ . . . The policy of this country ought to be to make everything national as far as possible; to nationalize our country, so that we shall love our country. If we are dependent on the United States for a currency and a medium of exchange, we shall have a broader and more generous nationality.

The original bank bill was passed in 1863 by narrow margins; the Senate vote was 23 for to 21 against; the House vote 78 for to 64 against. Democrats voted against the measure because they were hard-money men; Old Radicals like Thaddeus Stevens voted against because they were soft-money men and feared that the national bank notes (which had to be limited, because they were tied to bonds) would prevent the unlimited issue of greenbacks. The law was rewritten in 1864, but this time opposition to it was slight.

The important provisions of the National Banking Act were these:

1. Bank associations were to be formed upon application to the newly created Comptroller of the Currency. The minimum capitalization allowable was $50,000, and this was only for places of 6,000 population or less. (This was an obvious hardship for rural communities; too much capital was being required to serve farmer needs.) Fifty per cent of the capital stock was to be paid in at the time of commencement of the banking business; the rest was to be paid in at the rate of 10 per cent every month.

2. Such associations could engage in the banking business by "discounting and negotiating promissory notes, drafts, bills of exchange . . . ; by receiving deposits; by buying and selling exchange, coin and bullion; by loaning money on personal security; by obtaining, issuing and circulating notes." No person or company could borrow more than 10 per cent of the value of the bank's capital. Nor could banks lend on mortgages: a prohibition which hit agriculture hard, for farmers needed long-term loans—to buy their farms and equipment—which could be secured only by mortgage. (It became the practice, too, of the national banks to deal generally in short-term paper with 60-90-day maturities, and this hurt the farmers again as as well as new and expanding manufacturers.)

3. The associations were to deposit with the Treasury of the United States government bonds to an amount not less than $30,000 or not less than one-third of the capital stock paid in. In exchange, the associations were to receive circulating bank notes printed by the government, equal to 90 per cent of the current value (or par value, if the bonds were to sell at premiums) of the bonds. The bonds were to be held by the Treasurer. (It turned out that bank notes based on bonds had a reverse elasticity: when business was dull and credit expansion needed, bond prices would go up and banks would sell them, thus depriving themselves and the country of additional currency; when business was enjoying boom times, and brakes on credit expansion were needed, bond prices would be low and banks could and would acquire them to increase note circulation. That is to say, the bond-note connection threatened deflation when inflation was required and inflation when deflation was a prime necessity.)

4. The total amount of notes thus to be issued was to be $300 million, and these were to be apportioned among the States on the basis of population and previous banking capital, resources, and business. (This idea of apportionment was in the original Act of 1863, was dropped from the Act of 1864, and restored in 1865; in 1865, too, existing State banks—without limitation, and in disregard of the quotas set up—were given the right to become national banks.) It should be noted further—and this fact has already been commented on—that the ceiling of $300 million of notes was eliminated in 1875 and virtually free banking was established. But this had no effect on note issue; quite the reverse—between 1874 and 1878 the national currency decreased by about $50 million.

5. The reserve requirements created three different kinds of banks. At the bottom of the pyramid were the country banks, which were to keep on hand in "lawful" money 15 per cent of their notes and deposits; but three-fifths of this reserve could be maintained, at interest, in banks of so-called reserve cities, of which seventeen initially were designated. The banks of reserve cities, in turn, were to keep reserves of 25 per cent; they could, however, bank one-half of this with correspondents in New York (in the 1880s, Chicago and St. Louis were added). Finally, banks in central reserve cities were to maintain the 25 per cent reserves. This promised well—particularly when an amendment to the Banking Act in 1874 based reserves on deposits entirely. But the temptation on the part of country banks and reserve city banks to move such a large portion of

their assets to New York—they obtained interest for them—and the eagerness of the New York banks to put these funds out at call and thus finance stock-market operations, really undermined the whole reserve system. Stock-market manipulation, on the one hand, was made possible; and when the country banks, to finance the annual harvesting season, pulled back their balances, brokers' loans were suddenly curtailed and stock-market panics often followed.

6. In 1865, an excise tax of 10 per cent was put on bank notes issued by State banks; this drove such notes out of circulation, accelerated the movement into the national banking system, on the one hand, and forced the creation of new kinds of State banks, on the other.

In addition to these drawbacks in the national banking scheme, two others merit attention. The first had to do with note redemption, the second with the apportionment of notes regionally. Because no provision was made for central redemption, the same sort of weakness that had characterized the prewar State bank notes threatened: a floating note supply, not too sensitive to business needs, could become a powerful inflationary force. The contractionists raised this cry, and called for redemption in greenbacks in a central place like New York. Country banks, on the other hand, were opposed. When the issue of the amount of currency in circulation was resolved finally, in 1874, the Banking Act provided for redemption in "lawful" money by the United States Treasurer in Washington. To facilitate this, banks were called upon to deposit 5 per cent of their circulation in "lawful" money with that officer; and to prevent hardship, this deposit was to be considered part of the reserve requirements of banks. The step had two important consequences: it made the government, in effect, the guarantor of all the bank notes in circulation, for it really was being required to pay on demand all notes being presented and not simply those to the limit of the reserve it was holding; and it led to a rise in the deposit-reserve ratio.

The apportionment of the notes—really, their maldistribution—led to bitter attacks on the whole banking system, particularly on the part of inflationists like Carey, Stevens, and Kelley. Because of the rules laid down—notes were to be apportioned according to population and the amount of banking business—exactly those two sections of the country, New York and New England, which needed the new bank notes least (because their banks had already developed demand deposits, as a means of creating money, to a high degree) were the ones that were most favored. Carey pointed out that banks in these two regions, with a population of 7 million as against 30 million for the rest of the country, were allotted 60 per cent of the authorized circulation. Other ratios were even more disturbing; in 1866, for example, the per capita circulation for ten Southern States came to $1.70 and for seven Middle Western States to $6.36, while that for New England and New York came to $33.30. In the South and West—where demand deposits were still in embryonic form—money therefore was tight.

Two steps were taken to correct this injustice. The Act of 1870 increased the maximum amount of notes by $54 million, the whole of it being set aside for those States (notably, the Southern ones) which had suffered from the initial distribution. And in 1875, when free-banking was provided for by the elimination of the $354-million maximum, all banks theoretically could issue as many notes as they pleased—provided they were willing and able to buy the necessary bonds. But bond prices were going up; the profit that could be made on circulation, it has been estimated, was only 2.65 per cent in 1878.

State Banks   It was small wonder that all sorts of pressures, particularly from the country districts and the small towns, and from new industrial companies, were being brought to bear on State legislatures to revise and liberalize State banking laws. As far as these interests were concerned, the National Banking Act and its various amendments demanded too great a capitalization for the creation of banks, set the reserve requirements too inflexibly and too high (including the provision for redemption), made it impossible for new banks or modest banks to expand their circulation because of the mounting prices (and declining interest rate) of the government bonds, which were the only security permissible as a cover for notes, and forbade banks the right to lend on mortgages. Farmers, new manufacturers, small businessmen, those interested in the development and modernization of the growing cities of the land, needed more liberal credit terms.

These they obtained—from agencies created by the States and not the national government. Because this was so, the monetary supply of the country (the deposits of the State banks, added to the deposits of the national banks, plus the greenbacks, coin, and national bank notes in circulation) kept on increasing; in all likelihood, generally, it kept pace with the country's economic growth, the Populists and the Bryanites to the contrary notwithstanding. Did the absence of central banking devices (control over the rediscount rate and reserve requirements) permit too much money to be pumped into the economy—and thus help in bringing on booms and busts, notably the depressions of 1873-79 and 1893-96 and the bad recession of 1884-85? This, too, is to be doubted. It was an age of great exuberance and of daring innovators and business promoters; frequently, because their expectations were so high, they overextended themselves, but it was their optimism and their ability to make profits (plus the eagerness of European capital to finance new railroad construction, the opening up of new mines, and the throwing open of new lands to settlement) rather than the expanding money supply that was at the basis of this extraordinary growth. One should remember—as has already been pointed out—that prices during 1873-96 kept on falling in the midst of this expansion.

Beginning with the 1870s, a general movement to expand the country's State bank and trust company facilities took place. By special charters, and increasingly by general enabling laws, such banks—without the right of note issue, of course—were incorporated in great numbers all over the nation, in rural districts and in small towns as well as in cities. They appeared because of the low capitalization demanded and low cash-reserve requirements and because they were permitted to lend on land mortgages, the mortgages and bonds of manufacturing and mining companies, and on commercial paper longer than the 90-day maximum which had become the practice of the national banks.

In no instance did a State demand that any part of the capital of these banks be invested in federal government securities. At the same time supervision by State banking authorities was mild and frequently quite perfunctory (in Pennsylvania, for example, the office of superintendent of banking was not established until 1891). The result everywhere, including the back-country, was a great expansion of deposits by these new commercial banks.

In addition to the State commercial banks being permitted to lend on mortgages, one must note the increasing prominence of savings banks and insurance companies. Between 1875 and 1895, the total assets of savings banks increased from $896 million to $2,198 million.

Charles F. Dunbar was seeking to call attention to the increasingly important role being played by these new State banks, and while his figures are incomplete, the data he was collecting unmistakably showed the changing character of American banking. In 1897, for example, he demonstrated that there were in existence at least 549 State banks with a minimum capitalization of $10,000 or less; an equal number with a capitalization of over $10,000 and under $20,000; and at least 1,585 with capitalizations between $20,000 and $50,000. These same 2,700 banks had a total capitalization of $69.5 million; they are to be compared with the national banks of the minimum allowable capitalization of $50,000, whose number was 1,116 and whose total capitalization was $58.3 million. Kansas, Nebraska, and the Dakotas permitted banks to start with a capitalization of $5,000; Missouri and Minnesota put the minimum at $10,000, and Michigan at $15,000; while in New York and Iowa it was $25,000.

The office of the Comptroller of the Currency, too, tried to keep abreast of the trend—and this despite the fact that State banks no longer had to report to Washington. (In 1883, Congress repealed the tax on the capital and deposits of all banks, national, State, and private; from thence on reports to the Comptroller were incomplete.) In 1891, for example, he reported on 2,572 State banks (excluding trust companies): of these, 1,313 were in the Northwestern States; 444 were in the Southern

TABLE 13

	Deposits of State banks, millions	Deposits of national banks, millions
1870	$ 69.6	$ 705.5
1876	1,151.3	841.7
1888	2,174.9	1,716.2
1890	2,597.7	1,978.8
1892	2,970.2	2,327.3
1896	3,345.3	2,278.9

States—both regions the heart of the Populist agitation centering in more money; while only 196 were in the States of Ohio, Indiana, Illinois, and Michigan; 176 were in New York and 84 were in Pennsylvania. All these institutions were engaged in deposit banking.

Too, the deposits of State banks soon exceeded those of the national banks. (The figures in Table 13 were calculated by the Comptroller of the Currency, in fiscal 1930-31. They are not "adjusted" as are the figures cited later for deposits; hence the slight difference.)

The Size of the Money Supply   What, now, were the monetary resources of the United States, especially in those years when the money agitation was running high? Milton Friedman and Anna Jacobson Schwartz, in their monumental *A Monetary History of the United States, 1867-1960* (1963) have finally furnished us an authoritative answer. (Earlier estimates of theirs were· used in *Historical Statistics of the United States,* 1957 edition.) Professor Friedman and Mrs. Schwartz, in calculating the money supply, use the concepts "currency held by the public" and "seasonally adjusted deposits" to define the money of the period. The first included gold and silver coin and certificates, Treasury notes of 1890, greenbacks, national bank notes, and subsidiary coinage, but excluded currency in bank vaults and in the U.S. Treasury. The second included demand and time deposits of all commercial banks and deposits of mutual savings banks; but excluded interbank deposits and U.S. government deposits. (By this definition, savings-and-loan associations and credit unions—these were important in Massachusetts—were not banks.)

The figures in Table 14 are presented for the years 1870, 1876, 1888, 1890, 1892, and 1896. It will be observed that, in 1870, "currency held by the public" constituted almost 30 per cent of the total money supply; and that, by 1896, the ratio had fallen to less than 14 per cent. The magical formula of $50 per capita may now be tested in the light of actual experiences. In 1870, total money per capita stood at $43.20. In 1876 (a depression year), at $54.60. In 1880, at $76.00. In 1890, at $83.70. In 1892 (when the Populists were riding high) at $91.00 and in 1896 (a depression year) at $84.10. These values are in terms of current prices; but prices kept on falling from 1873 on. As the table shows, wholesale prices dropped 50 per cent from 1870 to 1896. If, then, *nominal* money is converted into *real* money, the result is even more arresting. For, by 1896, when the demand for an increase in the money supply reached its highest point, the per capita *real* money stood at $168.10.

Was there enough money to meet the country's expanding requirements? Except for the troughs of the depression years, the answer seems to be "yes." Thus, Professor Friedman and Mrs. Schwartz say: "The

TABLE 14
(In millions)

Year	Currency held by the public	Commercial bank deposits	Mutual savings bank deposits	Total nominal money supply[1]	Wholesale prices, 1870 = 100[2]	Population	Total real money supply[3]	Total nominal money per capita[4]	Total real money per capita[5]
1870	$510.	$ 779	$ 436	$1,725	100	39.9	$1,725	$43.20	$43.20
1876	516	1,158	842	2,516	81	46.1	3,106	54.60	67.40
1888	821	2,541	1,237	4,599	64	60.5	7,186	76.00	118.80
1890	888	3,020	1,373	5,281	61	63.1	8,657	83.70	137.20
1892	929	3,541	1,517	5,987	56	65.7	10,691	91.00	162.70
1896	832	3,434	1,693	5,959	50	70.9	11,918	84.10	168.10

1 The total nominal money supply is in terms of current values.

2 The wholesale prices are those of the Warren and Pearson Index, converted to 1870 as 100.

3 The total real money supply, deflated for wholesale prices.

4 Total nominal money per capita: the nominal money supply divided by the country's population. The figures are rounded.

5 Total real money per capita: the real money supply divided by the country's population. The figures are rounded.

SOURCE: From the Friedman and Schwartz book cited in the text, pp. 704-705; the calculations of real money supply and real and nominal money per capita made by the author.

stock of money displays a consistent cyclical behavior closely related to the cyclical behavior of the economy at large." See in Table 14, for example, the total nominal money supply in 1896 as compared with 1892.

Some State Bank Experiences   A brief examination of banking development in three States—Arkansas, Wisconsin, Massachusetts—demonstrates that some of the earlier unhappy memories of State banking had burned themselves out; in consequence, all sorts of devices were being employed to overcome the inadequacies of the national banking system. This resourcefulness (accompanied by governmental laxity, of course, so that the frequent recessions took a heavy toll of these poorly supervised banks) expanded credit facilities and encouraged business investment and hence economic growth.

Arkansas had had disastrous experiences in the ante-bellum period with two banks—one was the Real Estate Bank and the other was the State Bank; both were created in 1836 and both in part or wholly were financed from public funds. Both failed quickly, at the same time impairing for generations the credit of the State because of its inability to come to terms with its creditors. The result, because of the general prejudice against incorporated banks, was that the deposit-and-exchange business of its communities was carried out by merchants; these were, therefore, private bankers who did not have to submit to any regulation.

A few national banks appeared as a result of the passage of the National Banking Act of 1863-64; there were 6 in 1882. It was not until 1882 that a general incorporation law was passed which also permitted the creation of State joint-stock banks. The minimum capitalization was $300 for all corporations; and only three stockholders were required. Banks grew under this sanction, so that in 1899 there were 63 State banks (all with less than $50,000 capitalization); 14 private banks; and only 7 national banks. The deposits (largely demand in both instances) were $2.8 million for the national banks and $9.6 million for the State banks. It was not until 1913 that a general banking act was passed which, among other things, set minimum capitalization at $10,000, imposed a reserve requirement of 15 per cent, and created a State banking department.

Thus, Arkansas—a typically rural and Southern State—had more banking than one would ordinarily suppose. Private bankers also lent on land mortgages in the post-Civil War period; and with the appearance of State-chartered banks additional facilities were set up for the creation of both long-term and intermediate-term agricultural credit. The hostility to banks had largely disappeared, the deposits of State banks being sizable and more than three times those of the national banks. For the most part, these State banks were to be found in smaller communities, with their business rural in character.

Wisconsin went through the usual growing pains of a pioneer State. Just before the outbreak of the Civil War, it had some 108 State banks with a total capitalization of $7.6 million which had $4.4 million in notes in circulation and only $2.9 million in deposits. Many of the banks were wildcats, making no loans, accepting no deposits, and having no offices for redemption; they issued notes against securities—frequently of Southern States and hence of a highly dubious nature. In fact, as late as April, 1961, Chicago banks were refusing to accept the notes of some 40 Wisconsin banks for redemption.

National banks appeared tardily—the high capitalizations required and the small amount of bank notes allotted to Wisconsin being the chief deterrents. The result was, the State banks took a new lease on life after 1870; in that year only 17 had survived the 10-per-cent excise tax on their notes; but by 1880 there were 29 such institutions with resources of $19 million, and by 1893, there were 119 with resources of $50 million. This was due to the easy incorporation laws, the small capitalizations required (the law technically demanded a minimum of $25,000, but only 60 per cent had to be paid in, and frequently stockholders did this with personal notes), and the virtual absence of regulation. But more important was the great expansion in bank deposits; by 1870, checks against deposits were being generally accepted throughout the State. Thus, by 1896, the total bank deposits were almost $70 million, of which almost half was in State banks. Increases in banking resources and facilities marched side by side with Wisconsin's economic development, industrial diversification, and shift over from a wheat-growing to a dairying State (and therefore the greater cultivation of corn, oats, and hay). It was small wonder that Populism left Wisconsin almost untouched.

Although the depression of 1893 took a high toll among Wisconsin's banks—twenty-seven closed their doors permanently in 1893—the only step taken before the turn of the century to make banking supervision a little more rigorous was the creation of a bank examiner in 1895. It was not until 1903 that a comprehensive banking statute was enacted (Governor La Follette was the driving force here) which both abolished private banks and set up a system of supervision and control (a State Banking Department was established) patterned after that of the national banking laws as regards bank examinations, cash reserves behind deposits, restrictions on dividend payments and on loans. (Loans on mortgages, for example, were limited to 50 per cent of a bank's capital and surplus.) But low capitalizations were still permitted: banks in towns of less than 3,500 population could have a capitalization of $5,000; where the population was between 3,500 and 5,000, the capitalization could be $10,000.

Massachusetts' experiences followed another course—but with similar consequences, for the expansion of State banking facilities led to greater opportunities for loans and discounts and therefore the financing of all sorts of business ventures. Up to 1851, joint-stock banking was permitted only on the basis of special charter from the State's legislature; but in that year a free-banking system was authorized following generally the lines of that of New York State. State banking grew rapidly in consequence: whereas in 1850 there were 29 banks in Boston and 92 outside it with a total in deposits of $13.6 million and $4 million in mortgage loans; in 1860 the banks in Boston totaled 36, those outside Boston 138, deposits were $45 million, and mortgage loans $17.6 million.

The federal tax on State bank-note circulation naturally hit the State banks hard; by 1867, only two banks of issue still survived and these too soon disappeared. Massachusetts, however, made no effort to encourage State commercial banks. Its banking needs were met from the new national banks, of course; but more particularly—because of the longer-term paper they could handle, and because of their ability to underwrite real estate and mortgage loans—from private banks, the savings banks, trust companies (first appearing in 1871) and cooperative savings-and-loan associations (first appearing in 1877). The last made possible home ownership as a result of savings.

All these grew magnificently. By 1896, there were 187 savings banks (largely mutual) with assets of $482 million, 32 trust companies with assets of $110.4 million, and 122 cooperative banks with assets of $22.9 million. Savings banks alone had deposits of $453 million and had out on mortgage loans $202 million. Private banks also continued to flourish. Massachusetts is an interesting example of how State banking supplemented the activities of the national banks. In 1896, the demand deposits of the national banks were $176.8 million and time deposits less than $1 million; State commercial banks had demand deposits of $56.1 million and less than $2 million in time deposits. The time-deposit business was being done almost entirely by the mutual savings banks and the cooperative banks.

The Money Supply of the West and the South   It will be interesting, finally, to look more closely at the money supply (circulation of currency plus deposits) in those two regions where the money clamor had reached fever pitch by 1896. The Northern Alliance was most active in Iowa, Minnesota, Kansas, Nebraska, Colorado, North Dakota, and South Dakota—these had become the wheat-growing states of the nation. How much money did they have? In 1896, total bank deposits were $297.8 million; national bank notes came to another $13.8 million; and the circulation of coin, greenbacks and Treasury notes another $75 million (at a guess, representing 6 per cent of the total $1,271.4 million in national currency). The total was therefore $386.6 million, and with a population of about 7.3 million, the per capita was about $53 dollars. This comes right on the target the money reformers had set—$50 per capita.

Was it enough? We may assume that for the normal business requirements of the region—and these were for the greater part agricultural—the money supply was adequate. But the region had gone through difficulties, in part as a result of its growing pains, in part because of the changing international situation as far as wheat production was concerned. One should note overexpansion of the wheat-growing in the United States (and therefore the pressure of long-term agricultural debt as farmers acquired more land and machinery) at the same time that wheat acreage was increasing in Argentina, Canada, Australia, and in central and eastern Europe. The world price of wheat, therefore, dropped; in fact, the fall was greater, as we have seen, than for American farm products generally. At the same time, the American wheat country had had a series of bad crops from 1887 on, thus further involving the wheatgrowers in debt. We may say, in consequence, that the money

[273]

storm blew up in the Northern Alliance country because of debt, and because of its almost exclusive reliance on wheat, rather than because of an inadequate money supply.

The Southern States present another picture; here, too, we have the great growth and influence of the Southern Alliance, its origination of the Sub-Treasury scheme, and its entrance into the Populist movement. Cotton was of course the chief staple of the region and much of cotton-growing was financed through the crop lien system with the credit being furnished by the rural store owners who advanced the poorer farmers their supplies, taking a lien on the standing crop. How much book credit was made available every year in this fashion we do not know and cannot even estimate. The figures we have here are for the money supply in bank deposits, national bank notes, and a guess at the circulation of coin and Treasury notes. The states included are North Carolina, South Carolina, Georgia, Alabama, Florida, Mississippi, Louisiana, Texas, Arkansas, and Missouri. In 1896, total bank deposits were $277.6 million; national bank notes came to another $20 million; and the circulation of coin, greenbacks and Treasury notes (a guess) to another $150 million. The total was therefore $447.6 million, and with a population of about 16.5 million, this came to $27 per capita. Because we cannot say to what extent "store" credit added to this money supply, but it was sizable, the figure is undoubtedly too low. The coinage of silver would not have helped, as the experiences under the Sherman Silver Purchase Act indicated (unless "unlimited" meant coining all the world's silver at the ratio of 16 to 1). What the South clearly needed was more banks and more mortgage money; and these continued to increase during the early years of the next century.

A look at the corn country shows why Populism here had little effect. The Middle West, by the 1890s, had changed over from wheat to corn, general farming, and dairying. Ohio, Indiana, Illinois, Wisconsin, and Michigan in 1896 had deposits of $726.6 million; national bank notes circulation of $38.7 million; and the circulation of coin, greenbacks, and Treasury notes of an additional $200 million (a guess). The total was therefore $965.3 million and, with a population of about 15 million, a per capita of about $64.

The Middle Atlantic States (New York, New Jersey, Pennsylvania,

Delaware, and Maryland) furnish a further contrast. These were industrial and mercantile; agriculture was dairying and truck farming. In 1896, the deposits came to $2,387.5 million; national bank notes circulation to $86 million; and the circulation of other money to another $300 million (a guess). The total was therefore $2,674 million and, with a population of 15.5 million, the per capita was $177.

Here therefore was the heart of the enemy country as far as Populism was concerned; its intensive organization by the Republican party assured the defeat of Bryan.

CHAPTER NINE

EDUCATION

Education and Growth   Among the many ways that set off the American experience from the rest of the Western world, the commitment to the common school was the most interesting and, curiously, in economic terms, probably the most significant. Today, economists are beginning to point this out: education, because it is an investment in human capital, plays an important part in accelerating a nation's growth. Immediate income is foregone in keeping children and young people at school. But this is more than made up in time by the improvement in personal skills, thus making human labor more efficient and productive; equally, the increase in personal earnings over a normal lifetime, because of education, adds to disposable income and therefore consumption. Education pays; it should be begun earlier and continued later. Its effects can be measured, and economists are beginning to do so, thus adding another dimension to growth theory for the guidance of developing nations.

By 1900, this income foregone, or the so-called opportunity costs of education, had become quite considerable. An econometric reconstruction by Professor Albert Fishlow (in *The Journal of Economic History*, December, 1966) indicated that for all formal education, public and private, from the grade schools through all institutions of higher learning, total earnings foregone came to $213.9 million in 1900 as compared with $24.8 million in 1860 and $72.1 million in 1880. These were almost equal to the public expenditures for all formal education in 1880 and 1900 ($81.5 million and $229.6 million respectively) and somewhat greater than in 1860 ($19.9 million).

[276]

There are other elements in the educational process, however, that do not yield so easily to quantification. What of the contributions of home and church, for example? What of apprenticeship and on-the-job training? (The latter played a much more important role in America's development than the former because of the weaknesses of the trade-union movement and then, in those industries where the movement established itself, of its restrictive practices.) And what of the continuance of learning in systematic ways, after the school has been left behind, through the facilities furnished by philanthropic agencies and proprietary institutions—so many of which appeared in post-Civil War America—so that youths and young adults could acquire new skills, upgrading themselves and society itself in the process?

The years between 1865 and 1900 saw a vast expansion in such educational activities, and hundreds of thousands, if not millions, of Americans availed themselves of the opportunities they afforded. There were the educational programs of the Y.M.C.A.'s and Y.W.C.A.'s; those of the urban settlement houses; the work of the Chautauqua societies and the great publishing press Chautauqua established; the proprietary secondary schools which prepared working young men for civil-service examinations and for entrance to medical and law schools; the proprietary business schools which taught stenography, typewriting, and bookkeeping to hundreds of thousands of girls and tool, fabric, and garment design to large numbers of young men; the correspondence schools in mechanics, electricity, law, accounting, office management.

The settlement houses came into the great cities in the middle 1880s and multiplied in the 1890s. Established in the crowded slums where the immigrants lived, they set up educational programs at once—English and classes in citizenship for foreigners, arts and crafts and music, training in the industrial arts. The Y.M.C.A.'s and Y.W.C.A.'s—attracting young people and particularly a haven for country boys and girls coming to the cities for employment—in addition to lodging and athletic facilities, also installed educational programs, especially in commercial subjects. By 1894, in the United States and Canada, there were already 1,000 branches of the Y.'s, with 100,000 members. The Chautauqua movement, begun in 1874 as a summer training program for religious workers, expanded into literary and scientific fields. It developed a four-year reading course for adults, began to print its own books in all sorts of subjects of contemporary interest, and by 1892 was reaching 100,000 men and women through its lectures, extension services, and correspondence courses.

The proprietary business school, or "commercial college," was peculiarly American. It sprang up to train young people (girls particularly) who were not going to high school, in office work and procedures—stenography, typewriting, English, and spelling, business arithmetic, simple bookkeeping—and in a year's intensive instruction turned out competent office help. Those who wished to stay on a little longer were able to obtain courses in advanced bookkeeping, commercial law, and commercial geography. Some of these schools became more ambitious: they took to adding so-called preparatory departments, offering high-school subjects at night for workers seeking entrance into medical schools and law schools. There is no telling, with any measure of accuracy, how many students were being reached by these proprietary schools. The United States Commissioner of Education, in his report for the year 1896-97, gave the incomplete number as 77,700, in 341 such institutions. Eighty-two per cent of the students attended during the day, the rest at night.

Despite the continued advance of the common school, the young American—and the young immigrant—began working early. He could pick up, or indeed start his education in a great variety of ways and in educational institutions elsewhere, and did so. After-hours schooling and the lonely vigil of home study required an iron discipline and a driving ambition; the number of dropouts undoubtedly was large, but many survived to the end triumphantly. One who was brought up in early youth in an urban world where the immigrant and his children far outnumbered the native Americans can bear witness to the fact that again and again success crowned such heroic efforts.

In a very real sense, the presence of the common school in America gave spur to the creation of all the other kinds of educational activities. The common school started out by assuming that America's youth was educable; in fact, had to be educated, at public rather than private or philanthropic expense, if the democratic experiment was to prove viable. Whatever the backgrounds, the social, racial, religious origins of its students, it was the function of the common school to give them all a similar intellectual experience. (The early advocates also talked of moral training; the later, more sophisticated ones, of the disciplining of minds and social responses.)

The notion of the common school, in these terms, started with the elementary school and quickly was extended to the secondary school. It was to be open to all, its costs were to be borne by the whole community, and its broad policies were to be set by the community at large through its elective, representative bodies. From these first desiderata the others naturally followed: that attendance, for so many days of the year, up to a lengthening minimum age, was compulsory; that textbooks were to be furnished free; that teachers were to be trained at public expense; and that they, rather than special interest groups—churches, political organizations, chambers of commerce—were to devise curriculums and measure and certify performance.

Laurence A. Cremin, in his pioneering and thoughtful *The American Common School* (1951) is quick to point out that the intention of its leaders was not regimentation—to cast all from a single mold and thus fix permanently the character of the American—but the reverse. The impulse came from that same eighteenth-century Enlightenment which hailed man's rationality and capacity for improvement.

In essence [says Cremin], the proponents of the common school were seeking the nurture of a common core of sentiment, of value, and of practice, *within which* pluralism would not become anarchy . . . they were seeking to build and inculcate a sense of community which would function, not at the expense of individualism, but rather as a firm framework within which individuality might be most effectively preserved.

Cremin might have added that this was possible exactly because the American political scheme was a federalistic one: power resided in local and State authorities rather than in a centralizing one, so that experiments could be pushed and rapid, if uneven, progress made possible. A further thought: pre-Civil War humanitarians, workingmen's parties, businessmen individually and collectively, all joined hands. The reason why the common-school idea so quickly and so generally took hold was that the advocacy of Horace Mann—although he was only one among many—struck an immediate and universal responsive chord. Where judicial approval was sought, as we shall see, it was immediately given. Interestingly, it was the same Thomas W. Cooley, Michigan chief justice and law-text writer who committed the post-Civil War United States to the idea of constitutional limitations on the power of State governments, who laid down the rules for common-school expansion.

The Work of Horace Mann and William Torrey Harris   The common school, at the elementary level, got under way when Massachusetts in 1827 ordered local districts to support their schools from taxation. In 1834 a permanent State board of education was established; when Horace Mann was made its secretary, a forum and platform were created for the dissemination of his democratic and humanitarian ideas. A republic could not endure "without well-appointed and efficient means for the universal education of the people." This universal education would assure social stability; it would be the "great equalizer"; it would be "the creator of wealth undreamed of"; it would narrow the distance and diminish the hostilities between the rich and the poor; it would lessen crime—and not threaten property. If education, as Mann believed and proclaimed, would also accomplish moral triumphs ("the common schools would create a more far-seeing intelligence and a purer morality than has ever existed among communities of men"), he was only echoing the faith of that New England Transcendentalism which entertained so many lofty and absurd fancies.

Even more: with a prescience that curiously anticipated the current stressing by economists of the importance of human capital, Mann claimed that free, universal education would act "as the grand agent for the development or augmentation of natural resources; [it was] more powerful in the production and gainful employment of the total wealth of the country than all the other things mentioned in the works of the political economists."

According to Albert Fishlow's calculations, the national enrollment rate (total number of pupils in primary and secondary schools and colleges, divided by the white population 5-19 years of age) increased 60 per cent from 1840 to 1860. In 1840, it had been 38.4 per cent; in 1860, 57 per cent. Table 15, giving enrollment rates, shows how widespread the commitment to education was (but with the South lagging badly behind).

By 1860, in the North at any rate, the battle for the common school had been won; a majority of the States had provided for common schools. Some States (Massachusetts in 1852, New York in 1853) had even

TABLE 15

Regions	1840	1850	1860
New England	81.4	76.1	73.8
Middle Atlantic	54.7	61.9	61.3
South Atlantic	16.2	29.7	31.4
North Central	29.1	52.4	69.4
South Central	13.4	31.0	38.6
Totals	38.4	50.4	57.0

SOURCE: Albert Fishlow, "The American Common School Revival: Fact or Fancy?" in Henry Rosovsky, ed., *Industrialization in Two Systems*, 1966, p. 49.

enacted compulsory attendance laws. Massachusetts, New York, and Pennsylvania had authorized local authorities to establish public secondary schools. Michigan and Wisconsin had created public State universities. It was estimated that in 1850, in a total of 23.2 million whites, 3.6 million children and young people were enrolled in all types of educational facilities, and of these 3.4 million were in publicly supported institutions. Fully half of the country's white children were already getting some sort of formal education.

The great leap forward took place after the Civil War; and here again the common school had its eloquent protagonist. This was William Torrey Harris, superintendent of the St. Louis public schools from 1868 to 1880 and U.S. Commissioner of Education from 1889 to 1906. Harris was a professional philosopher who founded the *Journal of Speculative Philosophy* and was the source of inspiration of the so-called St. Louis philosophical revival. He was a Hegelian who saw in Hegel's quest for an orderly world as the only world in which freedom was possible, and in Hegel's dialectical logic of destruction and re-creation that at higher levels assured progress, not only the answer to his own searchings but to democracy's survival. As Cremin (in his *The Transformation of the School* [1961]) puts it: "Harris used Hegel to confirm what was worth conserving in a society pervaded by change; Hegel enabled him to accept a new America without repudiating the old. In Hegel's rationalism Harris found religion." The schools were to be an important agency to assure stability and growth.

It is idle to argue that Harris' devotion to Hegel made him adopt an essentially conservative position—the maintenance of property, the continued existence of inequality in men's talents and men's rewards; and that he used the schools to preserve the status quo. Those who are familiar with Marxian polemics are aware of the fact that there have been Left Hegelians (Marx the chief among them) and Right Hegelians. If society was to survive and freedom be maintained—in the midst of rapid change—the individual had to be prepared to play his proper role. He had to have a disciplined mind and orderly habits; his instincts had to be brought under the same controls to achieve that rational and free world which was Hegel's hope.

But Harris—like that other idealist Emerson—was a democrat; he believed in social mobility, and in an inspired and selfless leadership. He was also convinced that through a universal educational experience the American, as a thinking individual, could be prepared to take in his stride a world evolving through the dialectical processes. In our contemporary shorthand, Harris' educational scheme of things was "traditional" and not "progressive." Modern-day educationists shy away from Harris' constant stressing of discipline, the necessity for the mastery of fundamentals (he called them the "five windows of the soul"—these were mathematics, geography, literature and art, grammar, and history), the use of an essentially classical core for the construction of a high-school program. Harris' emphasizing of "regularity, punctuality, silence, conformity to order" (his own words) made him suspect, even to such an intelligent man as Cremin. Wasn't Harris condescending, possibly even somewhat sinister, when he said these things about the young American going by *Diktat* to school?

The pupil is taught to be regular and punctual in his attendance on school and in all his movements, not for the sake of the school alone, but for all his relations to his fellow-men. Social combination is made possible by these semi-mechanical virtues.

And this:

The work of the school produces self-respect, because the pupil makes himself the measure of his fellows and grows equal to them spiritually by the mastery of their wisdom. Self-respect is the root of the virtues and the active cause of a career of growth in power to know and power to do. Webster called the free public school "a wise and liberal system of police, by which property and the peace of society are secured." He explained the effect of the school as exciting "a feeling of responsibility and a sense of character. . . ."

[As] the school causes the pupil to put off his selfish promptings; and to prefer the forms of action based on a consideration of others—it is seen that the entire discipline of the school is ethical. Each youth educated in the school has been submitted in the habit of self-control and of obedience to social order. He has become to some extent conscious of two selves; the one his immediate animal impulse, and the second his moral sense of conformity to the order necessary for the harmonious action of all.

Harris was writing this around 1907. But he was also writing this:

The transformation of an illiterate population that reads the daily newspaper and perforce thinks on national and international interests, is thus far the greatest good accomplished by the free public school system of the United States.

We forget the measure of Harris' accomplishment in a long lifetime of pressing for these things—and for the graded school and the training of teachers in normal schools at public expense. Indeed, he was very much living in a changing United States and seeking to create in its people— becoming largely urbanized, made up increasingly of immigrants and the children of immigrants—a sense of community and at the same time of personal self-respect and of belonging. In 1900, the foreign stock (foreign-born and native-born of foreign or mixed parentage) of American white children of school-going age (five through eighteen) was already making up 31.5 per cent of its young people. But in the cities, the proportion was much greater: it was 55 per cent in Harris' own St. Louis and 73 per cent in New York. How better serve them—whose parents had alien tongues and ways, who yielded with bewilderment to compulsory school attendance, who were in no position to encourage, exhort, assist the growing young mind—than by Harris' rules of "regularity, punctuality, silence, conformity to order"?

The public school, certainly the urban elementary public school, was bright and clean and warm in the wintertime, it had running water and flush toilets—none of these too often encountered in the slum tenements in which so many children of foreign stock lived at the turn of the century. From the very first day of his enrollment, the child was taught cleanliness, orderly habits, the discipline of lessons done and recited. His classrooms were presided over by young women and older ones who never married (in New York, Chicago, Boston, the New England towns, many of them were Irish; becoming a schoolteacher was a very real step upward for the daughters and granddaughters of an earlier impoverished immigrant host) and who devoted themselves to their young charges; spurring on those who were bright and studious, lending them books, visiting their parents to talk of the necessity for going on to high school, perhaps even college, holding out the promise of greater usefulness as educated men and women.

This is what discipline and a formal curriculum, both in the elementary and in the high schools of America's cities, did for boys and girls who normally would have had no incentives for self-improvement. Everything in that course of study (so derided today) led to further steps: grammar to correct speech; writing to learn of, and for the fortunate to master, the great flexibility and the extraordinary nuances of the English language; reading to open the doors, through the public libraries, to so many new worlds. Did all this have a dark intention—to "Americanize" (i.e., standardize, regiment) the newcomer, to win him away from the traditions and values of his forebears?

As one looks back, it is hard to believe it. One of the most interesting phenomena of the American experience—for those who fell under the influence of Harris and several generations of schoolteachers trained in his regimen—was the voluntary return, as one grew older, to the heritage of one's ancestry. The child of foreign stock, if he went on with his education, had the benefits of both the New America and the Old Europe. All this was another aspect of the investment in human capital that must be marked up to the common school.

The Secondary School   No country in the Western World accepted as quickly and expanded as rapidly the public obligation to furnish free secondary education as did the United States. I. L. Kandel, writing in 1930, in the course of making a comparative study, was able to say:

The public high school of the United States is a unique institution. . . . In the history of education it is the first experiment in the attempt to provide a suitable education for all the children of all the people at public expense in a single institution. . . . Few secondary schools elsewhere have won the appreciation and support of the public as have the American high schools.

As early as 1874, a landmark judicial decision to extend the idea of the common school to secondary education opened the gates, and by the 1890s there were few States that had not enacted enabling legislation. From 1870 to 1900, progress was marked; it was not until the next fifty years, of course, that public secondary schooling became well-nigh universal. It was one thing to authorize such schools; it was another to raise the compulsory school-attending age from fourteen to seventeen and eighteen. Nevertheless, real beginnings were in evidence by the turn of the century.

The so-called *Kalamazoo* case originated in Michigan as a result of a suit against the State by the superintendent of schools of Kalamazoo to test the legality of a law permitting the establishment of a high school and the use of public funds to maintain it. The case ended in the State's Supreme Court when a unanimous bench, with the opinion written by Chief Justice Thomas M. Cooley, decided in 1874 that the legislature was exercising its constitutional rights; public high schools were legal and could be set up as long as the inhabitants of local school districts were prepared to tax themselves for their support. Decisions in other States took their lead from Cooley, and by 1900 there were at least a half dozen that made it very plain there was no opposition to his dictum.

Cooley's opinion was a reasoned statement of the American commitment to continuing education. Said he:

We supposed it has always been understood in this State that education, not merely the rudiments, but in an enlarged sense, was regarded as an important practical advantage to be supplied at their option to poor and rich alike, and not as something pertaining merely to culture and accomplishment, to be brought as such within the reach of those whose accumulated wealth enabled them to pay for it.

We content ourselves with the statement that neither in our State policy, in our constitution, nor in our laws, do we find the primary school districts restricted in the branches of knowledge which their officers may cause to be taught, or the grade of instruction that may be given, if their voters consent in regular form to bear the expense and raise the taxes for the purpose.

How far the United States was moving out of the mainstream may be noted from the fact that in 1901 the English Court of Queen's Bench, in *Queen v. Cockerton,* ruled exactly the reverse: that it was not within the power of a local education authority to expend money raised by local taxes upon any education other than the elementary schools.

Was the secondary school to have a particular role—to be a "people's college," as said the president of the National Education Association's Department of Secondary Education in 1891; to become the friend of the laboring man, "for he is coming to know that this is the institution which shall level the distinction between the rich and the poor, as far as power and place are concerned"? Was it to teach what came to be called "manual" subjects: the skills of particular crafts, so that America's youth could be trained for the building trades, machine shops, offices? From 1876 on—presumably inspired by the Russian exhibit at the Philadelphia Centennial Exposition of 1876, which contained examples of the accomplishments of technically trained young Muscovites in what the English called "arts and manufacture"—there was a flurry of debate over making secondary education "practical," which reached beyond schoolmen's meetings.

Businessmen criticized the narrow intellectual content of the secondary-school curriculum and expressed themselves in favor of a central place for manual training and vocational education. The national craft unions (as did later, when it was formed, the American Federation of Labor) on their part objected strenuously. The training of apprentices was their function, and for a long time they regarded with suspicion any effort to extend entry into the skills which they did not control. Thus, Samuel Gompers, president of the American Federation of Labor, declared in the early 1890s:

It is not only ridiculous but positively wrong for trade schools to continue turning out "botch" workmen who are ready and willing at the end of their so-called "graduation" to take the places of American workmen far below the wages prevailing in the trades. With practically half the toiling masses of our country unemployed, the continuance of the practice is tantamount to a crime.

But when a *modus operandi* was worked out—and this did not occur until the first decade of the twentieth century—trade unions consented to the introduction of manual-training courses in public high schools and the establishment of public vocational schools as long as they controlled the courses of study and made entry into jobs part and parcel of their apprenticeship requirement. The first such agreement was arrived at in Chicago in 1901, under which apprentices in the masons' and bricklayers' unions were to spend three months in every year of their training period in the public schools. In 1910, the AF of L formally gave its approval to public vocational education—if the unions participated in the program-making.

Meantime experiments in manual training, at the secondary level, and only to a limited degree, took place as a result of philanthropic effort. Perhaps the pioneer was the St. Louis Manual Training School of Washington University, which appeared in 1879. Tuskegee Institute, for Negroes, was another such; so were the Brooklyn Pratt Institute, the Baron de Hirsch School of New York (for Jewish boys and girls), the Drexel Institute of Philadelphia, and the Armour Institute of Technology of Chicago. There were similar schools, supported by local businessmen, in Baltimore, Toledo, Cleveland, Cincinnati, New Orleans. The St. Louis school was the model. It offered a three-year secondary-school program divided equally between traditional and manual subjects. The former included mathematics, science, languages, history, and literature. The latter (with an instruction shop for each art or trade), carpentry, wood turning, patternmaking, forge work, bench work, and machine work. A few cities sought to follow and established public manual-training schools; the better of these that survived shifted over to pure science and mathematics and turned out to be more useful in the long run. (The outstanding example was the Stuyvesant High School of New York.)

The opposition began to mobilize (Harris had always opposed the use of the secondary school for vocational training) and in 1893 won a signal victory. The Committee of Ten of the National Education Association, headed by President Charles W. Eliot of Harvard, created the pattern for the public high school that was to survive unchallenged for almost a half century. The purpose of the high school, said the report, was to give the student "four years of strong and effective mental training." And it went on:

The secondary schools of the United States, taken as a whole, do not exist for the purpose of preparing boys and girls for college. Only an insignificant percentage of the graduates of these schools go to colleges or scientific schools. Their main function is to prepare for the duties of life that small proportion of all children in the country—a proportion small in number, but very important to the welfare of the nation—who show themselves able to profit by an education prolonged to the eighteenth year, and whose parents are able to support them while they remain at school.

The Committee—Eliot's thinking was writ large in its deliberations and decisions—made the following proposals. The course of study was to last four years. Electives were to be permitted, as long as the equivalency principle was observed—that is, all subjects taught for the same length of time (three or five times a week; two to four years) were to be equal in value. But choices were to be strictly limited. The basic curriculum was to offer these subjects:

Languages: Latin, Greek, English, German, French (and, locally, Spanish).

Mathematics: Algebra, geometry, trigonometry.

History: General history, and the intensive study of special epochs. (This came to mean American history and modern European history.)

Natural history: Descriptive geometry, meteorology, botany, zoology, physiology, geology, and ethnology, "most of which subjects may conveniently be grouped under the title of physical geography."

Physical Sciences: Physics and chemistry.

All these subjects, said the report, "should be taught consecutively enough and intensively enough to make every subject yield that training that it is fitted best to yield." It can be seen that such a curriculum was no slavish imitation of the programs of the pre-Civil War private academies or the English public schools. It was "classical" to this extent—it recognized the importance of Latin and Greek, and in many great urban high schools, for many years, Latin at least was required of all pupils for the full four years. It was "modern" in its quick acceptance of the need for teaching modern history, mathematics, and the natural and physical sciences. It served the children of foreign stock well by making English—the regular writing of themes, the study of literature (at least two of Shakespeare's plays were to be found in every high-school course of study)—also obligatory for the entire four years.

The Committee was prepared to make concessions to the existing clamor. It proposed four four-year courses of study; these it called the

"classical," the "Latin-scientific," "modern languages," and "English."
It was clear, however, that it took a dim view of the third and the fourth.
Subjects "thought to have a practical importance in trade and the useful
arts" could be put in the fourth program as elective substitutes in the
last two years for the natural sciences. The Committee made its position
quite plain:

they desired to affirm expressly their unanimous opinion that, under
existing conditions in the United States as to the training of teachers and
the provision of necessary means of instruction, the two programmes
called respectively Modern Languages and English must in practice be
distinctly inferior to the other two.

Table 16 shows the three tracks the Cleveland High School of Ohio
was offering at about the turn of the century. (From Edwin G. Dexter,
A History of Education in the United States, 1904.) The numerals indicate meetings a week.

The number of pupils attending secondary schools (public and private)
was not large in the last two decades of the nineteenth century, but the
proportion registered to the population fourteen through seventeen
years of age grew impressively, as Table 17 shows.

The figures in Table 18 indicate the number of graduates of secondary
schools (public and private) over a longer period of years.

The Advances of the Common School   During the school year 1897-98,
the following was the total number of pupils and students of all grades
in both public and private schools and colleges: *

In the elementary schools, public 14,589,036
In the elementary schools, private 1,249,665
In the secondary schools, public 459,813
In the secondary schools, private 166,302
In universities and colleges, public 29,728
In universities and colleges, private 71,330
In schools of medicine, law, theology, public 8,096
In schools of medicine, law, theology, private 46,135
In normal schools (for teacher training, usually two
     years), public 46,225
In normal schools (for teacher training, usually two
     years), private 21,293

The very real growth of the common schools (elementary and secondary) is indicated by the figures in Tables 19 and 20.

* N. M. Butler, ed., *Education in the United States,* 1910, p. 126.

TABLE 16

FIRST YEAR		
Commercial course	*Scientific course*	*Classical course*
Bookkeeping, Business Forms and Commercial Correspondence 5	Natural History or Manual Training 5	Latin 4
English Composition, Reading, Literature .. 4	English Composition, Reading and Literature 4	English Composition, Reading, and Literature 4
Algebra 5	Algebra 5	Algebra 5
Natural History or Manual Training 5	Latin or German or American History 4	German 4 or Natural History 5

SECOND YEAR		
Commercial course	*Scientific course*	*Classical course*
Arithmetic, Bookkeeping, and Commercial Law 5	Physical Geography or Manual Training 5	Latin 5
English Composition, etc. 4	English Composition, etc. 4	Greek or German 5
Geometry 5	Geometry 5	Geometry 5
English History and Manual Training 5	Latin or German or English History 5	English 5

THIRD YEAR		
Commercial course	*Scientific course*	*Classical course*
Bookkeeping, Business Practice, and Commercial Geography 4	Physics 5	Latin 5
English Literature or German 5	Latin or German or English Literature ... 5	Greek or German 5
Physics 5	History 4	History 4 or Physics .. 5
Stenography and Typewriting or Manual Training 5	College English or Mathematics 3	College English 3

FOURTH YEAR		
Commercial course	*Scientific course*	*Classical course*
Office Practice, Banking, and Higher Accounting 4	Chemistry or Physiology and Botany 4	Latin 4
Economics and Civics . 4	Economics and Civics . 4	Greek or German 4
Stenography and Typewriting, with Commercial Correspondence .. 5	History or Advanced Mathematics 4	French or Physics 5
Spanish 5 or German or American Literature .. 4	French 5 or Latin or German or American Literature 4	History or Mathematics 4
	English 2	English 2

EDUCATION

TABLE 17

Year	Enrollment	No. enrolled per 100 of population 14–17 years old
1889–90	359,949	6.7
1899–1900	699,403	11.4
1955–56	7,774,951	84.2

SOURCE: *Annual Report of the U.S. Commissioner of Education,* various issues.

TABLE 18

Year	Graduates	Per cent of population 17 years old
1871	16,741	2.0
1880	23,634	2.5
1890	43,731	3.5
1900	94,883	6.4
1956	1,400.000	62.3

SOURCE: *Historical Statistics of the United States,* p. 207.

TABLE 19. REGIONAL ENROLLMENT VERSUS SCHOOL-AGE POPULATION FOR SELECTED SCHOOL YEARS BETWEEN 1870 AND 1898

	No. of pupils enrolled, millions				Per cent of school-age population (5-18 years old)			
	1870-71	1879-80	1889-90	1897-98	1870-71	1879-80	1889-90	1897-98
United States	7.56	9.86	12.70	15.02	61.45	65.50	68.61	70.08
North Atlantic States ..	2.74	2.93	3.11	3.61	77.95	75.17	70.45	70.38
South Atlantic States ..	.60	1.24	1.78	2.13	30.51	50.74	59.22	63.63
South Central States ..	.77	1.37	2.29	2.87	34.17	46.43	60.14	64.41
North Central States ..	3.30	4.03	5.01	5.67	76.87	75.84	76.46	75.25
Western States	.15	.29	.51	.74	54.77	64.96	70.01	76.73

SOURCE: N. M. Butler, ed., *Education in the United States,* 1910, p. 128.

TABLE 20. GROWTH OF THE UNITED STATES SCHOOL SYSTEM FOR SELECTED SCHOOL YEARS BETWEEN 1870 AND 1898

	1870–71	1879–80	1889–90	1897–98
Average daily attendance, millions	4.54	6.14	8.15	10.29
Ratio of same to enrollment	60.1	62.3	64.1	68.4
Average length of school term, days	132.1	130.3	134.7	143.1
Average number of days attended by each pupil enrolled	79.4	81.1	86.3	97.8
Number of teachers	220,225	286,593	336,922	409,103
Number of schoolhouses	132,119	178,222	222,526	242,340
Value of school property (millions of dollars)	$143.8	$209.6	$342.5	$492.7
Total expenditures for education (million of dollars)	$69.1	$78.1	$140.5	$194.0

SOURCE: N. M. Butler, ed., *Education in the United States,* 1910, p. 130.

It will be observed that from 1870 to 1898, the average length of the school term increased 11 days. Whereas for the whole country, it was 143.1 days in the school year 1897-98, there were wide variations among the States. In Rhode Island, it was 191 days, in Massachusetts 186 days, in New Jersey 185 days, in New York 176 days, in California 172 days, in Iowa, Michigan, and Wisconsin, 160 days; but in North Carolina and Arkansas, it was 69 days. At the turn of the century, on the average, the country's population was receiving school instruction for five years of 200 days each. This was not very much; on the other hand, it was a significant increase from the 3.36 years of 1870 and the 3.96 years of 1880. The greater part of this was in elementary and secondary education, for in 1898 the average amount of schooling of 200 school days each year was 4.46 years; but it was 2.91 years in 1870 and 3.45 years in 1880.

The first compulsory school-attendance law was passed by Massachusetts in 1852 and followed the next year by New York. Advances took place rapidly after the Civil War, so that by 1900, thirty-two States (largely in the North and West) had passed such laws. But sixteen States and one Territory had not. The most common period of required school attendance was eight to fourteen years; a few States started at age seven; a few ended at age fifteen. This did not mean attendance for the full term. Pennsylvania had the most rigorous requirement: 70 per cent of the full term was demanded. A few States stipulated twenty weeks in the year; most twelve; and Kentucky satisfied itself with eight.

Despite the fixing of minimum ages, at the turn of the century there were many exceptions and exemptions, so that it can scarcely be assumed that almost all of the country's children were at school from seven to fourteen years of age, or indeed finished elementary school. In 53 per cent of the States, there were no truant officers to enforce attendance laws; 65 per cent of the children lived in States that did not require seven years of schooling; 85 per cent were in States that did not have nine months as the minimum school year; 86 per cent lived in States which issued work permits before the completion of elementary school; and in 38 per cent of the States a child could begin working as early as the age of twelve if it could satisfy certain educational standards. In these presumably enlightened States, children could begin work at twelve years: Iowa, Kansas, Maine, Nebraska, New Hampshire, New Jersey, North Dakota, Rhode Island, Vermont.

EDUCATION

Unlike the general practice in continental Europe, the American federal government assumed no responsibilities toward the maintenance of the country's common schools. These became a charge upon the States (with State aid) and local school boards of education. In 1897, local taxes furnished $137.3 million for the public schools and State taxes $33.9 million. There was federal interest at only one point, and this was the creation of a Commissioner of Education in 1867. His powers were severely limited: he was authorized to issue an annual report (which, in time became very voluminous, running to as much as 2,500 pages); he gathered statistics (those used here come from these annual compilations); he and his assistants published pamphlets and tracts on educational matters. This was little enough, but in 1904 it was highly valued, for Edwin G. Dexter declared "that no other country makes such monumental contributions to the literature of education as we, through these [the Commissioner's] reports."

Twice, in the post-Civil War period, there was talk of federal aid to education. The two leading proposals that emerged in Congress were politically motivated, the discussions attending them produced much heat and little light, and when the reasons occasioning them disappeared, interest in Washington and in the country at large as quickly vanished and without trace. The first emanated from Representative George F. Hoar, Radical Republican from Massachusetts. The Reconstruction Congresses of the early 1870s had been passing Force Acts under which federal authority moved into the Southern States when Negro civil rights were being violated. Hoar sought to extend the same pattern to the schools and in 1870 introduced in the House a bill "to establish a national system of education." Its purpose, as Hoar said, was to compel the States to establish "a thorough and efficient system of public instruction." The federal government was to prescribe minimums; when standards fell below these, the President was given the power to designate the erring State "delinquent." He then could proceed to appoint a federal superintendent of schools for that State and federally designated school inspectors were to be named for Congressional and local school districts. Schoolhouses could be erected and textbooks published and distributed. Financing was to come from taxes on the delinquent States and from the interest of a permanent school fund that the bill provided. The Hoar bill never came to a vote in either house of Congress; like the rest of Southern Reconstruction, it was forgotten with the other lost causes of that brief period of high hopes and little accomplishment.

In 1881 Senator Henry W. Blair, Republican of New Hampshire, introduced a bill that called for the distribution of $77 million over eight years among the States in proportion to the number of illiterates over ten years of age in each State. The reason for this renewed interest in Congress in federal aid was the troublesome surpluses in the federal Treasury that the high protective tariffs were producing. The Blair bill was pretentious enough to attract interest; debates took place in the Senate; and the Senate Committee on Education and Labor held hearings. Blair proposed that a State, in order to become eligible for the public largess, maintain a system of common-school education (how quickly Reconstruction had been put aside may be seen from the fact that Southern States could do so through segregated schools); that its curriculum had to include "the art of reading, writing, and speaking the English language, arithmetic, geography, history of the United States, and such other branches of useful knowledge as may be taught under local laws"; and that sectarian schools were not to be assisted. The States would have to match the federal grants and were to administer the funds locally.

The Blair bill in its initial trial failed in the Senate in 1882, was passed in 1884, 1886, and 1888, and failed again in 1890. It never was carried in the House. By this time, Republicans had hit upon a more brilliant way of disposing of most of the surplus in one fell swoop—by paying service pensions to Civil War veterans—and education could be conveniently shelved. Besides, the Senate hearings had created too much disagreement and ill will. Important school and church leaders (from the Presbyterian and Catholic Churches in particular) were opposed; some farmer, labor, and business interests expressed mild approval; but businessmen really did not care seriously one way or another. A mild gesture was made in the direction of agriculture (the Southern Alliance in 1887 had asked for "a well-regulated system of industrial and agricultural education") by the passage of the second Morrill Act of 1890 for the further assistance of the State land-grant colleges. And thus the curtain was rung down.

Emergence of the Modern College and University   From the Jacksonian period of the 1830s and up to the 1880s, college attendance in the United

States had remained static. During the decade of the 1870s, the student body at twenty of the country's "oldest leading colleges" had increased only 3.5 per cent, while the nation's population had grown 23 per cent. In 1885, less than a quarter of all American Congressmen were college graduates; ten years later, the proportion had risen to 38 per cent. This showed a flurry of interest in collegiate education and in part indicated the response to the reforms that Presidents Charles W. Eliot of Harvard and Andrew D. White of Cornell were pushing in college curriculums. Nevertheless, enrollments remained low and the proportion of young men and women of college age (eighteen to twenty-one years) attending institutions of higher learning represented a tiny fraction, as Table 21 indicates.

TABLE 21. INSTITUTIONS OF HIGHER LEARNING

Year	No. of Institutions	Enrollment	Per cent of population 18-21 years old
1870	563	52,000	1.68
1880	811	116,000	2.72
1890	998	157,000	3.04
1900	977	238,000	4.01
1956	1,850	2,600,000	30.00

SOURCE: *Annual Report of the U.S. Commissioner of Education,* various issues.

There were many reasons for this. Courses of study in the "oldest leading colleges"—and they set the tone for the country—lay under the same blight that had been responsible for the stagnation of the English universities for more than a century. They were largely denominationally controlled and too frequently faculties were made up of clergymen with no particular skills in the subjects they professed to teach. The curriculums were the eighteenth-century ones of Greek, Latin, mathematics, and "moral philosophy," with instruction by set exercises. Despite the high moral tone characteristic of these institutions, there was plenty of time for idleness, and the popular prejudice that the four years spent in college led only to the cultivation of expensive and wasteful habits was not too far from the truth. Colleges were for the sons of the well to do. Unlike England, where a civil service already had begun to appear, the "mental discipline" which a college education was assumed to develop had no outlet in public affairs in the United States. The prevailing attitude of the business community was expressed by Andrew Carnegie in 1889, when he said:

While the college student has been learning a little about the barbarous and petty squabbles of a far-distant past, or trying to master languages which are dead, such knowledge as seems adapted for life upon another planet than this as far as business affairs are concerned, the future captain of industry is hotly engaged in the school of experience, obtaining the very knowledge required for his future triumphs. . . . College education as it exists is fatal to success in that domain.

Carnegie was writing at a time when reform was being pressed on many fronts; by 1900, these efforts had proved successful, so that a pattern was being set that was to be responsible for the very real triumphs of American higher education in the next half century. For one—as in the case of secondary education—it came to be accepted that institutions of higher learning should be readily available to all young people regardless of their circumstances or social origins.

Here, the public State universities played the leading role. President James B. Angell of the University of Michigan in 1879, when he announced the theme of his public address, said he was going to demonstrate "that it is of vital importance, especially in a republic, that the higher education, as well as common school education, be accessible to the poor as well as to the rich."

Secondly, a college education had utility, both as discipline and a preparation not only for public service but for a useful life in business as well. Charles Francis Adams, Jr., himself a Harvard product, received wide attention in 1883 when he delivered a Phi Beta Kappa address which he called "A College Fetish." The traditional classical curriculum was "fetish-worship, pure and simple." Said he, "I am practical and of this world enough to believe that in a utilitarian and scientific age the living will not forever be sacrificed to the dead." And he himself embarked upon a business career—as president of the Union Pacific Railroad—to demonstrate that it did no violence to his upbringing as a scion of the Adams family.

Thirdly, with the appearance of the university, only in part based on the German model, abstract research in the sciences and scholarship in the humanities properly were functions of higher education which the

American community had a responsibility to recognize and to support. By the turn of the century, Andrew Carnegie understood all this, as his munificent benefactions to colleges, universities, and research centers showed. (And so did other men of wealth—John D. Rockefeller, Leland Stanford, Jonas G. Clark, among a large host.)

Eliot, who had become president of Harvard in 1869, and White, named Cornell's first president in 1868, were the leaders—certainly as far as making utility the key to and the acceptance of a college education in the American scheme of things. In 1891, summing up his intellectual credo, Eliot said: "To impart information and cultivate the taste are indeed sought in education, but the great desideratum is the development of power in action." Through the elective system, Harvard proceeded to offer a broadened program in what came to be called the "liberal arts"; not eschewing Latin and Greek and "moral philosophy," it found an equal place in its curriculum—as did the many score small independent colleges in the East and the Middle West, following Harvard's lead—for modern languages, history, literature, political science, economics, the natural and physical sciences. White at Cornell leaned more heavily on the pure sciences and technology—and his influence on the State universities was marked.

Because graduate work (Eliot was less interested in basic research and scholarship, White more so) was added as an upper layer to many of the collegiate programs—at Columbia, Harvard, Yale, Princeton, Cornell— the devotion to utility and "service" did not drift into vocationalism, or the acceptance of the elective system into a riot of meaningless (and silly) courses of study.

For there were foolish as well as serious voices raised during the years of debate in the 1880s and 1890s. Said a New York University professor in 1890, "The college has ceased to be a cloister and has become a work shop." Calvin M. Woodward of Washington University, the leading advocate of vocational education in the secondary schools, proclaimed in 1901 that a university was "a place where everything useful in a high and broad sense may be taught." And as late as 1905, the president of the University of Illinois could declare:

[The State university must] stand simply, plainly, unequivocally and uncompromisingly for training for vocation, not training . . . even for scholarship *per se,* except as scholarship is a necessary incident to all proper training of a higher sort of vocation, or may be a vocation in itself, but training to perform an efficient service for society in and through some calling in which a man expresses himself and through which he works out some lasting good to society.

Even these calls to duty had their uses. Dedication to public service led to the formation of schools or faculties of political science (the serious and theoretical study of politics, economics, industrial relations, international law) at Columbia, Michigan, Wisconsin, and Chicago. Columbia, having been the first to establish a School of Political Science—at a higher level, and accepting research and the training of scholars and teachers as its chief purpose—followed this with a School of Pure Science. Applied science, largely although not entirely engineering, continued as a separate branch of Columbia College. Others followed the Columbia example; autonomous graduate schools, independent not financially but in curriculum-making, made their appearance as additions to colleges or within State universities also concerned with professional (or vocational) training. This was so of Columbia, Harvard, Yale, Chicago, Princeton, but also of Wisconsin and Michigan. To this extent, despite the influence of the German university, the American model was *sui generis*.

Many Americans went to Germany to seek the German university discipline. They enrolled in seminars—moving about frequently from institution to institution, listening to the lectures of favorite professors—and then stood for the Ph.D. degree at one of them on the basis of an oral examination and the writing of a thesis. During 1895-96, the peak year—after this a decline set in—517 American students were officially matriculated at German universities of high and low degree, for all were not first-class.

Americans in Germany either missed—or refused to take seriously—the German, characteristically cloudy notion of "pure science." They were too much children of British "common sense" to bring back with them German ideas of the roles of *Lehrfreiheit* and *Wissenschaft* as the basis of an underlying spiritual unity. Laurence R. Veysey, in his excellent *The Emergence of the American University* (1965), points out the differences between the American and German universities. Of the latter, he says:

German rhetoric about academic purpose appears to have centered upon three quite different conceptions [from the American idea of devotion to scientific research]: first, on the value of non-utilitarian learning . . . (hence "pure" learning, protected by *Lehrfreiheit*); second, on the value of *Wissenschaft*, or investigation and writing in a general sense, as opposed to teaching (*Wissenschaft* did not necessarily connote empirical research; it could just as easily comprehend Hegelian philosophy); finally, on their epistemological side, German statements of academic aim continued to run toward some form of all-encompassing idealism.

Two institutions—they never really justified the expectations of their founders—were set up on the German model in the United States. These were Johns Hopkins University in Baltimore in 1876 and Clark University in Worcester, Massachusetts, in 1889. Clark, even more than Johns Hopkins, for the latter had an undergraduate department, was entirely for graduate instruction and dedicated to the ideal of scientific research. But it succeeded, even after a whole decade, in enrolling at one time not more than fifty full-time students and about a dozen part-time ones.

The Ph.D. was offered as an American degree as early as 1884; but it was not until 1900 that the Ph.D. was expected of all those who wished to teach in a university and, before long, in the better of the independent colleges. The number of graduate students (apart from those in professional schools) began to mount: from 198 in the academic year 1871-72 to 935 for 1885-86, 2,499 for 1891-92, and 6,328 for 1900-1901. In the last two years cited one-fourth of the registered students were *in absentia*—because they went out to teach—and were presumably working on their theses.

What were the interests of these graduate students? An examination of twenty-four leading universities in 1897, where 3,204 students were registered, showed these concentrations: 35.4 per cent were working in literature and language studies, 20.6 per cent in history and social sciences, 14.2 per cent in natural and physical sciences, 18 per cent in philosophy and fine arts, and 1.1 per cent in mathematics. In 1900, it was reported that some 239 Ph.D.'s had been conferred throughout the country, the leaders among the private institutions being Chicago with 37, Harvard 36, Johns Hopkins 33, Yale 26, Columbia 21, Cornell 19, Pennsylvania 15, and Clark 9; and among the public institutions, Michigan, Wisconsin, and Minnesota with 5 each.

As has been said, the impact of all these stirrings at the collegiate and graduate levels during the 1880s and 1890s was quite slight; but the consequences to America in the next decade were immense. Despite their heterogeneity (there were hundreds of poor little colleges in the country not worthy of the name), and their confusions (particularly in the State universities), American institutions of higher learning were turning out far more well-educated young men and women than all of the institutions of Europe, including those of Great Britain. The devotion to easy entry for all those capable of further learning (with no social opprobrium attached to those who "worked their way through college") paid out.

Engineering Education   The training of engineers had an early start in the United States, but it was not until the end of the Civil War that engineering education took on serious proportions. Here, again as in the public high schools and in the colleges and universities, there were new beginnings and firm foundations. American leadership in technology, in the first half of the twentieth century, owed much to its engineering (and applied science) schools that sprang up after the Civil War. The first engineering program appeared in the United States Military Academy at West Point in 1817, the second at the Rensselaer Polytechnic Institute of Troy, New York, in 1824. Between them, up to 1847, they turned out many of the civil engineers who helped build the pioneer highways, bridges, canals, and railroads of the United States. In 1847, the Sheffield School was established at Yale, the Lawrence School at Harvard—both oriented toward the sciences but with courses in civil engineering—and the University of Michigan installed a civil engineering program. The Chandler School of Science was created at Dartmouth in 1851. And this was the lot until the early 1860s. In all, by the outbreak of the Civil War, among them these institutions had not graduated much more than 600 engineers, with Rensselaer responsible for 318 and West Point for 200, and Harvard's Lawrence for about 50.

The impetus for further growth came from two sources: from philanthropic giving (which created independent engineering schools) and from the Morrill Act of 1862, which encouraged land-grant colleges to set up engineering as well as agricultural programs of study. The first of the great private engineering schools was the Massachusetts Institute of

Technology, founded in 1861 but not opened until 1865. In 1868 the Worcester Polytechnic Institute (in Worcester, Mass.) began instruction; in 1866 Lehigh University (in Bethlehem, Pennsylvania); in 1871 the Stevens Institute of Technology (in Hoboken, New Jersey); in 1880 the Case School of Applied Science (in Cleveland, Ohio); in 1883 the Rose Polytechnic Institute (in Terre Haute, Indiana); in 1889 the Polytechnic Institute of Brooklyn; and in 1892 the Armour Institute of Technology (in Chicago).

The first president of M.I.T., William B. Rogers, in the prospectus for the new school, for which he solicited private support, set forth its purposes:

[It was to furnish] a systematic training in the applied sciences, which alone can give to the industrial classes a sure mastery over the materials and processes with which they are concerned. Such a training, forming what may be called the intellectual element in production, has, we believe, become indispensable to fit us for successful competition with other nations in the race of industrial activity. . . .

Rogers wanted money from men of wealth, and it was natural that he should appeal to their immediate interests. Nevertheless, the first curriculum of M.I.T., in 1865, contained a rigorous course of study in mathematics and the physical sciences. The first year required algebra, geometry, trigonometry, English, a foreign language, inorganic chemistry; the second year, analytics and calculus, general physics, chemistry, descriptive geometry, English, French, astronomy; the third year, calculus, physics, English, foreign languages.

Rensselaer had started with a three-year course of study and did not demand a secondary-school diploma. After the Civil War, all the schools mentioned—and they set the tone for the land-grant colleges—before long made their programs four years, accepted only secondary-school graduates, and expanded their courses of study to include mathematics, English, modern foreign languages, and the natural and physical sciences. Curriculums were usually divided in half—the first to lay the general scientific basis for all engineering instruction, the second to establish proficiency in a particular engineering field. All offered a general scientific training and civil engineering, and some stuck to only these two. Worcester, on the other hand, added mechanical engineering, electrical engineering, and chemical engineering. Stevens became famous for its mechanical engineering. Lehigh gave as well mining engineering and metallurgy. The Case School trained in eight fields—civil, mechanical, electrical, and mining engineering, and physics, chemistry, architecture, and general science. M.I.T. developed thirteen distinct programs—in all phases of engineering and in metallurgy, architecture, biology, physics, general science, sanitary engineering, and naval architecture.

The examples of Yale and Harvard were followed by other universities or private foundations. Columbia's School of Mines appeared in 1864, originally concentrating on mining engineering and metallurgy but before long expanding into civil, electrical, mechanical, and chemical engineering, and geology and architecture. Similar engineering and applied-science programs were set up at Princeton (1873) and Pennsylvania (1874).

Some notion of how many engineering and applied-science students were being reached by the leading independent private institutions may be gathered from Table 22.

TABLE 22

Institution	Founded	Graduated up to 1899	Students in 1899
Rensselaer	1824	1,219	143
M.I.T.	1865	2,000*	1,171
Worcester	1868	823	236
Lehigh	1866	1,000*	325
Stevens	1871	700*	214
Case	1880	230*	218
Rose	1883	260*	100
Polytechnic of Brooklyn	1889	100*	79
Armour	1892	60*	——†

*Approximately   † Unreported

SOURCE: *Annual Report of the U.S. Commissioner of Education,* various issues.

A far larger number of engineers was being turned out by State colleges and universities as a result of the Morrill Act. The idea of federal support of "industrial universities" originated in Illinois, the progenitor being J. B. Turner, the president of the Illinois State Teacher's Institute. In 1850 he delivered an address he called "A State University for the Industrial Classes," which he repeated a number of times to large audiences and which was taken up widely by farmers' organizations, agricultural journals, and many newspapers. Turner threw a much wider net than agricultural education alone; he spoke of all "the educational needs of the industrial classes of society," differentiating these from the professional classes. Instruction was to be for "thinking laborers" and should include, said he:

all those studies and sciences, of whatever sort, which tend to throw light upon any art or employment which any student may desire to master, or upon any duty he may be called to perform, or which may tend to secure his moral, civil, social, and industrial perfection as a man.

In 1852, a State convention called upon the Illinois legislature to memorialize Congress to "make an appropriation of public lands for each State in the Union for the appropriate endowment of universities for the liberal education of the industrial classes in their several pursuits in each State of the Union"; and so powerfully supported was this notion that the Illinois legislature did so in 1854. It was a bill along these lines that Congressman Justin S. Morrill of Vermont (he had become a member of the House in 1855) introduced in December, 1857. The bill passed the lower chamber but failed in the Senate. Two years later both houses of Congress voted for the bill only to have it vetoed by President Buchanan. At that time Morrill said of his measure:

Our great object was to arrest the degenerate and downward system of agriculture by which American soil is rapidly obtaining the rank of the poorest and least productive on the globe and to give to farmers and mechanics that prestige in life which liberal culture and the recognition of the government might afford.

The outbreak of the Civil War and Congress' control by the Republicans made it possible for Morrill to introduce his bill once more; it passed both Houses and was enacted with no real objection in 1862. To permit every State in the Union to establish an agricultural and mechanical college (or to add such a program to existing State universities), Congress voted to every State 30,000 acres from the public domain for each member of Congress (House and Senate) it possessed. The proceeds from the sale of the land, said the act, were to apply, using, almost verbatim, Turner's eloquent formulation,

to the endowment, support, and maintenance of at least one college where the leading object shall be, without excluding other scientific and

[303]

classical studies, and including military tactics, to teach such branches of learning as are related to agriculture and the mechanic arts, in such manner as the legislatures of the States may respectively prescribe, in order to promote the liberal and practical education of the industrial classes, in the several pursuits and professions in life.

As a result, in twenty-eight States, separate so-called A. and M. colleges were set up; in fifteen others, where State universities were already well established, the land grants were turned over to them to include the courses of study necessary to satisfy the requirements of the act. In three instances—Cornell University in New York, Rutgers University in New Jersey, M.I.T. in Massachusetts—the land grants were made to private institutions; M.I.T. quickly disaffiliated itself from the federal program, but Cornell and Rutgers remained permanently associated. To assist further agricultural and mechanical education, Congress passed the Hatch Act in 1887, under which States establishing agricultural experiment stations were to receive from the federal government $15,000 annually; and the second Morrill Act in 1890, also providing for an annual grant of $15,000 for each A. and M. college actually functioning. This latter act had a particular eye to the creation and maintenance of segregated Negro A. and M. colleges in the South; in all, seventeen such were set up.

Except for a few outstanding State universities (Michigan, Wisconsin, Illinois, Minnesota), the A. and M. colleges began at a low level, but by 1900 quite a number were already achieving the high standards and performance of the private independent technical institutes and the engineering and science departments of privately supported universities. A. and M. colleges, to attract students, began with preparatory departments, taught manual-training subjects for men and home economics for women, installed winter short courses on the campus and, off the campus, farmers' institutes—the latter two in order to fulfill their obligation to engage in agricultural education. (There were a few outstanding exceptions among the A. and M. colleges as regards scientific agricultural training. These were Iowa at Ames, Texas at College Station, Connecticut at Storrs, Rhode Island at Kingston, and Utah at Logan.) A. and M. colleges were doing increasingly better as regards engineering education, and here they could improve admission and performance requirements and embark on full three- and four-year courses of study. By 1900, it was estimated, there were more than 25,000 students (not all full-time) enrolled in the land-grant A. and M. colleges; two-thirds of these students were taking engineering courses of study.

It is easy enough to see why engineering was more attractive. There were not too many professional jobs in agriculture available. Nor had farming yet become so highly specialized—the growing of fruits and vegetables, poultry-raising, dairying; application of the lessons learned from chemistry, biology, and physiology—as to require particular and technical and scientific skills. Also, as we have seen, too many young people were leaving the land for the superior attractions—and, possibly, opportunities—of the cities. On the other hand, engineering was an expanding field with steady employment and where salaries were good: in railroad and bridge building, particularly in the 1870s and 1880s; and in serving the many needs of the exploding cities—laying down streets, development of municipal transit systems, construction of sewers and water-supply works, erection of the new, tall buildings using structural steel shapes. The railroad builders had been location engineers, following the jobs where they appeared, and frequently were self-employed. The sanitary and mechanical engineers, associated with urban growth, could establish themselves permanently in a fixed habitat, either as a member of or employed by a city firm, or they could become civil servants. The consequence was that, by the 1880s, the proportion of self-employed engineers had sharply decreased.

What kept down the number of professionally trained engineers in Great Britain was the long period of apprenticeship. A young man could become an engineer in Britain only by articling himself out to one already with a fixed practice, and who could find the time to give lectures in the necessary basic scientific knowledge. The probationer paid for the opportunity, and then served from five to seven years as an apprentice with nominal wages. This was necessary because certification to practice came only from the master engineers themselves. All this was a carry-over of the old (and monopolistic and restrictive) medieval guild system.

The apprenticeship system never took hold in engineering in the United States. The chief reasons were the fact that much of engineering had to do with railroad building, where theoretical instruction was impossible; and, of course, the existence of schools of engineering.

When the A. and M. colleges emerged, with free tuition, the opportunity cost of spending three to four years in an engineering school was quickly met after graduation. Further, professional engineering societies were not powerful enough, before the turn of the century, to affect the entrance and graduation requirements of the engineering schools. In short, they could not restrict entry, as the master engineers of Great Britain could.

Another interesting point to account for the attractiveness of engineering in the United States: an engineer with a college degree was a member of a profession (and not a trade, as in Britain) and had the social status accorded those of the other professions of law, medicine, and theology.

It has been said that in the United States opportunity costs were low and salaries were high. In the 1870s, 1880s, and 1890s, a young man technically or mechanically inclined could become a skilled worker—after training on the job or, in the few cases where the craft unions were powerful, the serving of an apprenticeship. A machinist's helper, for example, if an apprentice—the term was usually three years—obtained nominal wages during his probationary period. His opportunity cost during these years came to from $250 to $300. But a skilled machinist was paid on an average of $2.27 daily, or $680 annually.

The opportunity cost in attending an engineering school was several times higher than on-the-job or apprenticeship training, perhaps three to four times higher—but this is only a guess. (It would be a mistake to add tuition, books, and board and keep while being educated as the chief elements in the opportunity cost because American students in colleges and technical institutes worked their way in part or in whole through school.)

But once an engineer, even as a second or third assistant, the professionally trained young man quickly obtained as large if not a larger annual wage than the skilled machinist. And over a lifetime of engineering, as he moved upward in the scale, the earnings became very much greater. The figures are meager, but there are adequate evidences to support such conclusions. In 1875, the trade journal *Engineering News* published the salaries of municipal engineers for the leading cities of the country. Top salaries were $8,000 annually; the range for most was from $2,500 to $5,000. First assistants received from $1,000 to $5,000, with the majority falling between $1,700 and $3,000. Second assistants got $650 to $1,500; third assistants about the same. It should also be kept in mind that there was no objection to supplementation of fixed salaries from private consultation fees.

In the 1890s, when *Engineering News* from time to time discussed earnings, it reported that engineers in railroading were getting as much as $10,000 annually and those in mining from $6,000 to $25,000 a year. And it was able to say in 1893: "The average compensation of young American engineers is now generally in excess of corresponding grades in other countries, and fully equals, if it does not surpass, the average in income of beginners in other professions."

By 1900, engineering education (or education in "the applied sciences") had expanded impressively, the decade of the 1890s showing a very real leap forward. In addition to the dozen or so good private technological institutes, there existed programs in 36 schools supported in whole or in part by State appropriations, and technical schools or departments for such instruction in 102 colleges and universities.

A fairly good estimate, made in 1900, gave these totals for engineering graduates:

Before 1870	866
1871–80	2,259
1881–90	3,837
1891–1900	10,430

These figures were to expand impressively in the early decades of the twentieth century. This was notably so in the publicly supported institutions: another tribute to the broadening concept of the American idea of the common school.

CHAPTER TEN

URBANIZATION

The Economic Role of Preindustrial Cities   Cities, which have existed
in the Western World for at least 7,000 years, have been many things.
In the simplest sense, a city is a form of social organization whose population, living in a community, is engaged in nonagricultural pursuits.*
That does not mean that cities, from time immemorial, have been formed
to further more effective economic activity. Cities have appeared as the
seat of an administrative unit, whether military, political or religious.
This was so in the Roman Empire; and it was particularly so during the
Middle Ages when clusters of people collected under the walls of a
powerful lord or abbot and were either in his employ or were engaged
in services useful to his maintenance and those of his retainers, at the
same time getting protection. (Washington, Canberra, and Brasilia are
such modern-day cities without essentially an independent economic
life.) True, *faubourgs* or suburbs in time appeared outside of these
medieval towns where merchants and handicraftsmen gathered to engage
in commerce for a market, developing their own law and an international
medium of exchange (gold and silver coinage).

In addition, even in cultures which were noneconomic in the modern
market sense (and this was largely true of the feudalism of the Middle
Ages) cities rose up to foster commerce. Here, access to transportation
was the key factor. Such communities would appear on the seacoast or
up a navigable river or at a river's ford or in a great plain through

*This is Eric C. Lampard's definition, and it is a good one. See his very useful article
"The History of Cities in Economically Advanced Areas" in *Economic Development and
Cultural Change*, Vol. III, No. 2 (1955).

which a concourse of people regularly passed. The inhabitants of such settlements were seeking to develop a "more effective economic activity"—they were merchants or money changers or lawyers; they set up warehouses; working for them were artisans. But they were traders or merchant capitalists (Marx's useful category), and not industrialists. These merchants moved into the arteries of trade raw or semiprocessed materials (wool, hides, salt, wood products) and the slaves, precious metals and stones, fine textiles and spices they acquired as a result of their commercial intercourse with Africa and the Near and Middle East.

In the period in which merchant capitalism was dominant—from the thirteenth to the mid-eighteenth century—industry existed; but it was not generally urban. Location of plant was controlled by easy access to raw materials or water power; and this of necessity—before the appearance of the canals and railroads to provide through and cheap transportation—made industries country pursuits. Mills—gristmills, sawmills, fulling mills (for cleaning and shrinking cloth), paper mills—were established where there were falls of rivers; iron forges and furnaces appeared near large stands of timber to utilize the trees to be burned down to charcoal (the basic fuel for iron-making); potash and pearl ash were similarly made, as were barrels and staves; shipyards and ropewalks were founded; merchants collected the meat slaughtered and dressed by country butchers. Cottage industries—to weave woolen cloth, to make hats, shoes, broomstraw—were country activities. Access to raw materials and to labor (part-time country workers) made it possible for these industries to flourish before there was a factory system. The capitalist, again, was a merchant: he collected the necessary materials, let out their fabrication, advanced credit to and paid the workers, and shipped these manufactured (literally so, they were handmade) wares into commerce.

These merchants—undifferentiated rather than specialized—lived in cities. They were traders at both wholesale and retail; they financed the cottage industries; they engaged in money-changing and money-lending (hence the term, merchant, or private, bankers); they handled the insurance of ships and cargoes and erected warehouses; they bought into iron plantations and shipyards. The workers in the cities were of two kinds; those who were laborers around the wharves and in the warehouses and who were the city's coopers and draymen; and the skilled mechanics and artisans who were in the "bespoke" (custom-made) trades—building houses and making clothes, shoes, furniture, silver plate, carriages, to the order of their merchant patrons. And here too were gathered the printers (and newspaper publishers), lawyers, doctors, and private tutors who ministered to the other needs of the merchants and their families.

The predominant form of the economy in which merchant capitalism grew and thrived was agricultural. "The city was an island in a rural sea," as Scott Greer has picturesquely and properly put it in his *Governing the Metropolis* (1932). It provided services of one kind or another—the moving of surplus crops, banking, storage, education—for the vast rural hinterland; it sold to country people those goods they were not in a position to, or would not, produce for themselves.

These urban communities were preindustrial cities; they flourished as commercial centers in England right into the second half of the eighteenth century; and into the first half of the nineteenth century on the European continent and in the United States. The industrial revolution—brought on by the steam engine and power spinning and weaving (making possible the collection of workers wholly on the wage system and under supervision, in factories); and the creation of through and cheap transportation (first canals, then railroads)—accounted for the appearance of the modern city; at any rate, the city that was a unique phenomenon of the nineteenth century. This industrial city sprang up relatively late in the United States; right up to the 1850s, the large American cities were commercial rather than industrial in their orientation; this was true of New York, Baltimore, Boston, Charleston, New Orleans (which were seaports); Cincinnati, St. Louis, Pittsburgh, Louisville (which were river towns); Chicago and Buffalo (located on lakes).

I have called these cities "large"; that is, they had a population of 100,000 or over, and they were associated with a distinctive transportation facility. During 1800-1840, only the seaports of New York, Baltimore, Boston, and New Orleans, became "large" cities in this sense; during 1840-70, their company was expanded to include Philadelphia and San Francisco (seaports), Cincinnati, St. Louis, Pittsburgh, and Louisville (river towns), and Chicago and Buffalo (lake ports). In the last quarter of the nineteenth century, many of the earlier "large" cities also became significant industrial centers, notably New York, Philadelphia, St. Louis, Pittsburgh, Chicago, Buffalo, Cleveland. And these new ones emerged: Providence and Fall River (seaports); Memphis (a river town); Cleveland, Detroit, Milwaukee, Toledo (lake ports); and—made or largely developed by a new form of transportation, the railroad—Minneapolis, Rochester, Kansas City, Omaha, Indianapolis, Denver, Columbus, Worcester, Syracuse, New Haven, Paterson, Los Angeles, Scranton. In the case of the last group, these were truly and wholly industrial cities, whose destinies and fortunes were linked with one of the great attributes of the industrial age—specialization of function. Thus, when, in the last quarter of the nineteenth century, one thought of Minneapolis, it was in connection with flour milling; of Kansas City, meat packing; of New Haven, clockmaking; of Paterson, silk mills.*

The Rise of Industrial Cities   In the era of the dominance of industrial capitalism—that is, in the United States, in those years with which this book is concerned, from 1865 to 1900—cities played a particular economic role; and, as a result of their growth, cities contributed to the increasing efficiency of the American economy. Because of this, there were qualitative and quantitative changes.

The first force we must note—growing out of urbanization and in turn increasing industrialization—was specialization. With specialization of function, as industrial production moved from the country to the city, changes occurred in every aspect of society, creating at once uniformity and diversity. Industrial production was fragmented: an outstanding example, as we shall see later, was the diversified nature of the iron and steel industry. Light industry, where particular skills were needed and were attracted to or developed in cities, was a characteristic aspect of urbanization. It may be said that the larger a city became the more the tendency appeared for it to shift over from heavy to light industry and then to the services, or "tertiary" production. The occupational structure of the labor force was transformed. Exact service skills—another example of specialization and resulting greater efficiency—developed, for example, among bankers, lawyers, engineers, marketing specialists. And as urban populations grew, agriculture had to become specialized, not only producing the great farming staples but also—when farms were located near cities or within easy transportation reach—turning to dairying, poultry,

* This classification by "major transportation facility" is the work of Mark Jefferson in his article "Distribution of the World's City Folks" in *Geographic Review,* Vol. XXI (1931).

orcharding, and the growth of table vegetables. The cities, in the process, developed a unique intellectual, artistic, and political tone.

All this led to hostility and conflict. A good part of agrarian discontent stemmed from the awareness of—and helplessness in the face of—the increasing predominance of urban resourcefulness and leadership. In State legislatures, rural representatives lined up against urban representatives. To shake off urban dominance over banking, transportation, marketing, the particular national and State programs of the Grangers and Populists took form. But conflict also appeared in the cities, as the heterogeneity of the new urban population, made up more and more of European immigrants, rose to challenge the control over urban institutions of the older white, Anglo-Saxon, Protestant residents.

The second force was what the great English economist Alfred Marshall called the development of "external economies." Marshall saw that the concentration of industry in cities must "yield gratis to the manufactures . . . great advantages that are not easily to be had elsewhere." Such economies had factor indivisibility (it was impossible to differentiate their origin, whether from capital, labor, natural resources); and once appearing, they profligated in their effects. As Paul Samuelson has put it, an external economy "is a favorable effect on one or more persons that emanates from the action of a different person or firm." The result is, in economic terms, the lowering of input costs for other firms because they benefit from the appearance of a particular productive activity.

Marshall spoke eloquently of the widening of such "external economies" in cities because the urban climate was a powerful stimulus to innovation. Said he:

Good work is rightly appreciated, inventions and improvements in machinery, in processes and the general organization of business have their merits promptly discussed; if one man starts a new idea, it is taken up by others and combined with suggestions of their own; and thus becomes the sources of further new ideas. And subsidiary trades grow up in the neighborhood, supplying it with implements and materials, organizing its traffic, and in many ways to the economy of its materials.

But cities themselves, through their governmental activities, added to "external economies." They did so by the creation of "public goods," or what is called "social overhead capital"; that is, by improving transportation (paving streets, building bridges, making possible rapid transit); and by erecting hospitals, providing health and sanitation services, expanding education—thus adding to the betterment of "human capital." The contributions by municipalities to "social overhead capital," therefore, furnished general benefits to the city's population and workers and to its firms and industries. As a rule, they were provided free or at a nominal user charge; and the "external economies" they created were also indivisible.

Municipalities were able to expand their services, for increasing land values and growing business income made possible the widening and broadening of the city's tax base. Because this was so, municipalities could borrow; and this was one of the characteristics of the period.

Of greatest significance—to achieve "external economies"—was transportation: improved communications which reduced the cost and time in the factor movements entering into the cities, and communications within the city—bridges, ferries, rapid transit—that also made for greater efficiency in factor movements. Said Robert Murray Haig, in a pioneering article in 1926: *

[The pattern of settlement] is one which makes maximum use of territorial specialization within the limits set by the available means of transportation. The most favored points are those from which the richest resources can be tapped with the lowest transportation costs. At such points would develop the great cities.

Lampard summarizes Haig's contribution in this way:

cities were, from the standpoint of transfer efficiency, optimum points for production and consumption. While conceding certain diseconomies and "consumption advantages of non-urban locations" in particular cases, Haig made industrial-urban concentration the first premise of his spatial logic.

The third force accounting for the rise of industrial cities in the United States was the expansion of the market. The improvement in the agricultural processes leading to great surpluses in the staples gave another role to cities: the financing, warehousing, grading, processing, and marketing of the crops. The widening of the railroad net and the

---

* "Toward An Understanding of the Metropolis" in *Quarterly Journal of Economics,* Vol. XL (1926).

technological advances in railroad transport—the development of the refrigerator car was only one of these—further facilitated the movement of agricultural goods into local and foreign outlets. Cities now became the seats where flour was milled, livestock butchered and dressed, milk and eggs received and distributed, sugar refined and packaged. The widening of the market by transportation made it possible to shift plant location, so that steelmaking, for example, did not have to concentrate at Pittsburgh (because of propinquity to coal) but could spread out through Ohio and Illinois.

The emergence of a national capital market—which has already been discussed—lowered the costs of obtaining credit, and investment houses and the great institutional savers (the life insurance companies) found their proper locus of operations in cities. Urban commercial banks, in turn, developing specialization of function, studied the needs of their industrial customers on one hand and the financial resources of savers on the other to bring down the costs of credit. Reference has been made to the fact that municipalities were able to borrow to pay for the improvements invested in "social overhead capital." Because there was a national capital market, the interest rate municipalities had to pay on their bonds dropped from around 5.2 per cent in 1857 to 3.2 per cent in 1900. At the same time, the net municipal debt in the country grew from $200 million in 1860 to $725 million in 1880 and $1.4 billion in 1902.

And finally, we are to observe the appearance of an available labor force to make possible the growth of the industrial cities. This came from two sources: one being the internal migration of young people particularly from the country to the cities; the other being the natural gravitation of the "new" immigration, beginning in the 1890s, to the larger urban communities. In the rural-to-urban movement, we note that in the South young Negroes quit farming to settle in Birmingham, Atlanta, Memphis. (The Negro migration northward, again a farm-to-city movement, did not take place in force until the outbreak of World War I.) In the case of the immigrants, while most of them were young and unskilled, there were many with specific training (tailors, bakers, metalworkers, cabinetmakers) whose aptitudes could be utilized in cities depending for their "external economies" upon the ability to absorb and develop further specialization.

The Statistics of Urban Growth Between 1820 and 1860, the urban population of the United States increased 800 per cent and the national population 226 per cent. (In every case by "urban" is meant residence in incorporated places of 2,500 or over inhabitants.) Between 1840 and 1850, the urban population nearly doubled. By 1860, there were more than 100 cities with populations in excess of 10,000; 15 had 50,000 or more; 8 exceeded 100,000; and New York City (including Brooklyn) had more than 1 million residents.

The size of the "large" cities was not yet due to the location of manufactures in them, as the following figures for 1860, giving the proportion of population engaged in manufactures, indicate:

	%		%
Newark	26.2	Baltimore	8.0
Providence	20.0	Buffalo	6.9
Cincinnati	18.3	St. Louis	5.8
Philadelphia	17.5	Chicago	4.9
Boston	10.8	New Orleans	3.0
New York	9.5	San Francisco	2.6

Table 23 shows the advances urbanization made in the half century 1850-1900.

TABLE 23

Year	Incorporated places of 2,500 and over		Incorporated places of 100,000 and over		Incorporated places of 1,000,000 and over	
	No.	% of total population	No.	% of total population	No.	% of total population
1850	236	15.3	6	5.0		
1870	663	25.7	14	10.8		
1880	939	28.2	20	12.4	1	2.4
1890	1,348	35.1	28	15.4	3	5.8
1900	1,737	39.7	38	18.8	3	8.5

SOURCE: U.S. Bureau of the Census, *Urban Population of the United States*, 1930; and *Historical Statistics of the United States, passim*.

By 1900, the total urban population was not yet greater than the country's rural population. But as early as 1890, the number of gainfully employed workers ten years of age and over was already larger in nonfarm pursuits than those laboring on farms. In Table 24, note these figures in millions of population.

TABLE 24. TOTAL POPULATION AND POPULATION IN LABOR FORCE

Year	Total rural	Total urban	Total farm workers	Total nonfarm workers
1860	25.2	6.2	6.2	4.3
1870	28.7	9.9	6.8	6.0
1880	36.0	14.1	8.6	8.0
1890	40.8	22.1	9.9	13.4
1900	45.8	30.1	10.9	18.2

SOURCE: *Historical Statistics of the United States*, p. 72.

Over the half century, urbanization grew in every region of the country, but more rapidly in the North Central and Western States than in the Northeastern States, as Table 25 shows.

TABLE 25. PER CENT OF URBAN POPULATION BY REGIONS

Year	Total U.S.	Northeast	North Central	West	South
1850	15.3	27.1	9.2	6.4	6.0
1870	25.7	44.2	20.8	25.8	9.3
1880	28.2	50.5	24.2	30.8	9.4
1890	35.1	58.7	33.1	37.4	13.3
1900	39.7	65.5	38.6	40.6	15.2

SOURCE: U.S. Bureau of the Census, *Urban Population in the United States*, 1930, *passim*.

In Table 26, the size ordering of the country's ten largest cities, comparing 1860 with 1900, shows the growing importance of industrial cities west of the Appalachian Mountains.

TABLE 26. CITIES IN ORDER OF SIZE

1860	1900
New York	New York
Philadelphia	Chicago
Baltimore	Philadelphia
Boston	St. Louis
New Orleans	Boston
Cincinnati	Baltimore
St. Louis	Pittsburgh
Chicago	Cleveland
Buffalo	Buffalo
Newark	San Francisco

SOURCE: U.S. Bureau of the Census, *op. cit.*

As has been said, immigrants tended to locate in "large" cities, particularly in the 1890s, greatly adding to the country's labor force and contributing to some of the unique problems of urban America. Tables 27 and 28 differentiate between the population which is native white of native parentage and that which is foreign white stock (foreign-born or native-born of foreign or mixed parentage). Table 27 compares the two categories living in the country and living in cities. Table 28 shows the preponderance of foreign white stock in the country's great cities.

TABLE 27. PER CENT OF NATIVE WHITE AND FOREIGN WHITE STOCK IN
URBAN AND RURAL COMMUNITIES, 1900

	Urban	Rural
Total population	100.0	100.0
Total white	93.2	84.4
Native white of native parentage	40.0	63.1
Foreign white stock	53.2	21.3
Foreign-born white	22.2	7.6
Native white of foreign or mixed parentage	31.0	13.7

SOURCE: U.S. Bureau of the Census, *op. cit.*

TABLE 28. PER CENT OF TOTAL POPULATION

Cities	Native white of native parentage		Foreign white stock	
	1900	1890	1900	1890
New York	21.5	21.2	76.6	77.2
Chicago	20.9	20.3	77.3	78.4
Philadelphia	40.3	39.6	54.7	56.6
Detroit	21.5	20.8	77.1	77.5
Cleveland	23.0	23.6	75.4	75.2
St. Louis	32.9	26.3	60.9	67.7
Boston	26.1	30.3	71.7	67.8

SOURCE: U.S. Bureau of the Census, *op. cit.*

Social Overhead Capital City governments contributed to "external economies" and therefore to economic growth in a variety of ways. Perforce, part of this had to come from "social overhead capital." This included the creation of the "public goods"—laying streets, building bridges and docks, and provision for rapid transit, either by granting franchises to private companies to do so or by furnishing these facilities themselves. The maintenance of education, health services, and the improvement of sanitation—water supply systems, the treatment and disposal of garbage and sewage, the erection of hospitals—were the other important elements in the "public goods" whose capital outlays, costs, and maintenance cities assumed. Cities did not erect houses, but they took over the responsibility (with State help) of devising minimum codes for the protection of safety and health in multiple-dwelling buildings, and they budgeted for inspection services to assure compliance. Nor did cities, generally, furnish the public utilities of gas and electricity for lighting, cooking, and heat; again, however, they (or State authorities) established regulatory agencies to assure safety, proper service, and equitable rates.

Unfortunately, the federal Census Bureau did not begin publishing financial statistics on cities until 1902, and so we cannot record the systematic progress taking place in these activities over the years. But from the experiences of New York City (as a result of the investigations of E. D. Durand, *The Finances of New York City* [1898]), certain general observations are possible. New York's investments for "social overhead capital" at least kept up with its extraordinary population growth. From 1860 to 1890, in constant prices, such investments more than doubled while its population increased 90 per cent. In the 1890s and the 1900s, these took a great leap forward. Table 29 shows what was happening in New York City in the forty years 1850-90.

TABLE 29

	1850	1860	1870	1880	1890
Population (thousands)	515	805	942	1,206	1,515
Budget expenditures less state tax and debt payment (millions of dollars)	$2.8	$7.6	$18.2	$17.5	$24.3
Per capita expenditures	$6.53	$12.14	$28.14	$24.66	$23.09
Assessed valuation of real property (millions of dollars)	$286	$577	$964	$1,143	$1,696
Percentage of expenditures to valuation	1.18	1.70	2.75	2.60	2.06
Interest on borrowings (thousands of dollars)	$330	$837	$2,725	$8,422	$5,120
Debt redemption (thousands of dollars)	$90	$71	$1,115	$221	$2,080

SOURCE: E. D. Durand, *The Finances of New York City*, 1898, pp. 376-77.

Table 30 shows the particular purposes (selected) for which New York issued bonds in 1898 (or 1899), in 1900, and the total for all the years from 1898 to December 31, 1914, in millions of dollars.

TABLE 30

	1898	1900	1898-1914	Per cent of bonds issued
Water supply	$3.2	$3.5	$195.4	20.76
Rapid transit (subways)	—	1.0	105.3	11.20
Schools and sites	2.4	5.5	105.7	11.23
Public buildings	2.0	4.2	50.2	5.34
Bridges and approaches	3.4	5.2	80.8	8.58
Docks and ferries	3.0	2.5	95.2	10.12
Streets and roads	2.5	4.0	131.8	14.01
City parks	2.7	3.4	32.0	3.40
All purposes	$21.1	$32.7	$894.8	100.00

SOURCE: City of New York, Comptroller, *Annual Report and Financial Summaries,* various issues.

One of the early city services municipalities assumed was laying durable and cheap pavements for streets. Just about at the end of the Civil War, small granite blocks began to be used (New York put them down in 1869); these were the famous cobblestones which survived in many cities for a long time. But where stone was not easily available brick paving was employed; and beginning about 1870—following the example of London and Paris—asphalt was introduced. Streets had to be torn up constantly for sewers, water mains, gas lines and later electric conduits; asphalt lent itself easily to quick replacement and therefore was universally adopted when new streets began to be laid out. All this provided regular work for unskilled laborers, whether in the employ of the city or of private contractors. Keeping the streets in repair and clean—the use of horses by draymen and on the first forms of street transit created a stench as well as a health hazard—compelled cities to set up street-cleaning departments. The collection of garbage and its treatment and disposal, at about the same time, also became a normal city service—in the large cities handled by the municipalities themselves, in smaller ones let out to private contractors.

Furnishing a regular supply of water—for household and industrial uses, for fire fighting—had been an early concern of cities; Rome had had its aqueducts long before the Christian era. Its example had not persisted into the Middle Ages and early modern times, and cities fell back on wells or on the carriage of water in barrels from outside city walls. American cities began to experiment with the construction of their own aqueducts, tapping distant streams and installing pumping stations, long before the industrial city emerged—Philadelphia in 1801, New York in 1842; both were constructed and operated by the municipalities. This gave the lead to other cities, and in most of the large ones furnishing water was a municipal service. In 1896, this was true of forty-one of the fifty big cities of the country. But taking the total number of cities in the United States, only about 53 per cent owned their own water systems; in the others, private construction and management prevailed.

To keep water clean—as the lessons of bacterial research became common knowledge, notably the linking of typhoid fever with an unprotected water supply; as sanitation engineers saw the evidences of the pollution of streams from industrial wastes and sewage—steps were taken by municipalities to purify their water. Sand or mechanical filters began to appear in the 1880s; these devices were followed by the establishment of municipal bacteriological laboratories to test the city's water constantly (Providence was the first in 1888) and the use of chlorination (New York initiated this in 1893). The results were impressive. Chicago, for example, was able to reduce its typhoid rate, per 100,000 population, from 173 in 1891 to 7.5 in 1912.

The disposal of sewage became another important municipal concern. Early sewers had to be rebuilt and extended to make certain that their wastes did not pour into the waters also used for drinking. This was not enough, however; and the new sanitation engineers, usually on city payrolls, turned to the treatment of sewage in plants erected for that purpose before the effluvial flow was released. These were costly improvements and could be met only by municipal bond issues. But when new housing developments appeared in outlying districts, special assessments were laid on home owners to pay for the branch lines connecting with the main sewer trunks. (Even these assessments, before being collected, were financed by municipal borrowings.)

This attention to health and sanitation led to the establishment of boards of health—New York's appeared in 1866—to engage in health education and to supervise and lay down standards for the protection of the milk supply and other foods, to curb epidemics of contagious diseases, and—by the turn of the century—to quarantine homes whose inmates were reported by physicians or visiting nurses to have been stricken. To supplement municipal boards of health, State boards also were set up.

By 1900, these combined efforts had brought periodic crises involving health problems under control; the upshot was, mortality rates began to fall sharply, the greatest gains being achieved in the lowering of death rates for infants and for children under five years.

The establishment of large parks, as cities outgrew their original boundaries because of urban transportation, also was taken in charge by municipal authorities. Parks served important purposes: recreation, the planting of gardens, walks laid out in areas that simulated the country-side, and to allow escape from the noise and heat of congested sections—and more had to be done than the small city squares with trees and grass that America copied from London. New York set up the post of a park commissioner even before the Civil War; it was fortunate in obtaining for it the services of Frederick Law Olmsted, one of the great landscape gardeners of the nineteenth century. Breaking sharply with the French tradition of the formal garden and seeking to preserve the natural terrain of the country with its rocks, hilly slopes, trees, meadows, and lakes, Olmsted created New York's famous Central Park, Brooklyn's Prospect Park, and similar parks in Newark, Buffalo, Albany, and Chicago. He had many disciples and imitators, and other American cities followed New York's example.

Olmsted was also America's first city planner, and as early as 1871 he began to lay out New York clear north to the Westchester county line. True, the plan was the familiar rectangle, instead of great through north and south boulevards broken up by circles. If elegant vistas were impossible, the gridiron pattern permitted the handling of the automobile traffic of a later time. Olmsted also called for the elimination of railroad grade crossings from New York as it extended northward, thereby contributing much to its people's safety.

The municipalization of public utilities other than water supply made little progress in the United States before 1900. Public ownership of gas works and electric-light plants occasionally were to be found, but only in small cities. At the end of the century, Edward Bemis, in his *Municipal Monopolies* (1899), reported that only 13 cities ran their own gas plants and only 353 their own electric-light companies. These latter represented almost 13 per cent of such companies in the country and served about 5 per cent of its urban population. The same was true of municipal transit. Cities (authorized by State laws) granted franchises to private individuals and corporations to furnish this needed service, and private capital raised the funds in the expanding capital market.

Urban Transportation   In the early American cities, stages or omnibuses had appeared to carry passengers and express packages within the settled areas and out into the country. But as cities expanded, regular daily transportation facilities were required, following specified routes and regulated by municipal authorities as to uniformity of services and fares charged. The first such street railway to appear was New York's New York and Harlem Railroad, chartered for 30 years in 1831. Authorized by State laws, cities took to granting franchises—initially for 30 years, soon in perpetuity—under which privately-financed companies agreed to follow the specifications exactly laid out in their charters. Such companies were granted rights of way along which they laid the tracks on which cars were drawn, and received the benefit of a city's power of property condemnation so that they could erect their carbarns, repair yards, and stables. For the first streetcars were horse-drawn at a speed of about 6 miles an hour. During the 1860s, such horsecars appeared in all of America's large cities—New York had twelve lines by the end of the Civil War; by 1880, most cities with populations over 50,000, had horsecar lines. In that year, there were 18,000 streetcars on American city streets, using 100,000 horses.

This was just at the time that the cable car made its appearance. Chicago was the first city to introduce the cable car in 1882; Philadelphia came next in 1883, and then New York in 1886. By the mid-nineties, there were 157 miles of cable car routes in operation in Eastern cities, 252 miles in the Middle West, 6 miles in the South, and 217 miles in the Far West. (San Francisco's famous cable cars still linger on, to give thrills to a generation of Americans which has never seen the street trolley.)

Cables run by a stationary steam engine operating through a cable station were laid below the street surface and moved in a conduit midway between the rails at a regular speed of 10 to 15 miles an hour. The motorman, stationed on the car's front platform, engaged a "grip" on the cable by means of a control wheel, thus starting and keeping the car in motion. To stop, he disengaged the "grip." The cable car had certain advantages: regular speeds averaging 10 miles an hour; reductions in cost; and horses at last could be dispensed with. The disadvantages, however, were serious: the cable moved in a single direction, so that cars could not be sidetracked if they broke down; the cables snapped easily and the strands of the cables often broke.

The electric trolley overcame the problems of the cable car and largely superseded it. Efforts to utilize electricity for urban transit had been made from time to time in the 1870s, but none of these experiments had turned out to be practicable. The imagination, energy, and perseverance of Frank Julian Sprague—he was one of the truly outstanding innovators in the electrical industry, combining inventive with entrepreneurial ability—crowned these early attempts with success. Sprague had studied electrical engineering at the U. S. Naval Academy, had worked for Edison, and in 1884 left to set up his own organization. He had sought to persuade Jay Gould, the owner of New York's steam-driven Manhattan Elevated Railroad, to electrify; Gould had permitted Sprague to work on the installation of a centered third rail along which the current ran, whose costs Sprague had met; and then had called Sprague off. Gould did not believe electricity would work.

Sprague's opportunity came when Richmond, Virginia, called him in to electrify its surface cars in 1887. He was able to experiment with motors, controllers, trolleys which ran on overhead electric wires, and underground wires which supplied the current through a "shoe" attached to the car. As a result, Sprague was able to demonstrate that electricity was cheap and could be used on elevateds and surface cars (with the underground wire in congested areas and the overhead one in those more sparsely settled). Sprague installed the Richmond system in February, 1888, and it was an immediate success. On 12 miles of track, 40 surface cars ran, with power supplied from a central station whose steam engines operated a 640 kw. 500 volt Edison dynamo.

The Sprague Electric Motors Co. was in business, and it began to install electric street railways in hundreds of cities. In 1890, about 15 per cent of urban transit mileage was already electrified; by 1902, 97 per cent. Boston was the first large city to go over to electricity, and New York began the process of replacing horse-drawn and cable cars in 1895.

Elevated railroads first made their appearance in New York in 1871; the State legislature four years earlier had granted a franchise for the construction and operation of a line on Greenwich Street in lower Manhattan. Supported by a series of iron columns some 14 feet above the street pavement, a single-track railway was to be laid out with cars drawn by steam locomotives. The fare was to be 5 cents for any distance under 2 miles and 1 cent a mile thereafter. New York was to be compensated—a novel idea—by the payment of 5 per cent of the annual net income of the operating company. (This, presumably, was to make up for the loss in tax revenues because the existence of the elevated structure—shutting out air and light—and the noisy and dirty trains were likely to lead to property depreciation.) Some notion of the large costs involved may be noted from these figures. The erection of the iron superstructure, foundations, and stations, and the laying of double track, cost $700,000 per mile. The furnishing of engines and cars, for the initial four-mile El, came to another $200,000.

The elevated worked—despite the fact that passengers had to climb steep stairs to get to the stations and overcome their fears that the cars would jump the tracks—and the initial line was extended above Ninth Avenue as far north as 59th Street. By the middle 1870s, 40 trains were in daily operation, using 15 locomotives and 40 cars, over a 5-mile route. Similar railways were built on Second, Third and Sixth Avenues. In 1879, the Manhattan Railway Co. bought out the two companies running the four elevated lines and by 1881 was operating them under a single management, furnishing transportation—with a standard fare of 5 cents—from South Ferry to the Harlem River. When New York's first great suspension bridge, the Brooklyn Bridge, was opened in 1883, the elevated trains crossed the East River into the then incorporated city of Brooklyn; and, by special railway bridges, were able to open up the Bronx to rapid transit. Steam continued to be used until 1902 and then the "El"s were electrified. In 1910—when numbers of the El passengers began to fall off relatively—New York City's elevateds were carrying 450 million passengers a year as compared with 800 million riding on the street railways.

The electrification of the El prolonged its life; but city dwellers refused to countenance the chartering of new companies because of the nuisances the El created. New York was compelled to turn to other forms of rapid transit; the building of subways, or underground railways, was the most feasible one. The London underground, for a distance of 1⅓ miles, was opened in 1863. Boston, in 1895, began to construct a line of somewhat similar length, and completed it two years later at a cost of $4 million.

URBANIZATION

In 1901, New York (now Greater New York, made up of the five boroughs of Manhattan, Brooklyn, the Bronx, Queens, and Richmond, and with larger municipal revenues and heavier responsibilities, particularly for the movement of workers and shoppers over long distances into Manhattan) took the plunge and authorized the building of its first subway. It was to be municipally financed, and from 1901 to 1914 New York borrowed more than $100 million by bond issues to lay out subways. A construction company headed by August Belmont, the American representative of the Rothschilds, received the initial contract. In 1902, the Interborough Rapid Transit Co., capitalized at $25 million, was given an operating charter and proceeded to buy the necessary rolling stock. About the same time the Interborough acquired a 999-year lease from the Manhattan Railway Co. for all its elevated lines in Manhattan and its connections into the Bronx. The first New York subway, fully electrified, was opened in 1904.

A new phenomenon entered into the destinies of municipal traction in the late 1880s, and this was consolidation. Street railways had obtained their franchises from municipal authorities, the companies being given authority to operate individual lines. Originally the charters had been for brief periods, and only the sketchiest provisions had been included to protect passengers and the city itself. In the large cities, these franchises were valuable and corruption had almost at once appeared—the bribing of members of city councils and State legislatures, the suborning of courts, the acquisition by local politicians of contracts for construction and valuable building sites along proposed rights of way with the result that large fortunes could be and were made, to the neglect of services. When franchises expired, frequently they were renewed in perpetuity; no public hearings took place; no effort was made to use the street railways as a source of municipal income.

Scandals became so flagrant that State legislatures at last were forced to intervene. The New York State legislature, for example, in 1884 finally passed a General Street Railway Act which, in the case of renewals or new grants, called for public hearings, the consent of property owners along the rights of way, a uniform 5-cent fare with transfers, compensation to the city of 5 per cent out of gross receipts. Franchises could be forfeited for failures to comply. On the other hand, no specific terms were fixed for the charters, nor were consolidations forbidden.

These loopholes attracted a new company of promoters and financiers. First appearing in Philadelphia in 1880s—the group was headed by Peter A. B. Widener, Thomas Dolan and William L. Elkins—these men quickly consolidated more than half of the city's street railways and recapitalized the company, using some of the new funds to install cable cars but keeping most as entrepreneurial profits. Next, in association with a local financier, Charles T. Yerkes, they entered Chicago to perform a similar magic.. In the same year (in 1886) Widener, Dolan and Elkins joined hands with the New Yorkers William C. Whitney and Thomas F. Ryan and incorporated under a New Jersey charter the Metropolitan Traction Co., a holding company with the power to buy out (or exchange stock) or to lease the independent city traction companies. Originally capitalized at $10 million, after obtaining control by lease of the Manhattan Railway Co. the Metropolitan became a New York corporation, was capitalized at $45 million in 1898, and, to justify itself, began the electrification of the street railways and the elevated. In 1901, the New York consolidation was capitalized at $165 million, most of it really representing the value of the monopoly franchises the company held.

Municipal traction made money despite the overcapitalization of the lines, for unification afforded opportunities for efficiencies of operation and management. The successful experiences in Philadelphia, Chicago, and New York of the Widener-Elkins-Whitney-Ryan syndicate encouraged them to range wider. It was claimed in 1907 that they obtained control of the street-railway companies of one hundred cities from Maine to Pennsylvania, the total capitalization of their properties being in the neighborhood of $1 billion. These reaped a rich harvest.

The demand for municipal ownership of urban transportation—and it began to spread with the turn of the century—had its ironic consequences. Municipalities bought and operated street-railway lines just about the time when revenues began to decline and replacement of cars and equipment became heavy capital obligations. For the automobile was making its appearance on city streets. The promoters and financiers had been glad to leave the field and seek greener pastures. Municipal ownership—committed politically to low fares and compelled to recognize the trade unions of transportation workers—ended by producing deficits instead of profits.

Urban Housing The other great area in which private enterprise entered to help in the creation of "external economies" was the erection of housing for the booming urban populations. Taking the country at large, nonfarming residential construction mounted every decade but one for the half century, and this was the depression 1890s. An estimate of units built showed these figures: for the 1860s, 1,061,000; the 1870s, 1,333,000; the 1880s, 2,597,000; the 1890s, 2,491,000; the 1900s, 4,200,000. City houses, initially, had been made of wood or brick, had been for single-family occupancy, and had been constructed in leisurely fashion by skilled craftsmen who built carefully, presumably for eternity.

But as cities grew, other kinds of houses had to be erected: to provide for more families, to assure a modicum of protection against fire, and to be put up quickly. Around the Civil War the brownstone-front house—so called from the brownstone used to face the brick employed for the rest of the construction—made its appearance in neighborhoods where land values were still low. With a basement and two or three stories above (there was a long stone flight of stairs that led to the first floor), two or three families could be provided for. Interior structures—floors, beams, roofs—were of wood; but the roofs were covered either with slate or tar, for fireproofing.

As buildings, of necessity, had to rear upward and more stories had to be added—because of the increase in land values and to house the workers who were forced to live near places of employment—structural iron (and then steel) came into use. A metal frame or cage was put up; the brick or stone walls were added around the beams and columns. The manufacture of structural shapes gave a new lift to the iron and steel industry in the 1880s, after the country's railroads had been largely built. The production of pipe for plumbing and for the water mains, sewers, and gas and electric conduits also helped to account for the great expansion of the industry. Woodworking, to supply urban housing needs, moved over from a handicraft to factory manufacture.

The financing of multiple-family dwellings became one of the great outlets of savings—of individuals, savings and commercial banks, and life insurance companies, for, except for the small equities of builders, costs were met by mortgages, for which there was a ready market. In 1890, nonfarm mortgage debt stood at $3.8 billion; in 1900, at $4.6 billion. Builders, anticipating the spread of population as rapid-transit facilities began to be talked of or planned, took to developing areas—laying out streets, putting in water and sewer pipes—that were still in farms. And as populations followed, these speculative ventures—if the guessing or prior knowledge was correct—turned out to be highly profitable; thus, new urban fortunes emerged. These were some of the "external economies" resulting from the growth of cities.

An important development in American city building was the erection of the so-called tenement in which three or more families, all renters, were housed. These began to appear in large numbers in the 1870s, particularly in New York; the buildings—in the more congested districts—were five to six stories high with usually four apartments to a floor; they were of brick and were walk-ups; and the staircases, for fireproofing, were of stone and iron. City lots—because of the gridiron plan for the streets—were 100 feet deep and 25 feet wide. Before the 1870s, these lots had been utilized for the erection of front and rear houses, with a water pump and a large privy, or water closet, in the small court between. By 1879, it was estimated, New York had some 21,000 such tenements in which half a million people lived (and not infrequently worked, either in small industries like cigar-making or in the finishing of clothing).

An innovation in tenement-house construction appears in 1879. This was the so-called double-decker dumbbell building: dumbbell, because there were small air shafts on each side of the house. These tenements had some advantages over the front and rear houses: there were toilets on each floor; the staircases, as has been said, were fireproofed; iron balconies (called fire escapes) and exterior iron stairs leading from them down to the street did give added protection. But the interior rooms of the flats were laid out railroad fashion, with no windows for air and light facing on the outside. These rooms were either wholly dark and airless or had small transoms near the ceiling which opened on the interior hall of the floor. Into such a building were jammed at least one hundred men, women and children; frequently more, because many immigrant families in them took boarders—a new arrival from the same European town or village, whether a relative or a friend.

With such crowding, the poor ventilation, the sunless, ill-smelling air shafts, it was small wonder that death rates were so high. In New York in 1866, deaths totaled 34.92 per 1,000 population. In 1879, they had fallen to 24.13 per 1,000; but by 1889-93 they still stood at 24.01 per 1,000 annually.

Again and again, to cope with these problems, the New York State legislature set up investigating commissions and passed remedial laws. Such enactments appeared on the statute books in 1867, 1879, 1887, 1895, and 1901; it was the last that finally worked—in part because of the thoroughgoing nature of the reforms proposed, in part because New York City created in the same year a Tenement House Department, for inspection and reporting of violations to the law authorities.

The "new-law" tenements that could be constructed under the 1901 statute were to be entirely fireproofed buildings. Only 70 per cent of the lot could be used; and where a corner, 90 per cent. Buildings were to be no higher than one and one-half times the street width. There was to be at least one window in each room, opening onto a street, court, or yard. No room was to be less than 70 square feet in size; there were to be running water and toilets in each apartment; and each adult was to have at least 400 cubic feet of space and each child at least 200 cubic feet. Resident janitors, who were also handymen at minor repairs, were required for every building housing eight families or more.

As for the "old-law" tenements, certain renovations had to be made. Windows were to be cut in airless rooms and water closets installed in every apartment. So, at any rate, said the law; compliance was another matter. The new Tenement House Department had the authority to grant permits for new construction and the conversion or alteration of old buildings, and, along with the Board of Health, to enforce all the safety, health, and sanitation requirements of the new code. What New York City did was at once copied by other large communities; the future held out better promise for the housing of great masses of people. For private builders—except for a few "model" houses put up by philanthropic societies, public construction did not take place in the United States until the New Deal—frequently overbuilt, so that rents were low and flats were kept in reasonable shape and often repainted. In fact, to avoid the nuisance of living in an apartment while painters and plasterers were at work, New Yorkers took to moving—the months of May and September were given over to these hegiras—as apartments changed hands or new buildings were occupied.

The old buildings remained in New York City's Manhattan slums, where people continued to live, often for sentimental reasons. But new buildings were constructed as the city spread out—north, south, and east, into Manhattan's Washington Heights and into the Bronx, Brooklyn, and Queens. By 1900, even before the appearance of the "new-law tenements," Manhattan had only one-half of Greater New York's 83,000 tenement houses. In the next decade and one-half, particularly as a result of the building of subways, Manhattan's population and the number of its homes were to fall relatively.

Up to the end of the 1920s, the vitality of America's cities continued and their contributions to the country's "external economies" were large and important. Another kind of city, after the depression decade of the 1930s and the war years of the 1940s, was to emerge, with a different form of economic life. But that is not part of our story here.

In Praise of Cities   In 1899, Adna Ferrin Weber, a New York country boy who went to Cornell to study statistics and demography, published as a Columbia University Ph.D. thesis his classic *The Growth of Cities in the Nineteenth Century*. Weber's book has never been equaled; many of his acute observations still serve as the basis of the speculations of modern-day urban sociologists and economists. Weber saw the shadows as well as the sunshine of urban life, but he refused to succumb to the despair and hostilities that were already becoming characteristic of the writings of his contemporaries when they looked at cities and their new inhabitants. As he reflected on the broad sweep of urban development— for Weber wrote as learnedly of the cities of antiquity and the Middle Ages as he did of the nineteenth-century cities of Europe and America— again and again he was able to confirm his opinion that the progress of mankind (intellectual as well as economic) was an aspect of urban growth and supremacy. The quotation he printed on the flyleaf of his book set the tone for his own analysis and conclusions; he wrote in praise of cities. The quotation came from George Tucker's *Progress of the United States in Population and Wealth in Fifty Years* (1843):

The proportion between the rural and town population of a country is an important fact in its interior economy and condition. It determines, in a great degree, its capacity for manufactures, the extent of its commerce and the amount of its wealth. The growth of cities commonly marks the progress of intelligence and the arts, measures the sum of social enjoyment, and always implies excessive mental capacity, which is sometimes healthy and useful, sometimes distempered and pernicious. If these congregations of men diminish some of the comforts of life, they augment others; if they are less favorable to health than the country, they also provide better defense against disease and better means of cure. . . . In the eyes of the moralist, cities afford a wider field both for virtue and vice; and they are more prone to innovation, whether for good or evil. . . . Whatever may be the good or evil tendencies of populous cities, they are the result to which all countries that are at once fertile, free and intelligent, inevitably tend.

Weber handled with skill his economics as well as his demography and sociology. He knew unerringly why cities in modern times rose and flourished. Agricultural surpluses and their superior and efficient handling; the key parts played by transportation and communications; the movement of rural peoples into cities and the concentration of immigrants there, furnishing the needed additions to the labor force; specialization of function, particularly finance and marketing—these, in addition to the great improvements in medicine and sanitation, Weber saw, were what made cities grow in the nineteenth century. He caught the significance of manufactures, as opposed to the earlier commerce, in the appearance of the new industrial urban communities.

He did not hesitate to engage in broad generalizations when he commented on the advantages of urban living. Thus, on the intellectual life:

The village is dull not only to the man pursuing light amusements, but to him who seeks cultivated associations, for in these days the cities are the centers of intellect as of wealth. Even the college town with its intellectual atmosphere is to many high-minded people less stimulating than the city, where intellectual ability is much more varied.

And on morality:

On the whole, it is to be doubted if the cities are much worse than the rural districts as regards illegitimacy. . . . Infanticide, as the European criminal statistics have shown, is more prevalent in the country than in the city, while abortion seems to be less prevalent there.

Prostitution, regarded as a profession, is certainly a city institution, but many social workers doubt whether the sexual morality of the country is on a higher plane, from their knowledge of the large proportion of prostitutes who were first corrupted in country homes.

[331]

And on mortality (Weber had pointed out that death rates were higher in the city than in the country, and this was so in every period of life):

Death rates . . . vary with the degree of agglomeration of population. But there is no inherent reason for the relatively higher mortality except man's neglect and indifference. Recent tendencies show that the great cities are leading the way in making sanitary improvements. . . . This holds true of infant mortality, which is one of the most decisive indices of a locality's healthfulness.

He called attention to the drop in New York City's death rate, despite the growing density of its population. During 1856-65, deaths per 1,000 population stood at 32.19; by 1896, they had fallen to 21.52. He cited the case of the so-called notorious Tenth Ward, which was the most densely populated in the city, with 543 persons per acre as compared with 59 in the whole city. The average number of tenants in a house was 57.2; in the city 34. Yet, in 1896, its death rate was 17.14. That of children's deaths (under 5) was 58.32 per 1,000 of that age; for the city, 89.25; other wards showed rates as high as 183. This was so because the Tenth Ward was almost entirely inhabitated by Jews: "its people are careful in the observance of sanitary laws. Being Hebrews, they observe the strict Mosaic laws regarding cleanliness. . . ."

And, on congenital infirmities: there were more feeble-minded, more deaf mutes, more blind people in the country than in cities with 50,000 or more people.

And, on health:

There can be no doubt that down to very recent times the health and vigor of urbanites compared unfavorably with that of men who worked in the open air, just as their death rates did. But in the last quarter century the evidence in both cases has changed.

And he quoted with approval Alfred Marshall's comment:

it is not to be concluded that the race is degenerating physically, nor even that its nervous strength is, on the whole, decaying. On the contrary, the opposite is plainly true of those boys and girls who are able to enter fully into modern outdoor amusements, who frequently spend holidays in the country, and whose food, clothing and medical care are abundant and governed by the best knowledge.

Indeed, cities, particularly American cities, created opportunities; they allowed men to rise; talents here emerged to lead the nation. And Weber ended on this clear note of hope:

The salvation of society therefore depends upon a mobility sufficient to persist or even encourage the rise of individuals from the lower to the upper social ranks. The process of recruiting the real aristocracy of ability and character must be unimpeded. And it is the concentration of population *in cities which best promotes the process of bringing capable men to the front* [Italics in original].

The city proletariat appears to be recruited from the country-born rather than from the real city dwellers. In fact, the countryman coming to the city begins a slow ascent, rather than a descent; his children instead of being men of "lower physique with less power of persistent work," advance to a higher rank on the industrial and social scale, while the third generation, instead of dying out, is still more capable and efficient.

This was the same United States Adna Ferrin Weber, the young scholar, was saluting as had his older contemporaries William Graham Sumner and Andrew Carnegie. It was a country—exactly because it was now becoming urbanized—that welcomed talent and encouraged it to grow. And in the process, the United States itself was growing.

4

ENTREPRENEURSHIP—THE CASE OF ANDREW CARNEGIE

CHAPTER ELEVEN

CARNEGIE AND IRON AND STEEL

Technology of Iron and Steel   The Monongahela and Allegheny Rivers form a junction in western Pennsylvania, and at this point the great Ohio River originates to flow southwestward and join the Mississippi at Cairo, Illinois. In the triangle of land where the three rivers meet, Fort Pitt was established in 1753, and forty years later the town of Pittsburgh formally appeared; its population then was 1,400. In 1850, already a thriving mercantile center, with the movement of coal and lumber its chief activity, Pittsburgh's population was 46,000; it was here that the young Andrew Carnegie obtained his first employment and became familiar with the iron industry.

The terrain of the Pittsburgh area is irregular and cut up by sharp valleys through which run a series of swift streams. The natural routes of transportation follow these watercourses. Thirty-six miles southeast of Pittsburgh on the Youghiogheny River, which flows into the Mononga-hela at McKeesport (just 10 miles southeast of Pittsburgh), is Connells-ville, the center of the greatest coke ovens in the world; in the hills are limestone deposits; iron beds are to be found in close proximity, too. Pittsburgh, at the confluence of the Monongahela and the Allegheny, down which could float naturally the barges of coke, limestone, and iron, was destined to greatness.

The production of iron had appeared early in western Pennsylvania. Pittsburgh saw its first blast furnace (to make pig iron) erected in 1792; its first iron foundry in 1805; its first rolling mill in 1811. By 1850, there were some sixteen such mills in Pittsburgh and its vicinity with a capitalization in the neighborhood of $3 million, employing some 2,000 men and consuming about 65,000 tons of pig iron, blooms, and scrap. The plants were small and were operated as independent units—buying their pig iron or wrought iron from other similar small, individually owned foundries—and serving local markets entirely. Pittsburgh was to grow because of its propinquity to coal and iron-ore deposits; its ability to meet the requirements of the expanding railroad industry, which made the city one of its great centers; and because of the company of entrepreneurs who had come of age in it in the 1850s to seize the oppor- tunities offered by the Civil War, industrial growth, and particularly the development of the country's railroad net.

Iron is never found in a pure state. Other molecules exist in it: oxygen, carbon, phosphorous, silicon, manganese, sulphur. The efforts to remove one or all of these elements mark the progress from cast iron to wrought iron to steel. Cast iron was weak and brittle, because most of the offending elements were still there; wrought iron was an advance— it was stronger—because oxygen in the iron was got rid of. It was wrought iron that was used in America for rails and structural shapes (bridge parts, for example) until steel was perfected.

The making of wrought iron, in the United States, was a slow and costly process; that is why, until 1870, Great Britain manufactured more iron than the rest of the world combined and a good part of America's requirements were imported from her. Britain, very early, had solved the problem of fuel. The iron ore and with it the fuel (in the United States, charcoal; but in Britain, coke) were burned in a container, or blast furnace. This released the oxygen, which, however, was replaced by the carbon from the fuel. The result was the alloy pig iron—and cast iron when used for iron castings.

To convert the pig iron into wrought iron—thus expelling the carbon— a second process was necessary, and this the British devised by the inven- tion of the reverberating furnace and the employment of puddling. To quote Peter Temin (*Iron and Steel in Nineteenth-Century America,* 1964):

In this type of furnace, the iron was separated from the fuel by a low wall, and the flames from the burning fuel were conducted over the iron. The lack of contact between the fuel and the iron meant that a more impure fuel than the traditional charcoal could be used without contaminating the metal. This fuel was coke: too impure for use in refining by hammering, but not for use in puddling.

The puddler was able to work on the iron in the furnace while it was still under heat. He rolled and pushed around the hot iron, thus refining it; and the iron changed from a liquid to a pasty substance. Again to quote Temin:

Because the puddled iron could not be kept molten, it could not be rid of the bits and pieces of nonmetallic slag that it picked up in the course of puddling. Much of the slag was expelled by "squeezing" the iron after it was removed from the furnace, but a nonhomogenous composition remained a hallmark of wrought iron.

Up to about 1840, the United States made its pig iron with charcoal. Starting in the 1840s, Eastern ironmasters began to use anthracite as their fuel in their blast furnaces, and by 1854, almost one-half of the pig iron production was anthracite-based. Less than 10 per cent was made with bituminous coal (or coke); this meant that Western ironmasters, despite the large supplies of bituminous available to them, were still employing charcoal. Late in the 1850s and more particularly in the 1860s, the pattern began to change. The push of railroad construction across the Allegheny Mountains created the demand for more railroad iron; the existence of the great bituminous coal fields around Connellsville created the supply. The erection of coke ovens near the fields (the coal was burned down to coke in "baking" ovens, in the process freeing the coal of its sulphur) lowered costs and made coke pig iron as cheap to produce as anthracite pig iron; from then on, the former began to push ahead. But it was not until the middle 1870s—and the appearance of H. C. Frick (as we shall see), as the king of Connellsville—that the fuel made from bituminous began to exceed that coming from anthracite. Thus, up to the end of the Civil War, the iron industry was largely an Eastern one; after the Civil War, due to the leading demand for railroad iron, the location of the industry shifted to the West. And this was possible because of one of the great inventions of the nineteenth century: the Bessemer Converter, which, by the further refining of the crude ore, was able to turn iron into steel.

The invention of the Englishman Henry Bessemer's converter was announced in 1856; a similar converter was developed, at about the same time, by the American ironmaster William Kelly. In 1866, both patents were combined, and the commercial production of steel became possible in the United States. Bessemer found that by blowing cold air on molten pig iron, in a chamber with an acid lining, the carbon (as well as the silicon and sulphur) could be released. Hendrick described the chemical change as follows:

Finally a pure white flame, the reflection of the incandescence inside the vessel [the converter], shoots into the air; this is the symbol of victory; it means that practically all the carbon in the heated contents has vanished into thin gas. After a few minutes of steady illumination this glow extinguishes itself. The residue within the vessel is as liquid as water. The converter is mysteriously tilted, the molten stream trickles like a little river into a mold, and in due course appears as a gleaming rectangular ingot.

Steel was the result; the great difficulty with the original Bessemer process was that it did not remove the phosporus in the iron ore—and therefore only an iron with a low phosphorus content could be used in this process. Here the United States was fortunate: for the discovery of the great iron fields in the Lake Superior country—containing ore rich in metal, easily mined and as easily transported, and practically free of phosphorus—made Bessemer steel possible in the United States. At the western end of Lake Superior, spreading to the north and south in a vast area, lie ranges of hills made up of solid masses of iron ore. The seams are so soft and so near the surface that the ore can be scooped up with steam shovels. Steam cranes load the ore into waiting railroad cars; these are run to the Lake harbors of Duluth, Superior, Ashland, and Marquette, where mechanical contrivances empty the cars into the waiting ore ships.

The first of these iron ranges to have been discovered was the Marquette, and shipments of ore began to move out of it as early as 1855; the second was the Menominee, and its first shipments came out in 1877. Then came the Gogebic in 1884 and the Vermilion in the same year. It was the Mesabi, found in 1892, lying deep in St. Louis County, Minnesota, that was the greatest range of all. All these combined were the largest ore beds known—up to the middle of the twentieth century—and gave the United States a striking advantage, helping make it quickly the outstanding iron and steel producer of the world. The Mesabi alone, by 1900, furnished one-third of all the ore mined in the United States, one-sixth of the world's supply, and one-half of the total raw materials required to make steel.

A further set of refinements still had to occur; the first to lower the cost of making Bessemer steel, the second to eliminate phosphorus entirely from all kinds of iron ore and to do it quickly. It was the acid lining of the original Bessemer Converter that prevented its being able to remove phosphorus in the making of steel. This problem was overcome by the invention of the so-called "basic" process by the Englishmen Sidney Thomas and Percy Gilchrist in 1879; the basic lining, using lime and replacing the acid one, allowed the phosphorus in the iron to combine with the lining and be carried off in the slag.

The second was the invention of the open-hearth method of making steel. The work of two Germans working in England, William and Friedrich Siemens, and the Frenchman Pierre Martin, and appearing in the 1860s, this was based on a so-called gas regenerator furnace which, using extremely high temperatures, was able to utilize chemical control over the ore more effectively (and more cheaply) than the Bessemer process. This was so because the open-hearth furnace, generating heat which exceeded the melting point of the wrought iron, was able to eliminate puddling as a separate step. When the basic lining of Thomas and Gilchrist was added to the open-hearth furnace, then open-hearth steel with its clear certainty of getting rid of all the phosphorus was in a position to challenge the supremacy of Bessemer steel. Open-hearth steelmaking permitted the use of cheaper raw materials (including scrap) and cheaper equipment; it assured the making of steel of a higher and more uniform quality; it was faster. Basic steel began to appear in the late 1880s; by 1900, it was replacing Bessemer steel in the making of structural beams, armor plate, tin plate, and other important uses.

While these fundamental changes were occurring, technological innovation was being pressed on all fronts simultaneously—further reducing costs at the same time that it made possible the employment of less skilled workers. As W. Paul Strassmann in his *Risk and Technological Innovation* (1959) points out, in blast furnaces, labor costs were reduced by the increase in furnace capacity through stronger blast engines and hotter blast ovens. Fuel costs were reduced by the use of bituminous coke and the re-employment of furnace gas. At the same time, quality control came with the open-hearth method and with the introduction of nickel, tungsten, and chromium alloys. From 1860 to 1875, the daily output of the largest furnaces grew from 40 to 100 tons of pig iron. By 1900, the national average was 500 tons per furnace.

This industrial revolution, in the iron and steel industry, and in the economy generally, was accomplished by 1900. The results were apparent through such comparative figures as these: the price of pig iron was reduced from $38 a ton in 1810 to $14 in 1900, that of steel from $200 a ton to $19. In 1865, 100,000 tons of coke were consumed in the production of pig iron; in 1895, 9 million tons. In 1860, 114,400 tons of iron ore were shipped from the Lake Superior mines; in 1895, 10.4 million tons. In 1860, 820,000 tons of pig iron were produced; in 1895, 9.5 million tons. In 1872, the United States made 809,000 tons of iron rails and only 84,000 tons of steel rails; five years later, more steel rails were being turned out than iron rails; by 1895, iron rails were no longer being made, and so rapidly had replacement been pushed that 88 per cent of total railway trackage in the country was made of steel.

And here in Table 31 is the tale of American leadership.

TABLE 31. STEEL PRODUCTION
(In thousands of tons)

Countries	1870	1880	1890	1900
United States	69	1,247	4,277	10,188
Great Britain	292	1,375	3,679	5,050
Germany and Luxembourg	—	728	2,127	6,541
The world	692	4,205	11,902	28,273

Carnegie's Rise As a result of his training as a railroad man and his experiences in the War Department in the first two years of the Civil War, Andrew Carnegie saw clearly where his real opportunity lay: it was to be in iron. By 1863, at the age of twenty-seven and still working for the Pennsylvania Railroad as the superintendent of its western division, Carnegie was already the possessor of a small fortune. He had husbanded his earnings carefully, had made a number of sensationally successful investments (the largest in an oil company), and with these funds was helping in the financing of a group of iron companies—all working on war contracts or on the products (iron rails, axles, iron beams for bridges) that the railroad industry required. Just as the war was ending, Carnegie was the chief money man and the active manager of four such concerns, of which the one closest to his heart was the Keystone Bridge Co. The others were the Union Iron Mills (which rolled beams for railroad bridges), the Superior Rail Mill, and the Pittsburgh Locomotive Works.

In 1865 he quit the Pennsylvania Railroad and made his first return journey to Europe; in 1867, he moved to New York; and for the next five years he was in and out of the country—building up his financial resources at the same time that he expanded his iron interests primarily, but other interests as well. By 1868, Carnegie recorded an income of more than $50,000 from his partnerships in the iron companies and from stocks he owned. He was branching out in all sorts of directions—continuing his interest in the Columbia Oil Co.; acquiring a large block of stock in the Union Pacific Railroad; with George M. Pullman organizing the Pullman Palace Car Co.; and with investments in street-railway companies, coal companies, banks, grain elevators, the Western Union Telegraph Co.

But always, his eye continued to be on iron and railroading. For during the six years 1867-72—when the country's first large postwar railroad construction boom was taking place—Carnegie was helping in the organization of railroad bridge authorities to span some of the country's great rivers. For some he became the contractor, the Keystone Bridge Co. becoming a subcontractor to furnish the wrought and cast iron going into the bridge superstructures. In another role, Carnegie sought to peddle the mortgage bonds of these bridge authorities in the London and German money markets. During this period, he sold in all $30 million in bonds (their face value); most were those of bridge companies, but some were of railroad companies. These were gold bonds carrying 6 to 8 per cent interest, were offered by the European merchant bankers at 80 to 85, and were quickly snapped up. It is not unlikely that Carnegie made as much as a million dollars in these few years—in his dual capacity of contractor and financial agent—a stake with which he could go into the manufacture of steel.

His first venture of this sort was the building and financing of the Keokuk and Hamilton Bridge, chartered respectively by the States of Iowa and Illinois and approved by Congress. The bridge company was to construct and maintain a toll railroad, wagon, and pedestrian bridge across the Mississippi; the contract was awarded in December, 1868, and the bridge was completed in May, 1871. His second was his most spectacular one: the spanning of the Mississippi from St. Louis in Missouri to East St. Louis in Illinois. The bridge was decided upon in 1868, the regular constitutional formalities were cleared away, Carnegie obtained the contract, the Keystone Bridge Co. received the subcontract, and construction was begun in 1870 and completed in 1874. This was the famous Illinois and St. Louis Bridge which Captain James B. Eads built; and Carnegie went off to London in 1869 to dispose of the $4 million of first-mortgage bonds that had been issued. These he was able to move through the American merchant-banker Junius Spencer Morgan, who had settled in London. A similar bridge, across the Missouri, at Omaha, was financed in the same way, this one through the sale of $2.5 million in mortgage bonds. There were many smaller bridges which were made possible by the same devices—Carnegie the agent for the securities, Morgan the investment house placing the bonds among English banks. Some of the railroad securities Carnegie handled were in even larger blocks. Thus, he sold $5 million of first-mortgage Philadelphia Railroad bonds (guaranteed by the Pennsylvania Railroad) at 90—an excellent price—to Morgan; and from $9 million to $10 million bonds of the Allegheny Valley Railroad as well. Only once had he worked through the English merchant-banking firm of Baring Brothers; but the relationship had not turned out too well. As a result of these experiences with the House of Morgan—in which he had met with the son, J. Pierpont Morgan, his father's representative in New York—it was no wonder that the two joined hands thirty years later when the United States Steel Corporation came to be formed.

In England, Carnegie came to see that the future of iron was to be in steel—he had met Henry Bessemer and watched his converter at work— and in 1872 he announced his intention to organize a steel company to make steel rails. His iron-company partners (among them his brother Tom and his boyhood friend Henry Phipps) refused initially to join him; he sought out others, putting up $250,000 of his own funds to back his vision. Carnegie, McCandless and Co. was formed (its name was changed in 1874 to the Edgar Thomson Co., Ltd. after Carnegie's friend, the president of the Pennsylvania Railroad), and it began the erection of its first steel plant at Braddock, Pennsylvania, where the Pennsylvania Railroad, the Baltimore and Ohio Railroad, and the Ohio River met. In 1874, the company was capitalized at $700,000—of which Carnegie held $250,000, William Coleman $100,000, and seven other partners $50,000 each. Among these, now throwing in their lot with him, were his iron-company associates—his brother Tom, Phipps, and Andrew Kloman.

Carnegie kept on building Braddock during the depression, pouring his own resources into it (he sold out all his other interests; he backed his confidence in the country's recovery, and the future of railroading and of steel), raising funds from banks, and buying out faltering partners. Carnegie, in his *Autobiography*, described how he fought hard against the depression, resisting the temptation to sit idle until the storm spent itself, as so many of his competitors did. Said he:

But in a critical period like this there was one thought uppermost with me, to gather more capital and keep it in our business so that come what would we should never again be called upon to endure such nights and days of racking anxiety.

The Edgar Thomson Works—as Braddock was named—was in operation in September, 1875, still a deep depression year. Because the plant and equipment were new, Carnegie cut the market price for steel rails by $5 a ton; obtained orders—and kept in business. It was a practice he was never to surrender: of forcing the competition by costing-and-pricing policies. In 1878, still in depression, the company was recapitalized at $1.25 million, with Carnegie holding 59 per cent of the shares—a plan from which, thereafter, he never deviated. He was generous to his "associates" (as Carnegie designated these partners), seeking out talent everywhere and encouraging and assisting these younger men to become owners, but he was always the master, the one who set policy and took the risks, expanding vertically and constantly growing, so that from 1880 until 1900 Carnegie dominated the steel industry. By February 5, 1900, Carnegie had forty such partners. After the split with Frick, there were thirty-nine whose loyalty (and unquestioned acceptance of his leadership) was rewarded richly in 1901, when the Carnegie Steel Co. was absorbed by the United States Steel Corporation. Every one of these thirty-nine—most owning minute, fractional shares of the Carnegie

Company—emerged a millionaire. (Frick, of course, did far better on his own.)

In 1881 another consolidation took place, this time under the name of Carnegie Brothers and Co., Ltd., combining Edgar Thomson, the Union Iron Mills, and the Lucy Furnaces. The capitalization was $5 million, of which Carnegie owned $2.7 million and his brother Tom, $878,000. Expansion continued during the 1880s, the two most important being Carnegie's personal acquisition of the majority shares of the H. C. Frick Coke Co. and the purchase of the Homestead Mills, both in 1883. Frick and Homestead: this fateful combination was to have a profound effect on Andrew Carnegie—and cast a deep shadow over the reputation which he valued so highly.

Henry Clay Frick had started much like Carnegie. His schooling ended when he was seventeen; in 1870, at twenty-one, he was working as a bookkeeper in his grandfather's Overholt Distillery in western Pennsylvania—and already, out of his savings, branching out into other fields. The great bituminous coal lands of the area around Connellsville particularly attracted his attention and he began to buy into them. At the same time that Carnegie saw the potentialities of steel, so did Frick: to make steel, the basic fuel would have to be bituminous coal—coal burned down to coke (in the process, releasing the coal's sulphur) in "baking" ovens. Frick borrowed $10,000 on his personal note from the Pittsburgh Mellon Bank and built fifty coke ovens; in 1872 he quit the Distillery, established Frick and Co., and with further help from banks, bought more coal lands and built more ovens. Like Carnegie, he continued his ventures right through the depression, so that when it ended he owned more than 80 per cent of the coal mines of the Connellsville region and had erected a thousand coke ovens.

On January 1, 1882, the H. C. Frick Coke Co. was formally established, and into this Carnegie began to buy—thus furnishing the funds for Frick's great growth. In less than five years from Carnegie's entry into it, in 1887, the Frick Co. owned 5,000 acres of coal lands and was producing 6,000 tons of coke a day. At the same time Frick was admitted into a partnership in the Carnegie Co. (Tom had died in that year), being allotted $100,000 worth of stock, which—conforming to the pattern of all such arrangements with the Carnegie "associates"—was to be paid for out of earnings. This represented 2 per cent of the company's capitalization; in time, as Frick became more and more prominent in the Carnegie operations (he was made chairman of the Carnegie Co. in 1889), he came to own 11 per cent. Thus, he was Carnegie's leading partner.

There was another man whose star in the Carnegie constellation was to rise with Frick's: this was Charles M. Schwab, also Pennsylvania-born. Starting as not much more than a laborer in the Braddock works in 1880, when he was eighteen, Schwab's capacities were at once sensed and he was moved to posts of increasing responsibility. In 1887, at the age of twenty-five, he was superintendent of the Homestead Works and two years later an "associate" with a fractional share which, by 1900, was to become 3 per cent of the company's total capitalization. By that time, Schwab was the president of the Carnegie Steel Co.

Entrepreneur   One of the most interesting facets of Andrew Carnegie's entrepreneurship—there were many and they took bewildering and versatile forms—was this organization of young men, his "associates," that he created. When he appeared in 1911 before the House Stanley Committee—set up to investigate the steel industry—he explained this "organization revolution" of his in these words:

It has always been the policy of this association from its outset to regard itself as an association of individuals who have united together their fortune, their talents, and their industry to manufacture iron and steel in all its branches in the best form, by the best processes and at the most moderate cost. . . . It was the policy of those whose intelligence and faith in results founded the business to associate with themselves from time to time a number of young employees, who, by becoming directly members of the association, would be stimulated to the very best work.

On many occasions, he paid tribute to the younger men with whom he surrounded himself. At one time he declared that "the personnel of its organization was worth more than all the property of the company." At another time—in a relaxed mood—he remarked that "Mr. Morgan buys his partners, I grow my own." They grew because they were invested with responsibility in a departmentalized organization and their performances could be evaluated through an elaborate system of functional cost accounting. The Minutes of the company's managers—which Carnegie scrutinized very carefully when he was away and which he filled himself with the most exact detail when he was in attendance at the regular meetings—belie the too easy assumption that Carnegie was not absolute monarch in his own domain.

The successes of the Carnegie method were reluctantly attested to by the Stanley Committee Report, when it said:

All of the increase [in capital, of the Carnegie Co.] did not come from within. Capital had been added from without from time to time; but making due allowance for the added capital, the growth from within had been so remarkable as to read like a story from the Arabian Nights.

While this company had at times made agreements with its competitors as to prices and percentages of outputs . . . its general policy had been to rely on its superior advantages as to location, plant, and capital, coupled with the ability of its organization, and keep its mills running without much reference to the wishes or interests of its competitors.

It is too simple to assume that innovation consists of coming first into the field with a new revolutionary process; it is more important to be successful in its use, achieving the economies of scale that skillful management makes possible. Only then does such an entrepreneur leave the competition behind to become the leader, the pace-setter, in an industry. These things Carnegie did. Iron and steel were not the same again after his entry.

Part of the innovational procedure is process; part is organization. Carnegie was not the first to erect a blast furnace or a Bessemer steel converter or an open-heart steel mill. There were blast furnaces in western Pennsylvania dating back to the opening of the century. The first plant for the manufacture of Bessemer steel was put in operation in 1867 by the Cambria Iron Co., which began rolling steel rails in September of that year. The Siemens process for making open-heart steel was introduced by F. J. Slade in 1868 for Cooper, Hewitt and Co., then the country's largest ironmaster. Carnegie followed—and added all the other ingredients to make the mixture of business success and leadership work.

In 1870, while he was selling iron products and selling bonds, Carnegie made an important decision. To remain in iron, he had to make his own pig iron—erect his own blast furnace. The order was given to his partners in 1870 to put up the first of the two Lucy Furnaces; two years later they were in blast—and they were the first modern blast furnaces in the country.

To make pig iron required iron ore, coke as the fuel, and limestone as the flux. Carnegie's competitors knew only how to use the more expensive high-content ores. But low-content ores could be employed; and here chemistry came in. For a skilled chemist, by proper mixing, could overcome the high-phosphorus and high-silicon content of the cheaper ore; he could also use what had hitherto been looked upon as a waste product—the so-called "scale," the chips thrown off by the fiery metal as it passed through the rolls. Such a chemist, a German, was acquired to help in running the Lucy Furnaces.

Carnegie, in his *Autobiography*, described what the chemist did for his company:

We found a man in a learned German, Dr. Fricke, and great secrets did the doctor open for us. Iron stone from mines that had a high reputation was now found to contain ten, fifteen, and even twenty per cent less iron than it had been credited with. Mines that hitherto had a poor reputation were found to be yielding superior ore. The good was bad and the bad was good, and everything was topsy-turvy. Nine-tenths of all the uncertainties of pig-iron making were dispelled under the burning sun of chemical knowledge. . . . What fools we had been! But . . . we were not as great fools as our competitors. . . . We were the first to employ a chemist at blast furnaces. . . .

Phipps, Carnegie's iron partner, was responsible for the discovery of the use of the "scale." A low-grade iron and "scale" were combined with high-grade ore to turn out a first-class and a less expensive pig iron. This pig iron was sold through brokers to the trade at handsome profits; when the Edgar Thomson Works began to operate, it was used to make its steel. And here, the skills of Captain William R. Jones, the chief engineer of the Thomson Works, came into play, for his invention of the so-called Jones Mixer made possible the continuous feeding of the hot pig iron, kept molten until it was required, into a great caldron. The pig iron, as a result, did not have to be reheated—at a further saving in cost. It was no wonder that Carnegie, in his *Autobiography,* was able to say: "The Lucy Furnace became the most profitable branch of our business, because we had almost the entire monopoly of scientific management."

The same thing happened in the use of the open-hearth method for making steel. Carnegie had been following the work of the Englishmen,

Thomas and Gilchrist, who were seeking to overcome the inadequacies of the Bessemer process; in 1880, Carnegie paid the Englishmen $300,000 for the American rights to their patents and assigned them to the Bessemer Steel Association for the use of its members. Nothing came of this. The invention of the open-hearth furnace by the Siemans brothers and the addition to it of the Thomas-Gilchrist "basic lining" finally solved the problem of phosphorus ore. It was Carnegie who introduced these methods—the first to do so—into the newly acquired Homestead Mills in 1888.

Similarly, in 1896, at the Duquesne Mills (absorbed in 1890) automatic machines were installed to load the blast furnaces, to cast the pigs, and to dump them into freight cars. The consequences were two: blast furnaces could be built to a height of 100 feet and a saving of one-half the direct-labor cost in smelting iron was achieved. This was again during depression; as was the steady dismantling of Bessemer furnaces and their replacement by open-hearth ones. From 1893 on and right through the depression lasting to 1897, Carnegie expanded his steel production by almost three-quarters—and without impairment to his profits. In 1897, then a very junior partner, Charles Schwab was recorded as saying in the company's Minutes: "The great success with which we have always met in our business has been largely due to the fact that we have anticipated our competitors in manufacturing better and cheaper than they do."

To process were added organization and, with it, rationalization. Mass production was the key: larger plants, greater economies, the regular replacement of older equipment by the newest—costing less to operate—and new methods. This was so, as Fritz Redlich has pointed out, because Carnegie was "the new type of entrepreneur, the captain of business in contrast to the older captain of industry." To achieve such a role, he had to know the whole market, present and future, being ever alert to the potentialities of change. When the Carnegie Co. acquired Homestead, the country was in its third—and last—great postwar railroad building boom. In 1887, when the purchase of steel rails was almost at peak, Carnegie began to convert Homestead over from the making of rails to the fabrication of structural steel shapes.

The era of the modernization of America's cities had begun: tall buildings were being erected of stone and masonry (why not with steel skeletons?); new bridges were being built to speed urban rapid transit; elevated structures on which ran steam trains were being erected in cities; streets were constantly being torn up to lay great pipes for water and sewage disposal; the transmission of electricity, for lighting and power, the beginning of the urban electrical trolley—all required new and different kinds of steel for fabrication and operation. Again, Carnegie was in the van: it was no wonder that the profits of the company increased so sensationally in the 1890s—though almost one-half of the decade was in depression. Carnegie—himself, directly—sold his steel shapes, also in the depression of the 1890s, for the construction of New York's Brooklyn Bridge and its elevated railways, for the Washington Monument, and for the skyscrapers that were beginning to appear in American cities.

Frick played a large role in rationalizing the mass production Carnegie had introduced. The properties around Pittsburgh (Braddock, Homestead, Duquesne were the leading ones) were put under a common direction—but with departmentalization (and cost-accounting control) of purchasing, engineering, and marketing. It was Frick who watched all this at the plants level, while Carnegie ranged widely (by this time he was spending only half his time in the United States) as financier and as supersalesman. It was Frick who saw that vertical integration was possible, and at bargain prices in the depression years. After all, the first step had been taken earlier, with the joining of his coal lands and coke ovens to the Lucy Furnaces. The natural next step was the company's control of its own iron-ore mines in the Lake Superior country and their linking with the Pittsburgh complex by its own ore ships and railroads.

The Carnegie Co. profits in the 1890s had been extraordinary: in 1890, $5.3 million; in 1891, $4.3 million, in 1892, $4 million; during 1893-96 (all depression years) $3 million, $4 million, $5 million, $6 million respectively. During 1895, Carnegie's senior partners Henry Phipps and George Lauder, Jr., pressed for a distribution of dividends; they were fearful of keeping all the eggs in one basket (Carnegie's favorite phrase). Thus Lauder wrote to Carnegie on June 12, 1895:

I have a long communication from Phipps on the question of dividends versus improvements. His position seems to me unassailable. But apart from all he urges, I cannot see why you do not make dividends. . . . On the first of May we were about $1 million ahead with all fixed capital left out. Add May earnings with stocks and bonds which are really available assets, and there is between $6 and $7 million. If I am not right about this, I would like to know it. If I am, why do you not make dividends?

Carnegie's partners could only propose, somewhat plaintively (Phipps wrote in a similar vein, and ended: "I know it must annoy and bore you my giving opposite views, but I have not hesitated when it seemed to be my duty."); it was Carnegie who disposed. In 1896—profits undistributed, supplemented by personal borrowings from a New York bank on his own Frick Co. stock, Carnegie plunged ahead.

The famous, fabulous Mesabi Range, in Northern Minnesota, had been opened up in 1892 by the Merritt Brothers, to supplement and exceed with its prospects the earlier Marquette Range. (The first shipment out of the Marquette had been 1,500 tons of ore in 1855; by 1900, this had reached 3.4 million tons. The first shipment out of the Mesabi had been 4,200 tons in 1892; in 1900 it had been 7.8 million tons—and in 1911, 29 million!) Carnegie was aware of what was going on, for he had lent Henry W. Oliver $500,000 to help in the staking of the Merritts. But the Merritts could not hold out; they were compelled to sell in 1893 to John D. Rockefeller. In 1896, Rockefeller wanted to shorten his interest—and Carnegie had the cash. Carnegie refused to buy the ore properties; but he would lease for a long term, working the mines and using the Rockefeller railroads for shipment to Lake Superior, and the Rockefeller boats out of the Lake ports—paying royalties on the ore mined and going rates for railroad and ship transportation. To round out his holdings, Carnegie bought other mines in the Mesabi and in the Gogebic and Vermilion Ranges; and he acquired his own ore ships as well.

These ore lands were carried on the books as the Oliver Iron Mining Co. (named after the same Henry Oliver Carnegie had known as "my fellow messenger boy in the telegraph office," who had been associated with the Merritts). The Carnegie Co. owned five-sixths of the Oliver company; with its resources, despite the Rockefeller agreement, it went ahead buying and leasing lands in the Mesabi, until it controlled almost 100 million tons of ore reserves. In 1900, the Oliver Iron Mining Co. valuation was $20 million.

The Iron Age, the technical periodical of the industry, was watching what was going on with admiration. On Dec. 17, 1896, it reported that the Carnegie leases and other holdings gave his company "a position unequalled by any steel producer in the world."

The final link in the chain—to free him of dependence on the Pennsylvania Railroad—was the joining of Lake Erie with Pittsburgh. Carnegie bought the whole Lake shore front of the town of Conneaut, Ohio (thus controlling the harbor) and connected it (as we shall see) by railroad to his various plants around Pittsburgh. Pittsburgh had become a lake port.

Businessman   It is a pretty problem: shall we measure the length and breadth of Carnegie's achievement by what he said or by what he did? He was amazingly articulate, he wrote voluminously, and most of the things he said were a distillation of reflection, observation, and a long and varied experience. Occasionally—but not too often—he repeated by rote the "conventional wisdom." He was impressed by Herbert Spencer—as who was not in his generation in Britain and America? but to assume that the key to his conduct as businessman was the precepts of the "conventional wisdom" or Spencer's evolutionary ideas (what is today called "Social Darwinism") is to underrate Carnegie woefully.

He records in his *Autobiography* that he had read Macaulay and the American historian Bancroft; he knew his Bible, Burns, and Shakespeare —the last from reading and from his devotion to the theatre, and his one-time secretary J. H. Bridge reports that he could recite whole scenes from the Plays. According to Bridge, in a memory book—which represents some of his reading—Carnegie copied out bits and pieces from the Greeks, Milton, Goethe, Carlyle, Marcus Aurelius, Matthew Arnold, Tennyson, and the poet, James Thompson.

In his essays on topical subjects (less so in his *Autobiography*), one notes allusions in passing to "the law of supply and demand," "the law of wages and profits," "the law of ups and downs" in business. Edward C. Kirkland, in his *Business in the Gilded Age* (1952), in an acute observation, declares that "Carnegie's universe of law was partly the casual parroting of vernacular phrases." Having paid lip service to the economists of the day, Carnegie could also express impatience with the harmonies of their text books: they were, he said, "writers of the closet . . . removed from personal contact with every-day affairs." For when he talked of law governing the world of business, he meant the idea in terms of what he had seen and done himself. "The great natural laws," he said, "were the outgrowth of human nature and human needs." These were, as far as he was concerned in his role of businessman, the "law" of competition and the "law" of the aggregation of capital and establishments.

The first, he was convinced, was bound to prevent monopoly. Granted, trusts would be formed; prices would go up; but the very advantages large organizations obtained were bound to attract new capital and new enterprise to challenge the early comers. As for the second, individual enterprise, if successful, had to move through those rounds he himself had traveled—mass production, scientific organization, rationalization, with resulting lowering of prices and a more generally diffused raising of standards of living. True, inequalities continued to exist, and this made for labor hostility and industrial unrest.

On balance, there were advances: the ingenious, the intelligent (himself, as the example) survived and went on for self-improvement and improvement of the whole of society. And here Spencer explained all. He read Darwin, and Spencer in detail: *The Data of Ethics, First Principles, Social Statics.* Dramatically, in his *Autobiography,* he reports how understanding came to him.

Reaching the pages which explain how man has absorbed such mental foods as were favorable to him, retaining what was salutary, rejecting what was deleterious, I remember that light came as in a flood and all was clear. Not only had I got rid of theology and the supernatural [this had come in his youth, before he encountered Spencer] but I had found the truth of evolution. "All is well since all grows better" became my motto, my true source of comfort. Man was not created with an instinct for his own degradation, but from the lower he had risen to the higher forms. Nor is there any conceivable end to his march to perfection.

All this explained Carnegie to himself; it did not make him. What did, he himself knew, and one can piece out a fairly complete rationale of business conduct from his writings.

The successful businessman was the honest merchant in the market place. "I have never known a concern to make a decided success that did not do good, honest work, and even in these days of the fiercest competition, when everything would seem to be a matter of price, there

[354]

lics still at the root of great business success the very much more important factor of quality," he wrote in his *Autobiography*.

But price had to be scientifically determined—to reflect costs, to meet the competition, to make a profit. Cost accounting had to be installed; in the early 1860s, Carnegie was aware of this, and in his *Autobiography* he tells of how he grappled with the problem when the Union Iron Works began to grow.

Years were required before an accurate system was obtained, but eventually, by the aid of many clerks and the introduction of weighing scales at various points in the mill, we began to know not only what every department was doing, but what each one of the many men working at the furnaces was doing, and thus to compare one with the other. One of the chief sources of success in manufacturing is the introduction and strict maintenance of a perfect system of accounting so that responsibility for money or materials can be brought home to every man.

Carnegie followed costs with an exact, a niggling care. Those who worked under him knew this—and knew that, whether at home or abroad, Carnegie examined the cost sheets for each operation with microscopic attention. Charles Schwab, his chief lieutenant in the late 1890s, described to the Industrial Commission how exact the procedures were: "We made a careful statement of each manufacture, with the cost as compared with each department, and the reasons . . . had the manager of that department make such explanations as were necessary. . . . Greater economies are effected by strict supervision over all departments than in any other direction." And another associate, testifying before the Stanley Committee much later, recalled the constant driving presence of the head partner: "A careful record was kept of the costs. You are expected always to get it 10 cents cheaper the next year or the next month." And once, among many such occasions, Carnegie, looking at the reports sent to him in Scotland, caught an increase of 5 per cent in coke consumption. He wrote to the manager involved: "This is, at least, five per cent more than it should be, and perhaps more. It should be investigated, beginning at the beginning. . . . We should do better than that."

Affairs required the concentrated concern of the businessman; it worked best if there was no scattering of resources. He was contemptuous of those who assumed there was an easy road to fortune—through speculation, company promotions, book jobbery. Thus, on both points in the *Autobiography:*

I believe the true road to preeminent success in any line is to make yourself master in that line. . . .

It is surprising how few men appreciate the enormous dividends derivable from investment in their own business. There is scarcely a manufacturer in the world who has not in his works some machinery that should be thrown out and replaced by improved appliances. . . . And yet most businessmen whom I have known invest in bank shares and in far-away enterprises, while the true gold mine lies right in their own factories.

And again:

I have never bought or sold a share of stock speculatively in my life, except one small lot of Pennsylvania Railroad shares that I bought early in life for investment and for which I did not pay at the time because bankers offered to carry it for me at a low rate.

He was harsh and swift in his treatment of his associates whom he caught, or suspected of, diverting their energies into the stock market. He compelled one of his partners, J. A. Leishman, to surrender his shares in the Carnegie Co. when he learned that Leishman was trading in iron-ore shares. One of the reasons for the bitter quarrel with Frick was that the chairman of the Carnegie Co. sought to diversify his interests, using the large fortune he had built in the financing of other kinds of company promotions.

Carnegie's treatment of Leishman—who had become president of the company when Frick ascended to its chairmanship—was characteristic. When he learned what Leishman was up to, he wrote on December 24, 1894:

You have not treated me fairly as your partner. You know I often congratulated you on your *not* speculating in pig, and upon the fact that we were clear of purchases beyond this year. You kept silent and deluded me. You deceived your partner and friend, and only kept faith with him when you could deceive him no longer.

And when Leishman remonstrated, Carnegie pressed even harder, in his letter of January 4, 1896:

It appears you speculated for ore, in Minnesota ore stock, which you bought when already in debt, simply because you thought it would rise in value. . . . You do not realize what the Presidency means. . . . You say it was not a "speculation." We can't see what it was but that. No conservative businessman can have any other name for it.

Leishman was pushed out—to become United States Minister to Switzerland and later Ambassador to Italy and then Germany. There was no personal ill will; in fact, Leishman visited with Carnegie at Skibo Castle, and when Leishman, toward the end of his life, fell on hard times, Carnegie gave him a pension out of his own funds. It was simply that there were rules (which Carnegie made) for the deportment of his partners and they had to be observed. He warned another, who was straying: "Every dinner you attend, every lunch at the club at which you linger, every act, affects the Company; every word you speak, every financial step in your private affairs, has serious consequences."

Carnegie had no peer in his generation in one aspect of the conduct of business—and that was marketing, and this he was able to pursue from the vantage point of New York, where he maintained a private office. Here he met—informally at dinners and in clubs, and formally in their own offices—the heads of other large enterprises; and to them he himself sold his iron and steel. This was so especially in his dealings with the presidents of railway companies: he knew them personally, for he too had been a railroad man, and he knew their needs. He sold to them— and he was not above seeking and obtaining rebates from them when he moved the supplies they had purchased on their own lines. Because he was a man of large means he could assist in the financing of a contract, lending money to his buyers or taking their mortgage bonds to facilitate the purchases. When New York City was erecting its elevated structures for its street steam railways, because he was on the spot and knew exactly the steel beams required, he personally was able to obtain a large order for the structural shapes he was converting his rolling mills into making.

In line with this, Carnegie was convinced that the corporate form of business organization—in part because it put the investment banker, the promoter, close to the seat of decision-making—was not his cup of tea. The partnership was best; but there had to be a leading partner. So, in a conversation with Bernard Alderson, he said:

[357]

I do not believe any one man can make a success of a business nowadays. I am sure I never could have done so without my partners, of whom I had thirty-two, the brightest and cleverest young fellows in the world. All are equal to each other, as the members of the Cabinet are equal. The chief must only be first among equals. . . . No man will make a great business who wants to do it all himself or to get all the credit for doing it. I believe firmly in youths as executive agents. Older heads should be reserved for counsel.

Such a businessman was a risk-taker, or an adventurer in the early sixteenth-century sense. He was, Carnegie said in "Empire of Business," "chiefly dependent for his revenues not upon salary but upon profits. . . . The businessman pure and simple plunges into and tosses upon the waves of human affairs without a life-preserver in the shape of salary; he risks all."

Those who had been watching Carnegie at work for almost half a century knew all this; and they were unstinting in their praise. Thus, a witness before the Stanley Committee, in 1911, declared:

Mr. Carnegie was a genius in two points. In the first place he exceeded any man I ever knew in his ability to pick a man from one place and put him in another with the maximum effect. . . . His other point of genius was to realize that the real time to extend your operations was when nobody else was doing it.

The latter had been a guiding precept, as we have seen. Carnegie himself had summed it up in 1908 when he was testifying before a House Committee. He had said: "The man who has money during a panic [and invests it] is the wise and valuable citizen."

His famous article "Wealth," published in 1889, had created a furor throughout the English-speaking world. What attracted attention was Carnegie's bold asseveration that it was the duty of the rich man to get rid of his fortune, administering it himself, however, for the good of the community. More important for the argument being stressed here was his defense of the inequality of wealth and the economic role played by the businessman who invested his capital productively. He started off by saying that modern industrialization, mass production, resulted in the improvement of the quality of goods and reduction of prices. As a result: "The poor enjoy what the rich could not before afford. What were the luxuries have become the necessaries of life."

Among other things, "the law of competition" had made this possible. Its workings were harsh (as a result of it, using Spencer's famous phrase, "human society loses homogeneity"); but

the advantages of this law are also greater still than its cost—for it is to this law that we owe our wonderful material development, which brings improved conditions in its train. . . . We accept and welcome, therefore, as conditions to which we must accommodate ourselves, great inequality of environment; the concentration of business industrial and commercial, in the hands of a few; and the law of competition between these, as being not only beneficial, but essential to the future of the race.

Men engaged in such affairs, managing large concerns, could not stand still; their companies had to go forward—not simply earning interest on capital, but making profits. "It is a law, as certain as any of the others named, that men possessed of this peculiar talent for affairs, under the free play of economic forces must, of necessity, soon be in receipt of more revenue than can be judiciously expended upon themselves. . . ."

At this point he had left it. But the English pressed him hard; his first article and a second following it up were reprinted at once in Britain (it was here that the striking title "The Gospel of Wealth" was used) and elicited many comments and rejoinders, among them one by the Reverend Hugh Price Hughes, a Methodist minister. Hughes had said: "Whatever may be thought of Mr. Henry George's doctrines and deductions, no one can deny that his facts are indisputable, and that Mr. Carnegie's 'progress' is accompanied by the growing 'poverty' of his less fortunate fellow-countrymen."

Carnegie replied to his critics in an article published in the English review *Nineteenth Century* in 1891, which he boldly and characteristically—for he was no mean polemicist—called "The Advantages of Poverty." Here, spelled out in detail, with evidences from Britain's and America's industrial progress and its fruits, was presented the classical justification for the inequality of wealth as a result of entrepreneurship. Said Carnegie:

So far from its being a fact that "millionaires at one end of the scale means paupers at the other," as Mr. Hughes says, the reverse is obviously true. In a country where the millionaire exists there is little excuse for pauperism; the condition of the masses is satisfactory just in proportion as a country is blessed with millionaires. There is not a great millionaire among the whole four hundred millions of China, nor one in Japan, nor in India; one or two perhaps in the whole of Russia. . . . There are more millionaires upon the favored little isle of Britain than in the whole of Europe, and in the United States still more, of recent origin, than in Britain; and the revenues of the masses are just in proportion to the ease with which millionaires grow. The British laborer receives more for one day's handling of the shovel than the blacksmith or carpenter of China, Russia, India, or Japan receives for a whole week's labor, and double that of his Continental fellow-workman. The skilled artisan of America receives more than twice as much as the artisan of Britain. Millionaires can only grow amid general prosperity, and this very prosperity is largely promoted by their exertions. Their wealth is not made, as Mr. Hughes implies, at the expense of their fellow-countrymen. Millionaires make no money when they are compelled to pay low wages. Their profits accrue when wages are high, and the higher the wages that have to be paid, the higher the revenues of the employer.

He constantly reverted to his own experiences; how his own labors had direct effects on the community with which his fortunes had been associated. Alderson reports some remarks he made to his workers in Pittsburgh in 1893:

I made my first dollar in Pittsburgh, and expect to make my last dollar here also. I do not know any form of philanthropy so beneficial as this: there is no charity in it. I have hoarded nothing, and shall not die rich apart from my interest in the business. Unless the Pittsburgh works are prosperous, I shall have nothing. I have put all my eggs in one basket right here, and I have the satisfaction of knowing that the first charge on every dollar of my capital is the payment of the highest earnings paid for labor in any part of the world for similar services.

To an examination of the consequences of mass production, Carnegie returned, in detail, in an article called "Popular Illusions About Trusts," published in 1900. Again he rang the changes on his favorite theme, the limited partnership. But he took cognizance of the appearance of the corporation: it was able to use the mechanism of a national capital market, for it was able "to concentrate the small savings of the many and to direct them to one end." This massing of capital led to a lowering of costs and

If there be in human history one truth clearer and more indisputable than another, it is that the cheapening of articles . . . insures their more general distribution. . . . In no period of human activity has this great agency been so potent or so widespread as in our own. Now, the cheapening of all these good things . . . is rendered possible only through the operation of the law, which may be stated thus: Cheapness is in proportion to the scale of production. To make ten tons of steel a day would cost many times as much per ton as to make one-hundred tons. . . . Thus, the larger the scale of operation, the cheaper the product. . . . It is, fortunately, impossible for man to improve, much less to change, this great and beneficial law, from which flow most of his comforts and luxuries, and also most of the best and improving forces in his life.

Was his lack of concern over Bigness—concentration, integration, large aggregations of capital, the threat of monopoly—cant? He honestly believed, as he kept on saying again and again, that "Competition in all departments of human activity is not to be suppressed." But secretly his company engaged in pools—to fix (and, it was to be hoped, increase) prices and to promote (and limit) production among their members.

Pools in the steel industry began to appear significantly in the late 1880s and proliferated into all of the branches of steelmaking during the 1890s. The appearance of many new combinations and holding companies in the latter part of the decade—and the resulting disordering of markets—prompted those that were overcapitalized and probably overbuilt to seek some controls over prices and production. It should be kept in mind that pools were illegal and the agreements arrived at under them could not be enforced in the courts. They sought to improve their mandates by requiring that participants make financial contributions to a common fund: members were fined or forfeited what they paid in if they withdrew. Only small sums were lost for noncompliance. Pools were of relatively brief duration, in consequence, some of them lasting only a few months; none more than a few years. One of the important reasons for their instability was that the Carnegie Co. was in and out, and its refusal to stand by its commitments kept the whole industry in a state of turmoil.

There was a steel-rail pool that was organized in August, 1887, broke up in 1893, was revived (with new allotments) somewhat later and disappeared in February, 1897. A wire-nail pool made its appearance in 1895 and collapsed a year later. A steel-billet pool, organized in April, 1896, did not survive the year. There were pools in axles, beams and channels, angles. Testimony before the Stanley Committee indicated that a surprisingly small part of production was affected by these arrangements.

Before the Stanley Committee, Carnegie expressed his distaste for these collusive efforts. Schwab, who was his general superintendent during the second half of the 1890s, spoke at greater length to the Committee. He said: "I went into this business [steel] in 1880 and for the next twenty years I heard of agreements of this sort every few months in some direction. Most of them were never consummated, many of them lasted a day, some of them lasted until the gentlemen could go to the telephone from the room in which they were made, and some of them lasted a longer period."

During the depression of 1895-97, the Carnegie Co. meant to survive without these crutches. It continued to modernize, cutting costs, and its motto—Carnegie's own words—was "Take orders and run full." The company withdrew from the rail and beam pools, and prices went tumbling down. Carnegie explained his actions to Abram S. Hewitt, an important competitor: "I can make steel cheaper than any of you and undersell you. The market is mine whenever I want to take it. I see no reason why I should present you all my profits."

Hendrick, Carnegie's biographer, is right when he says that such efforts at the regulation of competition were unavailing. The Carnegie Co. was the price leader and it kept on pushing prices down—to the embarrassment of the new companies. To repeat, there is no doubt that Carnegie's aggressiveness was an important factor in the creation of the United States Steel Corporation; this was one way of controlling output and the market, and steadying prices.

CHAPTER TWELVE

THE WORLD CARNEGIE CREATED

The Development of Taste   Carnegie had matured early; the necessity for supplementing his father's meager earnings, the responsibility he quickly assumed for keeping the small household together, left firm and indelible impressions. He was determined to make a fortune, he wrote of himself when he was turning thirty—as who would not be who had been exposed to poverty from early childhood? He was going to settle in Oxford and get a "thorough education," he promised himself in another memorandum three years later: the spires, the bells, the beautifully maintained quadrangles, the medieval calm and presumably high learning of a society that had been permanently barred to the likes of him—these were dreams that of course never could be turned into reality.

But the want of formal schooling beyond childhood was a goad: he would improve himself, by reading, by going to the theatre, by listening to and developing a taste for music, by buying paintings, drawings, and sculpture, until he had sharpened his own senses of judgment and discrimination. If he could not sit under cultivated and scholarly men, he would seek them out—when he had made that fortune!—to converse with them and possibly acquire some of that wisdom he always thought he had missed when he was young. The company was large and somewhat curious: Herbert Spencer, Matthew Arnold, John Morley, William E. Gladstone, John Hay. The fact that the Englishmen were condescending about America—even John Morley, writing to Carnegie about his *Triumphant Democracy* referred to the United States as "too *aggressively* republican"—neither troubled him nor made him insecure; he took their disagreements and disapprovals with a good grace, and he continued to correspond with them and enjoy their company, for they were all first-class men with first-class minds.

He thought the American John Hay, too, was such a one, and here he was mistaken. He assumed that their views on American involvements overseas were similar, and of course they were not. Carnegie looked at American expansionism beyond the continent with disquietude; it must, inevitably, he had the vision to see, suck the United States into war, or what he called "the vortex of militarism." Hay—who never really faced up to realities as a writer and as a public figure, for the meager creative talents he had he did not use honestly—pretended to agree, yet he was the man who was responsible for American policy in the Far East and in the Caribbean. One is entitled to occasional lapses of judgment: Hay, Carnegie respected; of James G. Blaine—a far greater statesman with his notion of binding all the countries of the Western Hemisphere into a union of common political and economic interests—he was less certain and even suspicious.

Books, music, the fine arts, learning were important; if he himself had acquired access to these the hard way, he could ease the road for others. Here were some of the purposes for which a fortune could be used. (That a fortune gave social recognition and power Carnegie never quite saw or never admitted.) It is no occasion for surprise, therefore, that his chief benefactions—in his lifetime he gave away $350 million—had to do with libraries, museums and art institutes, pure research, education and college professors. "The improvement of mankind," was the oracular way in which he put it in the charters of the many trusts he set up; certainly what was knocking around in the back of his mind was that there were definite ways by which a democracy could prove itself, and one was to make the heritage of the race, the cultivation of the spirit and the mind, available to the largest possible number of people. The creation of "Free Public Libraries" (he gave the buildings, local communities maintained them) was the first of a series of magnificent acts—there were almost 3,000 of them and they were scattered over the English-speaking world. The Carnegie Institute of his adopted Pittsburgh, starting as a library, developed into a huge building also housing an art gallery, a natural history museum, and a music hall. Under the direction of the Institute were put the Technical Schools (in 1912 changed to the Carnegie Institute of Technology), which were also handsomely endowed. The Carnegie Institution of Washington was set up to encourage pure research in the natural and physical sciences. He made possible for New York its first (and still greatest) concert hall, which was named after him and happily survives against demolition as a publicly designated historic building. In addition—so important was music to him—he turned over the funds to build 8,000 organs in whatever churches and synagogues throughout the country bespoke his interest.

Carnegie's devotion to technology and science was no mere gesture: he had seen, at a crucial time in his newly chosen career as ironmaster, the advantages he was able to obtain and hold by the employment of a good chemist in his iron mill. He hailed the opportunities beginning to appear for the conversion of youthful apprentices into budding technologists. He gave generously to such programs and schools, for he understood, perhaps even better than the academics in charge of these new educational schemes, how they were contributing as much to a social as to an industrial revolution. The young men who would go to these new technical and scientific schools, but for such institutions, might have remained mechanics. Here was opportunity—the opportunity he always hailed if it meant that youth with talent, and training, could open up new doors.

As early as 1890, in an article he called "How to Make a Fortune," Carnegie was expressing himself along such lines. This was before he began to give his money away: in other words, the giving was based on reflection and conviction—he was not trying to buy his way into the Kingdom of Heaven because he had been a sinner. Organized charity he would not touch.

Carnegie was drawing a distinction between "the trained mechanic of the past" and his "rival," the "scientifically educated youth." The latter, he said:

have one important advantage over the apprenticed mechanic—they are open-minded and without prejudice. The scientific attitude of mind, that of the searcher after truth, renders them receptive of new ideas. . . . The scientifically trained boy . . . has no prejudices, and goes on for the latest invention or newest method, no matter if another has discovered it. He adopts the plan that will beat the record and discards his own devices or ideas, which the working mechanic can rarely be induced to do. Let no one therefore underrate the advantage of education; only it

[365]

must be education adapted to the end in view and must give instruction bearing upon a man's career.

By "career" obviously, Carnegie did not mean a better job: he meant a new life creatively satisfactory to its recipient and to society. He delighted in being surrounded by such young men, for they were widening their horizons through continuing education as they worked for him; and if they turned out well he gave them responsibilities, scolded them, and rewarded them munificently. In the article, he referred to two such men: Charles Schwab, superintendent of his Edgar Thomson Works, and John A. Potter, superintendent of Homestead. Both were examples of the "new product," each was under thirty; and he boasted, "Most of the chiefs of departments under them are of the same class."

This conception of the role of education and its fruits he gladly shared. He wrote to Joseph Chamberlain of Birmingham, who had become a political power in England in 1899, that Britain was falling behind in the race—in this case, the manufacture of iron and steel—because it was not breeding this new class of scientific experts working in industry. He was prepared to help Chamberlain establish a university in Birmingham, if Birmingham were to "make the scientific the principal department, the classical subsidiary."

Said he, seeking to take the sting out of the reproach:

If Birmingham were to accept the policy suggested, taking our Cornell University as its model, where the scientific has won first place in the number of students, and give degrees in science as in classics, I should be delighted to contribute the last $50,000 of the sum you have set aside to raise to establish a Scientific Department.

These—or so Englishmen thought—were still the years when Britain set the tone for the whole world. It was the richest nation, the most splendid, the most refined in matters of taste and learning, on the face of the globe. The classical education of Oxford and Cambridge prepared its upper classes to rule—in politics, in industry, in trade and banking. Matthew Arnold thought so; so did William Gladstone and John Morley. It took a second World War—a half century after Carnegie sought to set Britain on a new path—to make his birthland, facing up to its sharp descent from leadership and power, begin to think seriously of the kind of technical training at the university level of which Carnegie had been speaking—and the opening up thereby of doors to the children of lower middle-class and working families.

Carnegie had been asked to contribute to Oxford and Cambridge Universities and to their American counterparts; for him, they served the well-born and the well-heeled and he politely declined. But for little American country colleges, workingmen's institutes, the four Scottish universities—all reaching out to create educational opportunities for the deprived—he had an open purse. In institutions of higher learning, talents could be trained, and many such would remain in them to teach and conduct research; but salaries were not munificent, nor were there adequate funds for retirement: out of this understanding appeared full-grown the Foundation for the Advancement of Teaching, with an initial fund of $10 million for academic pensions. Before long the pension scheme was abandoned—there were too many actuarial problems; but out of it grew the more imaginative idea of the Teachers' Insurance and Annuity Association, to furnish life insurance and annuities at cost (with colleges and universities paying half the premium) for members of the teaching profession.

We are beginning to get some notion of the kind of person Andrew Carnegie was. This little man—five feet two inches tall, always slightly built, with a shock of flaxen, almost white, hair, and round, light blue, widely-spaced flashing eyes—could think for himself and could think fast and act fast. He loved to talk to the point of volubility; he bounced, his body was constantly in motion and he gesticulated as he walked or jumped; he gave orders. But those who talked back he listened to, and if they were right he yielded to them and gave them his confidence and affection. His former secretary, James A. Bridge—who came to dislike Carnegie and wrote a silly and untrue book about him, for he tried to prove that Carnegie's accomplishments were the work of his "associates"— confronted the recollections of his one-time employer with mixed feelings. He called him "a conceited man"; he thought Carnegie was aping Napoleon and compensating in the same way. (Because he was small? Because his origins were obscure? Because there were no limits to his ambition?)

Thus Bridge: "There is the same imperious demand for precedence, the same dislike of opposition, the same unfaltering faith in himself, the same paternal care for the active units of his army." And then Bridge becomes admiring, albeit grudgingly, for the rich, exciting personality of this "pony-built" man catches him almost by the throat. Carnegie, Bridge says, was " 'a star-spangled Scotchman' with none of the dour attributes of his race; a blithe urchin who never grew up, and ever rejoiced in verbal quips and thrusts. . . . Waving the flag in the sunlight and taking its glitter for his own, he always headed the procession and did it with joy."

Carnegie's biographer, Burton J. Hendrick, thinks there were many Carnegies—not one but a half dozen. Rather, one should say, here was a complex man, all of a piece but many-faceted. One notes, for example, a lifelong devotion to the companions of his hard youth whom he took along with him on his journey to success. Three of them—his younger brother Tom, Henry Phipps, his cousin George Lauder, Jr.—became partners (he financed them) and were never retainers but always equals. Tom died young (in 1886); his widow Lucy (after whom the great Lucy Furnaces had been named) continued to share in Carnegie's good fortune. Phipps he called "Squire"; Lauder, "Dod." They called him "Naig," and so he signed himself when writing to them from abroad, as he often did. Phipps and Lauder—as later, the much younger Schwab— talked back and disagreed, and Carnegie would flash out, and then listen. This was not the relationship of patron and client, of Bridge's Napoleonic imperiousness.

There was the devotion to his mother: he could never forget that she was a "heroic soul," for in the poverty-stricken household of Allegheny City, she had been "the mother, nurse, cook, governess, teacher, saint, all in one." There is a revealing and touching passage in the *Autobiography* in which she is referred to as the "slaving mother" to whom he meant to devote himself; she was to "live the life of ease hereafter, reading and visiting more and entertaining dear friends—in short, rising to her proper position as Her Ladyship." This was paying off the classbound, hide-bound Scotland of her birth, which had rejected her and her family and crushed the spirit of her husband. For there was no Scottish peeress who lived as splendidly and as generously as did Margaret Morrison Carnegie. One of Carnegie's early benefactions was to endow, and name after her, a college for girls, at the University of Pittsburgh. She died in 1886; a year later Carnegie married, at the age of fifty-two, and when his only child, a daughter, was born ten years later, she was named Margaret.

Carnegie's mother had another influence on him, and that was with respect to his attitude toward religion. Mother and father had rebelled against the stern Calvinism of their native Scotland: original sin, infant damnation, the predestination of the elect; the Shorter Catechism of the Presbyterian Church with its almost unending list (107 questions and answers) of the outward and inward duties that had to be performed to be brought into repentance. The father, needing spiritual consolation, drifted into the Swedenborgian church; the mother stayed at home, and when she sought religious guidance she read the *Sermons* of William Ellery Channing, that gentle New England Unitarian. But Margaret Carnegie did not try to dissuade her two sons from attending church and Sunday School. Carnegie followed his father for a time into Swedenborgianism: he wrote, "he became deeply interested in the mysterious doctrines of Swedenborg," but this could not last for this son of Scottish common sense and he drifted away, agreeing with his mother (as David Hume and Adam Smith undoubtedly would have) "that the writings of Swedenborg, and much of the Old and New Testament, had been discredited . . . as unworthy of divine authorship or of acceptance as authoritative guides for the conduct of life." Every experience, however, left some residue. The Swedenborgians in their Church of the New Jerusalem played music and sang: Carnegie learned about Handel—and from there went on by himself.

He ended up by being a mixture of agnostic and free-wheeling (but nonpracticing) Unitarian. Of his own religious faith he wrote in the *Autobiography:*

Let us therefore comfort ourselves with everlasting hope, "as with enchantment," as Plato recommends, never forgetting, however, that we all have our duties and that the kingdom of heaven is within us. It also passed into an axiom with us that he who proclaims there is no hereafter is so foolish as he who proclaims there is, since neither can know, though all may and should hope. Meanwhile "Home our heaven" instead of "Heaven our home" was our motto.

His distaste for sectarianism he never gave up and, characteristically, when it came to the establishment of the Foundation for the Advancement of Teaching one of the stipulations of the Trust was that church-related colleges were to be excluded—unless they divested themselves of denominational control. It is hard not to be admiring of such a person who will stand fast (as he did about the Spanish-American War and the following unhappy Philippine adventure) and let the good people fret and fume. He thought out courses of conduct; followed them; assumed he was right—and gave no more attention to, certainly made no effort to justify further, what he had said and done.

I have referred to Carnegie's taste. Occasionally, upon matters of art, he ventured an opinion, and it is impressive to see how right he usually was. At the World's Columbian Exposition in Chicago, to be held in 1893, the Carnegie Co. was to have a building. This is what Carnegie wrote to Frick in September, 1892, after he had seen what their architect proposed to do; his comments expose the silliness of the whole general conception—the erection of a shining white imperial Roman City in industrial, smoky, dirty, alive Chicago:

The proposed plans are altogether too Frenchy to suit my taste. It is most pretentious. The hanging chains upon it would do for a lot in a cemetery. . . . What is wanted is a pile that will impress people by its solidity—an armor plate for foundation, great 24-inch girders, etc. . . . I wonder what Stroble was about in employing a decorative artist, whose work is in the lightest and most delicate materials in shades and colors, to group massive forms of steel.

There is an amusing bit of correspondence to be found in Carnegie's papers in the Library of Congress. The Pittsburgh Carnegie Institute was sending a collection of its sculpture (bronze and plaster casts; many of these Carnegie had bought himself in Europe) on tour among a large number of museums. The plaster casts were full-size Greek and Roman statues, statuettes and busts copied from great European museum collections (part of them consisted of the British Museum's Elgin Marbles of the eastern pediment of the Parthenon); the bronzes, copied from those in the Naples National Museum, were of the finds then only recently dug up at the sites of Herculaneum and of Pompeii and Stabiae.

The director of the Institute wrote to Carnegie in dismay about the reception of the traveling exhibition; some of the museums were afraid of affronting their public because much of the statuary consisted of nude figures; permission was asked to drape them in the appropriate places. Carnegie wrote back, "let them"; but at Pittsburgh there was no compromise, no yielding—the statues stayed as they were.

The construction of the Pittsburgh Carnegie Institute and the purposes for which it was designed clearly demonstrate that Carnegie was a patron of the arts and sciences, as he was of letters and learning, in the grand manner. This was not the princely offhand gesture of a rich man, as too often maliciously has been said. Not only did he have excellent taste; he had an eye and ear for the contemporary and encouraged the officials of the Institute to show the work of living painters, American and European, and play the music of living composers.

In 1881, when he was still on the way up as steelmaster, Carnegie offered to furnish the funds for the building of a library in Pittsburgh provided the city would acquire the land and maintain the library. This was turned down. But the City of Allegheny accepted his terms, and on February 11, 1890, the Northside Carnegie Library building—the first of the thousands of municipally supported libraries he was to construct—was opened.

Thereupon Pittsburgh asked Carnegie to renew his original offer, the Pennsylvania legislature having cleared away the legal obstacles that had prompted the original refusal. Carnegie agreed to do so, but now his contribution would include provision for branch libraries and for an erection of a great building to include the central library, a museum of natural history, an art gallery, and a music hall. For this the city of Pittsburgh purchased 19 acres of land; and on this, with Carnegie's funds, was erected what came to be known as the Carnegie Institute—a handsome, massive, domed, sandstone edifice, in Renaissance style inspired from both French and Italian sources, which covered four and one-half acres. It was at that time the largest public building of its kind in the United States, and possibly it still is.

In 1895, construction was completed, and Carnegie delivered an address "Upon the Occasion of the Presentation of the Carnegie Institute to the People of Pittsburgh." He referred particularly to the Museum of Natural History and to the Art Gallery; these two departments of the Institute he planned to endow. The Art Gallery was to contain "casts of the world's masterpieces of sculpture . . . ultimately, there will be gathered from all parts of the world casts of those objects which take the highest rank."

From the endowment, pictures were to be purchased so that the Art Gallery "should eventually contain a chronological collection of American painting and sculpture." (By "chronological" he meant contemporary, for the "chronology" was to start with 1896.) And he went on: "It is provided that the commission shall purchase each year at least three works of American art exhibited in that year," to be added to the permanent collection. This was the founding—Carnegie's idea—of the famous Pittsburgh International (the first show of its kind in the western world) to which the outstanding American and European artists sent their work annually to compete for its three cash prizes and to offer their paintings for sale to the Institute.

The First Annual Exhibition, opening November 5, 1896, brought 312 paintings of which 173 were by European and the remainder by American artists. From this large display a Whistler and a Winslow Homer were purchased; before the century was over the Institute had also acquired paintings by the Americans Inness, Blakelock, Sargent, Harnett, and Chase, and by the French Degas, Pissarro, Boudin, and Sisley. Carnegie was also interested in early Dutch, German and Italian prints and had bought them; these started off the Institute's celebrated print collection, which Carnegie separately endowed.

The same was true of the Natural History Museum. In 1898 he financed an expedition to Wyoming that dug up and brought back the complete fossil remains of one of the great dinosaurs, now known as *Diplodocus Carnegiei*. This was erected in a special hall, and constant additions to the collection were made, so that now Dinosaur Hall houses one of the most complete exhibits of its kind in the world.

The Hall of Architecture and the Music Hall were Carnegie's particular pets. Into the former went the casts, those from the Naples National Museum consisting of literally hundreds of bronze reproductions of statues, statuettes, and busts found at Herculaneum, and household utensils, surgical and industrial implements, and musical instruments from Pompeii and Stabiae.

The Music Hall—still one of America's music showpieces—was constructed with a lavish hand. It was at once recognized as one of the perfect concert halls in America, accoustically speaking. Its foyer—patterned after the grand promenades of Europe's opera houses—was marble and gilt, in French neo-Baroque style. The hall could seat two thousand on three floors and its stage had room for a chorus of two hundred. The organ was large and fine. There were to be regular free organ recitals;

their purpose, said Carnegie, "is to meet each listener on his own plane and to lead him onward and upward through successive stages to a greater appreciation of the best in music."

Instruction from a man like that was not gratuitous. There can be no doubt that Carnegie, in the arts as in the sciences and learning, knew what he liked; and what he liked was very good indeed.

Homestead   Homestead, however, for a long time lay on Carnegie's conscience. Homestead had been built during 1880-81 by the Bessemer Steel Co. to make Bessemer steel rails, and had soon run into difficulties, for it was entering a market with overcapacity and overproduction in its product. The Carnegie Co. bought it in 1883 and within the space of a few years put $4 million into it for new furnaces and mills and new machinery. It reconverted the Homestead Works from Bessemer steel into the country's first great basic open-hearth plant, erecting twelve new furnaces; it shifted over from rails to structural shapes, beams, ship and tank plates, and armor plate (for the New Navy); it increased production by 60 per cent—and had a working force of 3,800 men. With proper pride, its young superintendent, J. A. Potter, could report in the Minutes of the Company that, as a result of Homestead's achievement, "The basic steel process was lifted from disgrace and made a recognized success." More; with increased production went increased productivity, for the continuous turning out of beams, which were rolled direct from the ingot in one heat, made it possible for unskilled and semiskilled workers to participate in automatic operations that previously had required highly trained manual workers. By 1892, there were, in all, only 280 such "heaters" and "rollers" left; and these, with an additional 500 or so, were the members of the Amalgamated Association of Iron and Steel Workers, a craft union which belonged to the American Federation of Labor.

The Amalgamated Association had appeared in 1876 as a merger of a number of craft unions of skilled workers, of which the Sons of Vulcan was the earliest and largest. It had, in 1892, a membership of some 24,000, but its strength was far greater than this, for the wage contracts it was able to negotiate included whole plants. The various Carnegie companies from 1875 on had not been antiunion. In 1875, for the Edgar Thomson Works at Braddock, Carnegie had signed a contract with the Sons of Vulcan, and similar ones had been negotiated, usually on a three-year basis, with the Amalgamated Association, so that the strikes which from time to time swept over the iron and steel industry—in 1877, in 1884, in 1886—left this great rail mill as well as Homestead untouched. Carnegie claimed—and this has not been challenged—that his wage scale for all his workers ran from 10 to 15 per cent above the rates prevailing in the industry, and for his skilled workers even higher.

At the Frick Coke Co., however, industrial peace was fitful. Frick Coke was the especial concern of Frick himself, and his labor relations were autocratic: he made it hard for unionism to survive, constantly feeding into his labor force—largely unskilled—Central and Eastern European immigrants from many lands and with different tongues, replacing them with newcomers when the earlier arrivals seemed to become adjusted. A strike had broken out, with accompanying violence, in the coal mines and coke ovens in 1887, when Carnegie was in Europe. Because he was the principal owner he had intervened, directing Frick to meet the workers' demands. The next year saw another strike and once more Carnegie gave orders to settle and they were obeyed. There was a third in 1890—and this time Carnegie remained silent and Frick fought it out and triumphed. (An unfortunate lapse, obviously; for had Carnegie talked up in 1890, perhaps Frick would have hesitated in 1892 at Homestead to keep the plants open when the strike and lockout occurred.) Violence, the customary pattern here, was met with violence. To quote Hendrick: "The resulting chapter was a fierce one; there were shootings, dynamitings, fire and murder; the sheriff this time did his duty; the Huns and the Slavs were held at bay; and Frick emerged a winner."

Carnegie had not wanted it this way. He had written two articles in 1886 called "An Employer's View of the Labor Question" and "Results of the Labor Struggle." This was the year of the famous May Day strikes for the eight-hour day, called by the American Federation of Labor's craft unions and participated in by the unskilled workers of the Knights of Labor assemblies. Carnegie had made some acute observations. He recognized the right of workers to negotiate with management through their unions—but at the plant (rather than industry-wide) level. He agreed that the workers had the right to use the most important weapon they had, the strike. Strikes were to be peaceful; when efforts at negotiation failed, management was to shut down the struck plants and make no efforts to hire strikebreakers or seek to protect them with private guards or deputy sheriffs. Just as strikers were to refrain from the use of illegal acts, management was not to do things that would lead to reprisals. Strikes should not degenerate into warfare; they were endurance tests and sooner or later, under these rules, one or the other side had to yield.

He did not disapprove of the eight-hour day; in fact, for two years, during 1885-87, he had tried to operate Braddock on that basis. The trouble with iron and steel was that the furnaces could not be banked—they had to be fired the clock around. If there were three shifts of eight hours instead of two of twelve, all ironmasters had to adopt the practice. As Carnegie explained to Alderson later:

We worked all the blast-furnace men on three shifts of 8 hours each, hoping that other iron manufacturers could be induced or compelled to follow our example. But only one firm in the whole country did so; and finally competition became so keen that we were forced to go back to the 12-hour shifts. It was a question whether we were to run the works at a loss or not, and after losing at least $500,000 by the experiment, we had to ask our men to return to the two shifts a day. We offered to divide with the men the extra cost of 33⅓ per cent . . . so that we might continue the 8-hour system, the firm paying 17 per cent and the men 16 per cent; but rather than do this they decided to go back to the two shifts of 12 hours a day.

In the 1886 articles Carnegie had made an interesting proposal. Because the price of steel rails and beams fluctuated sharply, he offered the establishment of what he called a "sliding scale" as the basis of wage determination. There would be a minimum rate; but the compensation of the workers would go up or down by a graded series of percentages as market prices for the product rose or fell. A committee of workmen was to have access periodically to the company's books and the adjustments in the rate scales would be made with their approval. Carnegie, of course, claimed far too much: The "sliding scale," he thought, "linked the destinies of management and workers, sharing prosperous and disastrous times together." It was, he said in his *Autobiography*, "the solution of the capital and labor problem, because it really makes them partners—alike in prosperity and adversity."

In 1887, the "sliding scale," with Amalgamated Association agreement, had been set up at the Edgar Thomson Works. In 1889, after a brief strike at Homestead (Carnegie again was in Europe), when strikebreakers were employed, discussions with the Amalgamated Association were resumed and a three-year contract was signed, including the "sliding scale." Carnegie had not liked what had happened, and had written to William L. Abbott, then chairman of Carnegie, Phipps and Co., from Berlin on August 7, 1889: "Whenever we are compelled to make a stand, we shall just have to shut down and *wait,* as at Edgar Thomson, until part of the men vote to work, then it is easy. I am glad however that we have three years' peace under sliding scale."

It was this contract that was terminating on July 1, 1892, and that the union sought to renegotiate—with the "sliding scale" as the basis for wage rates.

But Frick had prepared earlier a more elaborate proposal based on these considerations. The continued modernization of the plant had made possible the lowering in the cost of manufacturing steel billets and, at the same time, the reduction in the size of the crews in a number of operations; some departments, also, required clock-around work—the twelve-hour shift had to be maintained. Further, he wanted the date of the contract changed from June 30 to December 31. More specifically: the minimum in the "sliding scale" for billets was to be dropped from $25 to $22 a ton. Tonnage rates, at those furnaces and mills in which significant improvements had taken place and new machinery had been introduced—as a result of which productivity had been greatly increased— also were to be lowered.

By 1892, the company's cost sheets showed, the heaters and rollers, the skilled workers belonging to the Amalgamated Association, had increased their earnings by 60 per cent. This 60 per cent, Frick suggested, be cut in half, the company and the workers involved (this meant only some 300 men) sharing equally because of the large capital investments that had been made.

On May 30, Frick wrote to Potter, the superintendent of Homestead, that he was prepared to renew the three-year contract. On June 22, Frick wrote to the president of the Amalgamated Association saying that he was ready to meet with him, and with a committee of the Homestead workers, for the purposes of drawing up a new agreement.

The union, meanwhile, in its counterproposal, had raised only points of detail: the contract should end June 30, as before; if changes in dates were to take place, three-months' notice was to be given; the contract was to be a four-year instead of a three-year one. A meeting took place; there was no hint of possible compromise from either side; and on June 30, 1892, Homestead shut down. A lockout and a strike had simultaneously occurred. The Amalgamated Association—calling a strike which involved 3,800 men of which it represented not much more than 800— embarked on this trial of strength, as it had three years before. As Carroll D. Wright, in an article in the *Quarterly Journal of Economics,* said a year later: "With its affairs thoroughly systemized, with the prestige of a successful order, and with a satisfactory bank account, the Association entered the great contest of 1892 with the Carnegie Co." But then he went on, and there is no evidence of this in the backing and filling of May-June, 1892: "A mixed strike and lockout, that contest was waged more largely for the purpose of securing recognition of or defeating the Association than for any other reason. The question of wages and prices was subordinated, and the determination on the one hand to break the influence of the Amalgamated and on the other to crystallize and preserve it formed the real question at issue."

Wright did not explain what he meant by this willingness on both sides to test each other's strength. There was no doubt that after 1889 the Amalgamated Association was becoming more bellicose. David Brody in his *Steel Workers in America* (1960)—a work clearly favorably disposed toward the union—admits that the Amalgamated Association had been pressing the industry hard. To quote him: "John W. Gates, after running into trouble with the union in his Joliet plant, angrily urged another wiremaker to 'keep the Amal. Association out of your mill as they are certainly a bad lot.'"

This, then, seemed to be the company's position. As a result of sizable capital outlays, it had sought to improve its competitive role in a field (steel rails) confronted by overcapacity and sharp fluctuations in price. It was trying to develop new outlets—the manufacture of structural shapes and ship and armor plate—and to accomplish both purposes, it had introduced automatic processes and eliminated in considerable part its previous former dependence upon the skilled manual operations of the heaters, rollers, and puddlers. In short, it had taken large risks, yet it was willing to share the early successes of its reduced unit costs with the skilled workers. But the status quo (the 1889 contract) could not continue.

The company was prepared to run "full": to keep going twenty-four hours a day and for 95 per cent of the year. This promised a maintenance of wages, even in recession; and though this meant a twelve-hour day and lower piece rates, it did not mean lower average daily pay envelopes. (The company's records bore this out. For the first six months of 1892, when Homestead was operating under the Amalgamated Association contract, the average wage of every worker for every working day of the year was $2.43. At the beginning of 1893, wages were adjusted for that year— on the basis of the "sliding scale"—and averaged $2.44 daily. For 1894— the country was in deep depression; prices had fallen sharply—the adjustment led to an average daily wage of $2.24. Considering that the plant was running "full" and that the cost-of-living had dropped even lower than the 8 per cent, the Homestead workers were no worse off; in fact, they were much better off than those of other steel companies.)

On the other hand, the company as a whole (as we have seen) was making large profits—but not necessarily at Homestead. In strictly economic terms, Frick and Carnegie were right. Their high profits permitted them to keep on manufacturing and to survive the depression, to improve production and to expand and integrate (acquiring large ore properties, as we have seen), when their competitors were laid low. This was fortunate, for, after the depression, when new and more aggressive steel companies entered the industry, the Carnegie Co. was able to stand up to them successfully.

Now, what of the union? It had organized only the skilled workers. Its national officers sought to negotiate for all the workers of Homestead. At the same time, the heaters, rollers, puddlers were determined to maintain their privileged position when their skills were no longer at the basis of steel's growth and changing character. As Frick wrote to Carnegie: "The mills have never been able to turn out the product they should, owing to being held back by the Amalgamated men." In fact, the Amalgamated had deported itself like a medieval guild, insisting that its monopoly hold over its jobs at Homestead be respected. The Irish controlled the Bessemer and open-hearth furnaces; the Welsh, the rolling mills. When vacancies appeared, the Amalgamated made its own replacements, sending back to Britain for substitute workers. Even more;

its work rules in 1892 forbade the training of apprentices, limited the output of its members, and even prescribed the quality of pig iron to be used and the proportions of other materials entering into the mix.

To Carnegie himself, this was "feudalism," but his own paternalism—that "capital and labor" were partners—offered few realistic solutions in a complex situation where justice may have been on the company's side, but which demanded a willingness to compromise and to make concessions, for humanity's sake if for nothing else. Thus—and here were all the elements of a tragedy—the unskilled, those largely recruited by Frick from the "new immigration," were as much the victims of Amalgamated tyranny (they could not be trained for and moved into better jobs) as they were of Frick's hard labor policies.

They were undoubtedly hard. Steady wages were probably higher than elsewhere in the industry, but certainly low, as far as the maintenance of decent standards of living were concerned. The unskilled lived wretchedly in their "Hunkyvilles" in the river bottom, where houses had no running water and no sanitation facilities. The twelve-hour day (and Frick's speed-up) led to fatigue and a heavy toll of industrial accidents and deaths. The newcomers did not like the older immigrants; but they liked Frick less—and they went out on strike when the Amalgamated Association did.

Did Carnegie mean to crush the union? He quit the country in the spring of 1892—as had been his custom for many years—leaving Frick in charge of the company, for he had been made its chairman in 1889. Before going, Carnegie had issued a statement declaring that Homestead was to be nonunion, but then he had withdrawn it. What orders did he leave Frick? Certainly he had written Frick, as he had written Abbott three years before, that in the event of a strike there was to be a complete shutdown—and no scabs. Frick was to tell the workers: " 'Until a majority vote (secret ballot) to go to work, have a good time; when a majority vote to start, start it is!' I am satisfied that the employer or firm who gets the reputation of adhering to that will never have a prolonged stoppage, or much ill feeling."

On this crucial matter Frick insisted he had disagreed; he had argued for running the plant in the event of a strike—in short, for a showdown with the union. Carnegie had not challenged Frick; he had left no positive orders, and in consequence Carnegie's culpability cannot be

[379]

denied. When Frick, therefore, refused to meet with the union spokesmen a second time and in effect issued an ultimatum to them, he meant that thenceforth he was not going to brook the union's intervention. This was union-busting; and Carnegie's silence on this point, too, meant acceptance.

The Congressional Committee which investigated Homestead later was mild enough in calling attention to Frick's unyielding attitude. It said: "We do not think that the officers of the company exercised that degree of patience, indulgence, and solicitude which they should have done. . . . Mr. Frick, who is a business man of great energy and diligence, seemed to have been too stern, brusque and somewhat autocratic."

There had been disorders and turbulence at Homestead in the 1889 strike—but the mills had been kept running and scabs had been used. In anticipation of trouble and to protect company property, Frick had ordered built around the whole plant a high board fence, and this had been topped with barbed wire. On the fence, platforms had been erected and search lights mounted. Frick was prepared to move into the works, as Hendrick put it, a "garrison" of Pinkerton guards and watchmen who were to be armed. The rumor that Frick had been negotiating with the Pinkerton Agency was disquieting, for the reputation of its operatives was bad: they had been used increasingly in industrial disputes and where they had come there had been trouble. Says Hendrick of them:

Mercenaries have never been recruited from the cream of society or enjoyed much popularity, and Frick's "myrmidons" were no exception to the rule. The behavior of "Pinkertons" in several recent strikes had made them especially hateful to workingmen. These professional suppressors of rebellion seemingly enjoyed the trade; at any rate, the hostility raging between Mr. Pinkerton's assistants and union men had reached a stage that can be paralleled only in the feuds that kept Italian cities embroiled in the middle ages.

With the works closed on July 1, civil government ceased in the borough of Homestead. With the approval of the mayor, who was a Homestead worker and one of the strikers, an "Advisory Committee" was set up to replace the ordinary civil offices and functions; the Carnegie properties were sealed off (in effect, seized); no one—not even Carnegie supervisory and executive personnel—could enter or leave the city without passes. The sheriff of Allegheny County was ordered to leave when he put in an appearance; the "Advisory Committee" would maintain peace and order, and this it proceeded to do, it thought, by ringing the town with armed guards, and posting them on the hills and even in boats on the river. Frick's fence, barbed wire, and lookout stations appeared provocative, no more; but what the "Advisory Committee" did was illegal.

Frick was prepared to repossess the Company property: whether it was for the purpose of again starting the furnaces and mills with strike-breakers was not certain, for while the company had been advertising for new workers, none had yet been assembled; and he ordered the Pinkerton Agency to send the operatives he had ordered to the plant. These had been gathering at Pittsburgh from various parts of the country; but the roads to Homestead were blocked; the only ingress was by barges up the Monongahela River. At 2 A.M. of the morning of July 6, three hundred Pinkertons put out from Pittsburgh in two barges, with arms stowed on board; two hours later the boats were approaching Homestead when they were greeted with a fusillade of shots. Fire was returned with fire. Landing in force was impossible; those Pinkertons who did reach shore were driven back to their boats; and the Pinkertons trapped on the river were in danger of being burned alive, for the strikers had poured oil on the water. They surrendered, with the stipulation that they be permitted to quit the scene at once. In the melee, five strikers had been killed and three Pinkertons had been mortally wounded; there had been scores of injured on both sides. But the promise of safe-conduct to the Pinkertons was not observed, and they were badly beaten up as they sought to make their way to the Homestead railroad station. The strikers had won the Battle of Homestead and the company's property was still in their possession.

Five days later, Pennsylvania's governor intervened; 8,000 members of the state militia were sent to Homestead, order and civil government were restored, and the Carnegie plant was returned to the company. The Amalgamated Association, realizing that popular sympathy had turned against it, was ready to call off the strike—to surrender any demands about wages or hours; it would settle for recognition. Frick's reply was: "Under no circumstances will we have any further dealings with the Amalgamated Association as an organization. This is final." This was the first public statement a company official issued that henceforth

Homestead was to be nonunion. Carnegie's first word came to Pittsburgh in a letter to his partner George Lauder dated July 17. The somewhat cryptic message ran:

Matters at home *bad*—such a fiasco trying to send guards by Boat and then leaving space between river and fences for the men [the strikers] to get opposite landing and fire—Still we must keep quiet and do all we can to support Frick and those at Seat of War. . . . We shall win of course, but have to shut down for months.

Frick did not have to plan the next move—or wait months. Pittsburgh was not unfamiliar with anarchism; the American section of the Black International (as we have seen) had been organized here, and the doctrines of Bakunin and Most—of mutualism combined with the symbolical use of terror—had been heard in its workers' halls. Such an anarchist, in the person of the twenty-two-year-old Russian Alexander Berkman made his way to Pittsburgh from New York—he received a small sum from his young mistress, Emma Goldman, also an anarchist, to purchase a revolver—determined to assassinate Frick, who, said Hendrick, paraphrasing Berkman, "embodied the tyranny of capital." On a pretext—he posed as a representative of a New York strike-breaking agency—Berkman gained an appointment with Frick for the afternoon of Saturday, Juy 23. Frick was in conversation with J. G. A. Leishman, the company's president, when Berkman came in unannounced. Frick seemed apprehensive, noting Berkman's nervous behavior, for he arose and moved toward his visitor. At this point, Berkman drew his pistol and fired, the bullet hitting Frick in the neck. Frick fell to the floor, and Berkman fired again. Leishman grappled with Berkman, Frick staggered from the floor to come to Leishman's assistance, and now Berkman pulled a dagger from his pocket and stabbed Frick several times. Frick was not seriously hurt—surgeons quickly removed the bullets—and he remained at the office until he had completed the afternoon's work, including, Hendrick says, the negotiation of a loan by telephone. Then he issued a bulletin and coolly went home on a stretcher. He remained at home for three weeks, transacting the company's business.

Frick's bulletin said: "This incident will not change the attitude of the Carnegie Steel Co. toward the Amalgamated Association. I do not think I shall die, but, if I do or not, the company will pursue the same policy and it will win." The company did not have to exert itself, for Berkman's act had turned Frick from villain—his use of the Pinkertons had been widely condemned—into hero. Said Hugh O'Donnell, the local leader of the union men, who had been at the river when the Pinkertons had sought to land: "The bullet from Berkman's pistol went straight through the heart of the Homestead strike."

On July 27, the Homestead Works were reopened under military protection, and new workers were hired—1600 in all—while the old ones were permitted to apply, on an individual basis, for re-employment. The militia was withdrawn from Homestead in September; the Amalgamated Association called off the strike on November 20.

The aftermath? The Amalgamated Association's national membership dropped from 24,000 to 13,000 in 1893 and 10,000 in 1900. It was finished as a significant force in the steel industry. As Hendrick put it: "From that day the once powerful Amalgamated Association has been a pitiful remnant, only a few scattered bands here and there representing the hosts that once lorded it over American steel mills. Not a union man [this was written in 1932] has since entered the Carnegie Works." One hundred and sixty-seven strikers, who participated in the Battle of Homestead, were indicted on May 6 for conspiracy (not murder), but none was convicted. Berkman—he refused counsel—was brought to trial in Pittsburgh on six separate counts and found guilty on all of them, the jury not troubling to leave the jury box. He was sentenced to jail for twenty-two years by a vindictive judge who refused to take note that Berkman had made no attempt to protect his constitutional rights—and he served fourteen of them.

Carnegie suffered. He must have been aware of how Americans had turned against him, for this editorial in the St. Louis *Post-Dispatch* was only one of many in the same vein:

Three months ago Andrew Carnegie was a man to be envied. Today he is an object of mingled pity and contempt. . . . A single word from him might have saved the bloodshed—but the word was never spoken. Nor has he, from that bloody day until this, said anything except that he "had implicit confidence in the managers of the mills." The correspondent who finally obtained this valuable information expresses the opinion that "Mr. Carnegie has no intention of returning to America at present." He might have added that America can well spare Mr. Carnegie. Ten thousand "Carnegie Public Libraries" would not compensate the direct and indirect evils resulting from the Homestead lockout. Say what you will of Frick, he is a brave man. Say what you will of Carnegie, he is a coward.

Carnegie wrote agitated—and not very clear—letters to Whitelaw Reid, the publisher of the New York *Tribune* (the Republicans were worrying about the coming Presidential election), and to his English friends, among them William T. Stead, editor of the influential *Review of Reviews,* and the great man William E. Gladstone himself, who commiserated and sought information. To Gladstone he wrote:

This is the trial of my life (death's hand excepted). Such a foolish step—contrary to my ideas, repugnant to every feeling of my nature. Our firm offered all it could offer, even generous terms. Our other men had gratefully accepted them. They went as far as I could have wished, but the false step was made in trying to run the Homestead Works with new men.

Years later Carnegie wrote: "No pangs remain of any wound received in my business career save that of Homestead. . . . I was the controlling owner. That was sufficient to make my name a by-word for years."

CHAPTER THIRTEEN

THE NINETIES: TESTING TIME

Carnegie's Challenges   In 1889 Carnegie had sought to retire. He was immensely wealthy—his annual income was almost $2 million—he was married, and now was the time to cultivate his friends, his hobbies, and the development of that vast philanthropic program that was already shaping in his mind. As far back as the late 1860s, he had learned to take long holidays, for the most part in Europe, leaving New York in May and often not returning until October or November. To give himself a permanent summer home, he rented Cluny Castle in Scotland in 1888, and then Skibo Castle, also in Scotland, the next year. (Skibo did not become his until 1897, when he bought it and a great estate of 32,000 acres, and he put a million dollars into the restoration of its forests and streams and the renovation of the farms of its tenants.) In Scotland, he entertained, played golf, fished, and shot grouse—and followed closely what was transpiring in Pittsburgh, as we shall see, by reading with fussy care the Minutes of the Company's regular meetings, writing elaborate memorandums on them, and bombarding his intimates, Phipps, Lauder, Schwab, with personal letters and cables.

But in 1889, he felt his active business life was ready to be laid aside for that other life he thought he really wanted, about which he had written notes to himself in the 1860s and had prepared for by reading and sharpening his intellect and his tastes in the arts. He approached a group of English businessmen to ask if they would buy him out, but the proposal was too vague in his mind and in theirs and there were no further conversations. In 1892—the Carnegie Company had gone through a further reorganization in the middle of the year—he toyed with the idea again. Then came Homestead: and the outspoken criticism directed against him, the blows to his vanity, at home as well as in England, put him on the defensive, for the first time in his life. He had to redeem himself. But how? By the only way he knew: by showing that Carnegie the steelmaster, Carnegie the imaginative, aggressive, competitive businessman, was *primus inter pares*. He was the best in his field, who could make better steel at lower costs than any one else in the world and sell it at cheaper prices not only in America but in Europe as well, and thus profoundly change the nature of the whole economic, and therefore social, world in which he lived.

Carnegie ended, in the single decade of the nineties, by doing exactly that; and when he finally quit, in 1901, not only did he leave a magnificent property which not even the grossly overcapitalized United States Steel Corporation could hurt—but he was on the way to redeeming himself. In great things and in small: in connection with the former, as the recognized world leader in seeking to achieve international peace; in connection with the latter, by providing pensions (anonymously) to the strikers who had fought him so bitterly in 1892. From 1901 until he died in 1919, he was one of the foremost private citizens of the West.

Homestead was not the only challenge. There was the great depression of 1893-97: when his slogan to "run full" and his intention of maintaining wages—in the face of sharp curtailment in demand, wholesale bankruptcies among his leading customers the railroads, large scale unemployment and farmer distress and unrest—seemed impossible notions.

Yet he was able to do both: by pouring large sums into the modernization of his furnaces and mills, by pressing integration to command his own raw materials and transportation, and by meeting and underselling the competition at any point and at any price. As he explained it to the Stanley Committee in 1911:

It is the business of the manufacturer to get the highest price he can get. I was in business to make money. I was not a philanthropist at all. When rails were high we got the highest price we could get. When they were low we met the lowest price we had to meet.

There was restiveness among his partners: Phipps, his oldest friend and most reliable lieutenant, curiously, was the one to voice complaints—why not distribute profits? (And by that token, stop rebuilding and expansion.) But it was Frick who gave him the greatest trouble (he joined hands with Phipps) and whom he had to get rid of.

And there was a new competition when the depression's heavy pall finally lifted. The years 1897-1900 were frenetic years. A national capital market had emerged—the United States no longer had to look to Europe for long-term funds—and the large assets of life insurance companies and great commercial banks, under the leadership of investment bankers, J. P. Morgan and Co. the first, but new ones emerging in New York, Boston, and Chicago, were now available for the reorganization of old companies and the promotion of new ones.

Carnegie's rivals previously had been family-owned firms or limited partnerships like his own; they built and expanded out of undistributed earnings and occasional borrowings from banks. Now appearing were public corporations, heavily capitalized, whose securities were eagerly purchased by individual savers and whose stocks and bonds entered into the portfolios of these suddenly significant institutional savers. As for the investment bankers, what they were doing to the steel industry Carnegie disliked: they were "speculators," "manufacturers of securities," "Chicago adventurers." With their new ways and their immense resources, nevertheless, they had to be met and licked. He did both; it was war and it was superb.

The Growth of the Company   If the proper groundwork had not been prepared, if there had not been the accumulation of financial resources, Carnegie could not have succeeded. From 1870 to 1900, there had been a series of reorganizations in his companies with changes in partners. There were no formal "book" capitalizations as such until the mid-seventies; but we can piece out something of the growth of the Carnegie properties from the real worth of the partners and from the company properties, as they were recorded by Bridge, by Carnegie himself, and by the Minutes of the Company at the regular meetings of its directors (major partners). In July, 1871, Carnegie, Kloman & Co. was worth about $450,000, with its capital spread among Carnegie and his five partners as follows: Andrew Carnegie, $170,402 (37.6 per cent); Andrew Kloman, $90,639 (20 per cent); Thomas M. Carnegie, $87,014 (19.2 per cent); Henry Phipps, Jr., $87,014 (19.2 per cent); J. W. Vandevort, $13,595 (3 per cent); H. W. Borntraeger, $4,532 (1 per cent).

For a brief time, this company was replaced by Carnegie, McCandless & Co., and this was the one that erected the Braddock Works. In 1875, the first limited partnership was created when the blast furnaces were ready to make steel; this was the Edgar Thomson Steel Co., Ltd. Its capital stock was to be $1 million, of which $624,000 was to be paid in and used to buy out the real estate, buildings, and machinery of its predecessor. Of this sum, Carnegie contributed $250,000—he was therefore not yet the majority shareowner—and the rest was put up by eight other partners (Tom Carnegie and Henry Phipps among them). By January 1, 1880, the company's book value was $1,650,000 and Andrew Carnegie's share was 58.65 per cent.

On April 1, 1881, still another reorganization took place; in the form of Carnegie Brothers & Co., Ltd.; this time the capitalization was set at $4 million, of which $1 million was put up in cash by seven partners. (But the articles of association listed the assets that were combined as $4 million alone.) This company continued under the same name until 1892; when Tom Carnegie died in 1886, another company, Carnegie, Phipps & Co. was created in the same year, and this, too, survived until 1892. Carnegie, Phipps & Co. was capitalized at $3 million and this at the end of 1891 was raised to $5 million. The Carnegie, Phipps Co. started with seventeen partners; in 1891, there were twenty-one, of which the leading partners' shares were as follows: Andrew Carnegie, $2,800,000; Henry Phipps, $550,000; H. C. Frick, $550,000; George Lauder, $200,000. In January, 1889, Frick had been made a partner (originally assigned 3 per cent of the stock, which grew to 11 per cent in three years) and was designated at the same time chairman of Carnegie Brothers & Co., Ltd. It should be noted that while Carnegie Brothers & Co., Ltd. was a kind of holding company, it did not include the H. C. Frick Coke Co. Of this, of which Frick was president, Carnegie owned 52 per cent of the stock and Frick $33\frac{1}{3}$ per cent.

On July 1, 1892, there appeared the Carnegie Steel Co., Ltd.—another reorganization—this time capitalized at $25 million and with twenty-eight partners. (The capitalization was changed to $50 million toward the end of the decade.) In 1900—after Frick had arranged to leave, in order to buy him out at a new book value (his share of the company was now 6 per cent)—the Carnegie Co. of New Jersey was incorporated with a capitalization of $320 million, half in stocks and half in 5-per-cent mortgage bonds. All the subsidiary companies (including Frick Coke) were put under the umbrella of this holding company and the "Carnegie Association" as such was terminated. There were (after Frick left, and including Carnegie himself) forty partners, all of whom were stockholders; but the company was not a public one in the real sense, for only the forty were its owners. Carnegie's interest was $174,529,000; Phipp's, $34,904,000; Frick's, $31,284,000 (of which almost half represented what his share in the coke company stood for).

That the profits (not necessarily distributed) the various Carnegie companies were making plainly indicated that the book values had no relation to real worth, the following profit figures will show. They were drawn up by Bridge.

1875	$ 18,642	1888	$ 1,941,555
1876	171,790	1889	3,540,000
1877	190,379	1890	5,350,000
1878	300,353	1891	4,300,000
1879	512,068	1892	4,000,000
1880	1,557,771	1893	3,000,000
1881	2,000,377	1894	4,000,000
1882	2,128,422	1895	5,000,000
1883	1,019,233	1896	6,700,000
1884	1,301,180	1897	7,000,000
1885	1,191,993	1898	11,500,000
1886	2,925,350	1899	21,000,000
1887	3,441,887	1900	40,000,000

The Minutes of the Company give us glimpses of the processes of expansion and financial management, under Carnegie's tight control, during the nineties. So, a balance sheet of August 1, 1897, recorded assets as totaling $60 million, against a capitalization of $25 million and a book value of $43.5 million. The net earnings for the eight months, January 1-August 31, 1897 (the country was beginning to pull out of the depression), were $4 million, of which only $750,000 were earmarked for dividends. That is, the annual rate of new profits on the book value was 14 per cent, and the distribution among the partners 3 per cent. At the end of 1897—recovery in the economy had taken place—the profits turned out better than had been anticipated. The year ended with gross earnings of $7.7 million and net earnings of $7 million; and the dividends paid out were $2.5 million. The upshot was, the balance sheet of January 1, 1898, showed assets of $63.4 million; but the company's book value was only $45.3 million.

The advances continued at an accelerated rate. The balance sheet of January 1, 1899, listed assets at $77 million and book value at $58.3 million. And that for January 1, 1900, put the assets at $98 million and the book value at $74.3 million, against a capitalization of $50 million. The profits had been $21 million in 1899, and of this only $5 million had been distributed in dividends. That 1899 had been a boom year is shown by Table 32, giving the company's orders on hand at the opening of business.

TABLE 32
(In tons)

	April 1, 1898	March 31, 1899
Rails	344,692	474,991
Billets and blooms	229,017	336,441
Structural shapes and ship materials	103,964	268,502
Axles and bars	18,687	38,534
Plates	30,619	75,239
Total	726,979	1,193,707

On April 2, 1900, when the Carnegie Steel Co., Ltd. became the Carnegie Co. of New Jersey, the capitalization was increased from $50 million to $320 million. For their $50 million in capital stock and their interests in other companies, the Carnegie partners obtained $250 million in the new corporation made up of $125 million in its stock and $125 million in its 5 per cent bonds. How diversified and expanded the properties had become—as a result of the new acquisitions and expan-

TABLE 33

Carnegie Steel Co., Ltd.	$219,358,818
Oliver Iron Mining Co.	20,000,000
Pewabic Co.	100,000
Pittsburgh Steamship Co.	283,333
Carnegie Natural Gas Co.	1,500,000
Union Railroad Co.	2,107,257
Slackwater Connecting RR Co.	10,000
Pittsburgh, Bessemer & Lake Erie RR Co. ...	6,108,600
Conneaut Dock Co.	255,890
Pittsburgh Limestone Co.	45,000
Mingo Coal Co.	236,100
H. C. Frick Coke Co.	68,425,068
Youghiogheny Northern RR Co.	407,714
Youghiogheny Water Co.	113,636
Mt. Pleasant Water Co.	254,576
Trotter Water Co.	276,577
Union Supply Co.	522,426
Total	$320,000,000

sions of the years 1897-1900—was shown by the company's books as of April 1, 1900. Table 33 gives the outstanding values as listed by its journal.

This is what the United States Steel Corporation acquired a year later.

Carnegie, the Manager and Competitor   During the depression years of the nineties and in those following, when he was being so hard-pressed by his new competitors, a note of asperity became more and more evident in Carnegie's communications to his managers back home. The Minutes of the Company, transmitted to him, included every decision taken, no matter how insignificant; and his "Thoughts on the Minutes," as he called them, were equally detailed. His comments and his letters showed that nothing passed him by; he knew as much about the minutiae of operations and management as did those on the ground. He was sharp but not carping; insisted upon explanations—and then yielded with a good grace when he was proved wrong.

J. G. A. Leishman, the company's president, had written him in June, 1895, about matters at hand and pending business. Back came a note with queries, comment, and advice like this: "Did you contract for any Cornwall ore?" "What arrangements are being made for the new furnaces at Duquesne? . . . Also tell me whether the new engines have been put to work at Edgar Thomson, and with what result?" "Did you buy the 70 acres offered us, opposite Edgar Thomson? If so, at what price?" "Now is the time to buy mills because we are in for a boom and big profits for a time." "You may see pig in Pittsburgh district at $20 before our new furnaces can get in to increase supply. Remember pig at $10 was the lowest on record until recently. The country has been economizing for nearly three years, and a boom is the natural result."

Three weeks later, he wrote again to Leishman: his analyses of costs and the reports on blast-furnace products were not coming regularly; Mr. Frick had been doing so every month. ". . . these were very interesting. I wish you would kindly continue so." Pig iron was going to go higher; buy it at the market; "you can charge prices for finished material that will enable you to pay a good price for pig iron." This was on July 22. On July 24, again writing to Leishman, he was congratulating him on the sale of the Beaver Falls Mills—for his managers did not always get the rough side of his tongue—and then told him he would have no objection to seeing the Lucy Furnaces and the other two Pittsburgh mills sold. "If we could get from $2½ to $3 million for that property, we could put the money to much better use in other directions."

In August, there were seven different communications to Leishman, some having to do with trivia, some affecting major matters. The Illinois Steel Co. and the Pennsylvania Steel Co. were infringing the Jones

Mixer Patents; try to get $100,000 apiece from them; otherwise sue. Steal a march on all our competitors—and keep them off balance. Tell the Pittsburgh press that the Carnegie is building four new furnaces: "We expect to supply the general wants of the Pittsburgh district with pig iron." We are making natural gas; sell it, and use coal. Fire the manager at the Keystone Bridge Co.; his was a "sad showing." "The cost of pig both at Edgar Thomson and the Lucys is higher than I had expected, it is nearly a dollar beyond last year's price. Please give me the items justifying this." It was the same on September; one letter was particularly revealing about the lengths to which Carnegie was prepared to go to get business. Again to Leishman:

Have just cabled recommending that you fill with all orders you can get, up to the limit of our pig iron production, even if you can get no profit beyond that flowing from $17 pig.

And then praise: "Your cable received this morning for August is better than I had expected. . . . We are very unreasonable people if we are not profoundly grateful."

On December 9, 1895, he wrote to Thomas R. Lovejoy, secretary of the company: he wanted to know how every partner voted on the motions passed and the decisions taken at the meetings. "I have also suggested to the President that the Minutes record any reason or explanation which a member desires to give for his vote." Thus, "It would bring responsibility home to him direct, and I do not see any other way that will enable us to judge whether any of our partners have a good judgment or not." He repeated the same thing again to Leishman on December 23: "The shareholders should be able to read a record of proceedings which could enable them to judge of the judgment displayed, good or bad, by every manager." These directions were being carried out; for on January 20, 1896, he wrote to Lovejoy, with great satisfaction: "I think we never had the organization for managing our business so perfect as it is today."

And this was so; he had welded together a body of men who had mutual trust and confidence in one another, who were given the opportunity to rise because they were invested with responsibility. He watched the young men working for him closely and often fondly (this was true for example of Henry M. Curry, who had charge of the ore contracts with the Rockefellers, and of W. E. Corey, the general superintendent of Homestead, as it also was of Schwab), and he made them partners by lending them money. A large number of these men passed his tests and became members of the board of managers and co-owners. Those who did not come up to the high requirements had to go—some fifteen in all of the partners met this fate—but this occurred only when two-thirds of the shares owned voted to do so. Carnegie had to have the agreement of others when such decisions were taken.

Leishman, as we have seen, was one of these. His displeasure toward Leishman had been building up, not only because of his personal involvements in speculative ventures, but because he was using the same attitudes and frame of mind in handling the company's affairs. On February 4, 1896, he was very caustic with Leishman. The president had bought two bankrupt furnaces; Carnegie had not been consulted. Then: "I am sorry to have to write this, but I cannot live and have the Carnegie Steel Co. degraded to the level of speculators and Jim Cracks, men who pass as manufacturers but who look to the market and not to manufacturing, and who buy up bankrupt concerns only to show their incapacity."

He valued the repute of his organization and his own as well. When he himself strayed, he immediately admitted it and put on the hair shirt. On January 21, 1896, he confessed to Frick: "Mr. Thomson [president of the Pennsylvania Railroad, a friend, and the son of the man after whom he had named the Edgar Thomson Works] has just sent me an annual pass over the P.R.R., which on his account I felt I must accept, but it is probably the dearest luxury ever got for nothing."

Speculation was one thing, risk-taking was another; and when Carnegie embarked on a bold venture, he was willing to back up his judgment with his own resources. The Pennsylvania Railroad had been pushing him around, because it controlled the transportation from Pittsburgh to Lake Erie—and he did not like being bought off with a free pass! Early in January, 1896, still in the midst of depression, Carnegie decided now was the time to free himself. There was a small line, the Pittsburgh, Shenango and Lake Erie Railroad, which ran from the Erie Lake port of Conneaut, Ohio, to Butler, Pennsylvania, some thirty miles from Pittsburgh. Carnegie contracted to furnish this road a minimum of 1.5 million tons of traffic a year, moving coke to Conneaut and iron ore from Conneaut to his furnaces. But he wanted to build an extension from Butler right to his own works to save thirteen miles—and to escape from the Pennsylvania's grip, he wanted to buy the road and improve it. This would cost $3 million; Carnegie would assume personally $2 million of this, his partners and the company the other $1 million.

But Carnegie was short of cash. On April 18, 1896, he wrote to the president of the United States Trust Co., a New York bank, asking for a loan of a million dollars for one year on his personal note. He was prepared to post as collateral $1.5 million in Frick Coke Co. stock—it was, he wrote, worth three times that. And he went on to say: "You will have something unique—my notes. It is many years since I have had a personal obligation, and I have none now, nor do I intend to have any but this."

Carnegie got his million dollars at 5 per cent, and the extension was built in fifteen months. Out of this grew the renamed and rebuilt Pittsburgh, Bessemer and Lake Erie Railroad, which became one of the most strategic properties of the Carnegie company to be acquired by the United States Steel Corporation. Having got his loan, Carnegie now turned to Thomson and the Pennsylvania. In May, he wrote to Thomson reminding him that the Pennsylvania was charging him higher rates than it was his iron and steel competitors in Ohio and Illinois. He said he was freeing himself of his dependence on the Pennsylvania by building his own Pittsburgh and Butler Railroad; then he would be able to connect up with the Baltimore and Ohio, the New York and Erie, the Nickel Plate and Lake Shore railroads. And he said to Thomson: "I think the great Pennsylvania Railroad has come to a sad condition when it is [not] only not willing, but not anxious to stand behind its own customers, and give equal rates per ton mile to whose which its competitors receive." And he threatened Thomson that he would say publicly to the Pittsburgh community that this was one of the reasons why there was widespread unemployment there. The upshot was, Carnegie and Thomson came to terms—a peace that lasted only three years.

The years 1896 and 1897 were difficult; the country was beginning to move out of the depression—perhaps, for the nomination of William Jennings Bryan early in July created too much uncertainty. The outflow of gold, temporarily checked in 1895, might become a flood if he were elected. And America's balance of payments would then really be in serious jeopardy. In consequence, business marked time for the second half of 1896; one catches a note of caution in Carnegie's communications and at the same time a dogged insistence that competitors must be under-priced and the works kept running. On July 13, 1896, in his "Thoughts on Minutes," written from Scotland, he expressed doubts about con-verting Edgar Thomson into basic steel (as Homestead had been a decade before). Go slow, he said; and, "Nothing requires more con-servatism than the manufacture of steel. We tried coke dust, green blowing, direct rolling, and injured our reputation in each case. . . . The basic rail involves grave consequences, perhaps, and we should take no risks."

The proposal that sixteen additional furnaces be put in at Homestead was too optimistic. Cut it down to eight. "In this matter we should also go slowly, and have everything perfect before we begin." His managers were carrying too much inventory; it stood at $7 million—reduce it to $5 million. And watch the billet pool. If their membership in it prevents the company from taking orders, it would cost them dearly. "The policy today is what it always has been—'Scoop the market,' prices secondary; work to keep our mills running the essential thing."

On August 6, writing to his managers, once more he ordered that inventory be kept down. "Permit me to say again," he said, "that not a dollar's worth of anything should be bought, even if superintendents have to do the best they can with old things; and second, that we should sell off every dollar's worth of material that is not needed." There was too much to worry about. The board was voting dividends in anticipa-tion of an upturn in business. "I only wish, when the time comes, it will be seen that we have money to pay on these. It does not look so to me." And once more, the same battle cry:

There is one way to secure safety, but to pursue that, we must be free. *Billet and Boom Pools* must go, and we must step out boldly and take every order that presents itself, and be one of the few iron and steel works running. We should play for safety, not for profit.

With Presidential election over and Bryan and Free Silver defeated, he became perky once more. He wrote to Thomson of the Pennsylvania, on November 12, about his Pittsburgh and Butler Railroad. Because of it, "Pittsburgh is to be once more the best point for manufacturing and marketing steel, better even than Lorain. This railroad has saved our property." This was all very well to soften up Thomson. But on December 9, he reminded Frick that their real purpose was to compel competitive rates for the company's traffic. Said he: "If these have to be forced, it will not be our fault; peaceably if we can, forcibly if we must; but competitive rates we shall have."

Schwab had been made president of the company in 1897 (to replace Leishman) and was champing at the bit. He knew that Carnegie had been advising caution, but modernization had to be pushed not only to hold off the Pennsylvania companies but the newest and mightiest rival as well. This was the Illinois Steel Co., which had been formed in Chicago in 1889 with a capitalization of $25 million and two years later had doubled that. It had plants in Chicago, Milwaukee, and Joliet; and it owned thousands of acres of coal lands in Pennsylvania and West Virginia, iron mines in Wisconsin, forests in Michigan, and stone quarries in Indiana. Elbert H. Gary, a Chicago lawyer, was its general counsel, and he was wily and astute, where Carnegie was tough. Illinois Steel was to be watched, and this was no idle thought, for in 1898 J. P. Morgan stepped in and used Illinois Steel as the center and heart of the great Federal Steel Co., which was capitalized at $200 million.

Schwab put his ideas for immediate expansion and renovation before the board of managers on July 6, 1897. He proposed a new basic steel plant at Homestead, with sixteen to eighteen furnaces, to make only structural shapes; a new mill to make only angles; and a new plate mill. Carnegie liked Schwab and his spirit. Go ahead, he cabled: start with eight furnaces and get an option for eight more on January 1.

On August 31, 1897, the Minutes recorded that the managers, at Schwab's instigation, had passed a resolution calling for the immediate expenditure of $1 million for ten basic steel furnaces at Homestead, a new blooming mill there, the remodeling of the Duquesne mills, and the purchase of land for the erection of not only the angle mill but a universal plate mill as well. Schwab also wanted an aggressive campaign launched to challenge the English in export markets; he called attention to the possibilities of going into China and Australia, this business to be handled by commission houses.

The Minutes of August 31 prompted Carnegie to write again and again, with Schwab rejoining. The foils flashed with parry, riposte, and parry, as the older man and the young one tried each other out. Carnegie called Schwab "my dear young friend" and then attacked, openly and sharply. His "Thoughts on Minutes," written from Scotland on September 14, were highly detailed and critical. The president (Schwab) had proposed "sweeping changes which have never before been heard of; the board instantly approves; no word of criticism made." He did not like at all the plans for the Duquesne Mills and for a new reversible mill at Homestead; these called for the expenditure of $400,000. Their reasoning made no sense; if the billets made at Duquesne were not profitable, how would shifting over the same activity to Homestead pay out? And then: "A very large question is presented to us which should receive *months of study* and especially should time be given for the principal owners to hear all sides." And he reminded the managers four days later that the bylaws for important changes in machinery or methods of operation required a two-thirds vote of the stock distribution. Decisions were being taken with 75 per cent of the shareholders (himself, Phipps, Lauder, Singer) not having expressed their opinions. Then he ended: "Hearty congratulations upon August net. Great."

This was followed by a letter to Schwab, October 1:

Your report should have given the figures upon which you base the opinion that the "expenditure is desirable.". . .

What we have a right to ask is figures and not an expression of your opinion. . . .

The report should be full, accurate; facts, not opinions or impressions; really you do not [do] yourself justice in the apparent "slap-dash" manner in which you recommend this to the board.

Schwab had written on September 11 and again on September 18, pressing very hard; he gave Carnegie the full explanations the older man was demanding—and he did not yield an inch. He proposed to go ahead with the open-hearth furnaces at Homestead and a new blooming mill there to work with their Bessemer furnaces and produce four-inch billets. He meant to change over Duquesne entirely: it was to make smaller materials—billets, sheets, angle splice bars, materials for pipe-making. There would be new markets and real economies, among them the ability to supply the steel mill with fuel from the waste gas at the blast furnaces. There was to be a merchant mill at Duquesne, too.

It was Carnegie who gave way. On September 24 he wrote to Schwab, approving of the expenditures for Duquesne, including the merchant mill. Buy the extra land at Homestead. About the new plans for Homestead, he did not disapprove but simply said he doubted the wisdom of making only four-inch billets. "I believe they are to be the 'brown sugar' of the steel business, and that our pig iron can be put into more profitable forms." But Carnegie admired a powerful adversary and was ready to retire from the match. He ended his letter in this way:

I cannot tell you how much pleasure I have this morning in reading your letter, and learning there is such a great field yet to improve in, and that we ought to go on, not only increasing our work, but effecting greater economies in workers.

I think we are in for a great business next year. Nevertheless, I should fill up for the early months.

But Schwab sought complete surrender; and he wrote to Carnegie on October 1 and again on October 5. He explained why he wanted to make smaller billets: "there is going to be a greater consumption of this class of material and we have never been able to make a sufficiently large percentage of light stuff." He stuck by his guns as regards the universal mill and the angle mill. They were going to run full; what he was talking about were additions and not renovations.

On October 16, Carnegie cabled: "No objections Duquesne Homestead additions." And the same day and two days later he wrote to Schwab, conceding with great grace that the younger man had bested him. Here was a perfect example of why the Carnegie organization had no rival anywhere in the business world; his partners followed his lead, because he had given all of them marshal's batons. Said Carnegie to Schwab on October 16:

I am bound to say . . . that yours of 1 October puts a new face upon the matter and I am delighted to know that the additions are going forward. You are a hustler! Very much surprised to see by the photograph that you have done so much in one week at Open Hearth.

And more fully on October 18:

Blooming Mill at Homestead is all right. Go ahead. I am surprised but also pleased to know that the Reversing Mill will beat Duquesne.

In short, my dear fellow, I am thoroughly converted where I need conversion and hope you will go ahead with your improvements.

Believe me, I am rejoicing equally with yourself at your brilliant success and at the improvements which I am sure you are going to make.

Here is a letter from Lauder which I adopt as my own sentiments: "Everything about the business is in first-class shape." I do not have a single word of adverse criticism. There has never been a time on my return that I can recall when everything seemed moving so smoothly.

Carnegie Takes the Offensive   While this was going on, Carnegie was already thinking of taking the war into the enemy's camp; that is, invading the territory of the Illinois Steel Co. He did not think much about their foreign trade; it would be a sad day, he wrote to Schwab on October 18, "when we have to export." The home market was theirs to explore and exploit, and it had extraordinary possibilities. Let us move into the Middle West, he wrote on September 27 to the managers in his "Thoughts on Minutes" of September 14:

Our capacity is so great, and is to become even greater, that I think we should consider whether more finished steel can be made in any one locality to advantage. It is a question of distribution and all depends upon the cost of reaching far points. An improved Ohio River will benefit us after a time, and more so, year after year; but I think a line of boats from Conneaut to Chicago, making costs of freight about $1 per ton from Pittsburgh to Chicago, and later eastward via Canal, would do more than anything else to enlarge our market.

The managers looked forward to 1898 with confidence as a result of all these elaborate preparations. Corey, the general superintendent of Homestead, in a memorandum to Schwab in January, 1898, reported a large decrease in labor costs, in the expanded and new open-hearth departments particularly, but in the other departments as well. The average cost per ton per worker had dropped as much as 34 per cent, as compared with 1896 and 1897; the savings ran up to $500,000. Schwab came back from a visit with Carnegie in Cannes, and brought back this message to the managers on March 1. "Mr. Carnegie thinks that while we are making good profits [they were to be $11.5 million in 1898, as compared with $7 million in 1897], we should not hesitate to spend money freely for improvements, and in keeping our plants up to date in every respect." And he carried with him consent for the purchase of the Carrie Furnaces—which the board had ordered—to increase the company's pig-iron output. The Carrie Furnaces could be got for $750,000, only $50,000 to be paid in cash and the rest carried by a loan at 6 per cent.

Schwab presented these comparative figures; they showed how closely costs were watched and investments matched against each other. The Edgar Thomson furnaces cost $4,387,000 and were producing 2,770 tons of pig iron daily; this came to $1,584 in investment for one ton of iron a day. The Lucy Furnaces cost $1,250,000 and were turning out 657 tons of iron daily; this came to $1,900 investment per ton per day. The Carrie Furnaces, at a cost of $750,000, had a capacity of 589 tons daily; and this came to an investment of $1,273 per ton per day.

All this delighted Carnegie. He was still in Cannes on March 21 when he wrote to the managers: "The East is a clear field for us at $15 or $16 per ton for rails." He did not want to drive to the wall such an excellent company as Cambria Steel. Make an "amicable arrangement" with them; let them produce 150,000 tons of rails, we will turn out 600,000, and we can sell at the same price in Chicago, Pittsburgh, and at the eastern seaboard.

There was no doubt that the Carnegie pressure was hard and hurting. One clear evidence was the appearance of giant mergers in the industry in 1898 and 1889, as we shall see. Even then his competitors were not at all easy in their minds that they could stop Carnegie from expanding further and from taking their measure. In 1911, when Carnegie and others in the steel industry appeared before the Stanley Committee, all this was frankly admitted. After hearing Carnegie, Congressman Stanley said to him: "I am frank to say that I believe you would have captured the trade of the world if you had stayed in business. I am asking if you think so now." And Carnegie's reply was: "I am as certain of it as I can be certain of anything."

Said Elbert H. Gary, general counsel for Illinois Steel, in 1898 president of the giant Federal Steel Co., and in 1901 chairman of the United States Steel Corporation: "It is not at all certain that if the management that was in force at the time had continued, the Carnegie Company would not have driven entirely out of business every steel company in the United States." Said W. C. Temple, secretary of the Steel Plate Association (the plate pool): "Mr. Carnegie with his then plant, and his organization and his natural resources, was in a position where he could dominate the entire situation, and had the United States Steel Corporation not been formed at about the time it was, some ten years ago, the steel business not only of America but of the world today would be dominated by Andrew Carnegie."

At the end of 1898, Carnegie was almost prepared to be complacent; however, he was too clever, too much the infighter himself, ever to let his guard down. Schwab wrote to him on December 20: the greater part of the bridge and structural companies were talking of combining into one huge merger; they wanted Keystone Bridge in the consolidation; the managers looked favorably on the idea. Carnegie replied in two days. Once more he voiced his disdain of what Morgan and the Moore Brothers were doing; he would have no part of the proposal; in fact, now was the time to go into light steel as well as improving their position in heavy steel. Carnegie's letter, in little, expresses the principles that guided him as a steelmaster and his pride in the organization he had put together.

Surely my views about going into Trusts are pretty well known.

Our policy should be to make finished articles, Bridges among them. We should make the best bridge shop in the United States as soon as you get time to built it.

We want to sell finished cars as soon as you can do it. We shall want to make wire, and I think nails, as soon as we can. . . .

The concern that sells articles finished will be able to run all weathers and make some money while others are half idle and losing money.

The Carnegie Steel Co. should never in my opinion enter any Trust. It will do better attending to its own business in its own way; its officers devoting themselves, as they have so successfully done hitherto, to watching operations at home, keeping their eyes steadily fixed on these, and their minds also.

We hope our competitors will combine, for an independent concern always has the "Trust" at its mercy.

And he ended with this salute:

Please present to all my partners my cordial congratulation upon the prosperity of our concern, a concern which may now be said to have made a good start, the result of exceptionally able management by the most wonderful organization of young geniuses the world has to show, or ever had to show—I mean this, every word of it.

CHAPTER FOURTEEN

PLOTS AND STRATAGEMS AND QUARRELS

Conspiracies and Pools The years 1899 and 1900 were amazingly prosperous ones for the Carnegie Co., but Carnegie and his partners were aware that pressures on them were mounting from the new and powerful rivals that had entered the steel industry. The discussions among the managers ranged widely, and all sorts of tentative decisions were taken—frequently mutually contradictory—that showed some uncertainty as to the courses of action to be pursued. Should the company sell out—in whole or in part (as in the case of the Keystone Bridge Co.)? Should it reorganize (with outside financial help) to match the great resources of the Federal Steel Co.? Should it recognize the growing importance of the Illinois Steel Co. (Federal's subsidiary making heavy steel) and share the market with it in a new and gigantic rail pool? Should it meet the pressures of the new wire, hoop, rod, nail, tube companies, which were threatening to stop buying Carnegie steel unless their offered prices were met, by entering into competition with them as a·manufacturer of light steel? What to do about the Pennsylvania Railroad, which continued to favor Carnegie's Western competitors?

Toward the end of 1898, Frick reported to the managers that he had been approached by a syndicate: would the Carnegie Co. sell? The way to do it, said Frick, was to effect a complete reorganization and capitalize for $250 million under a New Jersey charter as a holding company. Such a corporation—ran the Frick proposal—would include Carnegie Steel, Frick Coke, the Bessemer Railroad, the Carnegie Natural Gas Co., and the Oliver Iron Mining Co. Half of the $250 million was to be paid in cash and half in 5-per-cent gold bonds. On January 5, 1899, at a meeting in Carnegie's New York home, where only the older partners were gathered, Carnegie reluctantly agreed, "yielding to the wishes of his oldest partner," Phipps: negotiate on those terms. But nothing came of the proposal, for the syndicate, while not objecting to the price, balked at the idea of putting up such a large sum as $125 million in cash.

Carnegie was delighted. Frick then reported an alternative; this was the establishment of Carnegie Co., Ltd., under a Pennsylvania charter as a limited partnership. Capitalization was to be $125 million, with the new company paying $60 million for all the properties of the Carnegie Steel Co. in cash and $35 million, also in cash, for Frick Coke. The money was to be raised by selling 5-per-cent gold bonds. Carnegie gave tentative approval and the managers appointed a committee to make the preliminary arrangements. But then Lauder—the only one—became sticky; $35 million was too much by $5 million for Frick Coke. Carnegie, having blown hot, now blew cold. On January 23, 1899, in his "Thoughts on Minutes," Carnegie said he was agreeing with Lauder. There was no hurry about the reorganization; the Coke company was being run very efficiently by Frick, why disturb the relationship? And then:

I should not like to see the Carnegie Steel Co. before the public as making a $100 million mortgage. Better postpone. . . . This seems to me a time for us to keep very quiet, pursue our business steadily, close five-year contracts as you are doing, and let the tumult in iron circles go on until it boils over.

The tumult went on. Part of it consisted of efforts to force Carnegie into new pools or collusive agreements to rig prices. He did not like them; he made every effort to keep out of them; sometimes he felt he had to yield. His correspondence and the Minutes of the Company record the backing and filling. In November, 1895, he wrote to Leishman, then president of the company, warning him against entering into any agreement with independent ore companies to keep up the price of ore. "I think our interests are," he said, "all in favor of the lowest price for ore." And then: "Surely our interest now is, to take the stand that, only as producers we have nothing to do with agreements or combinations."

Early in 1899, the American Tin Plate Co., one of the Moore corporations, threatened to terminate or sharply curtail its purchases of bars unless the Carnegie company agreed not to sell to other tin-plate companies. This aroused Carnegie's indignation and he sharply reprimanded the managers for entering into such a contract.

In a memorandum to them, dated January 30, 1899, he wrote:

In these days of Trusts and other swindles I think the Carnegie Steel Co. should keep a pure record. I do not favor the contract as made; I do not believe it is legal; I do not believe it is right; besides, I believe that independent concerns will soon beat the Trust and we shall lose more business ultimately by antagonizing these than by now trying to aid the Trust to maintain an unfair monopoly.

On February 23, 1899, the agreement was canceled. When he was again approached (this was in the same month) to sell out Keystone Bridge to a new combine, he set his terms so impossibly high that they could not be met: he would sell for $2 million; would stay out of bridge-making, viaducts, elevated railway structures for ten years; the new company would have to buy 50 per cent of its rolled steel from Carnegie; unless the combine got two-thirds of all the business, he would cut loose and re-enter. And he wrote to Lauder: "The failure of such a combination is not improbable."

He kept his freedom of action here; when he gave way, he exacted his pound of flesh. The Carnegie Co. had gone into the manufacture of pressed-steel cars in 1898; the American Car and Foundry Co., a new consolidation, had just appeared. Would the Carnegie Co. quit the field? Yes, said Frick, and Carnegie assented: pay us $1 million and $100,000 a year; and this was accepted.

In the fall of 1897, Carnegie was told by Frick that Illinois Steel and a group of Pennsylvania companies were suggesting an understanding that they agree to raise the price of steel, divide the heavy steel business among themselves, and freeze all other companies out. He wrote to Frick from Scotland September 20, 1897. He did not believe it would work; he would have nothing to do with Illinois Steel under its present management; he would not agree with any Eastern mill to curtail the Carnegie business in the East. "Our policy, in my opinion, is to stand by ourselves alone, just as we did last year. And take orders East and West. . . . And as for Illinois Steel: If you do arrange with them, you are simply bolstering a concern and enabling it to strike you in the near future."

Then he wrote on September 24 to Schwab, making it impossible for Illinois Steel to pursue the matter further. He would agree to a "private and confidential understanding" if Illinois Steel would divide equally with Carnegie the "competitive business" west of Chicago. But to include in the conspiracy the Eastern business or that east of Chicago, i.e., Ohio, "would be just throwing money away." As for the Pennsylvania companies, he wanted a full share of all the Eastern orders, which meant three shares to their one. And with his characteristic cockiness, he ended, "We have made the fight, the enemy is at our mercy, now do not let us be foolish enough to forego the fruits of victory."

But this was 1897; the next year saw the great Federal Steel Co. in the lists. The managers in Pittsburgh were for coming to terms, by entering a new and giant combine, really a cartel, under the guise of a New Jersey corporation to be called the Empire Rail Co., which was to buy and sell all steel rails for five years, obviously on the basis of carefully worked out prorations. At the least, Carnegie Steel should conspire with Federal Steel exclusively, wrote Schwab, in September, 1898, "by which we agree to jointly take rail orders on the basis of dividing the new proceeds from rails." And Schwab reported to Carnegie that the board of managers unanimously agreed to one or the other of these plans.

Carnegie cabled from Scotland October 3, asking for a postponement of any decisions until his return. Illinois Steel (the subsidiary now of Federal Steel) would not keep any agreement it signed its name to. As for Federal Steel, the parent company: "Believe a continuance of war much better for us than any peace; a good start for Federal being the last thing desired."

Carnegie Fights   Carnegie came home—an unusual procedure for him; he frequently stayed in Scotland well beyond the end of the year—and a meeting of the managers took place November 15, 1898. He would have no part of the proposed cartel; he said to them: "We should be having nothing to do with a formal trust of that kind." It would be attacked; it would put the company in a bad light. He persuaded Phipps and Lauder to go along with him, and because all three represented more than two-thirds of the company's stock, the managers voted to stay out. But Carnegie had to give in concerning the agreement with Federal Steel. Carnegie Steel entered into a "contract" with Federal Steel for five years (in which the Cambria Iron Co. and the Colorado Fuel and Iron Co. also joined) in which all agreed to pool the net proceeds from the sale of domestic rails (fixing the price) and divide equally—one-half to Federal, the second half to Carnegie and the other two—at the end of each month. This was quickly superseded by the so-called Rail Association, which included Carnegie, Illinois, Cambria, Colorado, Pennsylvania, Lackawanna, and National—the last a newcomer in heavy steel, put together by the Chicago Moore Brothers.

Presumably, the Carnegie Co. was to get 30 per cent of all the rail business; but the Illinois Co. was pressing and so was the National Co., as Carnegie had foretold, so that the Carnegie share was 25 per cent on September 21, 1900, and on November 27, 22 per cent.

Having yielded here, the effecting of similar arrangements in structural steel and plates was agreed to by the managers, Carnegie protesting all the while but not trying to force the issue his way, as he did in the case of the Empire Rail Co. Nevertheless, the Minutes of the Company reflected unusual disquietude. Said Schwab, at a meeting of the managers on June 6, 1900:

There is no question, of course, that if the business is left open and associations [pools] done away with that we can get our full share of the business and sufficient to keep our mills going at full speed. We should all think seriously upon this point.

The rail agreement was threatening their stability, Schwab reported to the managers six days later. National, the latest member of the Rail Association, wanted 10 to 12 per cent; this would reduce Carnegie's from 30 to 26 per cent (it fell even lower, as we have seen). And said Schwab: "We could not run full on such a percentage."

Carnegie, from Scotland, wrote long memorandums to his associates in Pittsburgh, June 20, and again on June 26 and July 11, on receiving this news. These are important as indicative of two things: that Carnegie was opposed to pools; and that he entered into them selectively, in the short run, to give him time to work out a basic strategy. Said he in the first (June 20):

In the former depressions we announced our policy, viz., take all the orders going and run full. Our competitors believed we meant what we said and this no doubt operated to clear the field. One after the other dropped out. . . .

We averaged $4 a ton profit on all our products in the worst of times.

I concur in the policy you are pursuing, trying to keep prices up as high as practicable owing to the large number of high-priced orders on the books yet unfilled. But it is probable you will be met by the problem before long whether to do as we did before or continue cooperating with others trying to keep up prices . . . even with rails it may be our best policy to meet low prices and run full.

Structural steel, probably one-half of all the steel made, at tolerable prices would be better than a large amount at lower prices, and it would be a pity to disturb an agreement that has worked so satisfactorily. In plates and all other things except these, I see nothing for it but the old policy, take the orders.

On June 26, he referred again to the new competitors in rails—Illinois and National, in the West, and Cambria, which was pushing hard in the East. He told the managers they ought to get out of the rail pool:

My opinion is that whatever temporary advantage might accrue from percentages, which would restrict our running, our property will be worth far more hence by deciding that come what may we shall run full as long as there are orders in the market. You know that we can run full and have a margin of profit.

And he issued the same spirited call to battle that he sounded for the guidance of his field officers on the firing line, in depression and in flush times. This on July 11:

Put your trust in the policy of attending to your own business in your own way and running your mills full regardless of prices and very little trust in the efficacy of artificial arrangements with your competitors, which have the serious result of strengthening them if they strengthen you.

On October 22, 1900, Schwab, at the same time that he was negotiating to enter a plate pool (against which Carnegie had advised), when speaking before the managers, agreed with the canny old man. It was apparent that Schwab had no intention of remaining in it too long, for he said:

the history of pools has been that where mills have been in a pool, and have made a great deal of money in any product, they have thought it unnecessary to economize in the manufacture of that product, but that has never been our history. When we have gone out of a pool, we have always been in good shape to follow the business.

Carnegie's competitors knew this. The secretary of the plate pool thus wryly confessed to the Stanley Committee in 1911 how the conspiracy really turned out:

The cooks who were preparing this meal for themselves and their associates found they had prepared and were ready to bake the finest pudding ever concocted financially, but that Mr. Carnegie had all the plums.

The battles in 1900 were not restricted to these limited engagements. They began to range over a very wide terrain, with Carnegie—now in the field himself, like the head of a large cavalry troop or (to be modern) like Patton's Tank Corps—striking again and again into the heart of enemy country. He hit in every direction, taking a number of his competitors on simultaneously and separately; and he succeeded in demoralizing all of them. What had got the wind up was the report to him from the managers in June, 1900, that a number of the newcomers in finished steel—American Hoop, American Steel and Wire, National Tube—were sharply cutting their purchases of steel billets or canceling their contracts. Carnegie's reply was: we will go into their business and manufacture, in competition with them, finished steel products.

On July 7, 1900, Carnegie cabled from Scotland: "Crisis has arrived." And he ordered that there be started at once at Duquesne, which was threatened with being shut down, the building of hoop, rod, wire, and nail mills. Then he went on:

Extend coal and coke roads, announce these; also tubes. Prevent others building; not until you furnish most staple articles can you get business among them to keep mines and furnaces in full operation; should also run boats Conneaut to Chicago. . . . Never been time when more prompt action essential, indeed absolutely necessary [in order] to maintain property. . . . Spend freely for finished mills, railroads, boat lines; continue to advise regularly by cable.

Lauder, in Pittsburgh, was the timid one and disapproved; Schwab, the good Marshal Ney, took the lead from his commander, and the resolutions were pushed through. Work was begun at Duquesne and a brand new tube factory was started on Lake Erie. Carnegie, encouraged, told his partners what the price was to be. On July 11 he wrote to the managers:

Briefly, if I were czar, I would make no dividends upon the common stock; save all surplus and spend it for a hoop and cotton-tie mill, for wire and nail mills, for tube mills, for lines of boats upon the Lakes. . . . If you are not going to cross the stream do not enter it at all and be content to dwindle into second place.

He had his way, of course; and he returned to Pittsburgh in September to cheer on his lieutenants. The tube mill alone, at Conneaut, was to cost $12 million. He planned to drive quickly to the wall these badly put-together and overcapitalized companies (largely the work of the Moore Brothers—they were to Carnegie "these Chicago adventurers") that were threatening him. He succeeded in terrorizing them; they ran to Morgan, asking for help. Carnegie was striking close to the bone, for one of the corporations Carnegie was putting in jeopardy was National Tube, a consolidation of nineteen companies, which Morgan had created with a capitalization of $80 million. (His own expert had told Morgan the nineteen were worth $19 million at the market.) It was Conneaut that worried the Morgan partners more than anything else, for they learned that Schwab had told Carnegie that he could make tubes at less than ten dollars a ton than National Tube.

As a Morgan partner said later: "When Andrew Carnegie gave his approval to the plant at Conneaut, he became at that moment an incorporated threat and menace to the steel trade of the United States." And when Carnegie was told this, his reply was: "I did not leave the National Tube Co.; the National Tube Co. left me."

Now, with disorder everywhere, Carnegie decided also to take on the Pennsylvania Railroad, his ancient tormentor. Carnegie had patched up a truce with Frank Thomson, its president, in 1896, following his construction and renovation of the Bessemer Railroad from Lake Erie to Pittsburgh. Thomson had died in 1899, and his successor, Alexander J. Cassatt, decided that the Pittsburgh business really was at his mercy; he ordered an increase in rates of 100 per cent for Carnegie traffic moving to the seaboard. In part, Cassatt felt confident in challenging Carnegie, because the Pennsylvania had bought into the Baltimore & Ohio, its leading Eastern competitor.

Carnegie had gone back to Scotland, and in October, he wrote at length to Schwab, asking for complete information about rates and how deep Cassatt had penetrated into the Baltimore & Ohio. He was certain Cassatt had violated the law; that Pittsburgh was now controlled by the railroad; and he intended to return, summon a "mass convention" of all the manufacturers and businessmen of Western Pennsylvania and Eastern Ohio, and raise the wind. He characterized Cassatt's action as "the most serious blow we have ever received, and it is a life and death struggle. If we are to be at the mercy of any one man our property is not worth having."

And he ended on the call to battle once more. "The deliverance of Pittsburgh is my next great work, and this time it will be thoroughly done, once for all, if I live."

Carnegie was clever enough not to be content with a public meeting. He made an alliance with George Gould, son of Jay Gould, who was planning to complete his father's work: to put together the family railroad properties of the Southwest and Middle West to be joined to a line running to the Eastern seaboard. He had gained control of the Western Maryland, running out of Baltimore to Wheeling and also to Cumberland in western Maryland. He announced he would build from this latter point to Pittsburgh—157 miles of road—and was already constructing a terminal at Pittsburgh. Carnegie encouraged this; he promised Gould one-fourth of his tonnage from Pittsburgh to Baltimore; there would be more assistance if called upon.

Cassatt had been aided and abetted by William H. Vanderbilt, president of the New York Central. The New York Central was a Morgan railroad, and the House of Morgan, as a result of its triumphs in reorganizing many of the Eastern railroads following the debacle of 1893-96, did not want to see the many "communities of interest" it had created disordered. (These "communities of interest" really worked through the partners of the Morgan firm, who sat on the boards and particularly the finance committees of many railroad companies.) Rates were steady; the railroads were prospering. If George Gould used his father's old and amazingly successful tactics of constant rate wars and the building of feeder lines into competitor's territory, the pretty pattern would be sadly disarranged. If the Pennsylvania Railroad was not worried, Morgan was. Morgan said to Schwab, to whom he had been talking at this time about Carnegie's plans: "Carnegie is going to demoralize railroads just as he has demoralized steel." Morgan liked order (and price stability); Carnegie stood for cutthroat competition—and threats to overcapitalized, rickety corporate structures. Events were moving to a denouement, with Morgan and Carnegie alone the protagonists in a great drama.

It was Frick who helped Carnegie make his decision.

Carnegie and Frick   In 1887, following the death of Tom Carnegie, the Carnegie Associates entered into a curious agreement that came to be known as the "Iron-Clad." Its purpose was to protect the other partners in the event of Carnegie's death. Its provisions were these: In the event of a partner's dying, his stock interest—at book value—was to be purchased by the company treasury and cash payments were to be made over an extended period (in the case of Carnegie, this was to be fifteen years). Also, at any time, the Associates, by a two-thirds vote (which meant two-thirds of the stock outstanding; the proportion was changed in 1892 to three-fourths) could decide to buy out, or oust, another partner. A partner seeking to retire was also to turn his stock in to the treasury and receive his proration of the book value. It was out of this accumulation in the treasury—and, as we have noted, during the course of the "Iron-Clad" some fifteen partners quit or were dissociated from the company's ownership—that new partners got their financial interest in the Carnegie organization. The new partners—younger men in every instance (except Frick, who put up a part of the allotment assigned to him in cash, borrowing for the rest from Carnegie personally)—were to pay for their shares, usually fractional, out of declared dividends. The result was, from time to time, the total of the stock was not distributed.

It will be noted that value was fixed "at the books." This presumably represented original costs, but the fact is, Carnegie himself kept the company property valuation down, so that it seriously underestimated earning capacity or market worth. We have observed how the recapitalizations that took place had no real relation to the enormous profits being made, or to the very valuable leases the company had on the Rockefeller ore lands, or to the successful integration of the Carnegie holdings, or to the company's leadership in new fields like the manufacture of structural steel and plates. At any given time, starting in the early 1880s, if the Carnegie Co. had been put on the market, its price would have been many times over—at least five times—the value "at the books."

In 1896, Phipps, the originator of the "Iron-Clad," had become restive and sought the agreement's dissolution; he had been opposed by all the partners including Frick, and even into June, 1898, Frick was supporting Carnegie. And then Frick shifted. Whereas Phipps and Carnegie, old friends, were able to live with their differences, their relationship always remaining on affectionate terms, Frick was something else again. When he surrendered the presidency in 1895, his stock ownership had been reduced from 11 to 6 per cent, and this undoubtedly must have stung, for now he ranked below Phipps among the senior partners. He saw himself being superseded by Schwab as Carnegie's closest adviser in the making of company policy. He had been following, more closely than the other associates, the corporate revolution taking place from 1897 on.

Old companies, like the Carnegie organization limited partnerships or individually owned, were being transformed into consolidations, as a result of the magic of financial promoters; their securities were being offered to the public and, despite overcapitalizations, were being eagerly snapped up. Large capital gains were to be made in the market by getting in on the ground floor of a reorganization, by trading in the securities of your own company—and control could still be maintained with minority ownership. At the same time, surplus funds obtained in this fashion could be used to acquire holdings in the new companies being formed every day (if one knew the promoters, and Frick was widening his acquaintance among them), before they were publicly launched. This was the new way of becoming wealthy; scores of millionaires, the House of Morgan, the Moore Brothers, Rockefeller (for he was allied with great commercial banks in New York also engaged in the investment-banking business), and those associated with them, had been made overnight with these processes. But it meant being a "capitalist" and not a manufacturer, with fingers in a hundred and one pies, and it meant being a Wall Street man and not a Pittsburgh steelmaster. All this had been at the back of Frick's mind when he had proposed the creation of a public New Jersey corporation, but nothing had come of it—in part because Carnegie had been cool to the proposal.

The relationship between Carnegie and Frick had been complex. Carnegie had the highest respect for Frick's managerial talents and in the early years of their association until 1895 had given him his head. Frick had been responsible for the initial rationalization of the company and had beaten down costs so successfully that a good deal of the credit for weathering the difficulties of the first half of the nineties was undoubtedly his. Carnegie knew this and was unstinted in his praise of Frick's accomplishments. Thus, he had written Frick from Scotland, August 1, 1893: "I'm glad we have you at the helm for you are the best financier I ever knew. If you get stuck Lord help the rest. . . ."

On the other hand, some of Frick's methods and some sides to Frick's character had made Carnegie uneasy. Carnegie did not like the way Frick handled his workers, as we have seen. He came—unjustly—to hold Frick responsible for Homestead. Frick was aloof in his relations with his management; he ruled over his lieutenants, the superintendents of the various works, with a quick temper and a harsh tongue. As Hendrick put it: "Frick lacked the quality which Carnegie regarded as the first requirement of leadership; he inspired little loyalty or affection in his subordinates."

At the same time there was a curious streak of instability in Frick. Normally taciturn in company and with little or no conversation, he could take umbrage at fancied slights and flash out (in writing to Carnegie) almost hysterically. Carnegie sensed this, for on December 18, 1894, after an exchange between them that was becoming increasingly heated on Frick's part, Carnegie wrote to Frick:

In a letter this A.M. I am sorry to note that an expression in a letter from me about Bethlehem being a sharp and lively competitor for *us* is considered as a reflection on your management—How groundless—You are not well my Friend you are not well. You would never have done me this injustice were you well.

Frick, on a number of occasions—he had been crossed; he had become angry—had threatened to resign his chairmanship. Finally, in 1895, Carnegie had yielded before one other such display of petulance and had acceded to Frick's stepping down as chairman of the Carnegie Steel Co.

He refused to accept Frick's offer to sell out to him his shares in the Frick Coke Co. and in the Carnegie Co. and insisted that Frick stay on as a partner. Frick, now seeking to save face—another example of instability of character—asked that he be given the title (really meaningless), "Chairman of the Board of Directors." Carnegie agreed, but the active head of the managers was to be the president—and this was first Leishman and then Schwab. Here was a further cause for irritation, and friction mounted between Frick and Schwab.

Carnegie had cabled Phipps about the strained relations and had hinted that Frick might quit. Phipps had replied on December 22, 1894, expressing dismay; he, Phipps, could not succeed. There were before them "troubles unnumbered—unending, life too short, the game not worth the candle." And he had ended:

When fair times come again, an arrangement can be made whereby we can have a haven of enjoyment and rest, instead of what may beset us any day, a sea of trouble, cares, anxieties. To some plan of sale and security you Dod [Lauder] and I should certainly look within the next year or two. . . . Our trio I think should confer fully and act only with unanimity. . . ."

At the bottom of the letter from Phipps, in Carnegie's handwriting, was this calculation. Did it mean, at the end of 1894, what Carnegie thought the company was really worth—when its capitalization was still $25 million?

$$
\begin{array}{r}
250 \\
585 \\
\hline
1250 \\
2000 \\
1250 \\
\hline
\$146{,}250{,}000
\end{array}
$$

Frick Looks for a Buyer   Frick showed his hand, finally, in April, 1899, when he and Phipps came to visit Carnegie; Frick had come to the conclusion, along with Phipps, that the old Association no longer would serve—Phipps because he wished to retire, Frick because he wanted to seek greener pastures. This time they had a firm offer. The Carnegie Co. and the Frick Co. were to be sold—the former for $250 million, the latter for $70 million—and presumably would be recapitalized and the new shares offered to the public. (Carnegie's share would be $157 million. He would receive $100 million in first-mortgage 5-per-cent bonds and $57 million in cash.) The two men asked for a 90-day option, presumably to give the purchasers time to raise the enormous sum. When Carnegie pressed for the names of the principals Frick and Phipps were representing, they demurred; they had promised not to tell. This nettled Carnegie; he asked that the negotiators post a deposit of $2 million for the option they sought, the sum to be forfeited to the Carnegie Steel Co. in the event that the cash could not be raised. On this basis an agreement was signed April 24, 1899, with $1.17 million put up as a binder by Frick and Phipps; this represented Carnegie's 58½ per cent ownership; the other partners waived their share.

At this point Carnegie left for Scotland. The story was too good to keep a secret for long, and all sorts of rumors reached and were printed by the press. John W. Gates was quoted as saying that the capitalization of the new corporation was to be $800 million; a New Jersey charter had been obtained; offices had already been engaged throughout the country to sell the stock. And then the name of William H. Moore came out; he was the principal Frick and Phipps were dealing for; he was the promoter who was hawking about the Carnegie name and using all of the skills and wiles of Wall Street to work up a public interest—and to obtain funds from banking firms—so that the option could be taken up.

This intelligence, when it arrived in Scotland, made Carnegie furious. He had only contempt for the Moore steel companies; the Moores and their associates were "Chicago adventurers." When Frick and Phipps journeyed to Scotland to seek an extension of the option in June, Carnegie turned them down: they had betrayed his trust in dealing with the Moores when they knew perfectly well what Carnegie thought of them and their companies. It was plain that the Moores had been unable to raise the $57 million; their deposit would be forfeited (a part of it, $170,000, Frick and Phipps themselves had to put up). And then—perhaps to taunt Frick (for Carnegie had also learned that Frick and Phipps were to get $5 million of the promotional profits if and when the new company was launched)—he declared the Carnegie Steel Co. was still up for sale. This time, the price of an option would be $5 million, however. What hurt Carnegie more than anything else was the fact that Frick, who had been such a great steelmaster, regarded Wall Street as more worthy of his talents.

Frick Is Bought Out   Carnegie returned to New York determined that Frick had to go. Other disputes between Frick and the Carnegie Co., involving the price of coke and Frick's efforts to buy a piece of land on the Monongahela for himself that the company had marked out for itself, only exacerbated the mounting ill will. Then Carnegie relented: he would let Frick resign from the chairmanship before the board of managers ousted him. This Carnegie told Frick personally and Frick sent in his resignation; he seemed thoroughly reconciled to his departure from the company's management.

It was the lull before the storm. There is no doubt that Carnegie was forcing Frick's hand by provocative acts. In the case of coke, it was decided to hold the Frick Coke Co. to an unjust contract—in which minimum prices had been fixed and no allowances had been made for upward market movements—and on January 4, 1900, the coke company (by vote of its own board, which Carnegie controlled) was ordered to sell to the Carnegie furnaces at $1.35 a ton when the going price was $3.50. Early, on January 8, the Carnegie board of managers, by resolution of Carnegie himself, reaffirmed the provisions of the 1892 "Iron-Clad" agreement—an effort had been made to liberalize it in 1897 but because it had not been signed, it was held not binding—which implied that Frick was going to be asked to sell his 6 per cent interest at the grossly under-valued capitalization "on the books." This would have come to a meager $4,900,000; at a capitalization of $250 million—which Frick had been insisting was the fair and reasonable one—his share would have been $15 million.

Frick, learning of this action, wrote to the board of managers on January 13:

At the instigation of A. C. you now specially seek without my knowledge or consent and after a serious personal disagreement between Mr. Carnegie and myself, and by proceedings purposely kept secret from me to make a contract for me under which Mr. Carnegie thinks he can unfairly take from me my interest in the Carnegie Steel Co., Ltd. Such proceeds are illegal and fraudulent as against me and I now give you a formal notice that I will hold all persons pretending to act thereunder liable for the same.

The board's reply on January 15 was a demand for the surrender of Frick's shares. Frick refused to answer and on February 1 his stock, again by order of the board, was ordered transferred to the treasury and a check rendered him. Meanwhile, Frick, now joined by Phipps, gave formal notice to the managers that further action was contemplated. They wrote jointly (Phipps signing first):

We desire to call your attention to the fact that the fair values of the properties of the Carnegie Steel Co., Ltd. are not shown on the books. In repeated instances, the values shown thereon are very far below what the real and fair values are, and in other instances, such values are not shown at all. If there are not now entries on those books showing the fair value of all outstanding and existing contracts [the reference was to the Rockefeller ore leases]; and of the earning power, and of the good will, there should be.

We insist that the books shall be so kept that they will, by an aggregation of all the accounts, fairly show the present real value, as a whole and going concern, of the Carnegie Steel Co., Ltd. . . .

We believe that said value considerably exceeds the sum of $250 million. If you dissent from this, we are willing to refer this question of value to three satisfactory and disinterested businessmen to be agreed upon by you and ourselves. . . .

On February 3 both men sent an emissary to Schwab saying they would settle for $250 million; this would have given Phipps $27.5 million and Frick $15 million. There was no reply. Frick alone then filed suit against the Carnegie Steel Co., Ltd. in the Court of Common Pleas of Allegheny County (the company was a Pennsylvania corporation) charging fraud because the transfer of his stock to the company treasury had been illegal and because the books of the company concealed assets.

The brief Frick's attorneys filed to support his claims elaborately recited the history, growth, and earnings of the Carnegie companies, in their various transformations, since 1881. It charged that many agreements over the period, spread on the Minutes, had not been carried out. That partners had been made—and given voting power—who had not actually paid for their shares. Particularly, those who had become members of the Association after July, 1892, "are all largely indebted to the Association for the amount of the contributions agreed by them to be made. The only members who hold fully paid up shares are Andrew Carnegie, Henry Phipps, George Lauder, W. H. Singer, and your orator [Frick]. The remaining members are largely indebted to the Association."

[417]

As for the value "at the books," the petition made serious charges. It said:

The books of said company do not now and have not recently contained a reasonable valuation of its assets. A very large quantity of its assets on Jan. 1, 1900, stood upon its books at very inadequate evaluations. Some of the assets do not there appear at any valuation. This was known to Mr. Carnegie and the other partners. The fair value of your orator's [Frick's] interest therein could not be determined from what now appears on the books of said company.

And Frick went on to point out the inequities to himself by the forced transfer of his stock under the "Iron-Clad." The price of his shares was to be set by the company. Payments were to be made to him in small installments "during a term of years of such duration as will, probably, not only enable the company to entirely pay for your orator's interests by using the share of the profits applicable to them, but having a surplus left to the company." This was not only sharp dealing; it was fraud as well. The petition to the court formally asked for Frick's reinstatement, the establishment of a receivership, and the liquidation of the property.

The brief, of course, was available to the press, and it led to a Roman holiday. Carnegie had his defenders and his detractors; and the debate ranged far and wide and with great glee. The Republican Party leaders—this was another Presidential election year, as 1892 had been when the Homestead scandal had shocked the country—and Mark Hanna, the Party's national chairman, were fearful of its effects on the campaign. It was pointed out, maliciously, that Carnegie's only defense could be to deny in detail the whole story Frick had spread on the record of the company's great advances and earnings—and thus repudiate his accomplishments as a steelmaster, which he had not only prided himself on but had boasted about.

Carnegie made a formal answer through his attorneys, March 14, and five days later—aware of the threatened damage to his reputation—settled with Frick. He was forced to do so by his chief partners; Charles M. Schwab, that faithful lieutenant, writing, "I can't help but think that reorganization at an early date is the proper step." On March 28, a joint statement was issued by the Carnegie Steel Co., Ltd., and the H. C. Frick

Coke Co., known as the "Atlantic City Agreement"; Frick not only had won but he had put an end to the "Iron-Clad."

By the agreement, a new corporation, the Carnegie Co., was to be chartered under the New Jersey law. The limited partnership of the Association was ended. Its capitalization was to be $320 million, of which all of the Carnegie Steel Co., Ltd. assets represented $250 million and those of the Frick Coke Co. $70 million. Technically—as was the fashion of the day (and the same device was employed by the United States Steel Corporation)—the Carnegie Co. was to be a holding company and the corporate entities of the Carnegie Steel Co., Ltd. and the H. C. Frick Coke Co. (although wholly owned by the parent) were to be preserved. The new corporation was to issue $160 million in common stock and $160 million in 5-per-cent first-mortgage bonds. There was to be no public offer of the securities and therefore no promotional profits for investment bankers. The consequence was that, except for Frick, the owners continued to be those who had built the two companies. Naturally, all the "associates" were to be paid off on a proration of their shares in the steel and coke companies but—because the New Jersey Corporation was a public one—they could legally dispose of their holdings at will. Parenthetically, this never occurred (in part because the par value of each share of stock was put at $1,000); the upshot was, there was no trading, and therefore no quotations listed, on the New York Stock Exchange. Carnegie's share was $174,529,000 (representing his stock in the two merged companies); Frick's was $31,284,000 (because he too owned stock in both); Phipps' was $34,804,000. Schwab became the chief officer of the new corporation. And $5 million of the new stocks was set aside for the creation of new partners and to take care of Carnegie's bright young men.

It is idle to assume that the story ended unhappily for Frick; he had lost Carnegie's friendship, and he never forgave Carnegie. But Frick got what he wanted: to be a capitalist and a Wall Street insider—to engage in company promotions and in plots and stratagems. When he died, he left an estate of $150 million—and one of New York's great art collections, each piece chosen with exquisite taste. It was turned over to the city by his daughters and housed in the handsome Renaissance building Frick had had erected for himself on Fifth Avenue when he had moved to New York. Frick, after all, left a permanent monument to himself, more. enduring than his coke ovens.

It will be interesting to record—before the curtain is rung down—what the last (private) balance sheet of the Carnegie Steel Co., Ltd. (Table 34), showed its assets to be (it will be remembered that these were capitalized at $250 million in the Carnegie Co.).

TABLE 34

Cash	$3,142,400
Bills receivable	6,764,910
Accounts receivable	18,922,970
Stocks	11,847,151
Works and properties	42,655,985
1900 improvements	1,513,854
Investments	9,449,330
Due from partners	2,407,565
Miscellaneous items	2,240,876
Total	$98,945,041

Sticking to his guns to the last, the value "at the books," with Carnegie's approval, was $64,883,783.

The next act in the drama was the absorption of the Carnegie Co. into the United States Steel Corporation—within the brief space of a year.

Carnegie's Forty Partners A final word about the partners, who profited so handsomely from the battle between the giants and from the creation of the United States Steel Corporation. Here is a list of the first thirty-six (headed by Carnegie himself, making the total thirty-seven), with the proportions they owned as of December 30, 1899. (The fractions stand for parts of one share. The total adds up to not quite one hundred. The difference was kept in the company treasury to be made available to new partners, when they were created.)

Andrew Carnegie	58½	James Gayley	11$\frac{1}{18}$
Henry Phipps	11	A. M. Moreland	11$\frac{1}{18}$
H. C. Frick	6	C. L. Taylor	½
George Lauder	4	A. R. Whitney	½
C. M. Schwab	3	W. W. Blackburn	⅓
H. M. Curry	2	J. C. Fleming	⅓
W. H. Singer	2	J. O. Hoffman	⅓
L. C. Phipps	2	Millard Hunseker	⅓
A. R. Peacock	2	G. E. McCague	⅓
F. T. G. Lovejoy	⅔	James Scott	⅓
Thomas Morrison	⅔	W. E. Corey	⅓
G. H. Wightman	⅔	J. E. Schwab	⅓
D. M. Clemson	⅔	L. T. Brown	2/9

H. P. Bope	⅑	G. D. Packer	⅑
D. G. Kern	⅑	W. B. Dickson	⅑
H. J. Lindsay	⅑	A. C. Case	⅑
E. F. Wood	⅑	John McLeod	⅑
H. E. Tener, Jr.	⅑	C. W. Baker	⅑
George Megrew	⅑		

On February 5, 1900, the following new partners, and their proportions, were named:

A. R. Hunt, Superintendent of the Plate Mills at Homestead	1/18
A. C. Dinkey, Assistant to the General Superintendent	1/18
P. T. Berg, Chief Engineer	1/18
Charles McCreery, Superintendent of the Blast Furnaces at Duquesne	1/18

This was the array of the partners with whom Carnegie had surrounded himself and almost all of whom he had chosen personally. The greater number—Phipps, Lauder, Singer retired; Frick went on to greener pastures—marched into the United States Steel Corporation, and many of them remained to become distinguished steelmasters in their own right.

Carnegie made a characteristically generous gesture in the case of Schwab, who had stood by so valiantly. Early in 1901, referring to the Carnegie Co. and before the United States Steel Corporation had yet emerged, he wrote Schwab:

I have set aside 2 per cent of my interest in the Carnegie Co. at par for the stock, the dividends from which and from the bonds going with the stock.

I shall credit, charging 5 per cent interest only on the par of the stock. This 2 per cent is wholly yours when it is paid under this plan—which involves you in no risk.

I make you this gift which will really give you the stock free as the bonds even at par meet the whole cost, to testify my appreciation of your splendid management so far of the chief office of the company.

CHAPTER FIFTEEN

THE UNITED STATES STEEL CORPORATION— THE PASSING OF A STEELMASTER

Mergers   There had been efforts, in the 1870s and 1880s, to control markets and prices—because of unchecked competition and consequently diminishing returns—in a number of industries. Initially these had taken the form of pools which were formal associations by which prorations for participating members were established and, sometimes, profits shared on the prorations assigned. Pools were common in railroading and from time to time appeared in iron and steel. In both instances, such collusive arrangements were short-lived: they were illegal under the common law of the States and therefore could not be enforced by the courts; and, too frequently, as we have seen in the case of Carnegie, aggressive competitors stayed as members only so long as they had learned, and were able to benefit from, the costs and pricing policies of their rivals—then they walked out.

Where pools took on the form of cartels—that is, profits were distributed by the associations themselves—they had somewhat better chances of survival. Such pools, in limited areas, were formed in the mining and working of salt, in the manufacture of cord, and in the distilling of whiskey, in the late 1870s. They worked fairly well, but they were superseded after not much more than ten years of existence.

This was because of the appearance of the trust, which was first popularized by Standard Oil in 1879. As amended by the trust agreement of January 2, 1882, the Standard Oil Trust had the following characteristics. Fourteen corporation and limited partnerships, by votes of all their stockholders, and another twenty-six companies, by votes of the majority of their stockholders, plus forty-six individuals, combined to form an association called a trust. This new organization was to be run by nine trustees, among whom the leaders were John D. Rockefeller, William Rockefeller, H. M. Flagler, and John Archbold. All the properties of the participants were combined—they represented 90 per cent of all the oil-refining and of all the oil transportation (largely pipe lines) of the country—and against them trust certificates were issued. Profits were distributed by the trustees on the basis of the original values of the companies entering into the agreement. The total number of Standard Oil certificates was 972,500 and, at $100 a share, the capitalization of the trust was $97.25 million. These could be traded in publicly and were listed on the New York Stock Exchange.

It should be noted that the Standard Oil Trust—and this was true of all the others which used it as a model—was put together by oil people themselves, without the participation of financial underwriters. There were, therefore, no promotional profits. Capital gains by the insiders, however, were to be made, as the values of the certificates increased. This was so because the trust had virtually monopoly-control of the market and could regulate prices and refined-oil production. Equally, because significant economies of scale were introduced: business practices were systemized; an elaborate and comprehensive marketing organization was established; sizable sums, out of the gross profits, were spent on technological improvements; by-products were developed. When the trust was dissolved in 1892 it was worth much more than its original capitalization.

There quickly followed similar associations and trust organizations (under various names) in these industries: cottonseed oil (1884), linseed oil (1885), lead mining and refining (1887), whiskey distilling (1887), cord manufacture (1887), and sugar refining (1887). The last was the largest of the imitators of Standard Oil, and, as in the case of Standard Oil, it was dominated by a single individual—Henry O. Havemeyer.

The trusts did not last, because they were outlawed, by State, and not federal, action. State law officers moved against the trusts not on the basis of statute but of common law, which held that agreements or contracts designed to restrain trade were void and therefore unenforceable. The common law did not provide for punitive fines or contributory damages, but State attorneys general and the courts did possess an impressive power: they could seek—and secure—the rescinding of the charters of the companies participating in such associations, and thus put them out of business.

Such proceedings were begun almost at once—in Louisiana against the cottonseed oil trust in 1887; in New York against the sugar trust in 1889; and in Ohio against the Standard Oil Trust in 1890. The decisions handed down by the highest State courts in New York in 1890 and in Ohio in 1892 had an instantaneous effect, and their examples were followed generally throughout the country. All trusts were dissolved.

The New York Court of Appeals, on the narrow issue that it was a violation of law for corporations created by the State to enter into partnership with other corporations, ordered the forfeiture of the North River Sugar Refining Co., the leading member of the Havemeyer sugar trust. It did not discuss the general question of the effects of the trust— that it sought the establishment of a monopoly in restraint of trade.

The Ohio Supreme Court went further. In the action against the Standard Oil Co. of Ohio, it found that the Ohio company, by entering into another association controlled by an outside body of trustees, was giving up its independence of action and thereby breaching the rights of its owners. But it also ruled that the trust's

object was to establish a virtual monopoly of the business of producing petroleum, and of manufacturing, refining and dealing in it and all its products, throughout the entire country, and by which it might not merely control the production but the price at its pleasure. All such associations are contrary to the policy of our State and void.

The Standard Oil Co. of Ohio was therefore ordered to withdraw from the trust. The implication was plain: failure to do so could lead to another suit and the forfeiture of its charter. The company immediately complied, and this led to the termination of the Standard Oil Trust in the same year.

Meanwhile, the State of New Jersey had come to the rescue of the merger movement. In 1889, its legislature had amended its corporation law to permit holding companies to purchase the bonds and stock of other companies and issue their own securities in payment for those thus acquired. The law was amended in 1896 in an important particular: a holding company, in this process of consolidating the properties of companies, was not confined to those chartered in New Jersey alone; it was legal for it to form a merger of corporations wherever chartered and in whatever States.

Holding companies receiving charters from New Jersey—and they were perpetual ones—did not necessarily have to control properties in that State. Offices had to be maintained there, and annual meetings of stockholders had to take place there. The holding-company device, because it offered so much freedom of action, was the pattern generally followed in the first great merger movement in the United States; that is, from 1895 (really 1897) to 1904. A holding company could either buy outright all the properties of individual companies entering into a merger, at the same time maintaining their separate corporate identities (this is what the United States Steel Corporation did), or it could acquire control of the combined companies by a purchase of majority stock, with a common board of directors sitting on the boards of all the participating companies.

The lead of New Jersey was quickly followed by other States—New York, Delaware, Pennsylvania, West Virginia, Maine, Nevada. New Jersey attracted the largest and most powerful mergers. In 1904, John Moody, in his *The Truth About the Trusts*, reported that of the 318 big combinations, 170 were incorporated in New Jersey.

This was one reason for the new impetus the merger movement in American industry received. Such early consolidations or holding companies were the Diamond Match Co. (1889)—the first large and successful effort of the Moore Brothers, American Tobacco Co. (1890), United States Rubber Co. (1892), General Electric Co. (1892), United States Leather Co. (1893). In these, and in the many mergers that took place in the decade following 1895, promoters and financial underwriters took the lead, and this was so because of two important considerations, as we shall see.

The movement toward combinations was held back in the first half of the nineties because of the continued depression and the uncertainties attending the legal interpretation of the Sherman Antitrust Act of 1890. The Sherman Act, in effect, translated State common law into federal statute law—with teeth in it. The eight sections of the act were the following: 1. "Every contract, combination in the form of trust or otherwise, or conspiracy in restraint of trade or commerce among the several States, or with foreign nations, is . . . illegal." 2. Persons monopolizing or combining or conspiring to monopolize any part of the trade or commerce among the several States, or with foreign nations, shall be deemed guilty of a misdemeanor and punished by fine or imprisonment. 3. Every contract in the form of a trust or otherwise, or conspiracy in restraint of trade or commerce among Territories and States or Territories and foreign nations is illegal. 4. The federal circuit courts are invested with jurisdiction; the federal district attorneys are empowered to institute proceedings in equity to restrain violations. 5. The courts may include other persons than those specifically enjoined under authority of Section 4. 6. Any property owned under a contract involved in a conspiracy in restraint of trade may be seized and condemned by the federal authorities. 7. A person injured by a company in restraint of trade may sue in the federal courts for three times the damage sustained by him, together with costs and attorneys' fees. 8. The word "person" shall be construed to include "corporations."

Labor and farmers' organizations were not excluded, as such, from the terms of the act, although an effort was made to do so. The Senate Judiciary Committee, writing the bill, felt this was unnecessary; yet, ironically, the first successful invocation of the law was against Eugene V. Debs' American Railway Union in 1894.

In 1895, the doubts of the business community were dispelled: the Supreme Court, in *U.S. v. E. C. Knight Co.*, virtually held that the Sherman Act was inoperative as far as combinations per se were concerned. The American Sugar Refining Co.—the successor to the Sugar Refineries Co., the Sugar Trust—was established as a New Jersey corporation in 1891, combining some twenty refineries in New York, Boston, New Orleans, St. Louis, San Francisco, and Portland, Oregon. The authorized capital at the time of consolidation was $37.5 million common and an equal amount of preferred. Its leading spirit and the president of the merger was Henry O. Havemeyer. In January, 1892, the corporation acquired a controlling interest of the four existing sugar refineries of Philadelphia, the E. C. Knight Co. among them. It was against this last company that the U.S. Attorney General brought suit under the Sherman Act.

Evidence was submitted to show that the new "Sugar Trust" had already obtained control of more than 95 per cent of the production of refined sugar in the country. But the heart of the government case did not rest in the practices of consolidation; it contented itself with arguing that the *purchase* of the four Philadelphia companies was enough to indicate that an illegal restraint on interstate commerce existed. On the basis of such a presentation the majority opinion of the Court was compelled to declare that the Sherman Act had not been violated. Manufacturing only was affected, and not foreign or interstate commerce.

Said Chief Justice Fuller, who wrote the Court's opinion: "The contracts and acts of the defendants related exclusively to the acquisition of the Philadelphia refineries and to the business of sugar refining in Pennsylvania, and bore no direct relation to commerce between the States or with foreign nations." And he went on:

Contracts, combinations, or conspiracies to control domestic enterprise in . . . production in all its forms, or to raise or lower prices or wages, might unquestionably tend to restrain external as well as domestic trade, but the restraint would be an indirect result. . . .

Here was a green light. According to Moody, by January 1, 1904, 318 industrial consolidations, with a total capitalization of $7.2 billion, had been formed. Of these, 82 (combined capitalization, $1.2 billion) had been organized before January 1, 1898; and 234 (combined capitalization, $6 billion) between 1898 and the end of 1903.

Ralph L. Nelson, in his authoritative *Merger Movements in American Industry, 1895-1956* (1959), presents a year-by-year analysis of what took place in this first great period of consolidating activity; that is, from 1895 through 1904 (Table 35), page 37. The prominence of New Jersey in this connection may be noted from the fact that, in terms of total new capitalization involved, in the decade in question, New Jersey was responsible for 79.1 per cent, as contrasted with New York, 3.7 per cent, Delaware, 2.6 per cent, and Pennsylvania, 3.2 per cent.

Helpful as the attitude of the federal government was, there were many more compelling reasons why this extraordinary activity took place. The first was the existence of a large-scale capital market, and the part played by stock exchanges in facilitating the distribution of industrial issues to the public. The second was the promotional profits the financial underwriters were able to obtain. And the third was the

TABLE 35

Year	Firm disappear-ances by merger	Merger capitaliza-tions, in millions
1895	43	$ 40.8
1896	26	24.7
1897	69	119.7
1898	303	650.6
1899	1,208	2,262.7
1900	340	442.4
1901	423	2,052.9
1902	379	910.8
1903	142	297.6
1904	79	110.5

control of the markets for their products, which participants in such consolidations were likely to acquire.

Nelson points out that during 1898-1902, 10.6 per cent of new stock issues of merged corporations, worth $360 million, was issued to the general public, and 89.4 per cent worth $3,026 million, was exchanged for the assets or securities of the companies entering into the combinations. The greater part of the bonds and stocks was listed on and traded in organized stock exchanges, New York's being the leading one. This facilitated, either directly or indirectly, the raising of capital. Perhaps of greater importance was the fact that the public, in the form of individual investors or institutional savers, purchased such securities, once they were listed, making it possible for the underwriters and the insiders to obtain large capital gains. As Nelson puts it: "The ability to readily 'cash in' securities received in exchange for assets of merged firms would have been an important factor in persuading entrepreneurs to join consolidations." And he cites the cases of a number of corporations the purchase of whose common stock led to sizable profits for investors. That of the United States Steel Corporation was typical. Organized April 1, 1901, its common stock issued at $50, the market price on December 1 was $43.50, and nine years later was $72.63. During these nine years dividends paid out totaled $21.75. The average annual rate of return was, in consequence, 9 per cent.

Nelson's conclusion on this point is worth noting:

The findings concerning the role of the capital market in the merger movement lend considerable support to the thesis that the development of the capital market was a major cause. The high correlation between merger activity and stock prices suggests that much of the merger activity of the period had its origin or was influenced by the stock market. Further examination indicated that capital market factors overrode the level of industrial activity in influencing merger activity.

The close links of the investment-banking houses with the expanding capital market has already been commented on. Their communities of interest with commercial banks and insurance companies gave them access to savings accumulated in these, including the banks' trust-company departments; and the return of prosperity and growing personal income further expanded the outlets for the new security issues. The business of underwriting required funds—for the legal work and initial costs of organization involved—as well as skills. There were legitimate expenses, but there is no doubt that the large profits possible from underwriting attracted merchant-banking houses like Morgan and the Moores. In the case of the United States Steel Corporation, Temin is convinced that possibly the most important motive for its appearance were the profits from the act of formation itself. (We must not forget that these went not only to Morgan, the organizer of the underwriting syndicate, but also to the Moores, Gary, Gates and all those others whose companies—already overcapitalized—were merged to form the huge combine.)

Nelson is further persuaded (as were Moody before him and Temin after him) that the necessity or desirability of avoiding the vigorous and often cutthroat competition so characteristic of American industry up to the 1890s constituted a powerful motive. Using the original estimates of Moody (with certain corrections and adjustments) Nelson's calculations show in Table 36 the high degree of market control achieved by merged firms (his page 102).

And Nelson draws the following conclusion: the desire for market control in all likelihood played at least a "permissive" role in the merger movement. And he adds:

The large proportion of merger activity resulting in market control suggests that the desire for the protection thus afforded to profits must have been a factor of substantial importance in inducing firms to merge. With the growth of the capital market this desire found an effective means of implementation.

TABLE 36. PROPORTION OF MERGER ACTIVITY ACCOUNTED FOR BY MERGED FIRMS
THAT ACHIEVED MARKET CONTROL, 1895–1904

Percentage of industry controlled	Consolidations and parent companies		Firm disappearances		Capitalizations (millions of dollars)	
	No.	% of total	No.	% of total	Value	% of total
42.5 – 62.5	21	6.7	291	9.7	$ 613.5	10.3
62.5 – 82.5	24	7.7	529	17.6	2,130.6	35.7
82.5 – over	16	5.1	343	11.4	998.0	16.7
"Large"	25	8.0	302	10.0	455.5	7.6
Total	86	27.5	1,465	48.6	$4,197.6	70.4
Total merger activity	313	100.0	3,012	100.0	5,960.9	100.0

What of economies of scale that merged firms presumably hoped to achieve? Nelson is not certain that positive evidence exists to substantiate the belief that these were accomplished—at least, in the short run. In the first place, Nelson calls attention to the fact that most of the mergers were horizontal. (Yet, as the history of Standard Oil indicated, more efficient marketing arrangements, and therefore economies, resulted from the consolidation.) True, when vertical integrations occurred, as in the case of the primary metals industries, economies could be achieved; but the numbers of such vertical combinations were quite few. Even here, the United States Steel Corporation is an example. Because so many of the mergers were holding companies, it took a fairly long time (usually well beyond a decade) for all elements of production to be closely meshed together and brought under tight accounting, and therefore costing, control. Indeed, United States Steel Corporation's central office was not completely overhauled until the 1930s.

On the other hand, Alfred D. Chandler, Jr., in his *Strategy and Structure: Chapters in the History of the Industrial Enterprise* (1962), by an intensive examination of a group of industries, submits evidence to demonstrate that the lowering of costs was a major motive for—and consequence of—consolidation. This was so in the activities of the Guggenheims (American Smelting and Refining Co.) who brought smelting and refining works to the copper mines and also controlled directly their shipping and marketing departments. The same was true of the manufacture of explosives and paper and the mining of coal.

Chandler cites the case of the DuPonts and explosives. From the 1870s, prices and production in the manufacture of explosives had been controlled by the Gunpowder Trade Association, a pool—which, however, was really dominated by E. I. DuPont deNemours & Co. In 1902, the DuPonts bought out most of the important independents in the industry, by exchanges of stock, and proceeded to set up a consolidation, in its strictest sense, and not a holding company. There was tight coordinated organization: plants were shut down, others were enlarged, new ones were built; and there were established centralized accounting, purchasing, engineering, traffic, and marketing departments. Once these processes were completed the DuPonts turned to obtaining control over their raw materials by the purchase of nitrate mines and guano deposits in Chile. Says Chandler:

In coal and explosives, and possibly copper, the major motive for combination, consolidation and the integration of supply with the manufacturing and marketing processes seems to have been an expectation of lowered costs through the creation of a national distributing organization, the consolidation of manufacturing activities and the effective coordination of the different industrial processes by one central office. In steel, the desire for an assured supply of raw materials [and the profits made from the maintenance of high iron-ore prices] appears to have been more significant in encouraging combination and integration.

In the case of steel, however, the prime reasons for the consolidation were Carnegie's intense competitiveness, his threats of overcapacity and price-cutting by his announced intention to go into the finished steel business, and his alliance with Gould in the projected building of a new Eastern railroad. As the U.S. Commissioner of Corporations testified before the Stanley Committee in 1911:

It was clear to everyone that no consolidation of this sort could be made successful unless it included the Carnegie Co., which was the most powerful factor in the situation, which had long been known for aggressive tactics, and which . . . had precipitated this crisis. Moreover, there can be little doubt that many interests in the steel industry regarded Mr. Carnegie's personal influence as a menace to their success and desired to secure his retirement from the trade.

The United States Steel Corporation On December 12, 1900, on the invitation of a group of bankers, a dinner took place at the New York

University Club at which assembled the financial and industrial elite of the city. Its purpose was to hear Charles W. Schwab, President of the Carnegie Co., talk about the future of the steel industry. J. P. Morgan came—it may very well be his partners had inspired the gathering; certainly his announced presence was responsible for the size and distinction of the audience. Carnegie looked in for a few minutes, pleased as Punch at the honor being conferred on one of his "young geniuses" but undoubtedly going there to see how all this talk of steel would sit with Morgan, for Schwab, among other things, meant to say that the recent intrusion of Wall Street was the disordering element in the steel world— and not Carnegie himself. Carnegie, despite his pretended naïvety, knew that the next move was up to Morgan.

Schwab's speech was not recorded; but there were plenty of persons there who were ready to report in detail the purport of Schwab's remarks. (Schwab, in 1911, furnished the Stanley Committee a summary of what he had said.) The promise of American steel, said Schwab, was great: its superior technology, its enormous, still really untapped, reserves of coal and iron ore, its aggressiveness, were leaving the steelmakers of Europe long distances behind. Nevertheless, much still remained to be done (and this was an oblique reference to the handiwork of Morgan and the Moores; that is, the banking community): rationalization had not been developed far enough; indeed, the reverse was taking place. If further economies were to be effected, specialization of plant and function had to be pushed, instead of the disarray—the multiplying duplication of the manufacture of both heavy and light steel—that was creeping into the industry. (All there knew of Carnegie's plans at Conneaut; Schwab was saying that Carnegie was being forced into the creation of excess capacity.)

Steel, therefore, said Schwab, had to do these things. Concentrate plant use on single products—whether rails, or structural steel or beams, or pipe. Relocate works to use transportation efficiently—a heavy cost in the industry—with better access to raw materials and consumers. Reorganize marketing and achieve the economies of a proper distribution system. How to do it? Not by the methods then prevailing in steel; not by pools and by secret, collusive understandings. Trusts, as Carnegie had said again and again, could not survive. The new consolidations— seeking to achieve monopoly holds on regional markets—were not going to work either. What was needed was a real amalgamation to accomplish the specialization of function and therefore the economies of scale Schwab had in mind. The consequences would be the lowering of prices and, out of profits, the exploration of new steel uses and the entry, large-scale, into world markets. (Schwab was talking as an engineer. He could not see that such a great company—as the United States Steel Corporation turned out to be—while not necessarily monopolistic in the classical sense, would be in effect oligopolistic. Its very presence, as leader, would result in stability of prices and not their reduction, and would restrict— if it could not prevent entirely—the entry of new firms.)

Morgan was impressed, for he took Schwab aside and engaged him in conversation at the end of the dinner. What was in Morgan's mind was clear; probably not so much Schwab's predictions about the consequences of his vision—the reduction of prices—as the necessity for protecting the consolidations he had built and his community of interest with them. If Carnegie, as lone wolf, were permitted to prowl freely, carrying on price wars and engaging in cutthroat competition, Morgan's overcapitalized companies and his great reputation as a financial reorganizer and promoter would both be in jeopardy. Morgan began to talk to his partners. As Carnegie had anticipated, it was Morgan who followed up the meeting. Could Schwab—this was suggested through John W. Gates— come to see him?

Schwab went to New York to Morgan's home and there found Gates and a Morgan partner, Robert Bacon. (Bacon was the man who subsequently took charge of all the arrangements for the formation of the United States Steel Corporation.) Morgan wanted details, but details about the things that interested him. What companies should go into this new amalgamation and why? What should their prices be in a recapitalization? Most important—and here he was frank, an embarrassment he did not usually suffer, for he was admitting his hand was being forced—would Carnegie come in, and at what price? In reply to the last, Schwab said he thought so, for Carnegie had been talking of retiring for at least ten years, but he would have to ask. It was a long meeting; when it broke up, Morgan said to Schwab: "Well, if Andy wants to sell, I'll buy. Go and find his price."

Schwab, despite his great successes at the company, was always in awe of the boss. He sounded Mrs. Carnegie out before going ahead. Should he put the question? Would he be rebuffed? Mrs. Carnegie said "yes" to the first; she thought not, to the second. Why not play a round of golf with Mr. Carnegie at the St. Andrews Club (in Westchester County, New York), then have lunch, and in that relaxed atmosphere convey the Morgan message? Carnegie listened—after all, it meant bowing out of an industry which he had been associated with for thirty-five years and dominated for twenty—and then told Schwab to return the next day. The reply was in the affirmative. In 1899, the negotiations with Frick and Phipps had put a price of $320 million on the Carnegie properties. The profits in 1900 had been $40 million; in 1901 they probably would be $50 million. Carnegie and Schwab decided their asking price would be $400 million.

Carnegie scratched out a memorandum for Morgan to read. The Carnegie Co. was capitalized at $320 million, $160 million in bonds and $160 million in stock. The new consolidation was to absorb the bonds dollar for dollar and exchange the stock with new preferred stock at a ratio of 1 to 1.5. Carnegie personally was to receive his share entirely in bonds. This Schwab took to Morgan, and this Morgan accepted without a single quibble. The terms of sale were essentially those originally drawn up by Carnegie, with one more condition (which was put into the legal agreement): that in the stock swap a bonus of common was to be put on top of the preferred—here Carnegie was adding a sweetener for his younger partners. The upshot was, the Carnegie price became $492 million. Andrew Carnegie, himself, received $225,639,000 all in the United States Steel Corporation first-mortgage, five-per-cent gold bonds. (This was in transfer for his $86,145,000 in bonds and $92,639,000 in stock.) His true share was somewhat smaller than this amount, for he was also acting for his sister-in-law, Lucy Carnegie, and his cousin and partner, George Lauder, Jr., who owned 4 per cent of the Carnegie Co. stock. The negotiations were completed early in January, 1901. When the new holding company was announced two months later—for eleven other corporations had to be brought into the fold—Andrew Carnegie, steelmaster and captain of industry par excellence, was through.

Carnegie hailed his passing from the scene in a letter he wrote to Henry Phipps, his oldest partner, some time early in March:

Mr. Stetson [the Morgan lawyer] has just called to tell me it is *closed,* all fixed—big times on Stock Exchange tomorrow.

Well, this is a step in my life—a great change, but *after a time,* when I sit down to new conditions, I shall become I believe a wiser and more useful man, and besides live a dignified old age as long as life is granted, something few reach.

Carnegie lived eighteen more years, and all his hopes for his older years were realized; he was wiser, he was useful, there was no question of the universal respect he was accorded. He died saddened, however, for the great task to which he gave so much fruitful thinking—the achievement of international peace—was as remote as when he had started on this high adventure.

As early as 1900, Carnegie had thought about, had become personally involved in, and had spent large sums on all sorts of proposals and measures to further the cause of world peace. In 1910, with great expectations, he had established the Carnegie Endowment for International Peace, setting aside $10 million as a trust to finance its activities. But then war had broken out in 1914; the United States had entered it in 1917; and by August 11, 1919, when Carnegie died, it was already clear that President Woodrow Wilson's efforts to get the United States into the League of Nations were to be unavailing.

On April 1, 1901, the United States Steel Corporation, chartered in New Jersey, was formally launched. It was capitalized at $1,403 million, as follows:

Common Stock	$510.2 million
Preferred Stock	508.2 million
First mortgage bonds	303.8 million
Underlying bonds	59.0 million
Purchase obligations and real estate mortgages	21.9 million
	$1,403.1 million

The principal corporations entering into the holding companies were these makers of heavy steel: Carnegie Co., Federal Steel Co., and National Steel Co. These fabricating companies: National Tube Co., American Steel and Wire Co., American Steel Hoop Co., American Tin Plate Co., American Sheet Steel Co., American Bridge Co., Shelby Steel Tube Co., and the Rockefeller properties, consisting of the Mesabi ore mines, railroads, and some one hundred ore-carrying ships, known as the Lake Superior Consolidated Iron Mines.

[435]

In the exchanges of stock that took place, all the merged companies, other than those of Carnegie and Rockefeller, got somewhat more than dollar for dollar of United States Steel securities for their original securities. Morgan took care of his own creations. For Federal Steel, the exchange was 110 for 100, for National Tube 125 for 100, for American Bridge 110 for 100. The Moores were covered, despite the obviously over-valued capitalization of their companies. For National Steel, the exchange was 125 for 100, for American Tin Plate the same ratio, and for American Steel Hoop and American Sheet Steel 100 for 100. Of the Moore companies, the Commissioner of Corporations in his Report on the Steel Industry in 1911 said: "[These] were the most heavily over-capitalized and suffered from a distinctly speculative backing." The Rockefeller Lake Superior Consolidated Iron Mines, a New Jersey Cor-poration created in 1893, had been capitalized at $30 million; for all his properties, and this included the Bessemer Steamship Co. as well as the iron mines, Rockefeller obtained $90 million in United States Steel securities. The promotional profits, largely going to J. P. Morgan & Co., were $62.5 million.

What was the worth of the new giant consolidation? It is hard to say. Moody, in 1904, put the figure at $760 million. The Bureau of Corpora-tion's valuation in 1911 was $676 million, representing the historical costs of the tangible properties. The market price of the securities of all the companies involved, prior to the consolidation, was $793 million. The corporation, itself, in 1902, placed the value of its tangible assets at $1,400.3 million as follows:

Ore properties	$700 million
Plants	300 million
Blast furnaces	48 million
Coal and coke fields	100 million
Transportation properties	80 million
Natural gas fields	20 million
Limestone properties	4 million
Cash and cash assets	148.3 million

This did not include, said the statement, "the value of the good-will and established business of the various plants and properties . . . nor the very valuable patents, trade-marks, and processes owned or controlled."

A royal domain was included in the assets of the corporation. These were made up of 78 blast furnaces and 150 steelworks and rolling mills;

ore lands whose reserves at the time were calculated to be three-quarters of a billion tons of iron ore; 70,000 acres of coal lands as well as limestone deposits; almost half of the coke ovens of the United States (about 20,000 out of 47,000), which produced more than one-half of the country's coke; 112 steamships and a thousand miles of railroad. The annual productive capacity of the United States Steel Corporation furnaces and plants was 7,400,000 tons of pig iron, 9,400,000 tons of steel ingots, and 7,900,000 tons of finished steel. Its pig-iron production represented one-half of the total output of the United States; its steel-rail production, about 68 per cent; its structural steel, 60 per cent; as much if not more, of the manufacture of steel plates, sheets, bars, wire and wire rods, hoops and cotton ties; nearly the entire manufacture of tin plates, tubes, wire nails, barbed wire, and woven-wire fence; and from 85 to 90 per cent of all the bridges made in the country.

A final word. It will be observed from the statistical table above that the capitalization of the corporation was largely in its natural resources, the ratio of fuel and ore property to plant and transportation facilities being about two to one. In short, it was writing up its enormous potentialities for the manufacture of much greater steel products than it was currently able to turn out. And if to this are added its strategic locations, and its improvements at Two Harbors on Lake Superior and at Conneaut, its great fleet of ships on Lake Erie, and its excellent double-tracked railroad from Conneaut to Pittsburgh—and the fact that its manufacturing plants were on or near the Great Lakes, at Milwaukee, Chicago, Duluth, Lorain, Cleveland, Conneaut, Erie, Buffalo, with the cheap transportation costs available to them—it is difficult to assume that Morgan was grossly overestimating the value of his most impressive accomplishment. He was wagering, in effect, that the country would grow up to what the United States Steel Corporation was capable of doing. It was a bold gamble; and he turned out to be right.

All this Carnegie was able to see accomplished—but from the sidelines. Other men, other policies, were directing the destinies of the steel industry. He had done his work.

The End of a Businessman and His World   Carnegie's retirement as businessman, entrepreneur, and innovator marked the end of an era in many ways. Thenceforth, large companies, managed less and less by owners and more and more by officers, chosen as frequently as not by the investment bankers responsible for their financing, were to dominate American corporate enterprise. Profit-making, to be assured by the continuance of steady prices and if necessary with less-than-capacity operations, and not the increase of productivity with the lowering of costs and prices, became the leading concern of business policy. A completely free market—certainly this was so of heavy industry—was replaced by oligopoly. This was the outcome of the so-called "corporate revolution": the control of the market by a small number of giant corporations whose business decisions were governed not by the reactions of buyers but by the reactions of one another. Price wars could be forestalled by collusive agreements or by a tacit sharing of the market or by the acceptance of price leadership by the largest of the firms in a particular industry. Thus, oligopoly was as effective as monopoly: it severely restricted competition.

Following 1904, such great companies came increasingly under attack, and this was so because the American climate of opinion, and its mores, changed. The Progressive Movement—and Theodore Roosevelt, now President in his own right, played a large part in inspiring it—started with "exposing" the machinations of the trusts (read, large corporations) and ended by throwing suspicion on business itself. The businessman as risk-taker, as innovator, was forgotten; now he was the exploiter of the workers and the farmers who got an unequal share of the jointly-created product. In part, he was able to accomplish this—so ran the charge—because he was in an unholy alliance with the "bosses" of the two dominant political parties, who controlled legislatures and judicial appointments.

The Protestant churches, now preaching the Social Gospel of responsibility toward the community rather than individual striving, did much to create this mood of hostility. The penetration of radicalism, whether Socialism or anarchosyndicalism, into the labor movement, was another contributory factor. Reform in the political processes to restore rule to the people; taxation of corporations and the successful movement toward the taxation of individual and company earnings to compel a social sharing of the national income; the invasion of the courts more and more into the realm of private decision-making and finally the successful antitrust suits of 1911 ending in the dissolution of the Oil and Tobacco Trusts—these were clear evidences of new times and new manners.

All this did not mean that oligopoly and the power of investment banking on the one hand, and expanding government intrusion on the other—to tax, to regulate, to forbid—put an end to entrepreneurship. A Henry Ford in automobiles and a Samuel Insull in electric power and light could break through the barriers of restraint in the 1920s. That much-maligned decade also saw the emergence of pioneering industries, some the product of research and development of great corporations, some the work of entirely "new men," in synthetic fibers, the radio, commercial aviation, the transformation of the movie industry by sound. And the 1950s, another decade we have been taught by the New Economics to regard askance, saw the challenging of old-established processes and mighty firms by another fresh company of innovators, and the great breakthroughs in electronics, data processing and systems, copying machines, aerospace, the development of rare alloys, antibiotics. Old companies, to survive, revitalized themselves by skillfully planned diversification; new companies used profits successfully in research to extend man's frontiers into the unknown.

Government helped (as in aerospace); government interfered (by using an outmoded antitrust law against business). Thus the simpler world of Andrew Carnegie had been superseded by one much more complex and more sophisticated. And unlike his counterpart in Carnegie's world, the businessman—having in mind the suspicions and hostility Carnegie never felt—walked more warily and was heard in the land much less frequently. The businessman continued to be a power; but the greatest power of all was Big Government. To this extent, even granting the continuance of private entrepreneurship and innovation into the foreseeable future, the United States will never behold an Andrew Carnegie again.

A SELECTED BIBLIOGRAPHY

General.

The broad political and economic backgrounds of the materials presented in this book may be found in these two works: for the political, S. E. Morison and H. S. Commager, *Growth of the American Republic*, 2 vols., various editions, and for the economics, C. W. Wright, *Economic History of the United States*, 1941. For economic data generally, the government's *Historical Statistics of the United States*, 1960, is indispensable. More specialized books covering the period from the Civil War to the end of the nineteenth century are these: C. A. and M. R. Beard, *Rise of American Civilization*, 1930; L. M. Hacker and B. B. Kendrick, *United States Since 1865*, 1932; Thomas Cochran and William Miller, *Age of Enterprise*, 1942; E. C. Kirkland, *Industry Comes of Age*, 1961; F. A. Shannon, *Farmer's Last Frontier*, 1945; Henry Clews, *Fifty Years of Wall Street*, 1908; A. D. Noyes, *Forty Years of American Finance*, 1925. J. H. Chamberlain, *Enterprising Americans*, 1961, is an excellent general treatment. A. F. Cole, *Business Enterprise in its Social Setting*, 1959, concerns itself with research in business leadership and has a very useful bibliography. The position of present-day econometricians, who stress almost entirely the role of theory in the analysis and writing of economic history, is to be found in Douglass North, *Economic Growth of the United States, 1790-1860*, 1961, and his *Growth and Welfare in the American Past*, 1966, and in L. E. Davis, J. R. T. Hughes, and D. M. McDougall, *American Economic History*, 1961. The beginnings of a critique of this "new economic history" are to be found in J. R. T. Hughes, "Fact and Theory in Economic History," in *Explorations in Entrepreneurial History*, Second Series, Vol. 3, No. 2, Winter, 1966, and in L. M. Hacker, "The New Revolution in Economic History," in *Explorations in Entrepreneurial History*, Second Series, Vol. 3, No. 3, Spring, 1966. Very useful pioneering essays in American economic history are in National Bureau of Economic Research, *Trends in the American Economy in the Nineteenth Century*, (Vol. 24 of "Studies in Income and Wealth"), 1960, and in same author, *Output, Employment, and Productivity in the United States after 1800*, (Vol. 30, of "Studies in Income and Wealth"), 1966.

In addition to the books mentioned in the text, the following works are recommended for further reading.

Introduction.
Balogh, Thomas, *Economics of Poverty*, 1966
Bhagwati, Jagdish, *Economics of Underdeveloped Countries*, 1966

A SELECTED BIBLIOGRAPHY

Davie, M. R., ed., *Sumner Today*, 1940
Davis, L. E., J. R. T. Hughes, and D. M. McDougall, *American Economic History*, 1961
Friedman, Milton, *Capitalism and Freedom*, 1962
Hayek, F. A., *Constitution of Liberty*, 1960
Hirschman, A. O., *Strategy of Economic Development*, 1958
Lewis, W. Arthur, *Development Planning*, 1966
Myint, H., *Economics of the Developing Countries*, 1964
Myrdal, Gunnar, *International Economy: Problems and Prospects*, 1956
Rostow, W. W., *Stages of Economic Growth*, 1960
———, ed., *Economics of Take-off into Sustained Growth*, 1964
Youngson, A. J., *Possibilities of Economic Progress*, 1959

Chapters 1 and 2.
Berthoff, R. T., *British Immigrants in Industrial America*, 1953
Commons, J. R., *Immigration and Labor Problems*, Vol. 7, *Making of America*, 1906
Dewey, D. R., *Financial History of the United States*, 1902
Ely, R. T., *Taxation in American Cities and States*, 1888
Erickson, Charlotte, *American Industry and the European Immigrant*, 1957
Gates, P. W., *Agriculture and the Civil War*, 1965
Hacker, L. M., *Triumph of American Capitalism*, 1940
Handlin, Oscar, *Uprooted*, 1951
Hansen, M. C., *Immigrant in American History*, 1948
Hibbard, B. H., *History of Public Land Policies*, 1924
Hutchinson, E. P., *Immigrants and Their Children*, 1952
James, E. J., *Origins of the Land Grant Act of 1862*, 1910
Mitchell, W. C., *History of Greenbacks*, 1903
Ratner, Sidney, *American Taxation: Its History as a Social Force in Democracy*, 1942
Robbins, R. M., *Our Landed Heritage*, 1924
Seligman, E. R. A., *Shifting Incidence of Taxation*, 1892
———, *Progressive Taxation*, 1894
Sharkey, R. P., *Money, Class and Power: an Economic Study of Civil War and Reconstruction*, 1959
Shipperson, W. S., *British Emigration to North America*, 1957
Taussig, F. W., *Tariff History of the United States*, 7th ed., 1923
Thomas, Brindley, *Migration and Economic Growth*, 1955
———, *International Migration*, 1958
Unger, Irwin, *Greenback Era*, 1964
Wells, D. A., *Theory and Practice of Taxation*, 1900
Yearly, C. K., *Britons in American Labor, 1820-1914*, 1957

Chapter 3.
Aaron, Daniel, *Men of Good Hope*, 1951
Alderson, Barnard, *Andrew Carnegie: The Man and His World*, 1902
Atkinson, Edward, *Industrial Progress of the Nation*, 1890
Bridge, J. H., *Millionaires and Grub Street*, 1931
Carnegie, Andrew, *Gospel of Wealth and Other Timely Essays*, edited by E. C. Kirkland, 1962
———, *Miscellaneous Writings*, edited by B. J. Hendrick, 2 vols., 1933

A SELECTED BIBLIOGRAPHY

Cochran, T. C., *Railroad Leaders, 1845-1890: The Business Mind in Action*, 1953
Commager, H. S., *American Mind*, 1950
Curti, Merle, *Growth of American Thought*, 1943
Dorfman, Joseph, *Economic Mind in American Civilization*, vol. 2 and 3, 1946, 1949
Fine, Sidney, *Laissez Faire and the General-Welfare State*, 1956
Harlow, A. F., *Andrew Carnegie*, 1953
Hofstadter, Richard, *Social Darwinism in American Thought, 1865-1915*, 1945
———, *Age of Reform*, 1955
Hendrick, B. J., *Life of Andrew Carnegie*, 2 vols., 1932
Kirkland, E. C., *Dream and Thought in the Business Community, 1860-1900*, 1956
Lester, R. MacD., *Forty Years of Carnegie Givings*, 1941
McCloskey, R. G., *American Conservatism in the Age of Enterprise*, "Conservatism and the American Mind: Andrew Carnegie," 1951
May, H. F., *Protestant Churches and Industrial America*, 1949
Wells, D. A., *Recent Economic Changes*, 1889
Winkler, J. K., *Incredible Carnegie*, 1931
Wright, C. D., *Industrial Evolution of the United States*, 1895

Chapter 4.
Cahn, Edward, ed., *Supreme Court and Supreme Law*, 1954
Corwin, E. S., *Court over Constitution*, 1938
Dillon, J. F., *Law of Municipal Bonds*, 1876
———, *Law of Municipal Corporations*, 2 vols., 1873
———, *Commentaries on the Law of Municipal Corporations*, 5th ed., 5 vols., 1911
Fairman, Charles, *Mr. Justice Miller and the Supreme Court, 1862-1890*, 1939
Freund, Ernest, *Police Power*, 1904
Haines, C. G., *American Doctrine of Judicial Supremacy*, 2nd ed., 1932
Hartz, Louis, *Liberal Tradition in America*, 1955
Paul, A. M., *Conservative Crisis and The Rule of Law*, 1960
Rodell, Fred, *Nine Men: A Political History of the Supreme Court from 1790 to 1955*, 1955
Symposium on John Marshall Harlan, 1883-1911, in *Kentucky Law Journal*, Vol. 46 (Spring, 1958)
Trimble, B. R., *Chief Justice Waite, Defender of the Public Interest*, 1938
Twiss, B. R., *Lawyers and the Constitution*, 1942
Wright, B. F., *Contract Clause of the Constitution*, 1938
———, *Growth of American Constitutional Law*, 1942

Chapter 5.
Brissenden, P. F., *I.W.W., A Study of American Syndicalism*, 1920
Brooks, J. G., *American Syndicalism. The I.W.W.*, 1913
Commons, J. R., et al., *History of Labour in the United States*, 4 vols., 1918-1935
Coombs, Whitney, *Wages of Unskilled Labor in Manufacturing, 1890-1924*, 1926
Crosser, Paul, *Ideologies and American Labor*, 1941
David, Henry, *History of the Haymarket Affair*, 1936
Destler, C. M., *American Radicalism, 1865-1901*, 1946
Egbert, D. D., and Stow Persons, ed., *Socialism and American Life*, 2 vols., 1952
Ely, R. T., *Labor Movement in America*, 1886

A SELECTED BIBLIOGRAPHY

Foner, P. G., *History of the Labor Movement in the United States*, 4 vols., 1947-1965

Grob, G. N., *Workers and Utopia*, 1961

Hillquit, Morris, *History of Socialism in the United States*, 1910

Joll, James, *The Anarchists*, 1964

Perlman, Selig, *Theory of the Labor Movement*, 1928

———, *History of Trade Unionism in the United States*, 1922

Powderly, Terence, *Path I Trod*, 1940

Quint, H. H., *Forging of American Socialism*, 1935

Rocker, Rudolf, *Pioneers of American Freedom*, 1949

Symes, Lillian, and Travers Clement, *Rebel America*, 1934

Taft, Philip, *A. F. of L. in the Time of Gompers*, 1957

———, *Organized Labor in American History*, 1964

Ulman, Lloyd, *Rise of the National Trade Union*, 1955

Ware, N. J., *Labor Movement in the United States, 1860-1895*, 1929

Wolman, Leo, *Growth of American Trade Unions*, 1924

Chapter 6.

Anderson, D. E., *Refrigeration in America*, 1953

Bogue, A. G., *From Prairie to Cornbelt: Farming in the Illinois and Iowa Prairies in the 19th Century*, 1963

———, *Money at Interest*, 1955

Buck, S. J., *The Granger Movement*, 1913

Clemen, R. A., *American Livestock and Meat Industry*, 1923

Dale, E. E., *Range Cattle Industry*, 1930

Gates, Paul, *Frontier Farmers and Pioneer Tenants*, 1945

Hicks, J. D., *Populist Revolt, A History of the Farmers' Alliance and the People's Party*, 1931

Hutchinson, W. T., *Cyrus Hall McCormick*, 2 vols., 1935

Mack, E. C., *Peter Cooper: Citizen of New York*, 1949

Osgood, E. S., *Day of the Cattleman*, 1929

Pollack, Norman, *Populist Response to Industrial America*, 1962

Ridge, Martin, *Ignatius Donnelly: The Portrait of a Politician*, 1962

Shannon, F. A., *Farmer's Last Frontier*, 1945

Taylor, C. C., *Farmers' Movement, 1620-1920*, 1953

Towne, M. W., and W. D. Rasmussen, "Farm Gross Product and Gross Investment in the Nineteenth Century," National Bureau of Economic Research, *Trends in the American Economy in the Nineteenth Century*, 1960

Webb, W. P., *Great Plains*, 1931

Wiest, Edward, *Agricultural Organization in the United States*, 1923

Woodward, C. Vann, *Tom Watson: Agrarian Rebel*, 1938

Chapter 7.

Allen, F. L., *Great Pierpont Morgan*, 1949

Baker, G. W., *Formation of the New England Railroad System*, 1937

Cairncross, A. K., *Home and Foreign Investment, 1870-1913*, 1953

Corey, Lewis, *House of Morgan*, 1930

Cleveland, F. S., and F. W. Powell, *Railroad Promotion and Capitalization in the United States*, 1909

A SELECTED BIBLIOGRAPHY

Decker, Leslie, *Railroads, Lands, and Politics: The Taxation of Railroad Land Grants,* 1964

Fogel, R. W., *Union Pacific Railroad: A Case of Premature Enterprise,* 1960

——, *Railroads and American Economic Growth,* 1964

Goodrich, Carter, *Government Promotion of American Canals and Railroads,* 1960

Haney, L. R., *A Congressional History of Railways in the United States, 1850-1887,* 1910

Hedges, J. B., *Henry Villard and the Railways of the Northwest,* 1930

Kennan, George, *E. H. Harriman,* 1922

Larson, Henrietta, *Jay Cooke,* 1936

Overton, R. C., *Burlington West,* 1941

Pyle, J. G., *Life of James J. Hill,* 1916

Stover, J. F., *Railroads of the South, 1865-1900,* 1955

——, *American Railroads,* 1961

Chapter 8.

Adams, H. C., *Science of Finance,* 1898

Andersen, T. A., *Century of Banking in Wisconsin,* 1954

Anderson, T. J., *Federal and State Control of Banking,* 1934

Barnett, G. E., *State Banking in the United States since 1864,* 1902

Cable, J. R., *Bank of the State of Missouri,* 1923

Davis, A. M., *Origin of the National Banking System,* 1910

Dunbar, C. F., *Economic Essays,* 1904

Helderman, L. C., *National and State Banks,* 1931

Hepburn, A. B., *History of Currency in the United States,* 1939

Knox, J. J., *History of Banking in the United States,* 1900

Laughlin, J. L., *Banking Reform,* 1912

Lewis, Cleona, *America's Stake in International Investment,* 1938

Merritt, F. D., *Early History of Banking in Iowa,* 1900

Redlich, Fritz, *Molding of American Banking—Men and Ideas,* Vol. 2, 1951

Smith, J. G., *Development of Trust Companies in the United States,* 1927

Sprague, O. M. W., *History of Crises under the National Banking System,* 1910

Studenski, Paul, and H. Krooss, *Financial History of the United States,* 1952

Taus, E. R., *Central Banking Functions of the U. S. Treasury,* 1943

Trescott, P. B., *Financing American Enterprise: The Story of Commercial Banking,* 1963

White, Horace, *Money and Banking,* 1936

Chapter 9.

Becker, G. S., *Human Capital,* 1964

Butler, N. M., ed., *Education in the United States. A Series of Monographs,* 1910

Butts, R. F., and Cremin, L. A., *History of Education in American Culture,* 1953

Dexter, E. G., *History of Education in the United States,* 1904

Finch, J. K., *Trends in Engineering Education,* 1948

Good, H. G., *History of American Education,* 1956

Hofstadter, Richard, and De Witt Hardy, *Development and Scope of Higher Education,* 1952

A SELECTED BIBLIOGRAPHY

Hofstader, Richard, and W. P. Metzger, *Development of Academic Freedom in the U.S.*, 1955

Kandel, I. L., *History of Secondary Education*, 1930

McGivern, J. G., *First Hundred Years of Engineering Education in the United States*, 1960

Ross, E. D., *Democracy's College: The Land-Grant Movement in the Formative Stage*, 1942

Schultz, T. W., *Economic Value of Education*, 1963

Chapter 10.

Barger, Harold, *Transportation Industries, 1889-1946*, 1951

Carman, H. J., *Street Surface Railway Franchises of New York City*, 1919

Gilmore, H. W., *Transportation and the Growth of Cities*, 1953

Green, C. McL., *American Cities in the Growth of the Nation*, 1957

——, *Rise of Urban America*, 1965

Haig, R. M., "Toward an Understanding of the Metropolis," *Quarterly Journal of Economics*, XL (February, May 1926)

Hirsch, Mark, *William C. Whitney*, 1948

McKelvey, Blake, *Urbanization of America, 1860-1915*, 1963

Moore, Jane, *Cityward Migration*, 1938

Passer, H. C., "Frank Julian Sprague, Father of Electric Traction," *Men in Business*, William Miller, ed., 1952

Queen, S. A., and D. B. Carpenter, *American City*, 1953

Schlesinger, A. M., *Rise of the City, 1878-1898*, 1933

Upson, L. D., *Growth of City Government*, 1931

Wilcox, D. F., *Municipal Franchises*, 2 vols., 1910, 1911

Zeublin, Charles, *American Municipal Progress*, 1916

Chapters 11–15.

A good part of the materials in these chapters is based on The Papers of Andrew Carnegie in the Manuscript Division of the Library of Congress, Washington, D.C.

Bain, J. S., *Industrial Organization*, 1959

Berglund, Abraham, *United States Steel Corporation*, 1907

Berglund, Abraham, and P. G. Wright, *Tariff on Iron and Steel*, 1929

British Iron Trade Association, *American Industrial Conditions and Competition*, 1902

Burn, D. L., *Economic History of Steelmaking, 1867-1939*, 1940

Casson, H. N., *Romance of Steel*, 1907

Clark, V. S., *History of Manufactures in the United States*, 3 vols., 1929

Corey, Lewis, *House of Morgan*, 1930

Ely, R. T., *Monopolies and Trusts*, 1900

Fritz, John, *Autobiography of John Fritz*, 1912

Garraty, J. A., *Right-Hand Man. The Life of George W. Perkins*, 1957

Habakkuk, H. J., *American and British Technology in the Nineteenth Century*, 1962

Harvey, George, *Henry Clay Frick*, 1928

Hughes, Jonathan, *Vital Few*, "Carnegie and the American Steel Industry" and "J. Pierpont Morgan, The Investment Banker as Statesman," 1966

Jones, Eliot, *Trust Problem*, 1924

Moody, John, *Masters of Capital*, 1929

A SELECTED BIBLIOGRAPHY

Nevins, Allan, *Abram S. Hewitt*, 1935

———, *Study in Power: John D. Rockefeller*, 2 vols., 1953

Pound, Arthur, and S. T. Moore, *They Told Barron*, 1930

———, *More They Told Barron*, 1931

Redlich, Fritz, *History of American Business Leaders*, Vol. 1. *Theory, Iron and Steel, Iron Ore Mining*, 1940

Ripley, W. Z., ed., *Trusts, Pools, and Corporations*, 1905

Seager, H. R., and C. A. Gulick, Jr., *Trust and Corporation Problems*, 1929

Swank, J. M., *History of the Manufacture of Iron in All Ages*, 2nd ed., 1892

Tarbell, I. M., *Life of Elbert H. Gary*, 1925

Taussig, F. W., *Some Aspects of the Tariff Question*, 1915

U.S. Commissioner of Corporations, *Report on the Steel Industry*, Pts. 1-3, 1911-1913

U.S. Steel Corporation Investigation, Special Committee for [The Stanley Committee], 62nd Cong. 2nd Sess., House of the Representatives, *Hearings, 1911-12*, 8 vols., 1912. Report No. 1127.

INDEX

INDEX

INDEX

INDEX

INDEX